Women of the Wild

Women of the Wild

Challenging Gender Disparities in Field Stations and Marine Laboratories

Edited by
Victoria M. McDermott, Jennifer M. Gee,
and Amy R. May

LEXINGTON BOOKS
Lanham • Boulder • New York • London

Chapter 5 Epigraph Permission to reprint this epigraph from Len Germinara
Published by Lexington Books
An imprint of The Rowman & Littlefield Publishing Group, Inc.
4501 Forbes Boulevard, Suite 200, Lanham, Maryland 20706

www.rowman.com

86-90 Paul Street, London EC2A 4NE

British Library Cataloguing in Publication Information Available

Library of Congress Cataloging-in-Publication Data

Names: McDermott, Victoria M., 1995- editor. | Gee, Jennifer M., 1980- editor. | May, Amy R., 1976- editor.
Title: Women of the wild : challenging gender disparities in field stations and marine laboratories / edited by Victoria M. McDermott, Jennifer M. Gee and Amy R. May.
Description: Lanham : Lexington Books, [2022] | Includes bibliographical references and index. | Summary: "Women of the Wild: Challenging Gender Disparities in Field Stations and Marine Laboratories (FSMLs) provides an interdisciplinary approach through the lens of communication to explore the gender disparities impacting women working at FSMLs"— Provided by publisher.
Identifiers: LCCN 2021056365 (print) | LCCN 2021056366 (ebook) | ISBN 9781793629401 (cloth) | ISBN 9781793629418 (ebook)
Subjects: LCSH: Women—Employment—United States—Case studies. | Sex discrimination against women—United States—Case studies. | Biological laboratories—United States. | Biological stations—United States.
Classification: LCC HD6095 .W6965 2022 (print) | LCC HD6095 (ebook) | DDC 331.4/1330973—dc23/eng/20211116
LC record available at https://lccn.loc.gov/2021056365
LC ebook record available at https://lccn.loc.gov/2021056366

This book is dedicated to those who support the critical mission of field stations and marine laboratories (FSMLs). May we learn from the experiences of the women who paved the way and create more inclusive and equitable paths for those yet to join our ranks.

Contents

Foreword

Marilyn L. Fogel

Fifty years ago when I first started to participate in fieldwork, no one seemed to be thinking about having diverse leadership at field stations or marine labs (FSML) in any way that I can recall. It was enough to be included, to join in. Working in remote places became a significant part of my research portfolio as I studied modern and ancient ecosystems and how they function on six continents. As I gained experience and stature, I opened my eyes to a system that fosters men over women and white people over people of color. I never took the reins at a field station or marine lab, choosing instead to build a serious analytical laboratory with an experimental component to complement my fieldwork. This afforded me the opportunity to lead while maintaining a field program.

This book edited by Victoria M. McDermott, Jennifer M. Gee, and Amy R. May ties together years of research and stories chronicling women's involvements in FSML. The authors are FSML leaders, researchers, and allies, forging a new legacy for women, and people of color, to work in remote places, to enjoy the solitude of being in a natural environment and appreciate all the world has to offer. Many of the stories describe the struggles that have beset women working at FSML, and it is sometimes disheartening to read these. However, the book details recommendations on how women can improve their situations and suggests policy changes for the better, including having parent-friendly policies and opportunities for mentorship. It is my hope that having a book like this will enable others to consider the importance of providing safe and inclusive spaces for everyone to embrace and enjoy meaningful work in the field.

As an undergraduate in the early 1970s, I was first interested in being chosen to participate in a field quarter at Penn State's newly formed Wallops Island Marine Laboratory in Tidewater, Virginia. One of just six women in a group of 40 students, we were probably self-selected as women who loved nature and academic challenges. Jumping off of a boat into chest high water then sinking into knee high mud was required. None of us were prissy women, realizing quickly that if we were, we didn't belong with this group. Fortunately for me, I liked working in mud, loved water, and had little fear of slimy critters. That experience propelled me to selecting a graduate program at the Port Aransas Marine Laboratory at the University of Texas, where I had envisioned continuing with a robust field program.

UT's Marine Lab was on a barrier island, a ferry ride from the mainland. The town of Port Aransas had about 1,000 residents, swelling to 20,000 in summer with tourists. Far from the main campus in Austin, I was one of only a few female PhD students. There were no role models who looked like me, as all the faculty were men, something not unusual at that time. My focus was strictly on my work, getting the degree, and moving up and on. I concentrated more on lab work than fieldwork. After three years, the marine laboratory that originally seemed like a haven for science, in fact, fostered a small community of scientists that I did not identify with. Although I now identified as a scientist, in particular a biogeoscientist, I felt out of place. I wasn't invited along on fishing trips or to evening poker games with the guys after work. My goal was to become a leading researcher, and I spent my time working toward that goal.

When I became a staff scientist at the Carnegie Institution of Washington's Geophysical Laboratory, I was once again a "fish out of water." I learned a few things about leading in science the hard way. These were very practical lessons that helped make my work in the field more productive and allow me to become a leader. I recommend that any women going into fieldwork as a significant part of their career think about nuts and bolts, literally, emergency planning, and how to deal with interpersonal situations. Spending time working on your Emotional Intelligence is needed.

As we assume leadership at more FSML, we should make ourselves as prepared as possible. At the Geophysical Lab, when I built my first lab, and most likely when women do their work at a FSML, I had to learn how to communicate with facilities guys. It was uncommon to have women in charge of a laboratory, so it took some effort for me to develop a way to communicate effectively with these men. Earning the respect of everyone involved in your success—from those who empty your trash and clean your floors to those who hold the purse strings—is fundamental. Working at, or leading, a FSML requires a lot of advance and daily logistical work. Familiarity with boats, tools, and practical knowledge about electricity and plumbing is a plus. Usually, because of FSML's remote locations, problems arise that require maintenance to get the power correct for an instrument or a boat motor that needs fixing. Women typically aren't in charge of these practical issues, yet find themselves beholden to those who are.

Working at Smithsonian's Carrie Bow Caye Field Station in Belize (1999–2010) brought up issues addressed in this book regarding male dominance, lack of support for parents, and emergency planning. The station was run by a male executive manager in Washington, DC, who set the rules, came down twice a year to post them around the field station, and set a very negative tone, assuming researchers were going to behave in unsafe ways. Station managers on site were always men, often with their wives who took on subservient roles. I traveled there as one of two or three principal investigators, all of us women. We had to assert our status every time we arrived on site, but none of us were shrinking violet types so we succeeded in having our field programs supported. Prior to having internet accessibility, our only mode of outside communication was via a very expensive telephone service. We were unable to contact our families during our stay there, unless there was an emergency. It did not lead to a parent-friendly policy and discouraged parents from spending time at the station.

Depending on how far away a FSML is from a hospital, having first-aid training is very important. It may be that women take on the role as caregiver more often than men. I traveled to field areas with a first-aid kit including antiseptic solutions, Band-Aids, antibiotic cream, insect repellant, and over-the-counter medicines for upset stomach, pain, and allergies. Over the years of going down to Belize, I dispensed them all. When one of our station managers had a small stroke, it really hit home that medical emergencies should be planned for. The Smithsonian had no doctor "on call" and no "in country" medical plan. We used the oxygen for scuba diving to stabilize the manager, who then rested in bed for a week. Had he deteriorated further, he would have needed an emergency flight to the United States.

Emotional issues are often more difficult to work through. Victoria McDermott writes that the women she interviewed had been "reprimanded, condescended, and underestimated" when they carried out their fieldwork. These behaviors aren't unique to doing fieldwork, and any woman who advances through the ranks of academia will encounter them. In Belize, when reprimanded by the Station manager for using the radio to relay our progress working on a remote island, I scoffed and answered, "Terribly sorry. Shan't happen again." I blew this off to the behavior of a person who wasn't very emotionally intelligent. As for condescension, I have experienced this from both women and men, and when I do, I switch on my demeanor that lets these people know that I've paid my dues and have accomplished something. I prefer to let my "don't take yourself too seriously" personality be my normal mode, but I can switch to a "National Academy of Sciences member" when I need to. For women who don't have that level of title, it's harder to get past this. Today we refer to these as microaggressions—small but hurtful quips that can prove very unpleasant. Having the wherewithal to respond to condescending behavior takes practice, something most of us really don't want to spend the time doing. But practicing this with safe people is a good idea.

I have been continuously underestimated throughout my career. When I interviewed fairly recently at a prestigious California university to head their marine lab, I was asked if I was capable of being a director and having a research program at the same time. I was taken aback by this question, because the men who had the position prior had done both. Why would they think I could not? I didn't get the job, which I consider fortunate, given what might have been an underestimation—and limitation—of my potential.

Fortunately for me, I did not encounter sexual harassment in any of the FSML that I studied at. But, on voyages to the far north Arctic on oceanographic ships, which are like marine lab outposts, I dealt with hypermasculinity or misogyny. The voyages were led by Norwegian scientists who thought of fieldwork as a test of physical strength. I was sidelined sometimes because they thought I wasn't "strong enough" to climb up a mountain or scale a glacier. In response to their male-dominated take on fieldwork, two other women and I formed the "Babes of Science" management group and insisted that we had a say in the fieldwork and the division of privileges. We struggled to make ourselves heard, which we did by consistently presenting our cases to be included, along with other women who were students or postdocs. I have to say this wasn't a "fun" chore, but when we succeeded in making our trips more inclusive and equitable, it was worth it.

Women of the Wild: Ending Gender Disparities in Field Stations and Marine Laboratories summarizes where we are today in a climate that is starting to favor inclusivity. Women are here to stay in field science. Realizing that we are competent leaders in the efforts to become directors at FSML and how our leadership will change the culture of doing work at the sites is highlighted in this work. With this publication, I hope that the barriers to open access and leadership by women will be overcome.

Acknowledgments

First, we celebrate the hard work and dedication of our contributors. We challenged you to translate your lived experience within the framework of an entirely different discipline, requiring you to learn qualitative research methods, APA formatting style, and foundational theories in communication and related disciplines. The end result far exceeded our expectations and underscored the importance of interdisciplinary research. Also, let's not forget you made all of this happen while navigating the uncertainty of a global pandemic.

Thank you to the research participants who allowed us to learn from your lived experiences, from the struggles to the triumphs and everything in between. Now, we challenge the readers to continue working to create more inclusive FSML communities through interdisciplinary relationships, research collaborations, and practical application of the recommendations presented by the scholars and practitioners who contributed to this edited volume.

Tori: Thank you, Chad, for your never-ending support of my research goals and career aspirations. Without you, the continuous adventures across the United States would not have been possible. I want to thank my family and friends for the emotional support from near and far. Thank you to my substitute husband Nike and my favorite little dude for keeping me sane during the editing process! I am incredibly grateful to Amy and Jen for their continued support, mentorship, and belief in my work, as well as my other academic colleagues and mentors who have supported my scholarly journey. Thank you to those at field stations and marine laboratories for letting me become a member of your amazing community. A special thanks to Toolik Field Station and the Organization of Biological Field Stations for the transformative experiences and meaningful relationships that spurred my interest in improving the FSML experience for all. Thank you to all the strong women who have paved the way for future generations of scientists to engage and succeed in field-based science! I hope to continue working to create more inclusive and equitable FSML communities.

Jen: I thank Elizabeth Long, Lisa Bush, Tori McDermott, and the Organization of Biological Field Station members for the inspiration, encouragement and support to take on the challenge of building a leadership program for women at Field Stations and Marine Labs, and I am grateful to the National Science Foundation for funding this effort. I also thank NSF for funding Women Evolving Biological Sciences (PI Claire Horner-Devine), which gave me the opportunity to participate in a symposium and planted the seed for our project. I have learned so much from the editors, the chapter authors and all of our focus group participants. Thank you all for crossing disciplines to chase this dream together. With this book, I believe we are taking important steps to begin to name and to navigate the barriers that some groups of us face in the field, and I am eager to continue to help open the door at FSMLs for people from all backgrounds.

Amy: Presley, you are my inspiration. You are always with me, "riding shotgun," encouraging me to keep going, helping me see the bigger picture, and reminding me to always watch out for the manholes. Tori, the student has become the teacher. Your leadership and vision were critical to the overall success of this project. Jen, I learned so much from your insights and thoughtful contributions. Your ability to navigate forest fires, forced evacuations, and power outages has become the stuff of legends. I feel privileged to be part of this editorial team, learning and communing with two incredibly talented scholars, practitioners, and women. Mom, Dad, and Baboo thank you for your unwavering love and support. Without your encouragement, I would not be here today. To my dear, sweet Vladimir, may your man bun always sit high. To COVID, thank you for challenging us to see this project through despite the setbacks and emotional uncertainty. We came out stronger on the other end and will never forget the lessons learned. #wedidit

Thank you Sarah Thompson, student editorial assistant, for your work on this project.

Introduction to Field Station and Marine Laboratories

Victoria M. McDermott,
Jennifer M. Gee, and Amy R. May

In an era filled with the overexploitation of natural resources, unstable food production, and rapid climate change, a strong and clear understanding of the natural world is more important than ever (Intergovernmental Panel on Climate Change IPCC, 2021; National Research Council NRC, 2014). Field stations and marine laboratories[1] (FSML) are sentinels of Earth's climate, environment, and biodiversity that provide scientists with the infrastructure to collect data in otherwise inaccessible areas of the globe. FSMLs offer a window into the increasingly unpredictable natural world that is challenged by progressively frequent natural disasters and extreme ecological changes. FSMLs provide vital support and "form a global infrastructure network which is critical for long-term environmental monitoring and research, education, and public information" (Tydecks et al., 2016, p. 88). A body of research underscores the impact and importance of FSMLs within the scientific community and society at large (Baker, 2015; NRC, 2014; Struminger et al., 2018; Tydeck et al., 2016). Collectively, findings indicate the types of science and questions that FSMLs allow researchers to ask and explore, along with the powerful iterative process of comparing field and laboratory research, provide crucial insights into ecological function that would not be possible strictly within a laboratory setting.

Although FSMLs provide vital insights into the increasingly unpredictable natural world, they remain exclusive, requiring economic, social, and networking capital to allow scientists and staff to live, work, and study in these often-isolated locations. Moreover, even though FSMLs provide invaluable access and opportunity for scientists to explore undisturbed terrains, the remoteness can be demanding on both professional and personal lives, and work at FSMLs often requires people to take extreme measures to adapt, survive, and thrive. Many FSMLs are located in isolated, confined, and extreme (ICE) environments, which pose logistical and social challenges for FSML staff, scientists, and local communities and that require multifaceted approaches to remain viable. Furthermore, FSMLs affiliated with universities may experience difficulties navigating campus politics and bureaucracy despite being located miles away. In general, these sites may be plagued by "financial insecurity, lack of public understanding and support, and weak governance" (Tydecks et al., 2016, p. 88).

Similarly, our stations must take into consideration our past histories. Many FSMLs were built around and continue to perpetuate male-dominated institutional ideologies, existing within traditionally male-dominated science, technology, engineering, and mathematics (STEM) disciplines, such as biology, oceanography, and terrestrial geological sciences. Furthermore, some FSMLs exist within Native and Indigenous communities that have been subjected to years of colonization and oppression, creating tension and conflict as FSMLs work to build equitable relationships with these populations and learn from their lived experiences. The result is an institution that makes it difficult for women, Black Indigenous and People of Color (BIPOC), and those with intersecting identities (i.e., gender, sexual orientation LGBTQIA+, race, ethnicity, differently abled, socio-economic status) to progress, succeed, and thrive. As communication researchers working with women scientists and practitioners navigating these spaces, we see an opportunity to bridge our collective disciplines to create different ways of knowing framed by gender, and organizational and intercultural communication theory. Our edited volume's goals are: (1) to document the gender history of FSMLs, (2) to provide a context for the current organizational culture and understand the current communication climate dynamics, (3) to explore current barriers to leadership, success, and factors that contribute to positive communication climates in FSMLs, (4) to explore strategies, programs, and interventions for supporting women's leadership roles, as well as, to develop best practices for policy, resource allocation, and FSML design to better support and increase women's leadership roles in FSMLs.

DEFINING IMPORTANT TERMS

Borrowing from our STEM research colleagues, the table below is a glossary box (see table 0.1). While not often seen in social science papers, this figure provides a useful legend for key terms throughout the book. We also invite future social scientists to adopt and mold communication norms from STEM fields and vice versa to begin creating a shared interdisciplinary language.

Table 0.1 Glossary Box

Term	*Definition*
FSML	Field Station and Marine Labs. Facilities can range from primitive campgrounds in protected or semi-protected areas to full facilities that offer meals and all the conveniences of modern urban life.
NC	Nature Centers. Similar to FSMLs these centers provide access and education to connect people with science. While FSMLs are thought to be more research-oriented institutions, NCs focus more on K-12 and citizen science engagement.
Fieldwork or field work	A broad term, referring to any work-related activities outside of a researcher's home institution ("In the field," 2018).
In the field	The terminology used to talk about when scholars are conducting fieldwork.
ICE	Isolated, confined, and extreme environments (see Golden et al., 2018 for more information)
PI	Principal Investigator. The leader in a laboratory that studies a particular scientific question with the help of lab members that include undergraduate and graduate students, postdoctoral fellows, and technicians who may act as lab managers.
STEM	Science, Technology, Engineering, and Math (sometimes referred to as STEMM, including Medicine or STEAM including Arts)
NSF	National Science Foundation
OBFS	Organization of Biological Field Stations. A prominent professional organization in which most of the contributors are active members. The mission of OBFS is to help member stations increase their effectiveness in supporting critical research, education, and outreach programs. They pursue this goal in a manner that maximizes diversity, inclusiveness, sustainability, and transparency (OBFS, n.d.).
BIPOC	Black, Indigenous, and People of Color
LGBTQIA+	Lesbian, Gay, Bisexual, Transgender, Queer/or Questioning, Intersex, Asexual/or Ally
Content Analysis	A tool used primarily by qualitative researchers to identify themes in text-based data, e.g., interview transcripts, surveys, social media posts, etc. (Hsieh & Shannon, 2005). Themes are interpreted within the context of the literature to gain additional insight into the lived experience of target populations.
Autoethnography	A tool used primarily by qualitative researchers to better understand their lived experience within the context of larger social institutions. Formally defined, autoethnography is a research method that uses personal experience ("auto") to describe and interpret ("graphy") cultural texts, experiences, beliefs, and practices ("ethno") (Adams et al., 2017, p. 1).
Grounded Theory	A generative approach to data analysis where theory emerges from the interpretation of a data set (see Bryant & Charmaz, 2007).

Note. For a more in-depth overview of FSMLs (e.g., how they work, who they serve, their mission, etc.), see chapter 1 in this edited volume.

The Value of Interdisciplinary Work

Snow (1959) is credited as one of the first scholars to describe the gap that exists between scientific culture and the culture of the humanities and arts. Due to this gap, people have been calling for an increase in interdisciplinary research for decades (Robinson et al., 2016). Diversity of bodies, identities, thoughts, and perspectives have been linked to scientific innovation, increased representation in leadership, and improved problem-solving capabilities (Swartz et al., 2019). Diversity can "generate new research questions that have yet to be asked by our field, develop methodical and analytical approaches to better understand study populations, and offer approaches to problem-solving from multiple and different perspectives" (Swartz et al., 2019, p. S33). Moreover, through interdisciplinary research, the strengths and weaknesses of disciplines can be leveraged to generate a better understanding of the research landscape and connect the public to the greater humanities and STEM scientific communities (Robinson et al., 2016; Shipley et al., 2017; Taebi et al., 2014).

Although the *concept* of interdisciplinary research is highly valued, there are a variety of barriers to completing interdisciplinary work. Interdisciplinary research "essentially involves bringing different disciplinary perspectives into contact with each other" (Robinson et al., 2016, p. 3); however, academics may often operate within academic silos (Miller et al., 2008) believing only one epistemological perspective is valid (Robinson et al., 2016). This can make it difficult to engage in interdisciplinary discussions surrounding rigor, theory, and methods. Furthermore, interdisciplinary research is systemically undervalued in traditional academic structures. It can be difficult to get interdisciplinary research published as journals and editors may be more cautious to accept interdisciplinary articles since many academic publications are silo-based, specialist outlets (Little, 2017). Stirling (2007) wrote, "The tendency for apparently technical questions over diversity to acquire high profile policy salience—as in fields like ecological conservation" (p. 710) can present a barrier to interdisciplinary research. Similarly, interdisciplinary research may also take more time, as extensive conversations have to be had in order to execute interdisciplinary research effectively (Little, 2017). This has resulted in some scholars, unfortunately, labeling interdisciplinary research as a "high risk venture" (Little, 2017, p. 7) and harder to assess and get funded (Stern, 2016). The result for scholars is that academic structures and criteria for career development make it extremely difficult for interdisciplinary researchers to be appointed, get tenure, and be promoted (National Academy of Sciences, 2005).

Fortunately, 2020–2021 years have brought social justice and equity to the forefront of society. As current academic structures and metrics for promotion are being challenged for systemic barriers to success for those with diverse and intersecting identities (e.g., women, BIPOC, LGBTQIA+, differently abled), we have the opportunity to redefine the value of interdisciplinary research in the academy. As we continue to break down the barriers for equity, access, inclusion, and diversity in the academy, interdisciplinary research provides an opportunity for reimagining the role and value of research inside and outside of academia. It is through these changes, we may be able to break down the barriers such as academic silos and promotion considerations that hinder the innovation needed to continue pushing the research community forward.

The Role of Communication in Facilitating Interdisciplinary Work

While we seek to redefine the value and increase the number of interdisciplinary collaborations, communication as a discipline may provide the tools necessary to bridge the "cultural divide" between STEM and the humanities. Previous work from communication scholars has posited the potential value of using communication theories and frameworks to evaluate STEM experiences. For example, Kisselburgh and colleagues (2009) explored how people make meaning of the value of STEM work through discourse, and Buzzanell et al. (2015) used communication to explore the role of mentorship for BIPOC academics; however, there is much more research to be done at the intersection of communication and STEM to fully explicate and support the continuation of innovative science and the individuals who complete this invaluable work. Therefore, this volume seeks to emphasize the value of interdisciplinary research. We seek to reinvigorate the conversation related to interdisciplinary research and highlight how interdisciplinary research can be facilitated to enhance the humanities and STEM science disciplines, as well as challenge and hold accountable the academic community to value interdisciplinary research.

Before embarking on this journey, we, as editors, had no idea how challenging and rewarding it would be to navigate the cultural divide (Snow, 1959). We learned a new language as contributors shared their research interests and experiences working at FSMLs. But just as important, our contributors provided invaluable social support as we navigated this project during a global pandemic and collaborated using technology-mediated communication. We want to acknowledge the great effort and work put in by our contributors who were asked to step outside of their comfort zone and frame their lived experience within the context of an entirely different discipline.

OVERVIEW OF CHAPTERS

Ultimately, FSMLs provide vital access to immersive scientific experiences. These experiences are crucial for retaining diverse populations within STEM (Bekki et al., 2008; Dahlberg et al., 2008; NRC, 2014; Vieyra et al., 2011). For many, FSMLs provide a first look into fieldwork and field-based research. As FSMLs continue to fight for funding and work to build more inclusive and equitable environments for scientists, support staff, and the communities they serve, identifying and addressing barriers becomes more urgent. This edited volume contains chapters from a variety of scholars within the FSML community. Below are brief descriptions of each chapter.

Setting the Stage of FSMLs

Chapter 1: Overview of the Field

In chapter 1, McDermott, Gee, and May provide an overview of field-based institutions. Beginning by defining FSMLs' role in the scientific process and community, this chapter concludes with an overview of historical gender disparities and the potential impact of ICE within FSML communities.

Chapter 2: The Isthmus

In The Isthmus, chapter contributor, Torti, tells the story of a female scientist joining two male scientists on a tropical island for the first time. In this fictional piece based on similar real-life experiences of women scientists, Torti uncovers the experiences of women attempting to navigate the male-dominated tropics.

Experiences in the Field

Chapter 3: "Brush your hair, apply for every grant, and get laid as much as possible": Sensemaking Women's Experiences Conducting Fieldwork in the Tropics

Moving from fictional to real-life experiences in the tropics, McDermott explores the narratives of four women scientists in the tropics. Through the lens of Muted Group Theory, McDermott explores how women scientists have been muted in tropical fieldwork ranging from the 1970s to today. This chapter concludes with research-based recommendations for improving the experiences of women scientists in the tropics.

Chapter 4: Make the Approach and Get the Data: Challenges, Teamwork, and Culture of Support for Women Who Are Scientists and Parents at Field Stations and Marine Labs

An often untold narrative, Debinski utilizes autoethnography to explore her experiences as a field-based scientist and parent. From her unique perspective, Debinski explains how she balanced parenthood and a scientific career with support from her partner and FSML community. Debinski closes her chapter with recommendations for cultivating family friend research teams and field station cultures and communities.

Chapter 5: Experiences of a Female Leader at Field Stations and Marine Labs

With almost 20 years of FSML leadership experience, Oktay seeks to answer the question *How can my leadership journey in FSMLs contribute to larger conversations about women in leadership at FSMLs?* Through the use of evocative autoethnography, Oktay shares the experiences and skills from her personal and professional life that have contributed to her growth as a leader. Her chapter concludes with individual recommendations for women seeking leadership positions in FSMLs.

Chapter 6: From the Standpoint of Women FSML Directors: Communication, Leadership, and the Impact of Gender Norms

In chapter 6, McDermott and May seek to understand women FSML directors' experiences and potential barriers to recruitment through the theoretical lens of standpoint theory. Beginning with the lived experiences of women directors, the authors seek to understand the role communication plays in the lives of three women directors within the same university system. These experiences are then compared with a decade of FSML director job descriptions to identify potential barriers to job recruitment, application, and retainment. From these findings, the authors suggest practical recommendations for job descriptions and training to increase the diverse pool of candidates qualified and available for directorship positions.

Chapter 7: Identifying Factors that Contribute to Positive and Negative Student Experiences at Field-Based Institutions

Serving in an equal first author role Becker, Griffin, and Miller seek to explicate the student experience at FSMLs. The experiences of students at FSMLs early in their careers have the potential to positively or negatively impact their long-term career trajectory in STEM. Thus, through the analysis of

402 qualitative survey responses, they find that five distinct factors have the potential to positively or negatively impact students' experiences at FSMLs. From these findings, the authors suggest solutions for improving the experiences of students at FSMLs.

Chapter 8: The Gift Relationship: How Mentoring Leads to Success for Women in Field Station Leadership

Through qualitative interviews with women in the FSML community, Oktay and Kloeppel explore the role of mentoring in the lives of women at FSMLs. Their results suggest that mentoring plays a critical role in the long-term trajectory and retention of women in field-based careers. From these findings, Oktay and Kloeppel provide recommendations for improving mentorship within the FSML community.

Chapter 9: Are Field Stations Gendered Work Spaces?

Often conflated, FSMLs and Nature Centers (NC) serve similar populations for engaging students and local communities in outdoor science. In this chapter, Roketenetz and Holliday delineate the gendered roles, perception, and status of FSML versus NCs and how each contributes to science education and communication. Through the analysis of survey responses, the authors find that gender impacts the perception of each organizations' overall mission, and subsequently their staffing compositions. From these results, Roketenetz and Holliday argue that the FSML and NC communities may enhance STEM engagement with more strategic, long-term partnership plans and goals.

Chapter 10: Women's Perspective on Building International Community–Field Station Partnerships

Struminger, Adame, & Shannan seek to address how best to advance FSML collaborations with local and international communities. Chapter 10 merges the unique perspectives of two leaders from the same field station through the assistance of a moderator and translator, to explore the ways in which identifying as women and mothers impacts their work and their shared goal of conservation, environmental health, and knowledge-building. From this conversation, the authors share how they have sought to engage in collaboration to bring together the work of El Centro de Investigaciones Científicas de las Huastecas "Aguazarca" (CICHAZ) and ASPac, to the greater international academic/research community and the local Calnali community that surrounds the CICHAZ field station.

Chapter 11: A Long (Community) Engagement: From Journalism to Field Stations

Author Busch illustrates a common theme among field station workers, namely, a nonlinear career path. Busch started her career as a successful science magazine writer and years later, she found herself in the position of field station director. She explains how her diverse background and training has impacted her values and programming as a field station leader. From the perspective of a seasoned journalist, Busch seeks to understand the importance and value of science communication within, the Native and Indigenous communities FSMLs occupy, the scientific community, and the general population at large.

Recommendations for FSMLs

Chapter 12: Recommendations for Developing More Diverse, Equitable, Accessible, and Inclusive FSMLs

In this final chapter, editors May, McDermott, and Gee provide overarching recommendations for administrators, FSML site directors, and individual scientists, based on the gaps identified in the above chapters, to make FSMLS more inclusive and equitable spaces to promote scientific discovery.

CONCLUSION

Although we recognize the incredible scholarship represented in the following chapters, we also acknowledge that this edited volume is simply a starting point for exploring the complex and dynamic experiences of marginalized individuals navigating the realities of FSMLs. We find it imperative to highlight what we consider "blind spots" in this edited volume, specifically the lack of diversity of the editorial team. From these blind spots, we provide opportunities for future research in the conclusion of this edited volume.

Overall, FSMLs have the potential to make science more accessible to people from all backgrounds (Billick et al., 2013) and through the use of immersive science, we can increase the engagement and retention rates of women and BIPOC individuals in the STEM disciplines (Dahlberg et al., 2008; Flowers et al., 2021; Gosztyla et al., 2021; NRC, 2014; Zavaleta et al., 2020). However, due to their undefined nature, we need to understand and acknowledge the many complex variables that negatively impact a FSMLs' climate to better support the science that occurs at and the scientists that visit them. We advocate that FSMLs take advantage of the unique and unbounded opportunities within these undefined spaces at the margins of the academic scientific community to engage in innovative interdisciplinary research to challenge and push the steadfast norms of the academic community. In order to continue developing cutting-edge research and science (Gosztyla et al., 2021), it is imperative that we diversify science, especially at FSMLs, to create more equitable, accessible, diverse, and inclusive climates. It is within this boundless place of scholarship, teaching, and outreach that we may shift the values of publication metric standards and impact factors (Davies et al. 2021) to an equitable space where we share the process of scientific inquiry with everyone.

NOTE

1. "FSML" is an abbreviation for field stations and marine laboratories used throughout the book.

REFERENCES

Adams, T. E., Ellis, C., & Holman Jones, S. (2017). Autoethnography. In J. Matthes, C. S. Davis, & R .F. Potter (Eds.), *The international encyclopedia of communication research methods*. John Wiley & Sons, Inc. https://onlinelibrary.wiley.com/doi/pdf/10.1002/9781118901731.iecrm0011

Baker, B. (2015). The way forward for biological field stations: Change needed to ensure survival and scientific relevance. *BioScience 65*(2), 123–129. https://doi.org/10.1093/biosci/biv003

Bekki, J. M., Bernstein, B. L., Ellison, K., Sridharan, A., Hita, L., & Spadola, Q. (2008). Work in progress: using case studies to increase the retention of female doctoral students in STEM fields. *38th Annual Frontiers in Education Conference*, T4F-9-T4F-10. https://doi.org/10.1109/FIE.2008.4720366.

Billick, I., Babb, I., Kloeppel, B., Leong, J. C., Hodder, J., Sanders, J., & Swain, H. (2013). Field stations and marine laboratories of the future: A Strategic vision. *National Association of Marine Laboratories and Organization of Biological Field Stations*. http://www.obfs.org/fsml-future.

Bryant, A., & Charmaz, K. (2007). *The SAGE handbook of grounded theory*. SAGE Publications LTD.

Buzzanell, P. M., Long, Z., Anderson, L. B., Kokini, K., & Batra, J. C. (2015). Mentoring in academe: A feminist poststructural lens on stories of women engineering faculty of color. *Management Communication Quarterly*, *29*(3), 440–457. https://doi.org/10.1177/0893318915574311

Dahlberg, T., Barnes, T., Rorrer, A., & Powell, E. (2008, March 12–15). *Improving retention and graduate recruitment through immersive research experiences for undergraduates* [Conference presentation]. *SIGCSE*, Portland, OR, United States.

Davies, S. W., Putnam, H. M., Ainsworth, T., Baum, J. K., Bove, C. B., Crosby, S. C., Côté, I. M., Duplouy, A., Fulweiler, R. W., Griffin, A. J., Hanley, T. C., Hill, T., Humanes, A., Mangubhai, S., Metaxas, A., Parker, L. M., Rivera, H. E., Silbiger, N. S., Smith, N. S., ... Bates, A. E. (2021). Promoting inclusive metrics of success and impact to dismantle a discriminatory reward system in science. *PLoS Biology, 19*(6), e3001282. https://doi.org/10.1371/journal.pbio.3001282

Flowers, S. K., O'Connell, K., & McDermott, V. M. (2021). Crafting field station and marine lab communities for undergraduate diversity, equity, and inclusion. *The Bulletin of the Ecological Society of America*, e01908. https://doi.org/10.1002/bes2.1908

Golden S. J., Chang, C., & Kozlowski, S. W. J. (2018). Teams in isolated, confined, and extreme (ICE) environments: Review and integration. *Journal of Organizational Behavior, 39*(6), 701–715. https://doi.org/10.1002/job.2288

Gosztyla, M. L., Kwong, L., Murray, N. A., Williams, C. E., Behnke, N., Curry, P., et al. (2021). Responses to 10 common criticisms of anti-racism action in STEMM. *PLoS Computational Biology, 17*(7), e1009141. https://doi.org/10.1371/journal.pcbi.1009141

Hsieh, H.-F., & Shannon, S. E. (2005). Three approaches to qualitative content analysis. *Qualitative Health Research, 15*(9), 1277–1288. https://doi.org/10.1177/1049732305276687

"In the field". (2018, September 25). *AdvanceGeo*. https://serc.carleton.edu/advance-geo/resources/field_work.html

Intergovernmental Panel on Climate Change [IPCC]. (2021). Climate change 2021. https://www.ipcc.ch/report/ar6/wg1/downloads/report/IPCC_AR6_WGI_SPM.pdf

Kisselburgh, L. G., Berkelaar, B. L., & Buzzanell, P. M. (2016). Discourse, gender, and the meaning of work rearticulating science, technology and engineering careers through communicative lenses. *Annals of the International Communication Association, 33*(1), 259–299. https://doi.org/10.1080/23808985.2009.11679089

Little, G. (2017). Connecting environmental humanities: Developing interdisciplinary collaborative method. *Humanities, 6*(91), 1–22. https://doi.org/10.3390/h6040091

Miller, T. R., Baird, T. D., Littlefield, C. M., Kofinas, G., Chapin III, F., & Redman, C. L. (2008). Epistemological pluralism: Reorganizing interdisciplinary research. *Ecology and Society, 13*, 46–62. https://www.jstor.org/stable/26268006

National Academy of Sciences, the National Academy of Engineering, and the Institute of Medicine. (2005). *Facilitating interdisciplinary research*. National Academies Press.

National Research Council [NRC]. (2014). Enhancing the value of sustainability of field stations and marine laboratories in the 21st century. https://www.nap.edu/catalog/18806/enhancing-the-value-and-sustainability-of-field-stations-and-marine-laboratories-in-the-21st-century

OBFS. (n.d.). *Home*. https://www.obfs.org/

Robinson, B., Vasko, S. E., Gonnerman, C., Christen M., O'Rourke, M., & Steel, D. (2016). Human values and the value of humanities in interdisciplinary research. *Cogent Arts & Humanities, 3*(1), 1–16. https://doi.org/10.1080/23311983.2015.1123080

Stirling, A. (2007). A general framework for analysing diversity in science, technology and society. *Journal of the Royal Society Interface, 4*, 707–719. https://doi.org/10.1098/rsif.2007.0213

Shipley, T. F., McConnell, D., McNeal, K. S., Petcovic, H. L., & St. John, K. E. (2017). Transdisciplinary science education research and practice: Opportunities for GER in a developing STEM discipline-based education research alliance (DBER-A). *Journal of Geoscience Education, 65*(4), 354–362. https://doi.org/10.5408/1089-9995-65.4.354

Snow, C. P. (1959). *The two cultures.* Cambridge University Press.

Stern, L. N. (2016). Building on success and learning from experience: An independent review of the research excellence framework. *Department for Business, Energy & Industrial Strategy.* https://www.gov.uk/government/publications/research-excellence-framework-review

Struminger, R., Zarestky, J., Short, R. A., & Lawing, A. M. (2018). A framework for informal STEM education outreach at field stations. *BioScience, 68*(12), 969–978. https://doi.org/10.1093/biosci/biy108.

Swartz, T. H., Palermo, A. S., Masur, S. K., & Aberg, J. A. (2019). The science of value of diversity: Closing the gaps in our understanding of inclusion and diversity. *Journal of Infectious Diseases, 220*, S33–S41. https://doi.org/10.1093/infdis/jiz174

Taebi, B., Correljé, A., Cuppen, E., Dignum, M., & Pesch, U. (2014). Responsible innovation as an endorsement of public values: the need for interdisciplinary research. *Journal of Responsible Innovation, 1*(1), 118–124. https://doi.org/10.1080/23299460.2014.882072

Tydecks, L., Bremerich, V., Jentschke, I., Likens, G. E., & Tockner, K. (2016). Biological field stations: A global infrastructure for research, education, and public engagement. *BioScience, 66*(2), 164–171. https://doi.org/10.1093/biosci/biv174

Vieyra, M., Gilmore, J., & Timmerman, B. (2011). Requiring research may improve retention in STEM fields for underrepresented women. *Council on Undergraduate Research Quarterly, 32*(1), 13–20.

Zavaleta, E. S., Beltran, R. S., & Borker, A. L. (2020). How field courses propel inclusion and collective excellence. *Scientific Life, 35*(11), 953–956. https://doi.org/10.1016/j.tree.2020.08.005

Part I

SETTING THE STAGE OF FSMLS

Chapter 1

Defining the Role and Value of FSMLs

Victoria M. McDermott, Jennifer M. Gee,
and Amy R. May

One of the most important ways to understand the altered state of our planet is through long-term data collection in relatively undisturbed living "libraries" that can only be found at field stations and marine laboratories (FSML). FSMLs provide access to students and researchers to further their knowledge of and contribute to our understanding of the changing environment (OBFS, 2018). Field stations are a "home for science" (Geissler & Kelly, 2016, p. 798), providing researchers a place of residence to study the natural world as our climatic conditions and the built environment continue to shift. Likened to anything from a research base camp to a research hotel, FSMLs are spread throughout the world in different forms with the sustained purpose and goal of protecting the environment and ecosystems (Geissler & Kelly, 2016). Found in all biomes, they tend to be heavily concentrated in marine, terrestrial, and freshwater systems (Billick et al., 2013; National Research Council NRC, 2014; Tydecks et al., 2016). FSMLs allow researchers to observe in real-time what is happening in the present ecological conditions and to compare it with similar data from the distant past as well as to make future observations (OBFS, 2018; Tydecks et al., 2016). This chapter begins with a brief overview of the purpose and value of FSMLs. We then explore the basics of FSMLs, as well as their past steeped in colonialism and male-dominated institutions. The chapter closes with an overview of the potential impacts of isolated, confined, and extreme (ICE) environments.

FSMLS AN OVERVIEW

Purpose and Value of FSMLs

The ultimate goal of FSMLs is to provide researchers with the opportunity for free and open inquiry into the natural world, supporting a culture of scientific research through offering a secure outdoor facility with all required infrastructure (i.e., living accommodations, food, laboratory space, etc.). With around 1,268 biological field stations located in 120 countries around the world, FSMLs encompass a wide range of ecological zones and conditions and FSMLs provide the necessary infrastructures to contribute crucial scientific information worldwide on environmental events (Billick, et al., 2013; NRC, 2014; Tydeck, et al. 2016). No matter the individual nature of the field location, FSMLs are on the front lines of understanding shifting climates and ecosystems to better understand the world's future conditions. Furthermore, FSMLs share the commitment to advance our understanding and mindful stewardship of the Earth through the support of teaching, research, and public education.

Teaching

FSMLs are a hub for undergraduate, graduate, and postdoctoral students to receive firsthand experience collecting and analyzing data under natural conditions in the field, and they are often affiliated with universities (Elser, 2016; Stevens & Gilson, 2016). In a 2008 survey of the 300 undergraduate geology students, 99% reported that they had to take a field course at some point in their college career (Drummond & Markin, 2008). The firsthand experience of fieldwork provides young students with educational opportunities and skills that cannot be replicated within a traditional academic college campus or classroom setting (Billick et al., 2013; Hodder, 2009; Janovy & Major, 2009; O'Brien et al., 2020; Tydeck et al., 2016; Zavaleta et al., 2020). For many students and researchers in training, spending a season in a remote field station collecting data can be a "life-changing experience" (Elser, 2016, p. 19). For example, James Elser, director of the Flathead Lake Biological Station of the University of Montana, stated that his summer at the University of Notre Dame's Environmental Research Station (UNDERC) was where he "found [his] life's vocation" (Elser, 2016, p. 19). This was a formative experience in Elser's life that shaped his future love of oceanography and FSML research. This is a common story for many emerging scientists who visit FSMLs. Overall, FSMLs are crucial for training the next generation of scientists and continuing training of educators and natural resource professionals (McNulty et al., 2017; NRC, 2014).

Research

FSMLs bridge the gap between the more controlled environment of laboratory science and the unpredictable science that researchers encounter in the field, connecting experimentalists and lab scientists to a real-world environmental context (NRC, 2014). The often remote locations of FSMLs provide the necessary settings for studying biodiversity and ecosystem processes untouched and within their natural settings (Billick et al., 2013; Tydeck et al., 2016). Field stations are living repositories of long-term data sets and plant and animal collections which are vital in understanding the factors associated with climate change (McNulty et al., 2017).

Additionally, FSMLs contribute scientific information to help key stakeholders (e.g., local ecological agencies, such as state and national parks, and governmental bodies, such as the U.S. Forest Service) tackle critical environmental issues and assist with evidence-based decision-making as at the local, national, and international level (OBFS, 2018). FSML staff and researchers also often play a critical role in ensuring that environmental considerations are factored into local and regional planning and development decisions. FSMLs may often act as a mediator between universities and local/federal government entities and the local communities they serve such as Native and Indigenous tribes and local peoples.

Finally, FSMLs also have an impact worldwide, providing a global network view of science to assist decision-makers in assessing and understanding environmental change. FSMLs play a fundamental role in supporting the search for long-term solutions when attempting to solve problems caused by global change (Perrings et al., 2011). The large intertwined network of research stations provides powerful collaborations across researchers, universities, stations, and countries.

Public Education

As living laboratories in the world of nature, FSMLs play an important role in giving K-12 students, members of the public, media, and elected officials direct access to research being conducted in the wilderness that surrounds the places we live and opportunities for engaging in citizen science (Baker, 2015). At the regional level, FSMLs often have an impact on the local communities where they are situated. Field stations provide local learning opportunities for students and the public to collaborate in the scientific process (Tydeck et al., 2016). The educational opportunities presented through a FSML may vary much more widely than a traditional academic setting, from courses for students and teachers to workshops for local farmers or conservation workers (see Struminger, Adame, & Shannan's chapter 10 in this edited volume; Whitesell et al., 2002).

Basics of FSMLs

A multitude of factors define and impact the climate and dynamics of a FSML. These factors include location, community support, stability of funding, staffing, availability of basic human necessities (i.e., power, water, and protection from the elements and wildlife), and the impacts of isolation. All of these have an effect on overall functioning at both the individual and organization-wide levels of a FSML.

How FSMLs Are Funded and Staffed

Much like the diversity among the specific objectives of each research station, funding sources also vary across FSMLs (Tydecks et al., 2016; Wyman et al., 2009). Many FSMLs are funded through grants awarded to individual scientists who wish to pursue a single lab's study question at the field station (research-based awards), to individual grantees awarded to the specific station (place-based award), or funding from the station's affiliated university or through governmental funding (institution-based awards). These forms of funding are highly volatile and lack long-term sustainability (Wyman et al., 2009). Furthermore, for many scientists and FSML staff receiving funding can be a barrier to access (Mansy et al., 2010). The cost of getting to a station, staying at a station for an extended period of time, and having the necessary equipment (i.e., hiking gear) for surviving in these remote natural environments requires social and monetary capital (NRC, 2014).

Therefore, the threat of closure and lack of funding for FSMLs has been a long-standing problem that threatens these irreplaceable study sites (NRC, 2014; Schubel, 2015; Tydeck et al., 2016). In 1945, there were 53 biological field stations operating in the United States. By 1966, only 20 of the original 53 biological field stations remained (Arvey & Riemer, 1966; Tydeck et al., 2016). FSMLs must always be on the lookout for grants, scientists, and educators from outside the managing institution who depend on access to FSMLs to pursue their scholarly and educational activities to stay afloat and steward the land for future research, teaching, and education.

The range of funding also translates to a variety of sizes and technological advancements of FSML, that is, from "trail networks to state-of-the-art laboratories" (OBFS, 2018, para. 2). Overall, the variability of staffing between FSMLs is high, with 60% of field stations having 10 or fewer employees and only 2% of all research stations having between 250 and 500 employees (Baker, 2015). Staffing at FSMLs tends to be minimal (Stevens & Gilson, 2016). This leads to staff having increased job responsibilities to keep the station running and safe for users. Overall, there is a dearth of research on the staffing of, and dynamics between, staff and scientists at FSMLs (see chapter 7 by Becker, Griffin, & Miller in this edited volume). Current research focuses more on the experiences and repercussions that scientists in the field must endure and not on the experiences of the staff themselves.

Where FSMLs Are Located

FSMLs are uniquely suited to studying a variety of environmental phenomena, ranging from global changes in climate, including in phenology, to the changing distributions of organisms (Baker, 2015; Raby, 2017). While FSMLs can be found in all climates and biomes (Baker, 2015), due to their often colonialist origins, they tend to be located in North America and Europe (Raby, 2017). For example, over one-third of all research stations are located in the United States alone (Baker, 2015). Stocks, Seales, Paniagua, Maehr, and Bruna (2008) suggested that the uneven representation of FSMLs across the globe has contributed to selective patterns of fieldwork, as well as across scientific inquiry and conservation in these neglected locations (Amano & Sutherland, 2013). Only 10% of published ecological studies are based at tropical field sites, although tropical countries make up about 40% of the global land area (Martin et al., 2012; Raby, 2017). Tropical field stations tend to cluster in a handful of locations in Central America, and there are sections of the world, such as tropical Africa and Asia, and tropical and subtropical dry forests, that remain under-represented in published fieldwork.

Colonialism

In addition to the lack of diversity in FSML locations, FSMLs often have a tenuous history with the village or community that surrounds them (Raby, 2017; Tydecks et al., 2016). Tense histories of scientists infiltrating and ruining Indigenous peoples' land and cultures are still readily felt today. Moreover, there is a long history of racially segregating the local populations after using them for their local resources and ages-old knowledge of the land (Anderson, 2009; Geissler, 2015; Geissler et al., 2016; Tilley, 2011). This use of imperialism has prevented Indigenous peoples from accessing FSMLs and collaborating on scientific discoveries.

In the mid-20th century, as tropical field stations in South America began to rise in prominence and popularity, it was made extremely clear to local scientists and Indigenous people that FSMLs were solely oriented toward the research goals of the United States (Raby, 2017). The implications of this domination of local communities and colonialism still impact the scientific community today. International field stations run by Western countries generate further distrust between science and society at large, especially with local communities that often form the infrastructure and local support system of FSMLs (see chapters 3 by McDermott and 10 by Struminger, Adame, & Shannan in this edited volume). Indigenous people have been treated more like servants by researchers and scientists than equal scientific counterparts. Furthermore, the potential clash of religious or cultural beliefs and practices (e.g., subsistence living) can result in conflicts between FSMLs and the communities in which they reside.

Much like the history of tropical FSMLs, polar stations also have a history of racially segregating local populations. Polar field stations were originally used as a way for countries to stake claim on land and compete with each other for knowledge, along with land, access to oil, and other natural resources (Geissler & Kelly, 2016). Unlike the tropical research stations, however, polar research stations members often had to work more closely with Indigenous communities to survive life-threatening conditions in places, such as Greenland and Alaska, to develop skills for adapting to the extreme cold while pursuing scientific data collection (Geissler & Kelly, 2016). One of the most prominent examples of colonialism and FSMLs is the geopolitical race surrounding the ownership of Antarctica, which is still felt today. Even though Antarctica is not owned by one specific country ("The Antarctic Treaty," 2011), many countries have their own research stations in Antarctica to maintain autonomy and national interests, even though resources might be better spent developing shared research stations.

Indigenous people and local communities are a part of the ecosystem that must be acknowledged for the survival of field stations. There is now a heightened focus on including both the local and remote public in field station activities, such as enrolling rural communities in research, building platforms for local citizens to engage in science, and enhancing K-12 engagement through media and schools (Graboyes, 2015; Moyi-Okwaro & Geissler, 2015). Scientists must explore the potential knowledge of Native and resident populations in order to collaborate and co-produce innovative, useful information (Geissler & Kelly, 2016; O'Reilly, 2016). Without the invaluable insights and support of local communities, scientific discoveries and research may remain at a standstill. Building trust and rapport with the local communities, as well as the general public, is a vital element for keeping field stations alive, communicating science to people who may not be able to access FSMLs, and ensuring the safety of the surrounding communities.

Male-dominated Institutions

Similar to their history of colonialism, FSMLs are often based in patriarchal norms and practices making it difficult for women to navigate and succeed in these organizations. While this edited volume is dedicated to documenting the experiences of women in FSMLs, we will provide a brief interlude to some of the most common barriers they face. These barriers include access to leadership, family-work balance, and harassment while in the field.

Leadership. Women leaders within FSMLs remain relatively rare compared to their male counterparts, leading to the different lived experiences and sense-making processes for both genders (Burns, 2001; Rothblum et al., 1998; Schmidt et al., 2005). In a study located at a remote station in Antarctica, findings suggested that women in leadership positions received less social support than other expeditioners (Rothblum et al., 1998). Previous research has suggested that the lack of social support for women in leadership can be an additional source of stress for leaders, especially for leaders who highly value group cohesion (Rothblum et al., 1998; Schmidt et al., 2005). The social roles assumed by males and females and the perceptions of interpersonal interactions and social support are consistent with prescriptive traditional gender roles (Burns, 2001; Rothblum et al., 1998; Weinstock, 1998). Women in FSMLs often become nurtures (McDermott, 2019), while men thrive in positions of power.

Work-life balance. Moreover, FSML life is often not conducive to families or relationships. McGuire, Primack, and Losos (2012) found a high proportion of single respondents for both men and women in their survey of field station life, which is a phenomenon that has been found in other disciplines of academia (Fox et al., 2011). The rigorous demands of academia and fieldwork do not assist in fostering or maintaining serious relationships and family development (McGuire et al., 2012). For those with families, women were more likely to bring children with them to the field, while men were more likely to have their spouses take care of their children at home (McGuire et al., 2012). Since the beginning of FSMLs, inequities in childcare responsibilities have contributed to higher observed rates of women leaving the field of science and lower levels of productivity, promotion, and salaries in comparison with those of men (Ceci & Williams, 2011; McGuire et al., 2012).

Harassment. Finally, previous research has demonstrated the concerning rates of sexual abuse and harassment that exist within FSMLs (Clancy et al., 2014; Gass, 2014; Gluckman, 2018; Wadman, 2017). Clancy and colleagues (2014) sounded an alarm for the scientific community and field camps alike when they conducted a 600-respondent survey that found 74.2% of respondents said they had seen firsthand or been told about colleagues making sexual comments at field sites. A further 64% of the respondents had personally been verbally sexually harassed and over 20% of the respondents had been sexually assaulted. Their findings suggest that women are 3.5 times more likely to report experiencing sexual harassment than men. Women were much more likely to report being sexually harassed or assaulted by men in positions of power; men were also likely to receive inappropriate sexual comments or actions but from peers of the same sex (Clancy et al., 2014). This study has since been replicated with similar findings in other disciplines that require fieldwork such as archaeology (Meyers et al., 2015) and the field of social work (Moylan & Wood, 2016). In 2017, Clancy and colleagues found that not only did these rates of sexual harassment and assault occur within the planetary sciences but that these experiences of hostility were even greater for women of color (Clancy et al., 2017).

As an extension of traditional academic environments, FSMLs create unique situations for individuals to navigate, especially when it comes to harassment. Unlike a classic 9-to-5 job, the remote nature of camps may make it next to impossible for victims to leave camp, talk with people within their normal support network, or even report the incident (Gluckman, 2018). FSMLs tend to rely on a hierarchy for both staff and researchers, meaning that sometimes only one person has access to vehicles or satellite phones to connect with the outside world (Gluckman, 2018). The remoteness can make it difficult to have a harasser removed from camp and the lack of clear boundaries can make certain rules seem less clear or less likely to be enforced (Gluckman, 2018). With the added complexity of colleagues spending days together for weeks on end, sleeping in close quarters and socializing together at night, the norms and customs that develop within a season at a FSML can be remarkably different than the rules within a normal workplace or academic setting (Gluckman, 2018). Remote fieldwork may even amplify the damaging effects of sexual harassment, as the distance from society may become both physical and emotional (Wadman, 2017).

Effects of Isolated, Confined, and Extreme Environments (ICE)

FSMLs are often located in ICE environments. Previous research has explored the impact of ICE environments through experiences such as military deployments and the work done by the National Aeronautics and Space Administration (NASA). Remote research stations, like those located in Antarctica, have been likened to extreme circumstances such as spaceflights and deep-sea exploration (Sandal et al., 2006; Suedfeld & Weiss, 2000; Yan et al., 2011). Current research on ICE has focused on the negative and positive impacts of ICE on those living and working in such conditions.

Isolation

People in ICE must deal with a lack of contact and connection to their normal social networks (Golden et al., 2017). For example, both staff and researchers living in remote field station must deal with the physical separation from friends and family. This extreme isolation can negatively impact individuals as well as how situations among groups are handled (see Golden et al., 2017). Long-term isolation has been linked to a reduction in sleep quality, impaired cognitive ability, and interpersonal tension (Palinkas & Suedfeld, 2007).

Confinement

A second defining factor of ICE environments is the lack of mobility and forced confinement within a socially closed "island" community of people, often due to dangerous outside conditions. The lack of private space and having to live and work in the same environment adds to the pervasive feeling of social confinement. In some FSMLs, people may be limited to living in just a few tents and laboratories for months at a time (Yan et al., 2011).

Extreme Environment

Finally, ICE situations present inhabitants with treacherous and life-threatening conditions (Golden et al., 2017). Extreme environments are defined as harsh and challenging conditions (Steinach et al., 2016). Some characteristics of extreme environments can be extremely high or low temperatures, absence of water and power, high or low atmospheric content of oxygen or carbon dioxide, or high levels of radiation and acidity. Examples of these locations include volcanoes, deep ocean trenches, extremely high elevation sites, deserts, polar regions, and even outer space (Golden et al., 2017; Steinach et al., 2016). These environments make it difficult for survival, requiring all species to adapt in order to survive.

Positive Impacts of ICE

A majority of research focuses on the negative aspects of ICE; however, ICE environments have the potential to provide some positive outcomes. Palinkas and Suedfeld (2007) suggested two major categories of positive outcomes from ICE expeditions; "the inherently enjoyable characteristics of the situation" (p. 158) and "positive reactions to challenges of the environment and having encountered and successfully surmounted these challenges" (p. 158). Many participants in previous studies and in personal ethnographies have acknowledged the grandeur and beauty of the landscape. People also noted the camaraderie and thrill of facing the life-threatening challenges of the environment alone and together with their peers (Mocellin & Suedfeld, 1991).

CONCLUSION

FSMLs usually center their mission around teaching, research, and public education. They provide an invaluable resource for continuing to push the limits of scientific research. While FSMLs as a whole seek to serve a similar purpose, there is great variability in the size, staffing, funding, and location of an individual FSML which can impact the overall culture and climate of an individual station. Two important factors impacting the structure and climate of FSMLs today are their roots in colonialism and male-dominated institutions. From this general overview, the rest of the book seeks to contribute more research to and challenge the conversation regarding experiences with and at FSMLs for people of all identities.

REFERENCES

Amano, T., & Sutherland, W. J. (2013). Four barriers to the global understanding of biodiversity conservation: Wealth, language, geographical location, and security. *Proceedings of the Royal Society of London: Biological Sciences, 280*(1756), 2022649. https://doi.org/10.1098/rspb.2012.2649

Anderson, W. (2009). From subjugated knowledge to conjugated subjects: Science and globalization, or postcolonial studies of science?. *Postcolonial Studies, 12*(4), 389–400. https://doi.org/10.1080/13688790903350641

Arvey, M. D., & Riemer, W. J. (1966). Inland biological field stations of the United States. *BioScience, 16*(4), 249–254. https://doi.org/10.2307/1293564

Baker, B. (2015). The way forward for biological field stations. *BioScience, 65*(2), 123–129. https://doi.org/10.1093/biosci/biu210

Becker, D. M., Griffin, J. E., & Miller, C. M. L. (2022). Identifying factors that contribute to positive and negative student experiences at field-based institutions. In V. McDermott, J. Gee, & A. R. May (Eds.), *Women of the wild: Challenging gender disparities in field stations and marine laboratories* (pp. 143–168). Lexington Books.

Billick, I., Babb, I., Kloeppel, B., Leong, J. C., Hodder, J., Sanders, J., & Swain, H. (2013). Field stations and marine laboratories of the future. *Organization of Biological Field Stations.* https://www.obfs.org/assets/docs/fsml_final_report.pdf

Burns, R. (2001). *'Just tell them I survived!': Women in Antarctica.* Allen & Unwin.

Ceci, S. J., & Williams, W. M. (2011). Understanding current causes of women's underrepresentation in science. *Proceedings of the National Academy of Sciences, 108*, 3157–3162. https://doi.org/10.1073/pnas.1014871108

Clancy, K. B. H., Nelson, R., Rutherford, J. N., & Hinde, K. (2014). Survey of academic field experiences (SAFE): Trainees report harassment and assault. *PLoS One, 9*(7), E102–E172. https://doi.org/10.1371/journal.pone.0102172

Clancy, K. B. H., Lee, K. M. N., Rodgers, E. M., & Richey, C. (2017). Double jeopardy in astronomy and planetary science: Women of color face greater risks of gendered and racial harassment. *Journal of Geophysical Research, 122*(7), 1610–1623. https://doi.org/10.1002/2017JE005256

Drummond, C. N., & Markin, J. N. (2008). An analysis of the bachelor of science in geology degree as offered in the United States. *Journal of Geoscience Education, 56*, 113–119. https://doi.org/10.5408/1089-9995-56.2.113

Elser, J. (2016). Message from the president: The future of field stations, the future of the aquatic sciences; some thanks to John Dolan. *Association for the Sciences of Limnology and Oceanography,* 19–20. https://aslopubs.onlinelibrary.wiley.com/doi/pdfdirect/10.1002/lob.10084

Fox, M. F., Fonseca, C., & Bao, J. (2011). Work and family conflict in academic science: Patterns and predictors among women and men in research universities. *Social Studies of Science, 41*, 715–735. https://doi.org/10.1177/0306312711417730

Gass, H. (2014, July 14). Sexual harassment and assault prove common during scientific field studies. *Scientific American.* https://www.scientificamerican.com/article/sexualharassment-and-assault-prove-common-during-scientific-field-studies/

Geissler, P. W. (2015). What future remains? Remembering an African place of science. In P. W. Geissler (Eds.), *Para-states and medical science: Making global health in Africa* (pp. 142–178). Duke University Press.

Geissler, P. W., & Kelly, A. H. (2016). A home for science: The life and times of Tropical and Polar field stations. *Social Studies of Science, 46*(6), 797–808. https://doi.org/10.1177/0306312716680767

Gluckman, N. (2018, July 15). Field sites are harassment hell. Here's how to improve them. *The Chronicle of Higher Education.* https://www.chronicle.com/article/Field-Sites-Are-Harassment/243914

Golden, S. J., Chang, C., & Kozlowski, S. W. J. (2017). Teams in isolated, confined, and extreme (ICE) environments: Review and integration. *Journal of Organizational Behavior, 39*, 701–715. https://doi.org/10.1002/job.2288

Graboyes, M. (2015) *The experiment must continue: Medical research and ethics in east Africa, 1940–2014.* Ohio University Press.

Hodder, J. (2009). What are undergraduates doing at biological field stations and marine laboratories? *BioScience*, *59*(8), 666–672. https://doi.org/10.1525/bio.2009.59.8.8

Janovy, J., & Major, K. M. (2009). Why we have field stations: Reflections on the cultivation of biologists. *BioScience*, *59*(3), 217–222. https://doi.org/10.1525/bio.2009.59.3.6

Mansy, K., Gundersen, G., & Palmer, M. W. (2010). *Design guidelines for sustainable biological field stations.* Oklahoma Academy of Sciences. https://hdl.handle.net/11244/317678

Martin, L., Blossey, B., & Ellis, E. (2012). Mapping where ecologists work: Biases in the global distribution of terrestrial ecological observations. *Frontiers in Ecology and the Environment, 10*, 195–201. https://doi.org/10.1890/110154

McDermott, V. (2019). *'It's a magnifying glass': The communication of power in a remote field station* [Unpublished master's thesis]. University of Alaska Fairbanks.

McDermott, V. (2022). "Brush your hair, apply for every grant, and get laid as much as possible": Sensemaking women's experiences conducting fieldwork in the tropics. In V. McDermott, J. Gee, & A. R. May (Eds.), *Women of the wild: Challenging gender disparities in field stations and marine laboratories* (pp. 31–52). Lexington Books.

McGuire, K. L., Primack, R. B., & Losos, E. C. (2012). Dramatic improvements and persistent challenges for women ecologists. *BioScience, 62*(2), 189–196. https://doi.org/10.1525/bio.2012.62.2.12

McNulty, S. A., White, D., Huft, M., & Foster, P. (2017). The organization of biological field stations at fifty. *Bulletin of the Ecological Society of America, 98*(4), 359–373. https://www.jstor.org/stable/90013298

Meyers, M., Boudreax, T., Carmody, S., Dekle, V., Horton, E., & Wright, A. (2015). Preliminary results of the SEAC sexual harassment survey. *Horizon and Tradition: The Newsletter of the Southeastern Archaeological Conference, 57*(1), 19–35.

Mocellin, J. S. P., & Suedfeld, P. (1991). Voices from the ice: Diaries of polar explorers. *Environmental Behavior, 23,* 704–722. https://doi.org/10.1177/0013916591236004

Moylan, C. A., & Wood, L. (2016). Sexual harassment in social work field placements, prevalence, and characteristics. *Journal of Women and Social Work, 31*(4): 405–417. https://doi.org/10.1177/0886109916644643

Moyi-Okwaro, F., & Geissler, P. W. (2015). In/dependent collaborations: Perceptions and experiences of African scientists in transnational HIV research. *Medical Anthropology Quarterly, 29*(4), 492–511. https://doi.org/10.1111/maq.12206

National Research Council [NRC]. (2014). Enhancing the value of sustainability of field stations and marine laboratories in the 21st century. https://www.nap.edu/catalog/18806/enhancing-the-value-and-sustainability-of-field-stations-and-marine-laboratories-in-the-21st-century

O'Brien, L. T., Bart, H. L., & Garcia, D. M. (2020). Why are there so few ethnic minorities in ecology and evolutionary biology? Challenges to inclusion and the role of sense of belonging. *Social Psychology of Education*, *23*(2), 449–447. https://doi.org/10.1007/s11218-019-09538-x

O'Reilly, J. (2016). Sensing the ice: Field science, models, and expert intimacy with knowledge. *Journal of the Royal Anthropological Institute, 22*(1), 27–45. https://doi.org/10.1111/1467-9655.12392

OBFS. (2018). *What are field stations.* https://www.obfs.org/what-s-a-fieldstation-

Palinkas, L. A., & Suedfeld, P. (2007). Psychological effects of polar expeditions. *Lancet, 379*, 153–163.

Perrings, C., Duraiappah, A., Larigauderie, A., & Mooney, H. (2011). The biodiversity and ecosystem services science–policy interface. *Science, 331*(6021), 1139–1140. https://doi/org/10.1126/science.1202400

Raby, M. (2017). The colonial origins of tropical field stations. *American Scientist, 105*(4), 216–223.

Rothblum, E., Weinstock, J. S., & Morris, J. F. (1998). Introduction. In E. Rothblum, J. S. Weinstock, & J. F. Morris (Eds.), *Women in the Antarctic* (pp. 1–14). Haworth Press Inc.

Sandal, G. M., Lean, G. R., & Palinkas, L. A. (2006) Human challenges in polar and space environments. *Review of Environmental Science and Biotechnology, 5*, 281–296. https://doi.org/10.1007/s11157-006-9000-8

Schmidt, L. L., Wood, J., & Lugg, D. J. (2005). Gender differences in leader and follower perceptions of social support in Antarctica. *Acta Astronnautica, 56*, 923–931. https://doi.org/10.1016/j.actaastro.2005.01.019

Schubel, J. R. (2015). Some thoughts on keeping field stations and marine labs afloat in turbulent times. *BioScience, 65*(5), 458–459. https://doi.org/10.1093/biosci/biv034

Steinach, M., Kohlberg, E., Maggioni, M. A., Mendt, S., Opatz, O., Stahn, A., & Gunga, H. (2016). Sleep quality changes during overwintering at the German Antarctic stations Neumayer II and III: The gender factor. *PLoS One*, *11*(2), e0150099. https://doi.org/10.1371/journal.pone.0150099

Stevens, M. T., & Gilson, G. G. (2016). An exploration of field–station partnerships: University operated field stations located in US National Parks. *BioScience, 66*(8), 693–701. https://doi.org/10.1093/biosci/biw053

Stocks, G., Seales, L., Paniagua, F., Maehr, E., & Bruna, E. M. (2008). The geographical and institutional distribution of ecological research in the tropics. *Biotropica, 40*(4), 397–404. https://doi.org/10.1111/j.1744-7429.2007.00393.x

Struminger, R., Adame, G. M. V., & Shannan, Y. H. (2022). Women's perspective on building international community-field station partnerships. In V. McDermott, J. Gee, & A. R. May (Eds.), *Women of the wild: Challenging gender disparities in field stations and marine laboratories* (pp. 225–254). Lexington Books.

Suedfeld, P., & Weiss, K. (2000). Antarctica: Natural laboratory and space analogue for psychological research. *Environment and Behavior, 32*, 7–17. https://doi.org/10.1177/00139160021972405

The Antarctic Treaty. (2011). *Secretariat of the antarctic treaty*. https://www.ats.aq/e/ats.htm

Tilley, H. (2011). *Africa as a living laboratory: Empire, development, and the problem of scientific knowledge*. University of Chicago Press.

Tydecks, L., Bremerich, V., Jentschke, I., Likens, G. E., & Tockner, K. (2016). Biological field stations: A global infrastructure for research, education, and public engagement. *BioScience, 66,* 164–171. https://doi.org/10.1093/biosci/biv174

Wadman, M. (2017, October 6). Disturbing allegations of sexual harassment in Antarctica leveled at noted scientist. *Science.* https://www.sciencemag.org/news/2017/10/disturbing-allegations-sexual-harassment-antarctica-leveled-noted-scientist

Weinstock, J. S. (1998). The psychology of social and personal life on an isolated frontier: U.S. women in the Antarctic. In E. Rothblum, J. S. Weinstock, & J. F., Morris (Eds.), *Women in the Antarctic* (pp. 221–236). Haworth Press Inc.

Whitesell, S., Liliehom, R. J., & Sharik, T. L. (2002). A global survey of tropical field stations. *BioScience, 52*, 55–64. https://www.jstor.org/stable/10.1641/0006-3568(2002)052[0055:agsotb]2.0.co;2

Wyman, R. L., Wallensky, E., & Blaine, M. (2009). The activities and importance of international field stations. *BioScience, 59*(7), 584–592. https://doi.org/10.1525/bio.2009.59.7.9

Yan, G., Ye, Q., & Tang, C. (2011). Adaptation and coping strategies in Chinese Antarctic expeditioners' winter-over life. *Advances in Polar Science, 22*(2), 111–117. https://doi.org/10.3724/SP.J.1085.2011.00111

Zavaleta, E. S., Beltran, R. S., & Borker, A. L. (2020). How field courses propel inclusion and collective excellence. *Scientific Life, 35*(11), 953–956. https://doi.org/10.1016/j.tree.2020.08.005

Chapter 2

The Isthmus

Sylvia Torti

Standing outside the bunkhouse, Alex looked out at the lake and saw the station's boat chugging toward the island. Behind the small boat, a massive freighter had emerged from the narrow canal and was moving toward the Pacific Ocean.[1] From there, it would go onto the port in San Diego or Long Beach. Slow beasts of human enterprise, engineers, and concrete were taking over the world.

He looked over at the *Cecropia* tree and saw that the three-toed sloth was still hanging there. A couple of moths fluttered about its back. Sloths are solitary creatures that sleep all day, eat leaves at night, and move only occasionally in slow motion. Their green hue comes from algae that live in the grooved hairs of their coats. This one had come and gone repeatedly over the months, and this afternoon, was hanging upside down, eyes shut, head tucked, likely sensing that the air had become heavy, and it would soon rain. Alex resented sloths; their ability to exist while doing almost nothing disturbed him.

There was a woman on the boat. The night before, José, the cook, had told him and Richard that they were to be joined by another scientist, "una mujer," he'd made a point to emphasize. Although Alex and Richard had gotten along well over the last few months together, the news that a woman would be joining them was acknowledged privately, with pleasure, by each man. Disciplined and tied to their research schedules, neither had left the island often. They talked about research and experiments, of course, and helped each other out with data collection from time to time. They also discussed politics and philosophies, movies and music, but never anything personal or emotional. Intending to preempt Richard's meeting of the woman, Alex had finished work early, showered, and was now ready to descend the 200 steps to the dock so that he would be the first to greet her.

The woman's name was Katherine, and the first thing she noticed from the boat was the whitewashed bunkhouse jutting out from the tall trees. Here she was finally, where she had long dreamed of being, in the middle of one of the most dynamic and exciting places on Earth. About three million years ago, the isthmus—this thin strip of land—had risen up via volcanic activity and bridged two continents, opening the door to The Great American Biotic Interchange. Species, once separated, moved north and south, and as they did so, they competed or mated, speciated, or were rendered extinct. The island had over 500 species of plants, 100 species of mammals, albeit mostly bats, 400 species of birds, and 500 distinct species of butterflies (Siedenburg, 2008).

Her mind settled on the ants she would study. She'd read everything about this species, *Eciton burchellii*, which so far, she'd only seen pinned or floating in tiny vials of alcohol. This was an ant species with a monthly cycle. The colony spent twenty-one days in one location, with daily raids out from the central nest to capture and bring back other ant species. And then, fourteen days in a nomadic phase, moving daily, consuming everything in their path, bivouacking at night. No one knew how many colonies there were on the island or how many ants were in each colony. She had argued to her dissertation committee that army ants were a keystone species, that their presence or absence in the system had the potential to change everything.

Beside her on the boat stood Richard, one of the two men she'd been told were on the island. He was lanky and pale with big eyes and an almost malnourished look. She could see the other one waiting at the dock, a stocky blond. The captain cut the boat's engine. Next to the dock, there was a crane whose weight, perched off-center from the dock, caused it to list slightly to one side. The boat's gears creaked with the rise and fall of the dock from the wake. The dock appeared to not have been used in some time.

Richard waved to the man on the dock. "That's Alex. He studies Howler monkeys."

Alex smiled, almost a grimace, and called out. "Well, well, Richard, he who never rises before 7:00 a.m., he who lives for the mating patterns of weevils, you went to town on the 5:30 a.m. trash boat."

"Shopping day," Richard said. He held up a crate of beer.

"Right," Alex said. "You went for the beer."

Alex reached out to shake Katherine's hand and then jumped on the boat to unload her bags. He hefted one onto each shoulder and made for the stairs, quickly ascending the 200 steps. She put on her backpack and began to climb after him wondering why they weren't using the obvious trolley next to the stairs. Richard huffed behind her. At the top, the men showed her the bunkhouse, an open room with wooden tables, two sitting chairs, and bookshelves along one wall, and then her room upstairs. Once she'd left her bags, she came down to the veranda. Richard was popping the top off a beer and was handing it to Alex, but when he saw her, he pivoted and gave her the beer. She took it to be polite, even though she didn't like the drink.

She looked out at the lake, which had been created when the canal was built.

"Crazy to think this island was once a hilltop," she said.

"And to think the Americans ruled this place like a colony," Richard said.

"And that the field station was only for men," Alex added.

"Well, at least *some* things have changed," she said.

"That's rather hopeful," Alex said. "Panama is still a kind of colony. And we've been the only scientists here for five months."

"Meaning?" she asked.

Alex shrugged.

Richard changed the subject. "We think the government funded our work so that we can record natural history before it disappears. We've been sent to this almost-past to mark down as much as we can one last time. In the future, people will read our work with nostalgia, like Egyptian and Mayan records deciphered and now mourned over."

"That's rather bleak," she said.

"Look at this place," Alex said. "It's obvious. They haven't upgraded the bunkhouse. We've got seven out-of-date, lousy solar panels that barely charge our computers. No internet. It's obvious they don't expect this place to be here in the future."

José, the cook, called them in for dinner. "Alice broke into the kitchen again," he said. "She ate the lettuce. No salad tonight."

"I thought there weren't other women on the island," Katherine said.

"Alice is a tapir," Richard explained.

José had a fondness for the 600-pound tapir and her speckled baby. Likely, the padlock on the kitchen door had only been half-forgotten. They sat down to dinner: two large serving bowls, one with rice, the other with soupy black beans.

"I didn't eat all day," Richard said as he served himself a mound of rice and pushed the bowl toward Alex, who passed it on with an eye roll to Katherine so that she could serve herself first. Alex reminded himself of what Darwin (1871) had written a hundred years before. ". . . and it could never have been anticipated that the power to charm the female has sometimes been more important than the power to conquer other males in battle" (p. 222). If it was about charm and female choice, even though he had met her first, Richard had no chance of winning.

Katherine knew that Alex worked on Howler monkeys and that Richard was studying a Brentid weevil. She was curious about both systems and kept up a steady stream of questions, but neither man seemed interested in talking.

"You guys all talked out about your research?" she asked.

"No, but you just got here. I feel like I'm going through my preliminary exams again," Alex said. "Are you always this intense?"

Katherine spooned the bland black beans and rice into her mouth and didn't say anything more. It was a critique she'd heard over and over about herself. Outside, Túngara frogs began to bleep like Star Trek lasers, and the big-eared bats swooped in front of the bunkhouse. On the other side of the island, the Howler monkeys quieted for the night.

The next morning Katherine woke to their thunderous roar. She took a breath and calmed herself. It was still dark outside. She heard the men getting up and moving around. She lay back for a few more minutes listening to the sounds of the rainforest in between the bellows of the monkeys and the clomping of men, feeling happier than she'd ever been in her life. She looked out her window. The morning mist had not yet begun to rise from the lake. The air was exceedingly humid. An agouti was at the edge of the forest rooting around for a nut or insect, and the three-toed sloth, which she'd seen when she arrived, had moved on.

At the table, Alex, surprised by Richard's early morning presence, lifted his eyebrows. He poured him coffee and slid the cup toward him. They ate in silence. A few minutes later, Katherine arrived, and then suddenly, in a torrent, the rain began.

"I thought this was the dry season," she said.

"Wettest dry season on record," Richard said.

Streams and gullies, normally parched from December to March, were filled with wet, blackened leaves, and the mud was thick, so much so that lately they'd been forced to wear rubber boots, which neither man liked. Their feet, sweaty during the day, barely dried out at night, and their wrinkled skin and soft toenails were vulnerable to fungal growth.

"I think it's going to end up in major monkey death," Alex said.

"How so?" Katharine asked.

"I'll explain later," Alex stood. "I'm heading out on Zetek Trail. If it's anything like yesterday, I'll walk the entire four thousand acres before I'm back for dinner."

"That's the advantage of lekking beetles. They don't move." Richard was studying a species of beetle that congregated and mated on rotting logs.

"But they're boring as hell," Alex said.

"I'll have to disagree there," Katharine said. "Weevils are fascinating."

"Would you like to come out to see them today?" Richard asked.

"Absolutely," she said. "I want to look for army ants and get oriented to the trail system."

"If you want to be oriented to the trail system, follow me instead," Alex said. "Richard goes 300 meters into the forest and stops."

"Another day," she said, "I'd definitely like that, to see what you're doing with the monkeys."

"Mostly just running after them," Alex said. "They're acting strange. The alpha male in troop seven is moving all over the place."

"He's obviously trying to find a mate," Richard said.

Alex looped the binoculars over his head. "Maybe."

Alex's advisor had convinced him to re-census the Howler monkeys, which had last been counted eleven years before. "Just go down to Barro Colorado Island and figure out who's still alive and which male is alpha," she'd said. Alex had thought that sounded simple and silly as he'd arrived with more ambitious plans, but it turned out that figuring out which animals were still alive was hard. Turns out that monkeys age too. The alpha males were pretty obvious, but the females seemed to be breaking all the rules, ignoring the males, and moving between troops. Alex zipped up his backpack. "See you beetle watchers at dinner."

Richard and Katherine hiked out along Snyder-Molino Trail, turning onto Shannon Trail, both named for the island's first biologists. For months, Richard had been hiking these trails out to the large, fallen tree trunk, home to his lekking Brentid beetles. The brown beetles were attracted to the rotting log, the females using their nose-like rostrums to drill into the soft red wood where, after mating, they laid an egg.

He set his field bag at the side of the trail and took out his notebook. With calipers in one hand, he picked up beetle after beetle and measured head to thorax, rostrums, and mandibles and noted the sex. Katherine offered to help, and together they measured and marked for most of the morning. The differences in beetle sizes were remarkable; females could be as small as 8 millimeters or as large as 27 millimeters. Males had an even larger range (Johnson, 1982). "The smallest I've measured was seven millimeters and the largest forty-nine," he mentioned in passing.

Further down on the log, they watched two males fighting, one bigger than the other, and he guessed the outcome.

"Size appears to be everything," he told Katherine. "So far, smaller males have only won four percent of the time."

A female moved along the log, probing the trunk as she went until she found a spot and began to drill into the soft wood with her rostrum. A male approached and mounted her.

"See," he said to Katherine, "she has lifted her rear, indicating receptivity. If she didn't want him, she would shake or scrape him off her back."

Another male, a larger one, came to the side of these mating beetles and probed the situation with his antennae. He inserted his rostrum between the male and female and tried to catapult his smaller competitor from her back, but to no avail. Instead, the larger beetle lost his balance and toppled over.

Katherine began to laugh. “He’s one of your 4%!”

Darwin (1871) had written, “but we are chiefly concerned with the structures by which one male is enabled to conquer another, either in battle or courtship, through his strength, pugnacity, ornaments or music” (p. 275). Darwin (1871) also knew that access was key. The male with first access, though not always the largest, was often the winner.

After a full day of beetle work and hiking trails but not finding army ants, Katherine and Richard returned to the bunkhouse. Alex was still out. They showered and sat on the veranda. Alex offered her a beer, but she shook her head. “I’m not a fan,” she said. “I prefer wine and whiskey.”

“Oh, in that case,” he said, jumping up. He returned with a bottle of whiskey and poured her a shot and one for himself, which he drank in one draw. She began to sip on hers. By the time Alex returned, showered, and they sat down for dinner, Richard had drunk several shots.

At dinner, she continued to probe Alex and Richard about their work, but Alex was tired and quiet, and Richard, it turned out, rather drunk.

“So, you’re both basically studying the same thing.”

“Not at all,” Alex said.

“Yes, you are.” She pointed her fork at Alex. “You’re interested in mating behavior in monkeys, and Richard is looking at sexual selection in weevils.”

“True,” Richard said, “but, really, the questions are so radically different in insects versus mammals. I’ve got a sexually dimorphic species; he doesn’t. He’s got social groups. I don’t.”

“The same principles apply. Charm or muscle? Which do you invest in?” She laid out her thinking, and when neither man responded, she stopped talking. “What’s wrong with you guys?”

Alex shrugged. “We’re guys. We don’t talk as much as women.”

Richard looked at her and smiled. Katherine felt his leg touch hers under the table. She repositioned herself away from him, laughed, and went back to her food. They finished their meal in silence, each said goodnight, and went to bed.

Katherine fell quickly into a deep, exhausted sleep but was awakened by a mostly naked Richard, who had snuck into her room, lifted the mosquito netting, and was climbing into her bed. His skin was sweaty, and his elbow jabbed the side of her head.

“Richard, what are you doing? Get out!”

He didn’t respond but groped at her. “Come on,” he said. “We need to end the good field day.”

He stank of whiskey. She slapped his hand away, pushed him over, and got out of the bed. She grabbed her headlamp and trained the spotlight on him. “Richard!” He had taken off his underwear and was reaching for her. She moved back. “Get out of here.”

He took hold of her pillow and wrapped himself around it and closed his eyes. "I like it here." Katherine grabbed some clothes, went down the hall to his room, and locked the door. She climbed into his bed, a musty disgusting smell, and it was only then that she let herself feel angry and realized that she was also scared.

What had her advisor, a pioneer woman tropical biologist, said? "There are three rules for success in graduate school: comb your hair, apply for every grant you can, and get laid as often as possible." Katherine wore her long hair pulled back, sometimes in a braid, and she was applying for lots of grants. The third rule, her advisor said, was a tactic that would lessen the blow from the constant rejection and criticism in science. Katherine had chalked up this advice to a different era; maybe her advisor, who had come of age with the second-wave feminism, when the pill was new and liberating, had found freedom as the only woman in a field of men.

Katherine certainly had no attraction for Richard and hadn't expected him to climb into her bed. Had Alex heard them? He must not have, she told herself; otherwise, what would explain him not coming to her rescue? She tossed and turned and finally gave up and went down to breakfast. She ate a banana quickly, stuffed a few pieces of bread into her field bag, and went out into the dark wet forest before either man was up. She trained her headlight down and stepped over the roots as she climbed the wet and slippery trail. It was not until she was deep into the forest and the sun was coming up that she realized how stressed she had felt. The forest was beautiful. She took a few deep breaths and felt herself start to relax.

At mid-morning, she found her first colony of army ants. From one moment to the next, there was a hum. The leaf litter began to tremble as if it were alive, and then there was a frenetic jumping and chirping of insects coming toward her. Behind the insects and trembling leaves came a flock of antbirds that flitted on and off the understory, feasting on the insects. And then she saw them, the carpet of black ants coming toward her. She felt her heart beat faster. She stood perfectly still while the mass flowed over the forest floor, toward her, crawled up her legs to her knees and then down again. She turned her head and watched them disappear behind her, like something out of a science fiction film, a magnificent creature made up of thousands upon thousands of individuals. For the next week, Katherine woke, ate a quick, silent breakfast in the morning before the men were up, and went into the forest alone. Out in the field, she looked up, down, counted, marked, and made notes. In the field, she was happy, engaged, and safe.

After a week of avoiding the men, she waited for Alex one morning at breakfast.

"Can I go out with you today?" she asked. She needed a bit of company and conversation.

They took Armour, Conrad, Zetek, and then the Standley trail. "One island. Sixty-five troops. An average of eighteen monkeys per troop, and I've managed to recognize each troop by its alpha male." He told her about 1951 when a yellow fever epidemic had reduced the population to 240 animals, but by 1959, it had grown back to 700 (Froehlich et al., 1981). Now, his estimate was just above a thousand. They followed one Howler troop after another to the water's edge and then turned and followed them back again. Alex made observations, and Katherine jotted down the data.

Just as they were finishing the work, a thundercloud clapped, and the afternoon rain let loose. In a moment, they were soaked. She laughed, enjoying the surprise storm, and so did he. They packed up quickly and trekked on the slippery trail toward the bunkhouse. Once or twice, she tripped on a root, fell into the mud, and still she was laughing. Alex reached over and gave her a hand. Back at the bunkhouse, he pointed toward the outdoor shower. "Ladies first."

"Appreciate it," she said. The hot water felt terrific after the rain, and she watched as the mud ran out of her hair, down her chest, and off her arms. She was getting ready to add conditioner to her hair when she felt a presence. She turned, and there, in front of her, was a naked Alex with a hard on. She jumped.

"I didn't mean to scare you," he said. He stepped into the shower.

Katherine felt panic. She considered her options. She didn't *want* to be like this with him, but here he was, moving toward her. She stepped away from the water and reached for her towel. "Alex, I can't," she said. It was a stupid thing to say. She didn't even know what she meant by it, but it was what came out of her mouth. She shook her head, pulled the towel around her tighter, and slipped past him. He flashed red, clearly having misunderstood. Later, when they met at dinner again, he avoided looking at her. He was irritated and argumentative with Richard that night.

Katherine went to bed immediately after dinner and locked her door. What had she done, what signal had she given? She went over and over in her mind trying to understand how Richard could have thought she wanted him in her bed that first night or how Alex could have understood he was to meet her in the shower. She had started by enjoying both of them, their company, and the conversations on the trails. Had they mistaken her interest in their research and general friendliness for interest in them? She began to cry, not knowing whether it was anger or sadness or fear that was overcoming her.

In the days that passed, she kept to herself and read in the evenings. The awkwardness with the two men continued. They were polite, as was she, but it was clear they didn't want her around, and so she spent the evenings in the station's library. One night she found copies of early papers and letters by the founders of the field station. In the 1920s, the biologists Barbour, Wheeler, Zetek, and Fairchild had debated the question of whether women should be allowed on the island. Fairchild, a primatologist and first director of the island, argued most adamantly against it. In a 1924 letter protesting the possibility of building a women's bunkhouse, Fairchild wrote:

> The question . . . is to whether it is possible, if we let women in, to keep there the one thing which to me is absolutely sacred. Let us keep a place where real research men can find quiet, keen intellectual stimulation, freedom from any outside distractions. (as cited in Henson, 2002, p. 586)

Poor Fairchild, Katherine thought. He would turn in his grave to know that the most notable primatologists of his century ended up being women. Only reading these letters and thinking about her experience with Richard then Alex, she felt a profound anger. Little had changed in 70 years. A woman still couldn't be only a scientist. She also had to be a distraction, and now, neither man would speak to her. She was outcast and rendered silent.

The last night on the island, she broke the usual dinner silence.

"What if," she said, "the male beetles are as choosey as the females? There's so much variation in female size. It doesn't make sense from an evolutionary perspective. If it's genetic, males should choose larger females. But then it can't really be genetic, can it? If it were, natural selection would eliminate the variation over time."

She'd hit on something Richard hadn't thought about. The question of the cost of mate guarding. Everything had been centered on female choice, and he hadn't paid attention to what it might cost a male to guard one female over another.

"You'll never know what's going on until you can measure that cost," she said.

She turned to Alex. "It's the same with Howlers. How do you know paternity? Just because a monkey is the alpha male doesn't mean that he's passing on his genes. I think your type of work will only become meaningful when you can measure paternity, do DNA analysis when you can subtract your own bias of what you think you know."

After dinner, she packed her bags with a profound sadness that she was leaving the island and her ants, but also with relief to not have to manage the solicitations, the looks, the challenges, the unfriendly responses to her scientific inquiries. In the dark morning, José offered to carry her bags down the 200 steps to the dock, but she declined, preferring to make the trips herself. As she went up and down, she noted that the sloth had returned to the *Cecropia* tree near the bunkhouse.

The tiny trash boat started its engine, and she felt it push off into the misty water. The unused crane rocked back and forth. She imagined the coming days on the island. Alex and Richard would continue their competitive banter, but now with her gone, they'd do so with more comfort. She had hoped for more from them, but perhaps it was impossible. As the island receded, she considered that perhaps her major professor said "get laid a lot" because this had been her strategy to deal with male scientists. Perhaps it had just been easier to sleep with them than to deal with their bruised egos and outright aggressions. Perhaps her advisor, in assuming control, had allowed herself agency, maybe even a kind of hard-won freedom, a way of being that Katherine was unwilling to embrace. Next year, she would recruit one, or maybe two, undergraduate women students to aid her (Larsen & Wcislo, 2019).

Eventually, the bizarre rainy, dry season would end, and the true rainy season would begin. The massive freighters would continue to pass through the canal, moving steel from one part of the planet to another. In the forest, the Howler monkeys roared morning and night. Below them, armies of ants unspooled from their bivouacs, set out in a carpet of quick moving legs and antennae, devouring every piece of protein in their path. The queen ant, bloated and fat with eggs, protected by a ball of sisters, was carried behind this fan of crawling ants and would be set down in a new pillow of ants that night. Insects and small frogs scurried away from the ant wave. White-spotted antbirds, perched above, picked off the katydids, beetles, and brown moths as they jumped to escape. A lumbering anteater, practically blind, stopped along the trail and inhaled through his long snout.

The algae-coated, three-toed sloth slowly unwrapped a paw from the *Cecropia* tree. His long sharp claws stretched wide, and he reached down to grasp lower. It was time to make the dangerous weekly descent to the ground. At the bottom, he dug a hole, defecated, and then covered it up. As if the effort were exhausting, he climbed back up even more slowly and then grasped his feet and arms onto the branch and tucked his head once more. The moths, which lived their entire lives on his back, fluttered into the air for a brief moment and then clung back onto his stiff green fur.

NOTE

1. This story is set on Barro Colorado Island. I have used historical and current documents throughout the story, and they are referenced at the end of the chapter. While set in a real place with references to real science, the timeframe and the characters are fictional; however, the story is based on similar events and experiences of women scientists in the tropics.

REFERENCES

Darwin, C. (1871). *The descent of man, and selection in relation to sex.* John Murray.

Froehlich, J. W., Thorington, R. W., & Otis, J. S. (1981). The demography of Howler Monkeys (*Alouatta palliata*) on Barro Colorado Island, Panamá. *International Journal of Primatology*, *2*, 207–236. https://doi.org/10.1007/BF02739331

Henson, P. (2002). Invading Arcadia: Women scientists in the field in Latin America, 1900-1950. *The Americas, 58*(4), 577–600. https://doi.org/10.1353/tam.2002.0045

Johnson, L. K. (1982). Sexual selection in a Brentid Weevil. *Evolution, 36,* 251–262. https://www.jstor.org/stable/2408043

Larsen, M. C., & Wcislo, W. T. (2019). *Biological and cultural diversity of the tropics. Strategic Plan 2019–2024.* https://stri.si.edu/sites/default/files/stri_strategic_plan_aug_2019.pdf

Siedenburg, J. (2008). *85th Anniversary BCI history and research.* https://stri.si.edu/sites/default/files/joan_bci.pdf

Part II

EXPERIENCES IN THE FIELD

Chapter 3

"Brush your hair, apply for every grant you can, get laid as often as possible"

Women's Muted Experiences Conducting Scientific Research in the Tropics

Victoria M. McDermott

INTRODUCTION

With a history of being a heavily white, male-dominated field, we, as a scientific community, are still working to diversify and make equitable many scientific disciplines both inside and outside of academia, notwithstanding outdated white, patriarchal norms, and practices that may still reify gender discrimination today. One interesting aspect of science that has had a tenuous history with gender discrimination is fieldwork and more specifically fieldwork in tropical locations. A quote that truly encapsulates the patriarchal history and culture of tropical field sites was written by David Fairchild in 1924 to his colleague Thomas Barbour, "Let us keep a place [the tropics] where real research men can find quiet, keen intellectual stimulation, freedom from any outside distraction" (Henson, 2002, p. 577). Although there may be more women present in fieldwork today, remnants of these cultural gender boundaries may still be impacting women's field experiences, especially in the tropics.

Thus, this chapter sought to learn about women's experiences with fieldwork in the tropics over three decades through the lives of four women scientists. This chapter begins with an overview of the history of fieldwork and the realities of life for researchers living and working at tropical field sites. I then explain my methodology for this chapter and the theoretical lens of Muted Group Theory (MGT) used to analyze the results of four in-depth interviews. Results indicate that women are and have been muted in their experiences with fieldwork in the tropics. From limited mentorship to being muted through socialization and isolation, women note that it is not "the science that is hard," it is the people and the culture. From these findings, I extend MGT and provide practical recommendations for improving the tropical fieldwork culture and communication climate to foster a safer, more inclusive environment for women, as well as anyone else who might fall outside of the hypermasculine identity.

LITERATURE REVIEW

Field stations are critical hubs for scientific discovery, providing opportunities for research, teaching, and community engagement (Janovy & Major, 2009; Tydeck et al., 2016, see chapter 1 by McDermott, Gee, & May in this edited volume for an overview of FSMLs). As stated by Janovy and Major (2009), field programs provide the opportunity for a "potentially life-changing and memorable encounter with the natural world" (p. 221). These memorable encounters with fieldwork have been known to increase student retention rates within sciences (Freeman et al., 2014). However, due to their often remote nature and the challenges FSMLs present requiring scientists to survive in the wilderness, field stations have unique cultures that have often come under scrutiny for exclusionary practices. Two key factors impacting field station culture are location and traditional gender roles.

Location: A Colonial Mindset

Currently, a majority of field stations are located in the Northern Hemisphere (Tydecks et al., 2016). This both biases the research scientists conduct, as well as limits the knowledge produced about diverse ecosystems. Over one-third of all research stations are located in the United States alone (Baker, 2015). This uneven representation of field stations across the globe has contributed to the unequal levels of scientific knowledge produced and the conservation efforts initiated, which often focus on ecosystems in the Northern Hemisphere (Amano & Sutherland, 2013; Stocks et al., 2008). It was only in the 20th century that tropical field stations in South America began to rise in prominence and popularity. Once identified as important scientific locations, however, it was made extremely clear to local scientists and indigenous peoples that the field stations built were solely oriented toward the research goals of the United States and that the lands and facilities were primarily for researchers from the United States (Geissler & Kelly, 206; Raby, 2017). For example, at the Barro Colorado Island field station in Panama, while Latin American researchers were "welcome" to research, they were racially segregated and relegated as assistants and translators to Western scientists (Raby,

2017). As the number of tropical field stations increased and more scientists went to the tropics to conduct research, the colonization norms and practices continue to plague these locations (Raby, 2017). This has led to a tense history in which local communities are wary of scientists. Although there are a significant number of authors within academia from across the globe, the Westernized countries still dominate research and paper authorship in comparison to small, tropical countries (Raby, 2017). Overall, undertones of the colonial mindset and values still impact how, where, and who can conduct scientific research in field stations and remote locations in the tropics and around the globe.

Traditional Gender Roles

The second major factor impacting FSML culture is the enactment of gender and reification of traditional gender roles. Although sex refers to the biological differences between males and females, gender is a socially constructed concept that defines the roles, behaviors, expressions, and identities of girls, women, boys, men, and gender-diverse people (CIHR, 2020). It is neither binary nor static; however, gender is institutionalized by society, impacting the ways in which it is performed (CIHR, 2020; Lester, 2008). Sex stereotypes or traditional gender roles are "socially shared beliefs about what qualities can be assigned to individuals based on their membership in the female or male half of the human race" (Lips, 2020, p. 4). In other words, there are culturally shared beliefs about how men and women should act, think, and behave (Lips, 2020). Previous research has found that some gender norms transcend culture. For example, Lips (2020) identified six defining characteristics of "manhood" shared across 25 countries: adventurous, dominant, forceful, independent, masculine, and strong. Likewise, there are shared cultural norms regarding womanhood, including sentimental, submissive, charming, emotional, fussy, and weak (Lips, 2020).

Due to these prescriptive, culturally normalized gender roles, gender has long been a defining factor in people's lives, determining access to and the experiences within social institutions, ranging from institutions of higher learning to the workplace (Koenig, 2018; McDermott, 2019). Gender gaps in fields such as mathematics and science that favor the masculine identity reinforce gender inequalities that fall in line with traditional Western gender roles (Tomasetto et al., 2011). For example, gender stereotypes such as "girls can't do math" create a threatening environment for women, resulting in poor performance, feelings of isolation, and internalized self-doubt (Tomasetto et al., 2011). Over time, these internalized biases can impact women when in the workforce, leading to dissatisfaction and turnover (Janssen & Backes-Gellner, 2015). Therefore, even though gender stereotypes are highly oversimplified binary categorizations of people's abilities and behaviors, women are more likely to hold jobs in caretaker roles, such as a nurse, teacher, secretary, whereas men are expected to hold more ambitious roles, such as managers and executives.

Hypermasculinity

Hypermasculinity is an extreme form of masculinity based on polarized traditional gender roles, power, competition, control, pain tolerance, and mandatory heterosexuality (Hunter, 2007). Mosher and Sirkin (1984) originally conceptualized hypermasculinity as calloused sexual attitudes toward women, the view that violence is manly and that danger is exciting. These beliefs also demonstrate the misogynistic perspective of male dominance over female submission. Hypermasculinity can lead to tense situations and harmful work environments for men and women who violate these traditional gender role norms (Rudman & Phelan, 2008). Moreover, those who identify with the hypermasculine identity may use violence and aggression to try to realign people to their prescriptive gender roles and reestablish power, leading to conflict, isolation, and tension among colleagues (Dodge et al., 2010).

Gender Roles in Field Stations

The enactment of gender and reification of traditional gender roles through communication has ultimately impacted the formation of field station culture. For example, one of the first women to have conducted fieldwork in the 19th century, Elizabeth Campbell, was given no credit for her work in her husband's memoirs (Pang, 1996). Pang (1996) analyzed a few other women's journals from the field during the 19th century and noted similar accounts from women, suggesting that "other women who received little mention in eclipse narratives may have done far more on their expeditions than the poverty of description of their roles would indicate" (p. 42).

Ultimately, the limited access and opportunities to participate in science continued into the 20th century (Henson, 2002; Pang, 1996). Henson (2002) documented the perceived culture of field stations in the tropics in the early 20th century, noting that it was thought to be an "inappropriate place for women" (p. 577), suggesting women, by their very nature, are incapable of contributing anything substantive to the scientific community. Communication constructs such as this demonstrate and perpetuate the exclusionary culture and barriers to access women faced in the early 20th century when attempting to engage in fieldwork science.

Moving into the 21st century, although there are now more women in science than ever, gender-based issues are still extremely prevalent especially in fieldwork environments (NSF, 2015; 2018). For example, Thornton and colleagues (2020) conducted an autoethnographic analysis of their experiences working at a specific location in the tropics known as the "peat swamp." In their reflection, the ten female scientists, all at different stages of their careers, mentioned how fieldwork is often seen as "dirty" and not for women. Seeking to "push the limits" of gender stereotypes at this field station through their own work, they noted that breaking the traditional mold of the feminine identity made others feel uncomfortable. In this piece, the women recount being reprimanded, condescended, and underestimated by "mostly male practitioners" for challenging the norm of who is allowed to engage in fieldwork (Thornton et al., 2020). Furthermore, the documentary *Picture a Scientist* (2020), released in 2020, recounted the hazing, abuse, and sexual harassment experienced by three prominent women scientists in the field (Cheney & Shattuck, 2020). The women featured recalled being pushed down hills, having rocks thrown at them while attempting to use the bathroom, and being told they were too dumb or stupid to be of any use to the research team in front of other researchers and peers (Cheney & Shattuck, 2020).

Furthermore, due to their isolated locations, sexual harassment and assault at field stations is a cause for concern (Clancy et al., 2014; McDermott, 2019; O'Donohue et al., 1996; Vechiu, 2019). In a groundbreaking study in 2014, Clancy and colleagues highlighted the rampant rates of sexual harassment and assault occurring in fieldwork. Of the 600 respondents surveyed, 74.2% said they had seen first-hand or been told about colleagues making sexual comments at field sites, and 64% of the respondents had personally been verbally sexually harassed (Clancy et al., 2014). Over 20% of the respondents had been sexually assaulted, defined as "physical sexual harassment, unwanted sexual contact, or sexual contact in which they could not or did not give consent or felt it would be unsafe to fight back or not give consent" (Clancy et al., 2014, para. 19). Overall, women were 3.5 times more likely to report experiencing sexual harassment than men, although men did report receiving inappropriate sexual comments or actions from peers of the same sex (Clancy et al., 2014). These findings continue to be replicated in fieldwork sites throughout different disciplines such as archaeology (Meyers et al., 2015), social work (Moylan & Wood, 2016), and astronomy and other planetary science-related fields (Clancy et al., 2017).

Communication scholars, such as Clair et al. (2019) and Keyton et al. (2018), have argued organizational culture can cultivate and allow sexual harassment and assault to occur. Due to the unique requirements and remoteness of field station life, targets may be unable to leave camp, talk to people within their normal support networks, and even report incidents of sexual violence (Gluckman, 2018). Overall, the field station organizational culture, history of colonization, and perpetuation of traditional gender roles can set the stage for sexual harassment, assault, and bullying to occur, ultimately supporting the harasser more than the harassed (Keyton et al., 2018). As the distance from society increases, fieldwork may foster a culture that allows gender discrimination and harassment behaviors to occur, negatively impacting those who identify outside of the traditional white, heterosexual male identity (McDermott, 2019; Wadman, 2017). Thus, it is vital to capture and understand the experiences of women scientists in the tropics to document and learn from how they communicated within a traditionally masculine environment that may have been trying to silence them.

Muted Group Theory

MGT provides a valuable framework for uncovering and evaluating the communicative interactions between dominant and subdominant groups (Barkman, 2018). MGT allows researchers to explore issues of power and the communication dynamics that may occur between men and women as a result of gendered socialization. As stated by Cheris Kramarae (1981), this theoretical framework "informs how power functions in speech, writing, and language in general" (as cited by Barkman, 2018, p. 3). Since language structures and practices have been primarily constructed by men to express their experiences, especially within the sciences, women are thus muted (Wood, 2005).

MGT provides three tenets for analyzing how dominant and subdominant groups communicate (Wood, 2005). These tenets include (1) dominance, (2) acceptability, and (3) subordination. *Dominance* is defined by the different experiences afforded to the dominant and subdominant groups. These experiences create and define how people perceive the world. *Acceptability* is defined by how the subdominant group's expression and language are less acceptable to and respected by the dominant group. This ultimately determines what meanings and communicative behaviors will be recognized and validated by the dominant group (Barkman, 2018). Finally, *subordination* characterizes how the subdominant group must use the dominant group's preferred modes of communication. This helps to maintain the dominant group's position and perpetuates the minimization, stigmatization, and the muting of the subdominant group's voice (Barkman, 2018; Wall & Gannon-Leary, 1999).

Previously, MGT has been used to understand how women manage their identities in primarily masculine environments (Razzante & Orbe, 2018). For instance, Lituchy and Wiswall (1991) explored if feminine speech patterns affected the "credibility and believability of women in organizations" (p. 453). Findings indicate that men's and women's speech patterns differ in several key areas, such as word choice and intonation, resulting in women being viewed by both males and females alike as less assertive, more uncertain, and lacking power. Other studies have used MGT to uncover microaggressions negatively impacting women of color in STEM (Wilkins-Yel et al., 2019) and the role of implicit and explicit gender bias in STEM (Farrell & McHugh, 2020). Ultimately, MGT argues the voice of the muted is often ignored or trivialized by the dominant group. In the case of gender, "the male model of society would be considered by the dominant group (men) to be accurate and true since they would see nothing lacking" (Ardener, 1975, p. 3). As such, researchers are challenged to make space for the stories of women. Narrative analysis, specifically, provides a useful lens for evaluating data and explicating the stories of women especially as gender intersects with race, sexuality, and other aspects of self.

Narrative Analysis and MGT

Narrative analysis has been used in conjunction with MGT to uncover sequestered voices (Chmieleswki, 2017; Clair, 1998). Clair and colleagues (1996) used narrative analysis to uncover silenced voices related to sexual harassment. The exploration of these often-hidden narratives provides vital insights into why targets of sexual harassment may stay silent and the long-term impacts of this silence. Findings indicate that through these sequestered narratives, targets of sexual violence inadvertently participate in the production and reproduction of the dominant ideology that promoted the environment allowing the original sexual harassment and assault to occur (Clair et al., 1996; 2019). More recently, scholars have used narrative analysis and MGT to explore how high visibility women in music have used personal narrative and feminine speaking to overcome mutedness (Heise, 2020), as well as used the in-depth narratives of unique feminine identities, such as Wiccans, to explore how marginalized groups of women are muted in often Euro-white, Christian-based societies (Shorey & Wickelgren, 2009). These studies provide a structure for using MGT in narrative analysis to uncover women's communicative experiences as the subdominant group in STEM environments.

Current Issue

For decades, people from around the world have been calling for changes to the current scientific community in regards to women and minorities in science (Leslie et al., 1998; Lucena, 2000). Although previous research has documented the experiences of women who attempted to conduct fieldwork and participate in science in the early 19th and 20th centuries (Henson, 2002; Pang, 1996), little to no research explores how women in the late 20th and early 21st centuries make sense of their experiences conducting fieldwork, specifically in the tropics. Thus, the current chapter seeks to explore how women scientists' experiences may have been muted while conducting research in the tropics. For a long period of time, the tropics were characterized as untamed environments that only men could survive in (Henson, 2002; Raby, 2017). During the late 20th and early 21st centuries, large social upheaval and movements, such as multiple waves of feminist movements, as well as the most recent #MeToo movement, greatly impacted academia, as well as reformed workplace culture (Bauer et al., 2020). Although these movements have led to the increase of women scientists conducting research in the tropics, this may not have resulted in their equal access or acceptance by others while in the field. Ultimately, a better understanding of women's experiences in the tropics may help to contextualize where fieldwork culture is today and how fieldwork sites and FSMLs must be challenged to continue to work on their accessibility and inclusion practices moving forward:

RQ: What are the experiences of women scientists working in tropical field sites?

METHODS

To answer the research question, I used qualitative research methods. Specifically, I conducted virtual interviews to gather data related to women's experiences working in the tropics. After transcribing participant responses, I used a narrative approach to data analysis that prioritized the women's telling of their field experiences.

Recruitment and Participants

To be eligible for an interview, participants had to be over age 18 and have experience as a woman scientist conducting fieldwork in the tropics. As this is a niche population, I used several different avenues for recruitment. First, I worked with a well-known contact in the industry. This contact allowed me to build trust with participants before asking them to participate in the study. Second, I used personal networks, as well as encouraged interview participants to share the recruitment call with others who fit the inclusion criteria. No incentives were offered for participation.

A total of four interviews were conducted. Due to the niche participant criteria, I argue—using the work of Buzzanell, Long, Anderson, Kokini, and Batra (2015)—that using a small sample of rich narratives provides vital insights into understanding people's experiences within organizations. Through these rich narratives, I sought to understand participants' scientific

Table 3.1 Participant Pseudonyms and Descriptions

Participant Pseudonym	*Participant Description*
Kelsey	Began working in the tropics in the late 1970s, left fieldwork to become an administrator in higher education in the 1990s
Sophia	Began working in the tropics in the 1980s, still visits tropical research sites throughout the year
Holly	Worked in the tropics in the 2010s, left after three field seasons ranging from a few weeks to months
Hannah	Began working in the tropics in the late 1980s, is currently a higher education administrator

Source: Author data.

careers in a more holistic, longitudinal sense. Pseudonyms were assigned to participants to ensure anonymity. Table 3.1 provides a general description of the participants' experience working in the tropics.

Interviews

An interview protocol was created to collect participant responses. The interview process contained open-ended, loosely constructed questions that explored women's experiences conducting fieldwork in the tropics. Each interview began with informed consent that provided an overview of the study, as well as an explanation of participants' rights. Following the informed consent portion of the interview, I asked questions that were designed to build rapport with the participants and gather background information. Sample questions included: *When did you get interested in science*? and *What got you interested in science?* After building rapport, the interview questions sought to explore topics such as career trajectory, gender dynamics, space variables, culture, and in-time messages. Some examples of the questions included: *How were you treated throughout your career as a woman working in the tropics?* and *How would you characterize fieldwork when you first started your career?* Overall, the interview protocol was developed to get a longitudinal overview of the participants' careers from their first exposure to science to their current position.

Interviews were conducted via Zoom and averaged 45 minutes per interview. Once the interviews were completed, the Zoom transcription feature was used to transcribe the audio, and the transcriptions were edited and cleaned before data analysis to remove any identifiable information, such as specific field stations names. Overall, the interviews totaled 177 minutes of audio and 139 pages of transcribed data.

Data Analysis Procedures

After transcribing the data, I began the qualitative data analysis process. As Riessman (2001) states, narrative analysis is "appropriate for studies of social movements, political change, and macro-level phenomena. Because storytelling 'promotes empathy across different social locations'" (p. 3). Therefore, narrative analysis was the most useful lens for analyzing the dataset. During the first read-through of the transcriptions, I sought to get a foundational understanding of the stories. I then began a second read-through of the data that included taking notes and highlighting important quotes (Riessman, 2005; 2016). Before completing the third round of analysis, I reviewed the theoretical framework of MGT (Barkman, 2018; Wood, 2005). With this framework in mind, I read through the dataset and my notes from my second review. I then developed codes to categorize the data (Lindolf & Taylor, 2017). Once the data were coded, I reorganized the codes into similar overarching patterns. For example, the quote "Looking around at our department there weren't very many women scientists" was coded under the category "limited female representation" which was merged into the larger overarching theme of *muted through a lack of representation.* I then pulled quotations from participants' interviews to exemplify each theme within the results section of my paper.

RESULTS

The subsequent section outlines the four overarching themes from the dataset: Muted through a lack of mentorship, muted through socialization and a culture of sexual harassment, muted through blurred lines of professionalism and isolation, and muted through a lack of representation.

Muted through a Lack of Mentorship

The women interviewed noted that conducting scientific research was easy; it was the lack of direction and mentorship that made it difficult for women to succeed. As Kelsey noted, "I did science when you were left on your own to figure it out." Kelsey mentioned how she believed science was an individual activity because of her lack of support from faculty. She stated, "I had to be a real self-starter and driver of your own agenda or you wouldn't have made it through." This ended up negatively impacting her ability to engage in collaborative work later on in her career and she eventually left fieldwork because she felt uncomfortable when science shifted to prioritizing larger group work in the early 1990s. Similarly, Sophia mentioned frequently how she had no mentors throughout her undergraduate and graduate careers, stating "they [the professors] just weren't the type that spent any time on supporting graduate students." Hannah mentioned when describing her mentor in graduate school that "[she was] a little bit old school, kind of hands-off. This was in the old days, where you would go work with someone, but you would define your own project." Hannah continued on to explain "they [the grad students] would just come in and students would often kind of flail around for a few years, exploring ideas." Hannah's story was not uncommon as all the participants mentioned being sent "into the field" without their advisor's guidance to conduct and collect research on their own.

Muted through Socialization and a Culture of Sexual Harassment

Not only did women believe that science was something you had to figure out on your own, they believed that sexual harassment was just "part" of science, and women's voices were often muted through the socialization and a culture of sexual harassment. When asked about the biggest challenges a new female scientist may face in the tropics, Holly noted that the culture and the people were the biggest obstacles. Things such as "sexual innuendos" frequently infiltrated the fieldwork culture making it difficult for women to feel safe while in the field. All participants mentioned feeling constantly on edge or on guard while in the field.

In order to rationalize how they were treated, participants stated, "that's just the way it was." From being left out of projects and bullied to sexual assault, this is just how women "thought" science was "supposed" to be. Sophia stated, "You just thought, that's the way it was, that there wasn't really an option to speak up and say, you know, you're being an asshole here." Hannah recalled a time when visiting a field station in Panama, "researchers started making comments about my breast size." Hannah continued, "I bet that would have happened more if I'd spent more time [there]." In a similar vein, Holly mentioned her traumatic experiences with sexual harassment in the field that caused her to take a year-long break from data collection in the tropics

> because if you have grueling experiences collecting your data or traumatic experiences collecting your data it's very unlikely that you ever want to like reach back and work with that data again. And so it took me a very long time after my second field season or my, I guess, that was my first field season to, to actually get up the courage to go back to collect more data and then also just to like work with that data that I was collecting

Holly mentioned in her interview that she was still working to process the sexual harassment and assault she experienced, as well as the lack of support she received from those in positions of authority after reporting her experiences.

Additionally, Kelsey talked about how overarching societal norms negatively impacted her understanding of what was acceptable for women. She stated, "I wanted to be a Park Ranger. And he [a university instructor] says, there aren't any women park rangers, you better go become a teacher. So I went and got my certificate and master's in teaching and then became a teacher." It was only after that there was a push to get more women in science that Kelsey was supported to go back to school for her doctorate.

Muted through Blurred Lines of Professionalism and Isolation

The theme of muted by blurred lines of professionalism and isolation is characterized by the lack of on vs. off work boundaries and the perceived impact of being in an isolated environment for an extended period of time. Everyone noted that in the field there is no time "off" work. As Kelsey mentioned, "Everybody worked extremely hard and you know you just use the occasional breaks that came to keep your sanity." When you are in the field, data collection is the number one priority.

This was also reinforced by the lack of physical boundaries and separation that occurred while in the field. For example, Holly mentioned during her experience in the tropics that she had no time to herself. Holly explained how her local guide slept in the same hut as her and on their days off was the only other person around to go on hikes with. Holly joked the only way she could "put a door between them" was to sit in the bathroom.

Additionally, living and working in the same area blurred the lines of professionalism. Men in power often thought that there were no rules when it came to women at the field station. Sophia recounted how an advisor attempted to use his power to seduce her, "he sort of grabs my hand and brings me into his bedroom and after having treated me dreadfully and you know I'm pulling away, but like, I'm sorry, [name]. I don't want to." Sophia went on to further internalize this incident believing it was her fault for his sexual harassment behavior.

The lack of boundaries for on vs. off work and the blurred lines of professionalism were compounded by the remoteness and isolation of many of these fieldwork experiences. The remoteness played a large role in women's feeling of safety, or lack thereof, at field stations and field sites. Often being stuck in a remote location with people for days to weeks to months on end, with no way to communicate outside the station, impacted women's willingness and ability to report sexual violence. As Hannah stated, "there was no

Internet. I could receive a fax once a week, which cost me $10 and I could send a fax. It cost me $20 to send a fax that was one paragraph when I was in the field." Similarly, Sophia explained how she felt the isolation exacerbated her experience being muted while in the field,

> He [her advisor] would use me as the scapegoat to sort of build-up you know their [the male students'] morale and you know you're stuck on an island. There's nothing to do. And you know, they were, I guess, going stir crazy. I thought it was wonderful, but except for, you know, this constant sort of undermining and harassment and making fun of me.

Sophia goes on to further state, "I [would] climb up in the mango tree in the backyard [and] spent hours up there crying, but, you know, we had to eat together so you couldn't really avoid him." Putting physical space between her and the perpetrator by sitting at the top of a tree was the only way to escape the harassment while at the field station.

Muted through a Lack of Representation

Although participants noted that science had changed over time, they still questioned where are all the women? Participants noted that in their graduate classes either a third or half of the students were women: however, those numbers of women are not being reflected in leadership today. As Kelsey stated:

> I went to NSF [National Science Foundation] panels and things like that. And I was always very aware of sitting in big board rooms with a huge desk and pictures on the walls all around me with these men looking down at me. And so I was very, very aware that the leaders are certainly not women. Very slowly over a 40-some-year career, I saw that women began to show up on those board walls.

The lack of women in positions of leadership was mentioned by all of the participants. Even participants who had started going to or still visited the tropics in the early 2000s and 2010s mentioned that there were limited women in positions of leadership.

All participants mentioned that the ratio of women in science and in leadership positions is not where it needs to be. They all mentioned that women still face many of the same barriers to success in science and obtaining leadership positions today. Even in the early 2010s, participants mentioned how sexual assault and harassment were still rampant in fieldwork. Kelsey, Holly, and Hannah all mentioned how the fieldwork culture led them and many female colleagues to leave for more progressive workplace climates. Those interviewed felt that science still had a long way to go in order to fully support women into successful scientific careers.

DISCUSSION

The findings of this study indicate that fieldwork and field stations are difficult places for women to navigate successfully, often due to the hypermasculine culture they foster. Women do not struggle with conducting science. Rather, they struggle to succeed in their fields because of the culture and communication climates that tolerate sexual harassment and bullying fostered in tropical fieldwork locations. Through the use of MGT (Barkman, 2018) and narrative analysis (Risseman, 2001), four women were able to share their experiences being silenced during their time conducting fieldwork in the tropics. All of the women interviewed mentioned that these interviews were the first time they were exploring, uncovering, and communicating their experiences in the tropics.

Through these narratives, I posit theoretical and practical findings for communication scholars and the STEM community to consider going forward to improve women's experiences conducting fieldwork. Theoretically, I propose an expansion of MGT to consider the role of isolation on the perpetuation of muted voices. Practically, I argue the cultural norms accepted and reinforced in fieldwork science may be contributing to the "leaky pipeline," leading women to leave the field of science as women may experience burnout as a result of being muted. Overall, these gendered cultural norms may be perpetuated under the guise of "grit," thus women need to recount the *true* stories of their experiences to bring attention to and challenge these seemingly steadfast norms. Finally, boundary management may provide an avenue for beginning to make field stations a safer and more inclusive place for women.

Theoretical Implications

Currently, MGT takes into account three tenets (1) dominance, (2) acceptability, (3) subordination (Wood, 2005); however, findings from this study call into question the impact of isolation on muting groups. Isolation could play a large role in women's perceived feelings of silence and safety as the subdominant group. When in isolated, confined, and extreme environments, women have less access to resources to communicate their negative experiences. Furthermore, these isolated locations may empower those in the dominant group to engage in more extreme behaviors (e.g., sexual harassment, bullying) that would not be tolerated or accepted on a university campus. When seeking to uncover muted voices, the impact or effect of isolation needs to be taken into account as it may exacerbate a dominant group's ability to engage in the muting of the subdominant group.

Applied Contributions

Practically, the findings from this study outline three overarching contributions, the impact of silence on women scientists' retention, the perpetuation of hypermasculinity under the guise of grit, and the potential use of boundary management for increasing safety and inclusivity. To begin, similar to the findings of Clancy and colleagues (2014), sexual harassment and assault are extremely prevalent within fieldwork in the tropics. All four of the participants in this study had one or more experiences with sexual harassment or assault while in the field. This sexual assault and harassment may occur in fieldwork due to the power dynamics within remote locations and due to the fact that women may not be seen as equals in the field (Clancy et al., 2014; Clancy et al., 2017; Meyers et al., 2015; Moylan & Wood, 2016). This lack of equity fosters a climate that allows sexual violence and bullying to occur. Additionally, the negative treatment of women is leading to a lack of women in leadership positions. As noted by the participants, although there were large numbers of women within their PhD cohorts, due to the "leaky pipeline" (Blickenstaff, 2005), these women do not often make it into positions of power.

Adding to this area of research, this study finds that the culture within fieldwork in the tropics often conflates "grit" with hypermasculinity and socializes women to assume, "this is just how science is." Under the guise of "grit," the hypermasculine identity is able to thrive in fieldwork scenarios. This masculine pride is built through the labeling of the tropics as wild, untamed, and dangerous, combined with the grueling nature of fieldwork and isolated locations. Built upon the history of promoting the tropics as an "inappropriate place for women" (Henson, 2002, p. 577), these cultural norms continue to be perpetuated today, impacting women's ability to conduct scientific research in the tropics. Moreover, through the use of the three tenets of MGT, dominance, acceptability, and subordination (Barkman, 2018), women are taught to expect to be sexually harassed and bullied in the field. Telling peers to stay silent about abuse to maintain their assistantships, constant experiences of sexual harassment from superiors, and a lack of intervention from bystanders reinforce that it is "okay" to sexually harass and assault women. Furthermore, equating silence of abuse to "grit" and "being able to handle anything" inadvertently furthers the production and reproduction of the toxic dominant culture that cultivated the harassment originally (Clair et al., 1996, 2019). In addition to silencing women's experiences, the dominant narrative that women don't belong in the tropics (Henson, 2002) led participants to internalize these experiences and place blame on themselves, questioning if they invited the sexual harassment or assault behaviors.

One of the ways in which the dominant narrative continues to be reinforced is through the silencing of alternative experiences (Barkman, 2018; Clair, 1998). The stories told and advice given about the tropics is often overgeneralized, polarized, and problematic. As Holly stated, people say either, "Oh, it's so exciting. That's so amazing" or "then on the other side, like, oh my god, be like, be careful. Be careful . . . neither of those perspectives is very useful." As mentioned previously, these interviews were the first time these women recounted their experiences working in the tropics. Often pushing bad memories aside for the sake of data collection in the name of science, true narratives remain silenced. Women need to share their stories of abuse and assault to call out the culture that is allowing these behaviors to occur (Clair, 1993; Farrell & McHugh, 2020). Calling out problematic behaviors and harassers will help to show young researchers that sexual harassment and bullying will not be tolerated (Wood, 2005). As mentioned in the results, many women rationalized their experiences as "this is just how science is." Making sure people are aware of what constitutes problematic behavior is the first step in beginning to end the current culture that is allowing it to occur.

Overall, the use of physical boundaries could play an important role in mitigating the potential for sexual harassment. Findings in this study indicate that participants felt isolated and confined by the fieldwork environment. Having to sleep and work in the same location with the same people for weeks to months on end led to the blurring of professional boundaries (Gluckman, 2018; McDermott, 2019). For those who were able to get away, lone walks, or sitting at the tops of trees were the only solace; however, not everyone had the ability to escape their fieldwork colleagues. Recently scholars have begun building and designing inclusive architecture (Judge, 2011; Price, 2016). These re-imagined spaces take into account issues such as boundaries and gendered layouts (e.g., avoiding closed-off corners or areas where assault could occur) (Judge, 2011). With a more inclusive, gender-neutral camp layout, people may be able to reestablish the boundaries of professionalism and on vs. off work when in the field (Price, 2016).

LIMITATIONS AND FUTURE RESEARCH

Ultimately, this research is just a starting point for understanding women's experiences with fieldwork in the tropics and has several limitations. First, narrative analysis has been criticized for the bias that may occur due to the interactions between the researcher and participants (Alvermann, 2000; Channa, 2015). To combat this potential limitation, I engaged in reflexivity throughout the data analysis process and acknowledge that my previous research experience and personal bias are study limitations. As a woman in academia who has previously studied women's experiences in fieldwork scenarios, my preconceived notions and lived experiences could have impacted the data analysis. To mitigate this bias, I read through the dataset three times, allowing themes to emerge organically from the narratives. Moreover, I suggest that future research look to quantitatively analyze women's experiences in fieldwork in the tropics or invite additional qualitative researchers to code data to increase interrater reliability.

Second, the sample size was small as the participant criteria created a limited pool of potential interviewees. However, the four interviews conducted provided rich data and vital insights into personal stories and painful experiences that could not have been uncovered otherwise (Buzzanell et al., 2015). Future research could use surveys or focus groups to learn more about women's experiences with harassment in the tropics. Future research should also seek to compare the experiences of women who conducted fieldwork in the tropics vs. other fieldwork locations, such as the arctic, to find similarities and differences among experiences. Finally, I would like to acknowledge that women are not the only targets of sexual violence. Future research should seek to uncover men's experiences with horizontal and vertical violence in the workplace setting. Future research should also include the experiences of gender-nonconforming researchers and practitioners working in FSMLs along with other marginalized and potentially muted groups.

CONCLUSION

Through the interviews of four female scientists, this chapter problematizes the culture of fieldwork that is being fostered in the tropics. As science continues to move toward increased accessibility and inclusion, it is important to enable women to share their experiences with sexual violence and bullying in the field using their words, their voices, and their stories. Continuing to silence women's stories will reinforce and perpetuate the negative cultural and communication norms that hinder women's success in fieldwork and in the sciences overall.

REFERENCES

Alvermann, D. (2000). Narrative approaches. In M. L. Kamil, P. B. Mosenthal, P. D., Pearson, & R. Barr (Eds.), *Handbook of reading research: Volume III* (pp. 123–139). Erlbaum.

Amano, T., & Sutherland, W. J. (2013). Four barriers to the global understanding of biodiversity conservation: Wealth, language, geographical location, and security. *Biological Sciences, 280*(1756), 2022649. https://doi.org/10.1098/rspb.2012.2649

Ardener, E. (1975). Belief and the problem of women. In S. Ardener (Eds.), *Perceiving women* (pp. 1–17). Malaby Press.

Baker, B. (2015). The way forward for biological field stations. *BioScience, 65*(2), 123–129. https://doi.org/10.1093/biosci/biu210

Barkman, L. L. S. (2018). Muted group theory: A tool for hearing marginalized voices. *Priscilla Paper, 32*(4), 3–7.

Bauer, K., Behjat, L., Brown, J. A., Gavrilova, M. L., Hayley, J. L., & Marasco, E. A. (2020). First wave, second wave, third wave: Women in science, technology, engineering, and mathematics. In S. Eaton & A. Burns (Eds.), *Women negotiating life in the academy* (pp. 101–115). Springer.

Blickenstaff, J. C. (2005). Women and science careers: leaky pipeline or gender filter? *Gender and Education, 17*(4), 369–386. https://doi.org/10.1080/09540250500145072

Buzzanell, P. M., Long, Z., Anderson, L. B., Kokini, K., & Batra, J. C. (2015). Mentoring in academe: A feminist poststructural lens on stories of women engineering faculty of color. *Management Communication Quarterly*, 1–18. http://doi.10.1177/0893318915574311

Canadian Institutes of Health Research [CIHR]. (2020, April 28). *What is gender? What is sex?*. https://cihr-irsc.gc.ca/e/48642.html

Channa, L. A. (2015). Narrative inquiry: A research tradition in qualitative research. *Kashmir Journal of Language Research*, *18*(1), 1–17.

Cheney, I., & Shattuck, S. (2020). *Picture a scientist* [Film]. Uprising Production.

Chmielewski, J. F. (2017). A listening guide analysis of lesbian and bisexual young women of color's experiences of sexual objectification. *Sex Roles*, *77*(7), 533–549. https://doi.org/10.1007/s11199-017-0740-4

Clair, R. P. (1993). The use of framing devices to sequester organizational narratives: Hegemony and harassment. *Communication Monographs, 60*(2), 113–136. https://doi.org/10.1080/03637759309376304

Clair, R. P. (1998). *Organizing silence: A world of possibilities*. SUNY Press.

Clair, R. P., Brown, N. E., Dougherty, D. S., Delemeester, H. K., Giest-Martin, P., Gorden, W. I., Sorg, T., & Turner, P. K. (2019). #MeToo, sexual harassment: an article, a forum, and a dream for the future. *Journal of Applied Communication Research, 47*(2), 111–129. https://doi.org.10.1080/00909882.2019.1567142

Clair, R. P., Chapman, P. A., & Kunkel, A. W. (1996). Narrative approaches to raising consciousness about sexual harassment: From research to pedagogy and back again. *Journal of Applied Communication Research, 24*, 241–259. https://doi.org/10.1080/00909889609365455

Clancy, K. B. H., Nelson, R., Rutherford, J. N., & Hinde, K. (2014). Survey of academic field experiences (SAFE): Trainees report harassment and assault. *PLoS One, 9*(7), E102–E172. https://doi.org/10.1371/journal.pone.0102172

Clancy, K. B. H., Lee, K. M. N., Rodgers, E. M., & Richey, C. (2017). Double jeopardy in astronomy and planetary science: Women of color face greater risks

of gendered and racial harassment. *Journal of Geophysical Research, 122*(7), 1610–1623. https://doi.org/10.1002/2017JE005256
Dodge, M., Valcore, L., & Gomez, F. (2010). Women on SWAT teams: separate but equal?. *Policing: An International Journal of Police Strategies & Management, 34*(4), 699–712. https://doi.org/10.1108/13639511111180298
Farrell, L., & McHugh, L. (2020). Exploring the relationship between implicit and explicit gender-STEM bias and behavior among STEM students using the implicit relational assessment procedure. *Journal of Contextual Behavioral Science, 15*, 142–152. https://doi.org/10.1016/j.jcbs.2019.12.008
Freeman, S., Eddy, S. L., McDonough, M., Smith, M. K., Okoroafor, N., Jordt, H., & Wenderoth, M. P. (2014). Active learning increases student performance in science, engineering, and mathematics. *Proceedings of the National Academy of Sciences of the United States of America, 111*(23), 8410–8415. https://doi.org.10.1073/pnas.1319030111
Geissler, P. W., & Kelly, A. H. (2016). A home for science: The life and times of Tropical and Polar field stations. *Social Studies of Science, 46*(6), 797–808. https://doi.org/10.1177/0306312716680767
Gluckman, N. (2018, July 15). *Field sites are harassment hell. Here's how to improve them.* The Chronicle of Higher Education. https://www.chronicle.com/article/Field-Sites-Are-Harassment/243914
Heise, N. A. (2020). *Halsey's a story like mine: Exploring the rhetorical constraints for muted group members and reframing rationality expectations for narratives about muted experiences* [Unpublished master's thesis]. Texas State University.
Henson, (2002). Invading arcadia: Women scientists in the field in Latin America, 1900-1950. *The Americas, 58*(4), 577–600. https://doi.org/10.1353/tam.2002.0045
Hunter, M. (2007). *Honor betrayed: Sexual abuse in America's military*. Barricade Books.
Janovy, J., & Major, K. M. (2009). Why we have field stations: Reflections on the cultivation of biologists. *BioScience, 59*(3), 217–222. https://doi.org/10.1525/bio.2009.59.3.6
Janssen, S., & Backes-Gellner, U. (2016). Occupational stereotypes and gender-specific job satisfaction. *Industrial Relations: A Journal of Economy and Society, 55*(1), 71–91. https://doi.org/10.1111/irel.12126
Judge, A. H. (2011). *Designing more inclusive streets: The bicycle, gender, and infrastructure*. [Unpublished master's thesis]. Macalester College.
Keyton, J., Clair, R., Compton, C. A., Dougherty, D. S., Forbes Berthoud, D., Manning, J., & Scarduzio, J. A. (2018). Addressing sexual harassment in a sexually charged national culture: a Journal of Applied Communication Research forum. *Journal of Applied Communication Research*, *46*(6), 665–683. https://doi.org/10.1080/00909882.2018.1546472
Koenig, A. M. (2018). Comparing prescriptive and descriptive gender stereotypes about Children, adults, and the elderly. *Frontiers in Psychology*, *9*, 1086. https://doi.org/10.3389/fpsyg.2018.01086
Leslie, L. L., McClure, G. T., & Oaxaca, R. L. (1998). Women and minorities in science and engineering: A life sequence. *The Journal of Higher Education, 69*(3), 239–276. https://doi.org/10.1080/00221546.1998.11775134

Lester, J. (2008). Performing gender in the workplace: Gender socialization, power, and Identity among women faculty members. *Community College Review, 35*(4), 277–305. https://doi.org/10.1177/0091552108314756

Lindolf, T. R., & Taylor, B. C. (2017). *Qualitative communication research.* Sage.

Lips, H. (2020). *Sex and gender: An introduction, seventh edition.* Waveland Press, Inc.

Lituchy, T. R., & Wiswall, W. J. (1991). The role of masculine and feminine speech patterns in proposal acceptance: A laboratory study. *Management Communication Quarterly, 4*(4), 450–465. https://doi.org/10.1177/0893318991004004003

Lucena, J. C. (2000). Making women and minorities in science and engineering for national purposes in the United States. *Journal of Women and Minorities in Science and Engineering, 6*(1), 1–32. https://doi.org/10.1615/JWomenMinorScienEng.v6.i1.10

McDermott, V. (2019). *'It's a magnifying glass': The communication of power in a remote Field station* [Unpublished master's thesis]. University of Alaska Fairbanks.

McDermott, V., Gee, J., & May, A. (2022). Defining the role and value of FMSLs. In V. McDermott, J. Gee, & A. R. May (Eds.), *Women of the wild: Challenging gender disparities in field stations and marine laboratories* (p. 3–15). Lexington Books.

Meyers, M., Boudreax, T., Carmody, S., Dekle, V., Horton, E., & Wright, A. (2015). Preliminary results of the SEAC sexual harassment survey. *Horizon and Tradition: The Newsletter of the Southeastern Archaeological Conference, 57*(1), 19–35.

Mosher, D. L., & Sirkin, M. (1984). Measuring a macho personality constellation. *Journal of Research in Personality, 18*, 150–163. https://doi.org/10.1016/0092-6566(84)90026-6

Moylan, C. A., & Wood, L. (2016). Sexual harassment in social work field placements, prevalence, and characteristics. *Journal of Women and Social Work, 31*(4), 405–417. https://doi.org/10.1177/0886109916644643

NSF. (2015). *Women, minorities, and persons with disabilities in science and engineering: 2015.* https://ngcproject.org/statistics

NSF. (2018). *Science and engineering indicators 2018.* https://nsf.gov/statistics/2018/nsb20181/

O'Donohue, W., McKay, J. S., & Schewe, P. A. (1996). Rape: the roles of outcome expectancies and hypermasculinity. *Sexual Abuse: A Journal of Research and Treatment, 8*(2), 133–141. https://doi.org/10.1007/BF02258006

Pang, A. S. (1996). Gender, culture, and astrophysical fieldwork: Elizabeth Campbell and the lick observatory–crocker eclipse expeditions. *Osiris, 11*, 17–43.

Price, M. (2016). Un/shared space: The dilemma of inclusive architecture. In J. Boys (Ed.), *Disability, Space, Architecture* (pp. 155–303). Routledge.

Raby, M. (2017). *The colonial origins of tropical field stations.* American Scientist. https://www.americanscientist.org/print/4056

Razzante, R. J., & Orbe, M. P. (2018). Two sides of the same coin: Conceptualizing dominant group theory in the context of co-cultural theory. *Communication Theory, 28*(3), 354–375. https://doi.org/10.1093/ct/qtx008

Riessman, C. K. (2001). Analysis of personal narrative. In J. F. Gubrium, & J. A. Holstein (Eds.), *Handbook of interviewing*. Sage.

Riessman, C. K. (2005). Narrative analysis. In N. Kelly, C. Horrocks, K. Milnes, B. Roberts, & D. Robinson (Eds.), *Narrative, memory & everyday life* (pp. 1–7). University of Huddersfield.

Riessman, C. K. (2016). Narrative data analysis and interpretation: "Flirting" with data. In J. Kim (Ed.), *Understanding Narrative Inquiry: The crafting and analysis of stories as research* (pp. 185–224). Sage.

Rudman, L. A., & Phelan, J. E. (2008). Backlash effects for disconfirming gender stereotypes in organizations. In A. P. Brief & B. M. Staw (Eds.), *Research in organizational behavior* (pp. 61–79). Elsevier.

Shorey, S. M., & Wickelgren, B. F. (2009). The muting of witches. *Intercultural Communication Studies, 18*(2), 136–146. https://web.uri.edu/iaics/files/10-Sarah-M.-Shorey-Bruce-F.-Wickelgren.pdf

Stocks, G., Seales, L., Paniagua, F., Maehr, E., & Bruna, E. M. (2008). The geographical and institutional distribution of ecological research in the tropics. *Biotropica, 40*, 397–404. https://doi.org/10.1111/j.1744-7429.2007.00393.x

Thornton, S. A., Cook, S., Astiani, D., Hapsari, K. A., Varkkey, H., Cole, L. E. S., Dargie, G. C., Sjogersten, S., Zawawi, N. Z., & Page, S. E. (2020). 'Pushing the limits': Experiences of women in tropical peatland research. *Marine and Freshwater Research, 71*(2), 170–178. https://doi.org/10.1071/MF19132

Tomasetto, C., Alparone, F. R., & Cadinu, M. (2011). Girls' math performance under stereotype threat: The moderating role of mothers' gender stereotypes. *Developmental psychology, 47*(4), 943.

Tydecks, L., Bremerich, V., Jentschke, I., Likens, G. E., & Tockner, K. (2016). Biological field stations: A global infrastructure for research, education, and public engagement. *BioScience, 66,* 164–171. https://doi.org/10.1093/biosci/biv174

Vechiu, C. (2019). The role of hypermasculinity as a risk factor in sexual assault perpetration. In W. O'Donohue, & P. Schewe (Eds.), *Handbook of Sexual Assault and Sexual Assault Prevention*. Springer.

Wadman, M. (2017, October 6). Disturbing allegations of sexual harassment in Antarctica leveled at noted scientist. *Science.* https://www.sciencemag.org/news/2017/10/disturbing-allegations-sexual-harassment-antarctica-leveled-noted-scientist

Wall, C. J., & Gannon-Leary, P. (1999). A sentence made by men: Muted group theory revisited. *European Journal of Women's Studies, 6*(1), 21–29. https://doi.org/10.1177/135050689900600103

Wilkins-Yel, K. G., Hyman, J., & Zounlome, N. O. O. (2019). Linking intersectional Invisibility and hypervisibility to experiences of microaggressions among graduate women of color in STEM. *Journal of Vocational Behavior, 113*, 51–61. https://doi.org/10.1016/j.jvb.2018.10.018

Wood, J. T. (2005). Feminist standpoint theory and muted group theory: Commonalities and divergences. *Women and Language, 28*(2), 61–72.

Chapter 4

Make the Approach and Get the Data

Challenges, Teamwork, and Cultures of Support for Women Who Are Scientists and Parents at Field Stations and Marine Labs

Diane Debinski

Every summer for 26 years, my family and I made an annual pilgrimage to the National Park Research Station, a field station supported by the University of Wyoming—some 1,200 miles (1,932 km) from our home in the Midwest. We packed up the vehicle with everything we would need for surviving six weeks at a remote field station. I still recall the year that we had to turn around, but luckily only 20 miles (32 km) west of our home, because we had forgotten the butterfly nets. As an ecologist, I cringe at the environmental impact of us driving well over 30,000 miles (48,280 km) during those years to get back to my field site each summer. But the commitment to this long-term research project and the scientific research that we were able to complete as a result were well worth the time, effort, and fossil fuel (e.g., Debinski 2010, 2013). Each mile tells a story and every summer represents an important moment in my life, both personally and professionally, that contributed in substantive ways to my career.

In this chapter, I summarize my perspectives on the incredible value of the field station, the culture created by the people there, and my experiences raising two children with my academic partner over multiple decades. My goal in this chapter is to reflect on my own experience as a field biologist with a very supportive partner and as a female field biologist with a family in hopes that my story provides a starting point for field stations to build more inclusive communities of inquiry. This chapter begins with a brief overview of literature related to women's experiences in science and engineering. I then explain the autoethnographic methodology used to frame my reflection and subsequent findings. Following my overview of the methodology, I explicate the three overarching themes found within my results, and from these themes, suggest recommendations for creating more inclusive field station cultures and how to navigate parenthood and a field-based research career.

LITERATURE REVIEW

The Backdrop: Women in Science and Engineering

Women in science have historically faced significant challenges and encountered barriers that limit career progression and the overall level of satisfaction with their respective disciplines (Bebbington, 2002; Makarem & Wang, 2019; Wanelik et al., 2020; Xie & Shauman, 2003). Over two decades ago, Virginia Valian (2000), in her book *Why So Slow?*, advanced the concept of accumulated disadvantage to define the experiences of women in science. Valian (2000) argues that the accumulation of many small disadvantages (e.g., a lower salary, lower rank when hired) can have substantial effects, akin to the concept of compounded interest. Although Valian's book is now 20 years old, the same disadvantages persist. As we continue to fight for equal and equitable pay, access, inclusion, and rights, disparities for those seeking to balance parenthood and a scientific career become even more pronounced (Cech & Blair-Loy, 2019; Lerman et al., 2021; Makarem & Wang, 2019; Wanelik et al., 2020; Williams, 2000). Women remain the primary caregivers for children, and they accomplish a disproportionate amount of the work that falls under the category of "unpaid care," including childcare, care for the elderly, cooking, and cleaning (Fogel, 2020). This has recently been exacerbated by the 2019 COVID pandemic as research has shown women have been disproportionately impacted in the wake of stay-at-home orders and online schooling (Madgavkar et al., 2020).

The material infrastructure as well as the policies and cultural norms that comprise academic institutions create environments that can serve to support or dissuade underrepresented groups. Field stations, similar to college campuses and laboratories, are part of this academic environment. The National Academy of Science report in 2014 on *Enhancing the Value and Sustainability of Biological Field Stations and Marine Laboratories in the 21st Century*, for which I was a coauthor, highlights the fact that field stations are excellent venues for discovery-based and active learning, pedagogical approaches that have been shown to promote diversity and persistence in science, technology, engineering, and math (STEM) fields (Schubel et al., 2014). However, if these spaces do not allow for equitable access, certain scientists, that is, women and other minoritized groups, may be disadvantaged. As such, it is essential that field stations are welcoming places to scientists at all phases of personal and professional development, from the start to the more senior periods of their careers.

Creating welcoming spaces for diverse identities, such as women and more specifically mothers, is important for continuing scientific innovation. There are many reasons why family and work can create conflicts (time constraints, multiple responsibilities, etc.), but one of the things we can do about it is to make field stations more welcoming to scientists with families, especially women scientists with families (Cech & Blair-Loy, 2019; Lerman et al., 2021). Previous research has explored the question of whether there are feminist methodologies in science that may be different from more traditional approaches (Rosser, 1992). I would argue that interdisciplinary research and observational research may be more "feminist" approaches that are valuable, relevant, and have the potential to be cultivated at field stations. Therefore, a lack of diverse representations of people, especially of women, may impede scientific progress. The National Science Foundation (NSF) has now supported ADVANCE grants for individuals and for institutional transformation for three decades "to enhance the systemic factors that support equity and inclusion and to mitigate the systemic factors that create inequities in the academic profession and workplaces" (NSF, 2021, Synopsis, para. 1). One of the take-home messages from these many efforts has been that we need to move away from trying to change the individual and move toward transforming the culture and policies of our institutions to be more supportive and welcoming of women and minorities in STEM. And a related goal raised by Baker (2011) is "having a life in science" (p. 1).

As I mentor the next generation of women in STEM, it is obvious to me that they are, indeed, looking for and expecting more balance between work and life. Field stations have their own infrastructure, culture, and policies that can help or hinder women in STEM and, because of limited budgets and isolated locations, they may be slower to change compared to more urbanized campuses. As you will see from the results of my autoethnography, field stations create a "work-life blur," but if navigated carefully and with the benefit of supportive leadership and partnerships, this lifestyle can be a fulfilling and productive blur. Currently, there is little research highlighting the experiences of women in field stations who seek to navigate parenthood and a career. In order to heed the call for change and showcase the value of work-life balance in supporting parenthood, I share my experiences as a scientist, woman, mother, and wife. Below I outline how these many ideas intersect at field stations and the potential for field stations to be even more effective in supporting women and underrepresented groups in science. Overarchingly, I seek to answer the research questions:

RQ1: What aspects of the approach that my partner and I took supported my work as a researcher and a parent?
RQ2: What aspects of field station culture supported my work as a researcher and a parent?
RQ3: What approaches to work-life balance and team management are most effective in creating successful field research teams for a scientist/parent?

METHODS

Autoethnography

This contribution is considered an analytic autoethnography (Anderson, 2006; Wall, 2006), which is a new style of scientific inquiry for me as a natural scientist, but it is appropriate relative to the goals of this book, that is, to reflect on the experiences of women working in remote field stations to design programs to support equity and inclusion. Adams and Hermann (2020) state: "'Autoethnography' consists of three interrelated components: 'auto,' 'ethno,' and 'graphy.' Thus, autoethnographic projects use selfhood, subjectivity, and personal experience ('auto') to describe, interpret, and represent ('graphy') beliefs, practices, and identities of a group or culture ('ethno')" (p. 2; see, Sparkes, 2020). Manning and Adams (2015) argue that autoethnography is defined in two ways:

> First, any work labeled 'autoethnography' should include personal experience and demonstrate, through thoughtful analysis, why this experience is meaningful and culturally significant. An essay that does not use or describe the importance of personal experience in a cultural context should not be considered an autoethnography. Second, this personal experience must be reflexively considered through the use of extant theory, other scholarly writings about the topic, fieldwork observations, analysis of artifacts (e.g. photographs), and/or involvement with others (e.g. interviews). If many of these elements are not evident, then a project should not be considered an autoethnography. (p. 205)

Thus, in maintaining Manning and Adams (2015) requirements for autoethnography, I have placed personalized accounts of my own experience in the context of the literature about women in science and engineering, field station research, and team science.

The Reflection Process

The process of reflection for writing this chapter came easily as if I had hit a "download" button in my head because field station–based research was a lifestyle that I had consciously chosen to continue on an annual basis as if renewing an important subscription. As argued by Holman et al. (2013), in autoethnography, the

> author takes the same experience, reflects on its nuances, and then writes intentionally to show how aspects of this experience illuminate more general cultural phenomena and/or to show how the experience works to diminish, silence, or deny certain people and stories, then the author writes autoethnographically. (p. 23)

Visiting the field station was a big commitment of time and energy, so I had to re-evaluate it each year. To engage in the reflection process I looked over old photos, dug into boxes and family photo albums for photos that had been taken prior to digitization, reviewed old slide presentations from scientific meetings, emails, journals, and publications. I reflected on the different aspects of the field experience and some of the most memorable events that had transpired. I selected a small number of photos that best captured the different stories and the stages of my life with my partner and two children in the field. As an ecologist who has taught classes on women in science and engineering, I pondered aspects of the field station lifestyle frequently from my own perspective as well as from the larger perspective of women in science. Additionally, to provide more in-depth insight, I asked each of my family members to share their perspectives of our time spent in the field by writing a paragraph about their own experiences after having been a part of this endeavor for many years. My goal in these reflections is to describe how these experiences played out for me, and in the end created a positive experience for me, my students, my family, and my career.

Every field station is different, and every woman scientist may experience some of the issues I discuss in different ways. So the transferability of this approach may be limited and highly dependent on the people involved, the particular research project, and the field station facilities. However, through this analytic autoethnography, I seek "to gain insight into some broader set of social phenomena than those provided by the data themselves" (Anderson, 2006, p. 387). Through the reflection of my experiences, and the added reflections from my family members, I hope that this story can provide some insight on creating a culture of support at field stations that can enable more women to balance family and career within the rich social and ecological backdrop of a field station.

Setting the Stage: Situating the Author

It was 1991. I was a newly minted PhD leaving Montana and heading for a postdoc at the University of Kansas. My goal at this phase of my career was to continue biodiversity research in the Rockies, building on my previous experiences at Glacier National Park. I teamed up with geographer Mark Jakubauskas and botanist Kelly Kindscher at the University of Kansas (KU) to brainstorm approaches. The goal was to use geographic information systems to classify land cover and use these maps to predict species distribution patterns of birds, butterflies, and plants within the Greater Yellowstone Ecosystem at a large landscape scale. During my time as an undergraduate and graduate student, I had learned the value of the associated scientific community and the supportive infrastructure that defines field station research.

I began conducting research on butterfly, plant, and bird communities at the University of Wyoming-National Park Service (UW-NPS) Research Station in Grand Teton National Park in 1992. I took a faculty position at Iowa State University in 1994 and continued to work at the field station. Over the years, I learned that the community of scientists who interact at field stations can provide rich opportunities for networking, mentoring, and the development of friendships. Traditionally, remote field stations are "adult-only" facilities where staff, researchers, and other stakeholders live and work to study a particular scientific phenomenon. When academics have children, fieldwork can be challenged, particularly for women who often assume primary caregiver roles. However, if orchestrated effectively, I argue that bringing partners and children along can enhance the field station community and help train the next generation of scientists who choose to parent while furthering their careers. I left Iowa to take a position as the Department Head of Ecology at Montana State University (MSU) in 2017. Upon reflection, having maintained my research in the Greater Yellowstone Ecosystem was a credential that probably helped me obtain the position at MSU. Collectively, my experiences underscore the importance of field stations and their associated communities of scholars as a major contributor to women in science, supporting their advancement into leadership positions and overall scientific progress.

FINDINGS/DISCUSSION

I have woven the findings of my reflection with the discussion of their larger implications. These findings resulted in three overarching themes to answer my research questions regarding my experiences navigating parenthood with a field-based research career. The following section will explicate the three major themes: (1) Adaptability and the Adventure of Parenthood, (2) Field Stations as Communities of Support, and (3) Acknowledging the Work-Life Blur, and weave together my reflection and experiences to the larger cultural context of field stations. From these reflections, I close the chapter with my recommendations for field stations to create more equitable, accessible, and inclusive cultures for those who seek to balance parenthood and a scientific career.

RQ1: What aspects of the approach that my partner and I took supported my work as a researcher and a parent?

Adaptability and the Adventure of Parenthood

When I met my husband-to-be, James Pritchard, we were both budding academics at MSU, he in environmental history, and me in conservation biology. I was conducting bird and butterfly biodiversity research in Glacier National Park, and he was interested in the history of Yellowstone National Park. We realized that we could both work in the same geographic region, thinking about national parks from slightly different perspectives. As our relationship became more "serious," as my mother would say, it became clear that his intent was to have children and mine was not. And the average (0.5 children) was simply not an option. For a short time, this question hung over us and threatened to end our relationship. Because my research required intense summer fieldwork, these topics weighed heavily on my decisions. As for many women, the choice of whether to even become a parent at all was a difficult one. But my partner promised from the start that if I wanted to be an academic and a field biologist, he would play more of the stay-at-home parent role and would be willing to be the parent in charge during field seasons. I joked that it took four years for me to get up the nerve to have each child. Although the concept was initially rather intimidating, I soon learned that parenthood would also be a highly fulfilling adventure that would be one of the best decisions in my life.

James and I got married two weeks after I defended my PhD, and we moved to our next academic home, the KU, a few weeks later. James started a PhD in environmental history, and I had a postdoc position at KU's Museum of Natural History. At KU, I teamed up with two new colleagues, geographer Mark Jakubauskas and botanist Kelly Kindscher, and we started fieldwork in the Greater Yellowstone Ecosystem. Our goal was to use remotely sensed data to classify montane meadows along a hydrological gradient (from wet to dry) and then determine how well we could predict the plant, bird, and butterfly communities (i.e., biodiversity) in these meadows. My fieldwork involved field surveys of plants, birds, and butterflies. My first field season at the UW-NPS field station on this project was in 1992. And I had a $500 grant! For the second field season in 1993, I had secured a $5,000 grant. As we say in academia, the trajectory was going in the right direction.

In 1994, James and I moved to Ames, Iowa, where I took a position as an assistant professor at Iowa State University. By then we were making the annual 1,200 mile (1,932 km) migration out to the UW-NPS field station each summer. And in 1997, after we became parents, our daughter Zoe headed out with us at the age of six months for her first field season. My colleagues and I had recently secured a much larger grant from the EPA Ecological Indicators program (hint: the trajectory from 1993 continued and we added two zeros to the grant magnitude). Now we could scale up our biodiversity and remote sensing research with multiple teams of scientists. There was no detailed conversation about bringing my child with my colleagues, students, or the director of the field station, but I knew each of them well and knew they were supportive. The one slightly humorous detail I recall is that I had two colleagues who didn't really like children and were slightly fearful of them. I recall staging a "would you please hold my baby?" and then passing her over just to try to help them get over their baby phobia as I secretly watched, trying to hide the smile creeping onto my face. Their worst fears of the baby spitting up on them did not occur, and it may have warmed them slightly to the idea that babies can be cute and endearing. Note that this is not an endeavor to be conducted with people one does not already know well and trust, but it was effective in my case.

Adaptability

Traveling across the country with a small child was memorable, to say the least. During the first field season with Zoe, James, who is an expert at camping and packing, decided to pack a folding rocking chair from Costa Rica in our Volkswagen (VW) van strapped on with bungee cords. I had initially looked at him in wonder, thinking *do we really need that?*, but it turned out to be a good idea. On the second day of our trip headed west from Iowa, Zoe was crying inconsolably in her car seat. We had no idea what the problem was, but being new parents, we presumed the worst. Stopping, we felt her forehead and worried about a fever. She looked pretty flushed after all. We pulled over at a rest stop near a small creek, cooked up some lentil soup, took the rocking chair out, and after a bit of soup and rest, everyone was fine. She was probably just not thrilled with that car seat.

James, aka "loadmaster," could always figure out how to fit one more thing into the vehicle when packing for a field trip. He is rather unflappable, patient, and simply loves an adventure. He also loves kids. So, he was pretty much the perfect partner for cross-country travel from Ames, Iowa, to a field station in Wyoming with a small child in tow. He would find parks with swing sets in obscure towns along the Pony Express route, small-town grocery stores where we could purchase fresh peaches in Nebraska, and lots of historic markers because he is a historian after all. For many years, we drove that VW across the Midwestern grasslands to the Tetons in late May or early

June. It was a great vehicle for camping along the way, but I always said that it worked best sitting still. It had no air conditioning, difficulty topping 55 mph, and a crash rating of "D" in the *Consumer Report* magazine. Given its limited ability to keep up with traffic on the major highways, we often took the secondary highways parallel to train tracks and tried to "race" the trains which were also traveling at approximately 55 miles an hour (we clocked them). Those cross-country trips were long, hot, and somewhat arduous. So, when our second child came along, we swapped out our VW for a vehicle that would keep up with the trucks on the freeway. We said goodbye to that awesome VW camper, but we may have lived longer for that decision.

Navigating Field Seasons with Children

James often hiked along with me to field sites with Zoe in the backpack.

I would do my bird or butterfly survey and then take a break to nurse Zoe. I admit that the first field season was a little difficult. I was tired, and bird surveys required early morning work, which didn't help with baby-related sleep deprivation. I suffered a case of mastitis (an inflammation of breast tissue that affects breastfeeding women and can involve an infection, fever, and chills)

Figure 4.1 Diane and Baby Zoe in the Field (Pritchard, 1997).

at one point, which negatively affected my data collection, but turned out to be an effective warning to slow down my pace for a few days and catch up on sleep. Luckily my field crew was very capable.

When Zoe was two or three years old, I recall going out on a solo survey up a trail in Yellowstone called "Bacon Rind" with Zoe in the backpack. I always chuckled at the name Bacon Rind, given that the area was also known for bear activity. It was a two-mile walk up the trail to the site, and I only had one bird survey to do that day. I just needed Zoe to be quiet for about 15 minutes while I did the bird survey. She was a big fan of peanut butter. So, I laid out a blanket for her with some toys, a small container of peanut butter, and some crackers, and asked her if she could try her best to be quiet for a few minutes. I conducted my bird survey standing just a few feet away from her. Zoe sat on her blanket peacefully, and when I was done, I looked over and her face and hands were completely covered with peanut butter! All I could do was laugh. That story was told a few more times over the years, and she remembers it well. She is still a big fan of peanut butter.

Adventures with Two Children. Thinking back on my decision to become a mom, as I said, it took me four years to get up the nerve to have each child. The first child, born pre-tenure, was the biggest hurdle, but I knew that adding a second child, even if it was post-tenure, would ramp that multivariate arithmetic of work-life balance up one more notch. When my son Hayden was born in mid-May 2001, I expected that James and I would be able to pack up the new baby and four-year-old Zoe a month or so after Hayden was born. The thing that I had not counted on was how absolutely tired I would be with the second child.

When you have one child, you sleep when they nap. When there are two children, that plan does not work quite so well. Because I had an inkling that there could potentially be worst-case scenarios, I had set up the field season to mainly be conducted by two strong, qualified people, one graduate student, and one field tech. I had told them that they should be ready to do the work without me, in case this new baby slowed me down and I could not go out in the field, and they were. The graduate student had worked on this project previously, so she was very capable and knowledgeable about the project. The hardest part for me was to admit that the best decision I could make would be simply to stay home that summer and be a mom and rest. I still recall sitting in bed, exhausted, thinking about the field season, and how difficult it was to make that decision about whether to make the trip west. My friends and family were polite but undoubtedly knew all along what the most rational choice was. So, after talking it over with my partner and a few women scientist friends who had had children and could understand my perspective, I convinced myself that missing one field season out of multiple decades would probably not set me back forever. I stayed home with my family. In the end, it was a good decision, and the field team brought back great data.

From Toddlers to Scientists in Training. When Hayden was just over one year old, we started taking two kids to the field station. As they grew up, the kids went to weekly barbecues and seminars every Thursday evening and met the other scientists at the field station. Overall, the culture of scientific inquiry within the field station impacted how the children played and engaged with their surroundings. When my son was just learning to talk, one of the phrases that we taught him to say was "Get the data!" That phrase had become a mantra for our team to emphasize the importance of trying to get the data even if weather conditions looked poor. At age two or three, Hayden would simply say "Get the data!" in the deepest voice that a toddler could muster, and everyone would burst into laughter.

As they got older, scientific inquiry remained a steadfast theme in their play and later in their identities. For example, when my kids had the chance to play with driftwood on the beach, they created a "Natural History Museum" in a little shack in the woods near our cabin. This three-sided shack, which was smaller than an average outhouse, was set up with bones, rocks, plants, soil samples, and notebooks. It was just barely big enough to house the two of them. They attached a string with a paper cup so that visitors could "call" to see if the curator was available and they would answer the other end of the phone.

Figure 4.2 Calling to See if the Curator Is in the Natural History Museum (Pritchard, 2005).

Figure 4.3 Mosquito Concoction (Debinski, 2005).

They would then give us a tour of the collection with all the pride of a curator at the Smithsonian Institution. They also became interested in ethnobotany and boiled up tinctures of sagebrush which they put into small containers so that we could spray ourselves with this concoction, presumably to keep the mosquitoes away.

In actuality, from a young age, my kids came out in the field and "helped" collect data. When they were young, the data that they collected had no scientific value. In fact, we sometimes took them to a different part of the meadow to do their own plant or butterfly "surveys." But it didn't take long before they were able to collect real data that was highly valuable.

Zoe began helping to collect real field data when she was 12. In middle school, she became a runner and so her aerobic capacity was soon put to good use as a person who could relieve one of the field techs in our butterfly mark-recapture survey plots. She was formally signed up as a university volunteer and did that for several summers until she had her own summer camp counselor job in Minnesota. Hayden, who was younger, did not get as many opportunities to help in the field during his early years. However, when he was in high school, he let me know that it was "his turn," and he served as a capable volunteer for several summers.

Both children learned all of the details of butterfly mark-recapture techniques, as well as plant phenology sampling.

Their data collection experience taught them to be sensitive and highly observant of the natural world, but they also learned the basics of the scientific method and appropriate ways to collect data. Over the years, they have

Figure 4.4 Zoe and Hayden as Butterfly Catchers (Pritchard, 2004).

Figure 4.5 Zoe helping with a butterfly mark-recapture survey, and holding a butterfly with forceps (Szcodronski, 2012).

been excellent additions to my field crew because having a volunteer to assist would allow us to relieve one of the field technicians or graduate students, either during part of a day or for a full day. Because the work that I do has intense periods of required continuous data collection, and butterfly surveys actually do require running with a net, it is always good to have an extra person on hand who can help out. The kids kept track of their hours, usually only helping 10–24 hrs/week. I paid them out of my own money, and they were proud of their contributions.

At a certain age, depending upon the child and the project, it may be possible to allow the child to participate as a volunteer. This is a great opportunity for them to learn how science is done and may help the research team by giving someone else on the team a break for a part of the day. Research has shown that "hands-on" field-based scientific experiences build children's scientific self-efficacy, achievement, and increases the likelihood of children staying within a STEM career path (Caglak, 2017; James & Williams, 2017; Webb-Williams, 2018). However, in order to protect everyone, it is essential that university protocols are followed and that the minor is formally signed up as a university volunteer. The last thing that any field station director would want is a tragic outcome of a child volunteering on a research project.

Moreover, assuming that children are well behaved, the opportunity for them to spend time at a field station can be transformative. Sitting at a dinner table listening to a group of scientists talk about their research in the evening could plant the seed that sparks their own interest in pursuing a career in science. It makes science less formidable, and intelligent conversations seem normal when children listen to the people that they get to know in their daily pursuits at the field station. As it turns out, several of the children that grew up visiting the UW-NPS Research Station with our kids went into STEM fields.

The summers in the field were transformational for many of the children who visited, including my own. Below, Zoe and Hayden explain how they perceived summers in the field:

Zoe:

> The UW-NPS Field Station is a unique thread in our family's story that binds our shared curiosity about the natural world, our love of adventures, and our time together in a cabin and an ecosystem. I looked forward to the trips each year and feel the same excitement and nostalgia of driving into the park every time I come back. Our dad was always keen for an excursion with my brother and I: canoeing to buy ice cream down the lakeshore, mapping out hikes, my first backpacking trip, swimming, and skipping rocks. As a young girl, I also loved catching butterflies and feeling that I was part of a scientific mission, surrounded by graduate students and scientists that I looked up to. By sharing

meals, car trips, and community with scientists, I developed comfort in the scientific world and my own interest in science. I became confident in living remotely and working outdoors, which contributed to my later pursuits leading outdoor trips and working as a field technician in a bee lab. The interest stuck with me—I am now a graduate student at Montana State University studying wild bees, still running around with a net!

Hayden:

Trips to the AMK Ranch (UW-NPS field station) were a much-anticipated portion of every summer and somewhat a part of my identity growing up. The Grand Tetons possessed a landscape, flora and fauna entirely different from our home in Iowa. I took great pride in "discovering" flowers, hiking trails, insects, and interestingly shaped sticks, and showing my parents what I'd found. We spent our days canoeing, swimming, and hiking, and as I grew older, helping with plant and butterfly surveys in Pilgrim Creek. I was even referenced in a master's thesis for finding a counterexample to our previous theory that the Parnassius butterflies did not travel far within their lifespans. As a result of spending time with my parents' scientific colleagues, I developed an affinity for interacting with adults that many of my peers did not have. I always looked forward to talking with the students on the team, the staff on the ranch, and other researchers at the station. All of these groups would co-mingle for a game of cards, an evening walk to historical graves near the station, watching the sunset from the boat dock, or a discussion of science. I most vividly remember communal dinners, pinecone tic-tac-toe, storytelling, jam sessions, and moth hunts with the incredible people I met over the summers, and further developing our friendships the following years. Living at the station was certainly one of the factors that has shaped me into an academic who is passionate about the outdoors.

RQ2: What aspects of field station culture supported my work as a researcher and a parent?

A Community of Support

Field Stations as a Scientific Community

Field stations provide a place where scientists from a broad set of institutions come together to conduct independent research in the same geographic region. As Geissler and Kelly (2016) note, field stations serve as a "halfway house" between the laboratory and the field where nature can be accessed. When living at a field station, scientists interact in laboratory settings, seminars, or simply by walking across the property. These seemingly happenstance interactions provide valuable opportunities for sharing ideas about how to conduct science, how to use a new instrument, or where in the region to find a particular species or plant community. For example, I am always looking for species sightings of particular rare plants and butterflies. "*You saw Dicentra uniflora where?*" would be a topic of interest to me and my field crew.

Field stations also provide informal opportunities for hatching new research ideas and for mentoring. Because the living situation at a field station is relatively informal, it breaks down some of the barriers that might otherwise exist between scientists at different stages of their careers (McDermott, 2019). Furthermore, at field stations, scientists from different institutions often come together and share their research findings, providing an opportunity to identify shared interests (Schubel et al., 2014). This type of networking opportunity happened for me over a decade ago. A visiting seminar speaker at the field station presented an idea that resonated with a future direction of research that I was interested in. I made a beeline to talk with the seminar speaker afterward, visiting by the lake that evening, and thereby initiating what would turn out to be a long-term research partnership.

Field Stations as a Place to Support Women in Science with Children

For many women scientists, the decision to parent is a significant one and the question of how we create a field station culture that supports women who are both scientists and mothers has been very important to me. As a newly hired assistant professor in the mid-1990s I recall asking a highly respected tenured-women faculty member from another institution about the concept of women faculty having children. I was the only tenure track woman faculty member in my department, so there were not very many role models. She responded something to the effect of "Oh, the women that I know who had children all dropped out of academia." She herself had no children. It took some time for me to process her observations. I knew that her statement was probably well-founded based on her experiences, but I also was hopeful that the world was slowly changing to a climate more supportive for women in science.

In essence, there was an unspoken expectation that it would be difficult to balance a family and an academic career in science (Mason & Goulden, 2004; Williams, 2000). I honestly could not envision how one could be both a good scientist and a good mother, not to mention adding the dimension of the large chunk of time annually required to conduct fieldwork. And so, as an academically driven person, my solution had been simply not to get interested in having any children and to plan specifically to focus on a career unfettered by children.

This is a significant issue because women who are at the beginning of their scientific career are often at the age when they are also considering whether or not they want to parent. Although there is a "leaky pipeline" all along the way, marriage and childbirth account for one of the largest leaks in the pipeline from graduate school to the acquisition of tenure for women in the sciences (Goulden et al., 2011). Even today, 43% of women leave full-time STEM employment after their first child and new mothers are more likely than new fathers to leave STEM, switch to part-time work, or exit the labor force entirely (Cech & Blair-Loy, 2019). The result of this leaky pipeline is that the numbers of women full professors are still low in many areas of science, and sometimes this is blatantly obvious (Lerman et al., 2021). For example, in academia, there is a culture of having a seminar room displaying portraits of leaders from the beginning of the institution to the present. When I would look at the portraits of deans, department chairs, or field station directors displayed in these spaces, there was an obvious lack of representation of women and people of color. Changing that not-so-subtle message requires a change of culture. Providing women and people of color the opportunity to find a likeness in the portrait hall in universities and at field stations requires the unbending of gender (Williams, 2000), creative solutions (Baker, 2011; Mason & Goulden, 2004), and a broader awareness of the challenges facing underrepresented groups (Demery & Pipkin, 2021).

Implementing Formal/Informal Support. For women and for many scientists with young children, it may not be deemed reasonable or desirable to leave a child behind for several weeks when one goes to the field. This issue is particularly applicable to breastfeeding mothers. Allowing scientists to bring their family along to a field station allows them to balance work-family needs and can also serve in training the next generation of scientists. It is important to note that while some field stations allow families, and there are some field stations that are not at all conducive to having a family come along on a scientific endeavor. In virtually all cases, there are numerous health and safety issues to be considered; for example, children and their caregivers need to have a comprehensive understanding of the dangers of the outdoors. One of our family legends recounts the night our daughter at an age around seven years old and a young friend from another family were walking from the lake to our cabin (which is a very short distance) when they were surprised by a bear. We will never know exactly how close the parties to this encounter were, but everyone heard the bear safety lecture one more time!

Overall, when children are present, the challenges of fieldwork may be compounded because a faculty member who is leading a research crew must be attentive to their family, as well as their research team. Therefore, formal and informal support structures need to be in place for women to successfully navigate parenthood and a scientific career. In my case, my partner and I took our family out in the field with us every year from the time that our first child was six months old. As an environmental historian, James has focused, to a large degree, on researching the history of science in national parks (e.g., Pritchard, 1997). This was convenient because it meant that he could also do research based out of the same field station. For many years, we took a "tag-team" approach, that is, trading off work time to take care of the kids so that the other person could do research. But James was very generous and made my research the priority. It is really not as easy to keep two full-blown academic careers going at full tilt with kids, and he deferred to mine on many occasions. He spent much more time with the kids during the day when we were at the field station. He would sometimes tag along with my students and I on our data collection adventures so that the entire group of us could be in the field together, but he was always the primary person on kid-duty when we were in the field on one of my projects. Over the years, sometimes I would wonder if we were missing out on other things in committing to this annual field endeavor. My kids would point out that we had never taken them to see the ocean, for example. So, I would ask James, "Are you *sure* you want to keep going out to the UW-NPS Research Station every summer?" and he would respond simply and definitively with a *"This is what we do."* In other words, we had committed to this long-term project, both in terms of data collection and in terms of our family traveling together. His unwavering support is something that I am very thankful for. I should also note that I recognize that we were lucky to be in such a privileged position to have the economic and career-based flexibility to accomplish this. Many two-career couples

Figure 4.6 James at the Field Station (Debinski, 2012).

don't have this as an option. To provide additional depth and perspective, James has reflected on our field adventures from his perspective.

James:

One hot and humid summer day around 1995 I was parking my car at Drake University (a very good school) in Des Moines where I was teaching a summer course. I called my spouse who was conducting her summer fieldwork in Grand Teton National Park, and I thought, "there is something amiss here." Why was I sweating while sitting still in this humid place, and she was in The Park? I never missed another summer research season in the Tetons. When the kids came along, my duty became clear. My mission became supporting Diane in her research and enhancing a cohesive family unit. The kids and I explored the station, learned about the historic architecture, local legends, and visited gravesites nearby. We hiked the trails as frequently as we could, puzzling over scats and tracks, observing how birds flew, and of course noticing the butterflies. To this day, I'm amazed at my son's sharp eye for the small things in nature. As appropriate, we'd stop by where Diane and her crew were surveying, so from an early age, both kids learned how to catch and handle butterflies. Eventually, our young researchers officially volunteered as assistants.

My own interests led me to the archives at Grand Teton National Park, and the Murie Center nearby. I completed a study on the patrol cabins of Grand Teton National Park (Pritchard, 2009), and a report on the development of the park's trail system (Pritchard, 2010). That study led to an article in the *Annals of Wyoming*, about the first park naturalist in Grand Teton National Park, Fritiof Fryxell (Pritchard, 2013). I also pursued information on Olaus and Mardie Murie, wilderness advocates. When convenient for the butterfly crew, I would dash off to the archives or sequester myself in the research station's library. This library was managed by the University of Wyoming, and as luck would have it, the spouse of the station director (Mary Ann) was a librarian! The library was an integral part of life at the field station, holding lots of interesting titles about wildlife and the parks, and enjoying frequent use by everyone at the station. Thus, I was able to pursue worthwhile research when not engaged as activities director!

From two to six weeks every summer, our family made the trip to Grand Teton National Park to "chase butterflies" and participate in the life of the field station. Being able to go to the field as a family was a wonderful experience for all of us. Our children wandered among the Principal Investigators (PIs), grad students, undergrad field techs, and during some years interacted with another family or two, hearing conversations about science and nature all the day long. Eventually, Hayden brought along a clarinet and serenaded anyone

> within earshot from the porch. I would like to think our family added something positive to the remarkable ambiance and integrated experience of the field station, and to the social world of science at the AMK Ranch. (UW/NPS Research Station)

Children always need supervision at some level, so it is the parent's responsibility to make sure that that is accomplished. In some cases, two faculty members might both be conducting field research at a station and be able to trade-off in caring for their children. Another model is to bring a grandparent or babysitter along. During our years visiting the station, there were a few families that also visited and brought along caregivers. For example, there was one other woman scientist who had children, and her mother would come along with her to take care of the children while she did her fieldwork. There was also a male scientist who brought his wife and two young daughters to the station for some years. And the director of the field station annually brought his wife and two sons along. In general, there was an informal cultural norm of support for children at the station. The children would sometimes play together with a parent or grandmother supervising while the scientist parents were in the field. One summer my family shared a house briefly with another woman scientist who had children, creating another layer of informal support.

Lerman and colleagues (2021) argue for more caregiver grants for scientists who are parents to increase their access to fieldwork. Providing caregiver grants is an important way to break down one of the largest barriers (i.e., childcare) to engagement in fieldwork for scientist parents. Moreover, caregiver grants may help to formalize support structures for scientist parents. While we did not have formal grants for bringing along caregivers when academic colleagues joined us for field seasons some acted almost as adopted academic grandparents. I have fond memories of our colleague Dr. John Clark, an environmental historian from the KU and one of James' mentors, who after hearing about our annual summer treks westward announced "*I've decided to come with you*" one spring. Dumbfounded, we didn't quite know what to say, so we hesitatingly went through the drill of what he needed to bring along, and he packed his bags and joined us. He huffed and puffed along on the trails, but kept up with us. He joined us for several years, both before and after we were parents. I have a particularly sweet memory of him helping me out on a bird survey in the Custer Gallatin National Forest, holding baby Zoe while I went down the hill into an aspen grove to do a bird survey. The idea was we would not be very far away from each other, but if Zoe made any noises, she would not scare the birds away. It worked!

RQ3: What approaches to work-life balance and team management are most effective in creating successful field research teams for a scientist/parent?

Acknowledging the Work-Life Blur

There are many beneficial aspects of field stations, but there are also challenges inherent in working out of these kinds of remote facilities. Long hours, the uncertainty of the weather, the stress of obtaining adequate amounts of high-quality data, and living in rustic conditions with limited phone, internet, and other facilities can be taxing. Before the advent of cell phones, people would line up, sitting on a log by the single outdoor payphone, to check in with friends, family, or their sweetheart in the evenings. There wasn't much chance for privacy with your conversation! We now have cell phones, but at this field station, there is one 6 ft diameter region next to a particular tree at the top of a hill where the reception works best. So, the privacy issue continues.

The Work-Life Blur

Field crews often have to live and work together for weeks, which can test even the best of teams (Golden et al., 2018). Defining time on the clock is virtually impossible when working in a field station. Regardless of whether a person is actually working or just present when one is at the field station, the lines between work and personal life become very much blurred. And even though a team of scientists may need to drive, hike, or boat to a particular field site to collect data, there is the planning, the revising of planning, the data entry, data analysis, and writing that all happen at the field station. Because butterfly surveys are so weather-dependent, the plans for a particular day are usually made after checking the weather the evening before, but if clouds show up in the morning and the temperature is too cool, the plans may have to be adjusted. Butterflies are "solar-powered," and they simply don't fly if the weather is too cool. There is also the issue of wildlife that can affect access to survey sites. In Grand Teton National Park, we have had mornings where we drive to our field site only to find that it is inhabited by a grizzly bear. This can change the activities for the day because we may need to wait and see if the bear leaves or simply go back to the field station and try to collect the data on the next day. There are often interactions among members of the team during the "off time." And that is just the way it has to be. But when someone is at their house at the field station, they can be working or not working and that may not be clear to other people at the station or even those on the team. As McDermott (2019) describes, "due to the blurred lines between being on and off, both men and women are expected to be ready to work and personable 24/7 when they are at camp" (p. 90). This can be a tiring set of circumstances. Work hours can be long and fieldwork can be unpredictable.

Sometimes there is an intense effort of work that has to occur for several weeks. For example, with butterfly mark-recapture surveys to estimate population sizes, our goal is to get data every day that the *Parnassius clodius* butterflies are flying, for about three to four weeks. Ideally, if there are enough people on the research team, people can alternate taking a day off. But often, the days off are determined by the weather. A rainy day may spontaneously be a day off for the entire crew. It is important to explain these kinds of work situations to all of the people involved before they agree to become part of the team.

Furthermore, responsible use of alcohol among all field station residents and dedication to getting the hard work done is essential in order to maintain the professional integrity of a field station. Field station directors, as well as faculty and team leaders, need to set an appropriate tone and expectations and be clear about when boundaries are crossed with respect to professionalism, use of alcohol, and safety. Because of the blurred lines between work and home life, unprofessional behavior can lead to bad public relationships or much more problematic issues.

Boundary Management

One way to deal with the fuzzy line between work and personal life is to set boundaries (McDermott, 2019). Faculty may set physical boundaries by staying in separate dwellings from graduate students and technicians or by setting verbal boundaries such as when they will consider themselves unavailable during the day. When living and working at a field station, the choices of housing can be limited, making it difficult to set physical boundaries. Whenever possible I tried to live in a house separate from my students and field crew. Some years there was only one house available, and it was shared by the team. In our work within the Custer Gallatin National Forest, we were lucky to get one cabin, and of the two possibilities, one had no running water. For many years, the water source for washing dishes and bodies came from a small creek a short walk from the cabin. Drinking water came from a large tank that we filled from a nearby campground. As such, the luxury of having a separate space was not an option. We were just glad to have a hard-sided building to live in in bear country, and a roof above our heads was very much a welcome commodity when the sleet and snow predictably came in June. So, one light bulb hanging from a cord, a woodstove, and solid walls did not provide much for privacy. But it was easier than working from a tent. The UW-NPS field station where we worked for part of the field season had multiple houses and they all had heat; some had running water.

Depending upon availability, some years my family lived with my graduate students, but for many years we did have our own separate cabin at the

UW-NPS Research Station. This was a welcome respite after a long day in the field or even a long day in the library at the research station. As Geissler and Kelly (2016) note, the "intimacies attendant in sharing a home" (p. 804) for scientists at field stations from cooking and eating together to waiting to use the bathroom breaks down the barriers, but can also create awkward situations. McDermott (2019) goes so far as to say that in isolated, confined, and extreme (ICE) field station conditions, "you cannot just have co-workers when you live and work with people; you have to become friends with them to survive" (p. 68). My experience was not an ICE field station, so the level of remoteness was not extreme, but there are parallels. When my children were with me in the field, I found that it was particularly helpful to separate out time and space for the "parent role" vs. the "professor role." Of course, I always wanted my children to be on their best behavior when my graduate students were present, but toddler meltdowns don't occur on such schedules. And when children are small, they often want all of a parent's attention, so having that personal space to focus entirely on one's family is valuable, particularly in the evenings. Even when one gets along quite well with their students, that separation can be healthy for everyone. In general, having some level of privacy with my family was helpful and sometimes we would have students over for dinner and a card game of "Ruckus" or Butterfly Bingo (we could not help ourselves).

Verbally, boundaries can be set by working out ways that people can take breaks and knowing when the formal workday is over (Golden et al., 2018; Lerman et al., 2021). When clear breaks are set early in the field season, team members can be expected to respect each other's time for relaxation and only initiate brief interruptions if needed to plan the next day's activity. Similarly, keeping an eye on the weather and declaring a day off early in the day or the day before is a way to let people know that they have the full day to do personal activities. In addition, many researchers have important personal events (there are a lot of weddings that overlap with prime butterfly field season!) for which they will need particular days off. If major scheduling can be done before the field season and everyone agrees to that schedule, work can be covered and each team member can have some vacation time. Overall, it is valuable for team members to set work boundaries before heading into the field and talk about when they might want to specifically take some time off in order to mitigate the potential impacts of the work/life blur.

RECOMMENDATIONS

The section above contains reflections from myself and my family regarding how we navigated and balanced family-career needs while in the field.

From my reflections and discussion, I suggest four overarching recommendations for effective science when parenthood and research are combined at field stations. Many of these recommendations are valuable outside the context of parenthood simply to have effective research teams. These recommendations stem from the support systems and experiences that assisted me in succeeding the most while in the field. The recommendations are broken down into techniques for building effective field teams, empowering graduate students, having a mantra, and creating a culture of support through leadership.

Techniques for Building Effective Field Teams

Field research can push people to the edge because the work is stressful, the conditions are challenging, and there are often narrow windows of time when a lot of data collection needs to occur. Furthermore, adding children into the mix adds layers of complexity. As such, it is important to be clear about the roles that each team member will play, about the expectations and conditions of the fieldwork, and about the communication strategies that will be used so that conflicts can be minimized and field seasons can be successful (Read et al., 2016). Collectively, these recommendations work together to support a culture of inclusion for not only researchers but also for their families.

Assigning Roles to Field Team Members

The stress of fieldwork can sometimes test people's ability to work well as a team. Even when children are well behaved and disciplined, they may add a layer of stress. Over the years, I have refined my thinking on this subject when people on our crew experienced some friction and disagreements that were difficult to resolve. I'm still learning myself, but I have become more proactive in thinking about where tensions could arise. Before the field season begins, it may be helpful to assign specific roles to individual members of the team and discuss the presence of children. These roles can be assigned based on roles within the team, experience, or a particular type of expertise. In some cases, there may be one person who serves as the "broker" or point person among all of the other team members, but in other cases, there may be multiple "brokers" who each have expertise in different areas (Cheruvelil et al., 2014). For example, in my teams, one person may be better at identifying plants and another may be better at identifying butterflies. Both are important skills. If a graduate student is leading a team, it is important for them to have ownership of the project and be able to lead the people they are supervising. However, in some cases, a seasoned technician may have more experience on a project than a new graduate student. This kind of situation can set the stage for awkward interactions if the role of each team member is not well defined. One way to deal with this may be to say that the graduate student has the decision-making role in the context of experimental design, but the seasoned technician may be expected to make decisions that require expertise with a particular technique. These roles may also have to change over the course of the field season.

Additionally, having conversations about how to approach concerns regarding children may be warranted. Some graduate students and technicians may avoid raising concerns regarding children for fear of offending the parent-researcher and losing favor. Ensuring open communication is critical. The bottom line is that if a discussion and definition of the roles and expectations occurs before the field season, everyone can know what to expect before they are in the midst of data collection, which can facilitate smoother teamwork. And in linking back to the scenario where the faculty member brings a child along on a field project, in my opinion, it goes without saying, but giving a graduate student or technician the responsibility to take care of a faculty member's child is not part of their job description. Childcare responsibilities are best left to a family member or someone specifically employed for that purpose. This is part of boundary management.

Having and Setting Realistic Expectations

Setting realistic expectations is critical for creating a culture of inclusion. Careful pre-planning and preparation of realistic expectations so that field technicians and students are not surprised by field conditions or the presence of a small human can prevent second thoughts or even mutiny. For example, in some field conditions, workers are expected to confront cold or hot environmental conditions that are outside of their previous experience. They may be expected to work in locations where there are large predators that could harm them. There may be an abundance of ticks, toxic plants, barbed wire, or cow pies that they need to contend with on a daily basis. Accessing the field sites may require driving on muddy or icy roads. Being realistic about describing the conditions that a field technician or graduate student will need to contend with on a daily basis and asking the difficult questions about whether these are conditions that they will be comfortable with is a minimum requirement. Sometimes after a week or two, it may become apparent that the conditions are not something that this person can deal with. Those events can be avoided or minimized by proactive planning and discussions. Moreover, for researchers bringing their children to the field, disclosing they will be present is important to ensure a level of comfort and willingness to engage with children. Some graduate students may fear they will be required to babysit or otherwise share responsibility for the safety of the child.

Once when I was interviewing for a field job in the Aleutian Islands of Alaska, the interviewer kept asking me questions in a way that sounded like they were trying to talk me out of the job. I was confused at the end of the interview but did indeed get offered and accept the job. The motivation for this line of questioning only became clear many years later, when I realized how costly it could be if a field technician did not work out in the middle of a field season. Careful vetting prior to fieldwork can mitigate some of these problems, but the reality of the situation only becomes 100% clear after the team is in the field. Understanding these challenges and being ready for them is just one of the things that a faculty member or graduate student needs to keep in mind when hiring.

Similar to setting field expectations during the recruiting and hiring process, it is important to set realistic expectations for how to deal with and overcome potential problems when in the field. Most field ecologists can think of examples where they designed an experiment in the comfort of their office or lab, probably in the company of graduate students or colleagues, that when they tried to implement in the field, it just did not work. Whiteboards and brainstorming sessions can be some of the most enjoyable parts of starting a new field project. We think about the sampling design, the number of replicates, the variables that we hope to focus on, the kinds of plots that we want to install. However, what happens when the plan from the Whiteboard doesn't match the reality in the field? This is the classic issue of "armchair ecology"—when sitting in the armchair, away from the field, things may seem simpler than they are in reality. I can think of several examples of this issue with respect to the research design. In the early days of our EPA-funded research, our research team categorized six meadow types using remotely sensed imagery, printed out a dozen maps, and then tried to find 10 examples of each meadow type on the landscape within a 3–4-mile distance of a road. As it turned out, some of the polygons that were defined as "mesic meadows" on our map, when visited, turned out to have stands of aspens intermingled in the meadow. This meant that instead of finding a mesic meadow, we were in a forested habitat, which was unusable for the purposes that we had planned. That meant we had to refine our mapping algorithm. In another instance, in 2020, when COVID modified our field plans, my graduate student and I tried to replicate an experiment that we had done in the Tetons in a field near Bozeman, Montana. Our plan was to measure plant photosynthesis before the sun came over the horizon. I had done this in the Tetons and usually had from 5:30 to 9:00 am to get the sampling done. We were rather surprised to find out that the work needed to be *completed* by 6 AM in this different locality due to the way that the sunlight hit our plots so much earlier in the day. The implications for the timing of data collection were significant.

If we add children to the mix, the unpredictability of fieldwork can make fulfilling expectations even more challenging. I recall sitting in the back of a vehicle with baby Hayden, taking a tour of Minnesota riparian habitats for a new research project on filter strips. Pre-trip planning did not allow me to know how long the trip would take and that there would be no comfortable option for breastfeeding while in the car, on a long trip that went very late, with several collaborators that I had not previously met. Eventually, I just breastfed the baby while the tour continued and ignored seat belt regulations. All of these types of reality checks that occur when implementing a new protocol or setting up a new research project can provide stress for the research team. Sometimes it means that people need to do more work or completely change their schedule. Communicating about how each of these challenges will be dealt with is essential. If not, the regular stress of fieldwork can be compounded by the realization that it is much more difficult to collect the data than one originally expected.

Field stations are often located in extreme environments where the technology and infrastructure that we use on a daily basis at universities are much less available (Golden et al., 2018; McDermott, 2019). One acronym that is used is ICE: Isolation, Confined, and Extreme. Simply having water for cooking and bathing, temperature control in a living situation, access to grocery stores, hardware stores (essential for field experiments), internet, and good cell phone service become luxuries in many cases. Children require the equivalent of a small department store's worth of goods to meet their basic needs, from diapers to baby food and other sundries. Planning ahead is essential so that resources are available, people know what to do if someone gets hurt, and the team can meet the challenges of doing fieldwork in a remote location. For example, if you are standing in a meadow an hour's drive from any hardware store and you realize that you don't have the correct screwdriver required for setting up an experimental structure or a child is out of diapers, that can halt progress for an entire day. Mardy Murie (2003, p. 212) summarized this same issue relative to families in the field in northern Alaska in 1926 when she wrote, "Looking back on it, I'm surprised that we didn't panic over those lists and that outfit. What if we had forgotten something vital, such as spare engine parts or extra baby bottles?" Yes, having a good supply of research and other gear is essential when working remotely.

Using Effective Communication Strategies

Research on building effective communication in interdisciplinary research teams has highlighted that group communication must balance between the goals of building group cohesion and accomplishing the tasks at hand (Thompson, 2009). In ecological fieldwork, it may be worthwhile to invest in building group cohesion prior to the team being in a remote locale. Cheruvelil et al. (2014) encourage investment in team-building exercises to establish good time management and conflict management practices.

Scheduled Communication. Communication may become difficult if the team members are not all working in the same location. For example, a faculty member may send a team out to the field, but they may not be working with that team for the entire field season. Given the rapidly changing environments and conditions of fieldwork, it is important for faculty who are not present in the field to check in with their field crews on a regular basis. Although many field stations and field sites are located in remote places where cell service is limited, the advent of cell phones and technology adoptions from COVID-19 have created new avenues for teams to stay in touch remotely. Such remote interactions could be a benefit to women with children because they can involve less travel prior to the meeting, allowing women scientists to work from home and/or breastfeed more conveniently, but they can also add stress if children in the background need attention at the same time as their colleagues.

In general, scheduling specific times to communicate with field teams can be important for keeping projects moving and maintaining team morale. One approach to this check-in that I have used is a combination of a team check-in as well as one-on-one check-ins. The team check-in allows for the entire group to visit with the faculty member and talk about research progress. The one-on-one check-ins allow individuals to privately discuss any challenges that they may not want to bring up within the team meeting. Both of these events can occur consecutively, and phone calls don't need to be extensive, but this allows for a more thorough assessment of how the work is progressing and how the team is functioning. It is also important to remember that subtle messages can be lost on the phone or in emails. There is no substitute for in-person communication, and research has shown that face-to-face communication is important for effective communication and productivity in research teams (Cheruvelil et al., 2014).

Setting a Tone. Communication can also be used to set the team culture and tone. When faculty are present in the field with their graduate students for extended periods of time, they can contribute to understanding how an ecological system may be changing based upon multiple years of observation, they can assist with problem-solving when experimental manipulations are not working as planned, and they can help build a positive working environment. It may not be possible for faculty to be involved in fieldwork in all situations, and as graduate students become more competent to work on their own, oversight can be reduced. But in a way similar to the field station director setting a tone at the field station, the faculty mentor sets a tone for the research team, that if done properly can help facilitate smoother functioning of the team. One strategy for setting the tone when a researcher's attention may be split between caring for the child and caring for the research may include division of priorities for each task based on the time of day, where certain times are prioritized for research and other times for childcare, if possible. In addition, there may be times when these two responsibilities will just have to overlap and the expectation for the speed of accomplishing a research activity may have to be reduced.

Empowering Graduate Students and Graduate Student Mentoring

The process of training graduate students allows them to learn firsthand how to design, implement, and carry out a field study. In many cases, it allows them to learn how to write their own grant proposal and even manage their own budget. Providing graduate students with the appropriate level of information about the funding, introducing them to research partners in agencies or nongovernmental organizations, and allowing them to work as colleagues are excellent ways to train them for the next step in their careers. There may be some aspects of the project that a major advisor would prefer that the student does not get involved in. This choice may be in the student's best interest so that they can focus on getting their degree completed. There may also be particular roles that the major advisor needs to play as the PI of the grant which are inappropriate for the graduate student to be involved in. However, there are many aspects of the research that are appropriate for the graduate student to participate in, and learning about these aspects provides a fertile training ground for graduate students as independent researchers. For a scientist juggling science and parenthood, providing capable and willing graduate students with additional responsibilities may provide important experiences and curriculum vita lines, while lessening the load on the faculty member. It is important to note that communicating with graduate students about additional responsibilities and giving graduate students credit for their work is important if they are asked to take on extra responsibilities.

Moreover, field stations provide valuable opportunities where networking and mentor/mentee relationships can occur. A valuable aspect of field stations is that faculty from a variety of institutions may come together encouraging inter-institutional cross-pollination to talk about everything from career opportunities, to ways of better understanding the academic landscape, to swapping suggestions for recruiting new graduate students. In some cases, prominent scholars in the field may have a history of conducting research at a particular field station. Because they may also have a regular schedule of visiting that field station, this provides an opportunity for graduate students and junior faculty to interact with senior faculty in a more relaxed venue.

Whereas the graduate student or junior faculty might never have considered contacting this senior faculty on a college campus, if they're both living at the same field station and happen to cross paths while walking from the library to their housing, there is an opportunity for more informal interaction. Although everyone is busy, there are usually some periods of "down" time at field stations. This may allow for informal conversations about manuscripts, data collection, or professional development. These informal interactions can break down some of the institutional barriers that may otherwise inhibit a graduate student or junior faculty from reaching out to that senior faculty member. This may allow graduate students and junior faculty to ask questions about the way academic systems work that they would feel less comfortable asking peers at their own institution. In the best of examples, a new mentor/mentee relationship may be developed.

Having a Mantra

As I noted earlier, the phrase "Get the data," coined by my partner James, became a mantra for our team to emphasize the importance of trying to get the data even if weather conditions looked poor. It came from a mountaineer's mantra "Make the approach." In other words, if one wants to climb a mountain, you can't get to the top without making the approach. You may have to turn back if the weather becomes unfavorable, but the time you spend making the approach may be valuable if the weather shifts to a better state. We used both of these mantras jokingly sometimes when we really didn't want to go out in bad weather, but we knew that we may be able to get some data. I have fond memories of a bird survey where we made the approach and it was so cold that it started snowing in the middle of the bird survey. For context, summer bird surveys are not usually done in the rain, and definitely not in the snow. One of my students turned to me and said, "Diane, it's *snowing* and the birds are *not singing*." At last, I conceded that it was time to call it quits, but we laughed about it and took a photo to commemorate the odd weather when we did, at least, make the approach to get the data. Mantras can be used to build cohesion among teams and lift team morale.

Creating a Culture of Support at Field Stations through Directorship

Because field stations create and provide the infrastructure that is supportive of long-term research projects, many scientists spend decades working out of the same field station each year. Because of this ritualistic behavior, groups of people that may not even have much in common from a scientific disciplinary perspective may create bonds of friendship that are strengthened by this annual return to the field station. Shared meals combined with humorous stories from fieldwork serve to create strong bonds.

Besides the infrastructure, the human dimension of the community at a field station is also a critical variable. The field station director sets a particular tone based upon their position, personality, and background, and this person can be critical in fashioning the culture of the field station, which can include cultivating a *family-friendly culture*. As such, the director can facilitate new research or introduce new scientists to researchers or agency collaborators in the area. We were lucky in that during many of our field seasons, the UW-NPS Research Station was directed by Dr. Hank Harlow, who set a high bar for field station directors. With commitment, humor, practical know-how, strong science, and a weekly barbeque, he set a positive tone at the station that enhanced its scientific mission. Along with his spouse Mary Anne, their family also successfully navigated the academic year and life between a university and a field station.

One summer there was talk of a potential future policy of "putting a researcher in every bed" by administrators at the University of Wyoming. This would maximize the amount of research conducted, but would effectively eliminate the option for families to come along. James, ever the historian, quickly responded that Olaus and Margaret Murie (2003) had traveled by boat with their baby down the Old Crow River in northern Alaska while studying geese in 1926. James and I wrote a letter to the provost of the University of Wyoming referencing this story and providing it as justification that there was a precedent for children coming along on fieldwork by a famous wildlife biologist from Jackson, Wyoming. We never got a response to that letter, but any further discussion of changing a policy quietly went away.

Aspects of a productive field station culture include the creation of a welcoming community for all, support for new researchers, and defining by example what is appropriate behavior. A field station director who is effective is a *presence* at that field station. In my opinion, this person should ideally also have strong scientific credentials and a good understanding of the myriad of ways that other scientists may need to collect data, design experiments, and run the teams that collect data. This person also serves as the face of the field station to the local and broader community and communicates with partners and with the public about the value of what is being done at the field station. The director may facilitate public lectures, meetings that are held at the field station, and the planning of the annual events. They also set an essential example, defining what it means to be a professional, a scientist, and a colleague. Because the lines between personal and professional activities are blurred, the field station director is a role model for others in the context of moderation in the use of alcohol, behavior on days off, risk-taking, and interaction with others at the field station. Recent literature by anthropologists studying issues of harassment, assault, and other inappropriate behavior at field stations highlights the importance of both clarity and enforcement of appropriate professional behavior and rules and provides suggested policies, procedures, and paradigms that field station directors and PIs can implement to improve field experiences and better achieve equal opportunity in field research settings (Nelson et al., 2017). Ignoring such issues has the potential to endanger the credibility and efficacy of the field station.

Facilitating the development of careers for underrepresented groups is a particularly valuable way that a field station director can provide leadership. Casting a broad net when hiring interns or announcing small grant opportunities are ways that a field station director can encourage underrepresented groups or scientists with fewer financial assets to become more involved in research at a field station. Field stations can also be more inclusive by creating spaces for nursing mothers, equipping the bathrooms with changing tables, or giving priority for particular housing to scientists with families. These practical resources, including physically transforming the space, or making certain living arrangements possible can make a big difference.

FUTURE DIRECTIONS

Improving the success of women in science at research field stations requires effort on the part of PIs, field station directors, and associated academic institutions. The PIs must be intentional in building an effective research team and being responsible if family members join them in their field endeavors. The director of the field station needs to cultivate a welcoming, yet professional atmosphere. Institutions likewise need to be proactive in supporting scientists at all levels of their careers and from a broad diversity of backgrounds, racial groups, and genders. There are challenges and safety issues associated with allowing scientists to bring their families to a field station that must be adequately addressed, but without such an allowance, young parents are potentially excluded from the opportunity to even consider participating in field station–based science. The ability to bring children along to field stations can have a particularly significant effect on young mothers who are also scientists and it challenges the narrative that accomplished women in science cannot also be excellent mothers. Challenging some of these narratives is essential if we want women and underrepresented groups of all kinds who are parents to find a likeness in the portrait hall of the future. As Phoebe Leboy, professor emeritus of biochemistry at University of Pennsylvania and past president of the Association for Women in Science is quoted in Baker (2011), "The workplace—in academia at least—is still constructed for men with stay-at-home wives, and even a lot of American men are rebelling about that" (p. 430). Indeed, the ADVANCE programs have "changed the conversation" regarding ways to improve the recruitment and retention of women in STEM (Bowen & Debinski, 2013). There are several sources that address ways to work toward work-life balance, such as The University of California Faculty Family Friendly Edge (Berkeley, n.d.), and many institutions are modifying the tenure clock in the context of supporting women in academia (Mason, 2009).

Overall, field stations provide a rich environment for cultivating creativity, friendships, mentoring opportunities, and the advancement of science. Long-term field station–based research has been a major contributor to the careers of many environmental scientists. The institutional support for such facilities should be continued, if not enhanced, and the culture and policies should be examined to determine if they are supportive of women, underrepresented groups, and parents in STEM.

FINAL THOUGHTS

Note that my main goal in writing this chapter was to advocate for supporting women scientists who are parents at field stations. However, I would like to reiterate that not all field stations are amenable to bringing children due to safety or logistical concerns. And when I make arguments in favor of having children at a field station, I am assuming that parent(s) will be very responsible about taking care of their child(ren) living at a field station. Inappropriate behavior could result in restrictions on the culture and policies that support these privileges.

REFERENCES

Adams, T., & Herrmann, A. (2020). Expanding our autoethnographic future. *Journal of Autoethnography, 1*, 1–8. https://doi.org/10.1525/joae.2020.1.1.1

Anderson, L. (2006). Analytic autoethnography. *Journal of Contemporary Ethnography, 35*, 373–395. https://doi.org/10.1177/ 0891241605280449.

Baker, B. (2011). Having a life in science. *Bioscience, 61*(6), 429–433. https://doi.org/10.1525/bio.2011.61.6.4

Bebbington, D. (2002). Women in science, engineering and technology: A review of the issues. *Higher Education Quarterly, 56*(4), 360–375. https://doi.org/10.1111/1468-2273.00225

Berkeley. (n.d.). *The UC faculty family friendly edge*. https://ucfamilyedge.berkeley.edu/

Bowen, B. S., & Debinski, D. M. (2013). *ISU ADVANCE NSF final report* (Grant no. HRD-0600399). National Science Foundation. https://www.advance.iastate.edu

/sites/default/files/Additional%20Resources/History/IowaStateADV-FinalReport-Public-Approved-2013.pdf
Caglak, S. (2017). Does hands-on science practices make an ımpact on achievement in science? A meta-analysis. *Journal of Education in Science, Environment and Health, 3*(1), 69–87. https://doi.org/10.21891/jeseh.275708
Cech, E. A., & Blair-Loy, M. (2019). The changing career trajectories of new parents in STEM. *Proceedings of the National Academy of Science of the United States of America, 116*(10), 4182–4187. https://doi.org/10.1073/pnas.1810862116
Cheruvelil, K. S., Soranno, P. A., Weathers, K. C., Hanson, P. C., Goring, S. J., Filstrup, C. T., & Read, E. K. (2014). Creating and maintaining high-performing collaborative research teams: the importance of diversity and interpersonal skills. *Frontiers in Ecology and the Environment, 12*, 31–38. https://doi.org/10.1890/130001
Debinski, D. M., Caruthers, J. C., Cook, D., Crowley, J., & Wickham, H. (2013). Gradient-based habitat affinities predict species vulnerability to climate change. *Ecology, 94*(5), 1036–1045. https://www.jstor.org/stable/23435946
Debinski, D. M., Wickham, H., Kindscher, K., Caruthers, J. C., & Germino, M. (2010). Montane meadow change during drought varies with background hydrologic regime and plant functional group. *Ecology, 91*(6), 1672–1681. https://doi.org/10.1890/09-0567.1
Demery, A. J. C., & Pipkin, M. A. (2021). Safe fieldwork strategies for at-risk individuals, their supervisors and institutions. *Nature Ecology & Evolution, 5*, 1–5. https://doi.org/10.1038/s41559-020-01328-5
Fogel, M. L. (2020). *Advice from the Isotope Queen: Building a meaningful career while enjoying a full life*. Yaqui Gulch Press.
Geissler, P. W., & Kelly, A. H. (2016). A home for science: The life and times of Tropical and Polar field stations. *Social Studies of Science, 46*(6), 797–808. https://www.jstor.org/stable/26107053
Golden, S. J., Chang, C., & Kozlowski, S. (2018). Isolated, confined, and extreme (ICE) environments: Review and integration. *Journal of Organizational Behavior, 39*, 701–715. https://doi.org/10.1002/job.2288
Goulden, M., Mason, M. A., & Frasch, K. (2011). Keeping women in the science pipeline. *The ANNALS of the American Academy of Political and Social Science, 638*(1), 141–162. https://doi.org/10.1177/0002716211416925
Holman, S., Adams, T., & Ellis, C. (2013). Introduction: Coming to know autoethnography as more than a method. In S. Holman, T. Adams, & C. Ellis (Eds.), *Handbook of autoethnography* (pp. 17–47). Left Coast Press.
James, J. K., & Williams, T. (2017). School-based experiential outdoor education: A neglected necessity. *Journal of Experiential Education, 40*(1), 58–71. https:doi.org/10.1177/1053825916676190
Lerman, S. B., Pejchar, L., Benedict, L., Covino, K. M., Dickinson, J. L., Fantle-Lepczyk, J. E., Rodewald, A. D., & Vleck, C. (2021). Juggling parenthood and ornithology: A full lifecycle approach to supporting mothers through the American Ornithological Society. *Ornithological Applications, 123*(2), 1–9. https://doi.org/10.1093/ornithapp/duab001

Madgavkar, A., White, O., Krishnan, M., Mahajan, D., & Azcue, X. (2020). COVID-19 an gender equality: Countering the regressive effects. *McKinsey Global Institute*. https://www.mckinsey.com/featured-insights/future-of-work/covid-19-and-gender-equality-countering-the-regressive-effects

Makarem, Y., & Wang, J. (2020). Career experiences of women in science, technology, engineering, and mathematics fields: A systematic literature review. *Human Resource Development Quarterly, 31*(1), 91–111. https://doi.org/10.1002/hrdq.21380

Manning, J., & Adams, T. (2015). Popular cultural studies and autoethnography: An essay on method. *The Popular Culture Studies Journal, 3*, 187–211. http://commons.lib.niu.edu/handle/10843/14754

Mason, M. A. (2009, May 28). Rethinking the tenure clock - dealing with the rigidities of the tenure system is a key reform facing academe, if we want tenure to persist. *Chronicle of Higher Education*. https://www.chronicle.com/article/rethinking-the-tenure-clock/

Mason, M. A., & Goulden, M. (2004). Marriage and baby blues: Redefining gender equity in the academy. *The ANNALS of the American Academy of Political and Social Science, 596*, 86-103. https://doi.org/10.1177/0002716204268744

McDermott, V. (2019). *'It's a magnifying glass': the communication of power in a remote field station* [Unpublished master's thesis]. University of Alaska Fairbanks.

Murie, M. E. (2003). *Two in the far north*. Alaska Northwest Books.

National Science Foundation. (2021). ADVANCE: Organizational change for gender equity in STEM Academic Professions. https://www.nsf.gov/funding/pgm_summ.jsp?pims_id=5383

Nelson, R. G., Rutherford, J. N., Hinde, K., & Clancy, K. B. (2017). Signaling safety: Characterizing fieldwork experiences and their implications for career trajectories. *American Anthropologist, 119*(4), 710–722. https://doi.org/10.1111/aman.12929

Pritchard, J. A. (1997). *Preserving natural conditions: Science and the perception of nature in Yellowstone National Park*. University of Nebraska Press.

Pritchard, J. A., & Longfield, K. (2009). *The Northern backcountry patrol cabins of grand Teton National Park*. Report to the University of Wyoming-National Park Service Research Center, Moran, Wyoming. https://journals.uwyo.edu/index.php/uwnpsrc/article/view/3699

Pritchard, J. A. (2010). *A brief history of the trails of Grand Teton National Park*. Report to the University of Wyoming-National Park Service Research Center, Moran, Wyoming. https://journals.uwyo.edu/index.php/uwnpsrc/article/view/3749

Pritchard, J. A. (2013). Irresistible fascination: Fritiof fryxell and the development of Grand Teton National Park. *Annals of Wyoming, 85*(4), 2–16.

Read, E. K., O'Rourke, M., Hong, G. S., Hanson, P. C., Winslow, L. A., Crowley, S., Brewer, C. A., & Weathers, K. C. (2016). Building the team for team science. *Ecosphere, 7*(3), e01291. https://doi.org/10.1002/ecs2.1291

Rosser, S. V. (1992). Are there feminist methodologies appropriate for the natural science and do they make a difference? *Women's Studies International Forum, 15*, 535–550. https://doi.org/10.1016/0277-5395(92)90057-3

Schubel, J. R., Coleman, F. C., Conrad, C., Debinski, D. M., Kareiva, P. M., Matsumoto, G. I. Mcknight, D. M., Parmesan, C., Plowes, R., Power, A. G., Power, M., Sisk, T. D., & Stromberg, M. R. (2014). Enhancing the value and sustainability of biological field stations and marine laboratories in the 21st century. *National Academy of Sciences Report.* http://dels.nas.edu/Report/Enhancing-Value-Sustainability/18806

Sparkes, A. C. (2020). Autoethnography: accept, revise, reject? An evaluative self reflects, *Qualitative Research in Sport, Exercise and Health, 12*(20), 289–302. https://doi.org/10.1080/2159676X.2020.1732453

Thompson, J. L. (2009). Building collective communication competence in interdisciplinary research teams. *Journal of Applied Communication Research, 37*(3), 278–297. https://doi.org/10.1080/00909880903025911

Valian, V. (2000). *Why so slow? The advancement of women.* The MIT Press.

Wall, S. (2006). An autoethnography on learning about autoethnography. *International Journal of Qualitative Methods, 5*(2), 146–160. https://doi.org/10.1177/160940690600500205

Wanelik, K. M., Griffin, J. S., Head, M. L., Ingleby, F. C., & Lewis, Z. (2020). Breaking barriers? Ethnicity and socioeconomic background impact on early career progression in the fields of ecology and evolution. *Ecology and Evolution, 10*(14), 6870–6880. https://doi.org/10.1002/ece3.6423

Webb-Williams, J. (2018). Science self-efficacy in the primary classroom: Using mixed methods to investigate sources of self-efficacy. *Research in Science Education, 48*, 939–961. https://doi.org/10.1007/s11165-016-9592-0

Williams, J. (2000). *Unbending gender. Why family and work conflict and what to do about it.* Oxford University Press.

Xie, Y., & Shauman, K. A. (2003). *Women in science: Career processes and outcomes.* Harvard University.

Chapter 5

Experiences of a Female Leader at Field Stations and Marine Labs

Sarah D. Oktay

Woman in Charge
by Len Germinara

Nevertheless she
Persisted against all odds
No job too daunting

INTRODUCTION

Only 27% of workers in science, technology, engineering and mathematics (STEM) in the United States are women, despite comprising 48% of our nation's workforce (Martinez & Christnacht, 2021). In STEM-related leadership positions, the data indicate an even wider gender gap (McCollough, 2011). Although the number of women in leadership positions at field stations and marine labs (FSMLs) is increasing, they still have not reached parity (NSF, 2018), providing further evidence that systemic disparities remain.

The factors contributing to these disparities are complex and not fully explicated in the literature. Discrimination, implicit bias, family obligations, and lack of mentorship (see Oktay & Kloeppel, chapter 8 in this volume) are significant and persistent impediments to equality and integration that have been identified in the literature, but research is lacking (McCollough, 2011), especially for women in STEM working at FSMLs. Collectively, women earn over half of all bachelor's, master's, and doctoral degrees in STEM; however, numbers dwindle significantly in leadership positions (AWIS, 2019). There are structural issues, such as harassment and lack of representation on hiring committees (AWIS, 2019), but also cultural and societal norms that may negatively impact women and how they perceive themselves as leaders in STEM. Inherent stereotyping and centuries of bias and discrimination have limited the opportunities for women in corporations, academia, the military, and to a lesser extent, nonprofits. Eagly and Carli (2007) identified a labyrinth of challenges for women seeking leadership roles and dismissed the "glass ceiling" concept as overly simplistic. Carli (2007) found that "vestiges of prejudice against women, issues of leadership style and authenticity, and family responsibilities are just a few of the challenges" that women in the workplace continue to face.

The American Association of University Women (AAUW) is one of several large professional organizations that have identified the gender leadership gap as a significant and persistent problem, publishing their findings in a research report entitled *Barriers & Bias: The Status of Women in Leadership* (AAUW, 2016). Members of the Organization of Biological Field Stations (OBFS) contributed to this report (AAUW, 2016), and the organization as a whole recognizes the importance of increasing diversity in the leadership and staffing of FSMLs (OBFS, 2020).

Complicating scholarship in the area of leadership is the sheer volume of discussion of it in both the academic and popular presses. A quick search on Amazon.com, for example, shows 60,000 titles currently available with "leadership" in the title. However, of the 60,000 available options, only 187 titles (0.3%) specifically address barriers to women in leadership, underscoring the lack of research and focus for both academics and practitioners. Collectively, the abundance of leadership-focused publications and lack thereof for women and other marginalized groups illustrates the need for discussion and scholarship addressing these populations. Leadership can mean many things depending on the individual, context, industry, and discipline; moreover, leaders may emerge in the midst of an emergency or develop over time through education, experience, and/or an established hierarchy. This vast breadth of definitions and styles of leadership complicates the examination of leaders, leadership, and what it means to be led. The University of Minnesota (2013) distinguished between the roles of a leader and leadership itself as:

> The leader is a group role that is associated with a high-status position and may be formally or informally recognized by group members. Leadership is a complex of beliefs, communication patterns, and behaviors that influence the functioning of a group and move a group toward the completion of its task. A person in the role of leader may provide no or poor leadership. Likewise, a person who is not recognized as a "leader" in title can provide excellent leadership. (Chapter 14.1, para. 1)

An in-depth discussion of types of leadership, leadership strategies, and emerging trends is beyond the scope of this chapter, however. Instead, this chapter focuses on positional leadership, in which people, in this case women, occupy positions of power that are recognized and rewarded in observable ways. Identifying paths to leadership and creating opportunities for women and underrepresented populations are critical to building sustainability in any organization (Hunt et al. 2015, 2018). In their research, Hunt et al. (2018) analyzed data from over 100 companies in twelve countries. They measured "sustainability" for a corporation using two measures of financial performance, profitability (measured as average EBIT margin, i.e., operating earnings over operating sales) and value creation (measured as economic profit margin). Findings suggest that positive financial outcomes were significantly higher for corporations with more diverse leadership and corporations in which diversity was defined as "a greater proportion of women and ethnically/culturally diverse individuals" (Hunt et al., 2015, p. 1). In other words, having diversity in leadership roles leads to more profitability in addition to introducing diverse perspectives into the workplace that more fully represent the general population (Gender Insite, 2018).

As a woman with almost 20 years of experience in leadership positions at FSMLs, I often reflect on how I was able to navigate and thrive in institutions historically designed to exclude me. Taking an evocative autoethnographic approach and guided by the following RQ: *How can my leadership journey in FSMLs contribute to larger conversations about women in leadership at FSMLs?*" I systematically analyzed my lived experience, both personally and professionally, sharing my story to explore how the FSML community may seek to better support women into leadership positions.

LITERATURE REVIEW

Women's Experiences with Leadership

Like other personality traits, some innate leadership ability exists, but eventual success in a leadership role is a function of upbringing, environment, and influenced by parents and mentors (Drummond et al., 2002, p. 4). As previously noted, there are many definitions of leadership, and female leaders often report dramatically different experiences than their male counterparts (Taylor et al., 2020). Contrary to what the media or a lifetime of biases may tell you, leadership traits are not gender specific and are, in fact, statistically identical for men and women (Barling, 2014). In other words, women are as predisposed to leadership as men (Barling, 2014). Johnson et al. (1998) identified leadership traits as being heritable, especially when it comes to transformational leadership traits. Yukl (2006) states

> that the trait approach emphasizes leaders' attributes such as personality, motives, values, and skills. Underlying this approach was the assumption that some people are natural leaders, endowed with certain traits not possessed by other people. This is very different from describing leadership as a process. In essence, the trait viewpoint suggests that leadership is inherent in a few select people and that leadership is restricted to only those few who have special talents with which they are born. (p. 13)

However, just as many researchers view leadership as a process that may be helped along with inherent traits, but also learned and developed over time through education and experience. Rowe (2007), for example, argues

> viewing leadership as a process implies that leadership is a phenomenon that is contextual and suggests that everyone is capable of exercising leadership. This suggests that leadership can be learned and that leadership is observable through what leaders do or how they behave. (p. 3)

Whether leadership is innate or developed over time, women are under-represented in leadership positions, suggesting the lack of opportunities or other barriers may be preventing women from achieving leadership-related goals. Researchers have identified four types of barriers to leadership for women: structural barriers, institutional mindsets, individual mindsets, and lifestyle choices (Andrews, 2013; Barsh & Yee, 2012). Barling (2014) concludes that unconscious biases against women in our society are the significant cause of why women are not rising to leadership positions, and further argues that men, women, and the media must work together if we hope to achieve gender parity anytime soon. Simon and Hoyt (2013) found that women internalized what they visualized, in other words, *you are what you see*, and media representations of women leaders may be problematic. They completed two studies to see if women responded positively to seeing other women in non-stereotypical roles. In the first study, they showed images of women in counter-stereotypical roles, for example, as professional athletes, entrepreneurs, and doctors. They found that women who viewed "media images of women in counter-stereotypical roles subsequently reported more nontraditional, egalitarian gender role beliefs about women than women who viewed media images of women in stereotypical roles" (Simon & Hoyt, 2013, p. 241). In the second study, they explored how women's leadership was affected. Female participants who viewed images of women in counter-stereotypical roles reported lower negative self-perceptions and greater leadership aspirations after performing a leadership task than participants who viewed images of women in the stereotypical roles of homemaker and caregiver. In other words, if you watch "Wonder Woman" and other representations of women in positions of power and leadership, you will feel empowered.

Andrews (2018) clearly defined this problem as having an *institutional mindset*: Institutional mindsets describe a variety of gender biases and stereotypical viewpoints. This was first described by Eagly and Karau (2002):

> For example, role incongruity occurs when someone holds beliefs or stereotypes about a group that are inconsistent with the behavior thought to be necessary to succeed in a specific role. In other words, there is a common belief that gender differences make women and men effective in different roles. Thus, women are less effective to the extent that the leader role is masculinized, and men are less effective when the role is feminized. (as cited by Andrews, 2018, p. 37)

Women's Leadership Styles

A separate body of literature focuses on whether women and men differ in their leadership styles. The styles that have been studied most are transformational (i.e., innovative leadership in which the leader serves as a positive role model based on gaining the trust of the followers), transactional (i.e., leadership by administering rewards for good behaviors and punishments or corrections for poor performance), and laissez-faire (i.e., the leader is neglectful and uninvolved). Transformational style is a concept that has emerged over the past two decades and has been seen to positively contribute to organizational effectiveness.

In a meta-analysis of literature comparing men and women leaders, mainly in the business and educational sectors with leaders defined as supervising or directing the work of others, Eagly et al. (2003) found that women were more likely to have a transformational leadership style. The authors suggest that women may favor this style of leadership because it is both effective and consistent with the female gender role of nurturing relationships, thus providing a way of overcoming the previous stereotype or "role incongruity" of being in a leadership position. According to Eagly and Karau's (2002) role congruity theory, prejudice against female leaders results from the incongruity between the *take charge*, or *agentic*, stereotype linked with leadership and the *take care*, or *communal*, stereotype often associated with women (p. 574).

Interestingly, the transformational leadership style that many women employ focuses on inspiration and motivation as key components. Transformational leaders are those that "use ethical behavior, create a positive shared vision, and motivate followers to achieve that shared vision through strong emotional appeals" (PSU, 2014, para. 12). Several researchers have shown that women leaders tend to use transformational leadership styles in interacting with their employees (Silva & Mendis, 2017). Bilal et al. (2021) found that women leaders inspired a much deeper level of trust and connectivity with their workforce, which allowed for greater creativity and innovation. Eagly et al. (2003) showed that employees show more innovative behavior under female leadership compared to male leadership. Hyde (2014) found that "although leadership is stereotyped as masculine, there is no evidence that women are incompetent as leaders, whether measured by effectiveness or by the use of optimal styles such as transformational leadership" (p. 388).

Hyde (2014) summarized earlier work by Eagly et al. (1995; 2003) in which a series of meta-analyses were conducted on gender and leadership. The comparisons among papers showed no significant gender difference in leadership effectiveness although in certain situations women may be more effective than men (see Hyde, 2014; Eagly et al., 1995; 2003).

Women's Experiences in Field Work

Most of the literature that addresses women in science has concentrated on the lab (Else, 2019; Hartley & Tansey, 2015), the academy (Casad et al., 2021; Mansfield et al., 2019; Fitzgerald & Ormerod, 1993), and industry (Taylor et al., 2020). The challenges that other women and I have experienced and identified while working in FSMLs and in the field, however, are different and represent a reality not structured and defined by the confines of a physical building or campus. Some of the unique challenges women face while working in FSMLs are safety concerns, lack of bathroom or sleeping facilities, assumed bias when it comes to physical tasks, and fewer overall opportunities due to arranging travel and sleeping arrangements (Demery & Pipkin, 2021). Recent increased interest in diversity and inclusion in STEM has fueled research, unraveling the many of the ways in which field-based experiences can be problematic, unsafe, and unwelcoming for people of all gender identities as well as other marginalized groups (Demery & Pipkin, 2021). Despite the growing body of research that focuses on the experiences of women working in FSMLs, a significant gap remains when it comes to women in positions of leadership at FSMLs.

Current Issue

Focusing specifically on women leaders in field stations, there is a dearth of research explicating barriers and identifying solutions to leadership of women and other marginalized groups at FSMLs. The "leaky pipeline" has been a consistent focus in the popular and academic press for decades; however, women are still underrepresented in STEM and STEM leadership. We need to identify and address how we can best increase the footprint of women, especially in leadership positions. As a woman working in field station leadership, sharing my experiences provides a starting point for uncovering not only barriers but also opportunities and strategies for supporting women throughout their careers so that the highest levels of achievement are a natural progression. Using autoethnography, I reflected on my twenty years of leadership experience in conjunction with my research question: *How can my leadership journey in FSMLs contribute to larger conversations about women in leadership at FSMLs?*

METHODS

Autoethnographies "are highly personalized accounts that draw upon the experience of the author/researcher for the purposes of extending sociological understanding" (Sparkes, 2000, p. 21). They can be especially useful when an experience is relatively rare and of interest to others (Ellis et al., 2011). In order to answer the research question (*RQ: How can my leadership journey in FSMLs contribute to larger conversations about women in leadership at FSMLs?*) and fill the dearth of research on women's experiences with leadership roles in field-based institutions, autoethnography was determined to be the optimal data collection method.

For this topic and my place within the research context, I concentrated on an evocative ethnography approach. Méndez (2013) describes the different approaches as the following: "Analytic autoethnography is directed towards objective writing and analysis of a particular group, whereas evocative autoethnography aims toward researchers' introspection on a particular topic to allow readers to make a connection with the researchers' feelings and experiences" (p. 281).

As a scientist myself, using past experiences and comparing them to the available literature is, at least for this topic, most appropriate. I identify as half-white, half middle-eastern cisgender women and have a total of 17 years of leadership experience in field sciences with a doctorate in chemical oceanography. I have been the executive director of a field station in a remote location off the coast of Massachusetts on the island of Nantucket for twelve years and held leadership roles at the Rocky Mountain Biological Laboratory in Gothic, Colorado, and for the University of California Davis' Natural Reserve System.

In order to engage in the autoethnographic process, I created seven question prompts to guide my reflection and chronicle my leadership journey:

1. What was my experience with leadership before working in FSMLs?
2. How did I get started in a career in FSMLs?
3. How did my personal life impact my experiences at FSMLs?

4. What factors impacted my success as a leader throughout my career?
5. What strategies have been successful in overcoming any potential barriers to leadership success?
6. What other factors have impacted my experiences and career within FSMLs?
7. Looking forward, what changes are needed to support future leaders and sustain FSMLs?

Following the creation of the discussion prompts, two neutral third-party facilitators with experience in autoethnography were invited to ask the questions as I reflected out loud and recorded answers using Zoom's built-in recording feature. Using this approach, I was able to spontaneously share my lived experience without having to stop and take notes, allowing me to engage in the free flow of ideas. The process of talking through my lived experiences was more conversational and honest than might have occurred from a more formal, written reflection. Moreover, inviting third-party facilitators resulted in spontaneous follow-up prompts that allowed me to dive deeper into my lived experiences. At the conclusion of the guided reflection, I used the transcription feature in Zoom to generate transcripts. The recording resulted in 58 minutes of audio and 46 pages of transcribed data. As a first step in data analysis, I read the transcript line by line and corrected any transcription errors and removed any information that was deemed too personal or identifiable. Next, I reread the transcripts and added additional reflections to fill in any gaps or missing details from the data. I also received additional notes from the third-party facilitators, which allowed me to further explore the data.

After scrubbing the transcript using this iterative process, I encountered two challenges which required me to engage in additional reflection prior to moving forward with data analysis. First, I struggled to extract information I felt was pertinent to other women working in FSMLs during the initial coding process; I felt like I was forcing themes to emerge vs. sharing my leadership story in a way that might resonate with other women working in FSMLs, undermining the tenants of evocative autoethnography (Méndez, 2013). To address this concern, I read the transcript several more times and decided a more meaningful way "to allow readers to make a connection" (Méndez, 2013, p. 281) was to answer each reflective prompt, that is, tell my story, vs. trying to identify overarching themes. In addition, I was somewhat astonished to find how deep my own biases were regarding male and female roles as leaders. I referenced the literature to further define and challenge my biases before moving forward with data analysis. Although I consider myself to be a feminist, I still had preconceived stereotypical ideas which Andrews (2018) described as an "institutional mindset." This was most clearly seen, for example, when trying to ascertain whether my "masculine traits'' might have made leadership roles simpler for me to achieve. Assuming leadership traits are masculine is part of the deep-seated gender bias experienced by women in roles of leadership (see Barling, 2014, pp. 209-212).

With a deeper understanding of my personal biases and an approach to sharing my story that felt more authentic and relatable, I moved forward by summarizing my reflections to substantively answer each reflective prompt. In the results and discussion section, I summarize my findings and provide space for readers to draw their own conclusions and connect with my "feelings and experiences" (Méndez, 2013, p. 281).

RESULTS AND DISCUSSION

The subsequent section interweaves my lived experiences with relevant literature to explore how my experiences with leadership may help other women move into and succeed when in positions of power at FSMLs. From these reflections, I seek to challenge the traditional gender norm value that women are not "born" to be leaders, explore the intersection of personal and professional lived experiences for building networks of support, and provide examples from my own life for building valuable leadership skills through confidence-building activities.

Q1: "What was my experience with leadership before working in FSMLs?"

Experiences in leadership accumulate throughout one's lifetime. I have always been, as far back as I can recall, a "natural" leader. Yukl's (2006) review of leadership literature says that a statement like "She/he was born a natural leader" indicates that leadership is innate. Additional traits of leaders may include extroversion, being comfortable in public speaking, bossiness, decisiveness, organizational or mediation skills. As with many other personality traits, the literature is awash in theories of both nature and nurture and whether these tendencies are inherent or acquired traits (Johnson et al., 1998). Regardless, women in leadership may be perceived as having fewer or less developed leadership traits, reaffirming gender stereotypes (Eagly et al., 2020).

As I reflect on the leadership traits defined in the literature (Yukl, 2006; Johnson et al., 1998), I've never had the problem of being under-respected. I've actually had the opposite problem, most of the time. In fact, even at a very young age I would often be given adult-like responsibilities. I call this the "curse of competency." Regardless of the situation, people would defer to me. From nursery school to high school and through early adulthood, I would often be thrust into responsibilities that were "above my pay grade." In high school, the teachers would sometimes have me take over and teach AP English/Shakespeare. I directed several plays in high school and also directed a community production in my last semester of high school. I would joke that it made more sense for me to direct than to act. I am not the greatest actor, but in reality, I usually would memorize the script and could read music. In addition, I did not mind telling the actors what to do, so it made sense for me to direct. Maybe no one else wanted the workload or responsibility, but I was comfortable in the leadership role. I became responsible at a very young age (nine) for the family after the death of my father, so by the age of 16, assuming leadership roles seemed pretty natural to me.

Another example of being thrust into leadership was a time when I was promoted to shift manager at the age of 16 at Wendy's, my first serious part-time job. Later on, at the hard chrome-plating company that I worked at in Tulsa, Oklahoma, during my 20s, I became Director of Purchasing, Safety, and the Lab in addition to working as a chrome plater. I would just see a problem and say, "we really need to have someone in charge of safety and they're like, well, it's your bright idea. So I guess you're in charge," and the same was true for purchasing. People give me power based on my willingness to identify a problem and generate potential solutions. Because I am not the kind of person who learned early on to say "no," I accept power and responsibility. It can be frustrating at times to feel like the only person who wants to step forward and do things, but later on in life, these experiences made it easier for me to transition into larger leadership roles.

An excellent example of this occurred on the first research cruise I participated in as an undergraduate student. During both my undergraduate and graduate degree careers, I would participate in oceanographic research cruises sailing out of Texas A&M Galveston facilities. On one such cruise on the research vessel (RV) Gyre, we left the dock and headed out into the Gulf of Mexico for a weeklong oceanographic survey. In oceanography, you "drive around" in straight lines (feels kind of like plowing the ocean) measuring the water chemistry and physical traits at various depths and collecting water, sediment, and organic matter, including sea creatures. In this case, the seas were pretty high and almost everyone on board was either in the bunks asleep or nauseous. Benadryl and other drugs used for seasickness, such as scopolamine patches, cause substantial drowsiness in most people. Although not immune, I typically do not suffer serious drowsiness. A combination of wakefulness and a strong constitution meant I was the only person awake to run the surveys and monitor the seafloor using a sub-bottom profiler and multibeam echosounder. Basically, it was the equivalent of a high-stress video game; I had to stay awake, watch the screen and maneuver the line holding the profiler up and down to keep from dragging the equipment through the mud on the seafloor. I was not the least bit prepared or qualified, but as usual,

I looked more competent than I am, so for the night I was in charge of the ship's science. Fortunately, I was able to rise to the occasion and perform the functions needed without additional guidance.

I was given power even while traveling and working in cultures where women were not considered for leadership roles. I traveled throughout mainland China in 1994 with my advisor, Peter Santschi, PhD, to give talks and provide training in trace metal chemistry and radiochemistry protocols. I was a 30-year-old brand-new graduate student and looked to be about 20. I learned about 100–150 words of Mandarin. On at least one occasion, I was given the check for our table of 15 dignitaries, all but two of which were men and all but one older than me. In all my lectures, I was accorded respect in a society which typically did not value young women. This respect accorded to me was in no small part also a result of the confidence my advisor placed in me to bring me and my spouse on this trip. As is described in chapter 8 (Oktay & Kloeppel, 2022) of this book, the mentorship that occurs early on in one's career can significantly support later success. Lastly, my spouse also accorded me full respect and an active listening stance that likely bolstered my confidence and modeled appropriate behavior on the part of other males.

I joke about this now, but I can be in New York City on the street for a few minutes and people will come up to me and ask for directions. The same phenomenon occurs in grocery stores. Everyone assumes that I know the answer to their question and apparently I have a welcoming persona that makes strangers feel comfortable asking questions. If Godzilla was attacking Tokyo and I was in the control room, everyone in the room would turn to me and expect me to find an immediate solution. I guarantee it. There's something about me, where people want to give me stuff to do and want to give me leadership roles. They voluntarily give me power, and I am willing to take responsibility in almost any situation. That can be a scary thing, because if you fail and you are in charge, people can lose their research, their livelihood, even their life in some circumstances.

There is evidence that people perceive inherent leadership traits to be defined by communication style, decisiveness, and organizational skills (Yukl, 2006; Johnson et al., 1998), challenging gender stereotypes (Eagly et al., 2020). In my case, this predisposition by others may have resulted in more leadership development opportunities within the context of patriarchal cultures.

Q2: How did I get started in a career in FSMLs?

I completed my undergraduate and graduate degrees at Texas A&M University at Galveston which is a marine orientated university. I led school and public field trips exploring the marshes and the ocean as a part-time job in Sea Camp and led tours for visitors through a sea turtle hatchery and recovery program. It was a very hands-on degree with full-scale lab work available so that I could publish in the peer review literature as an undergraduate student. As part of my undergraduate and graduate degrees, I was able to visit marine labs around the country including the Louisiana Consortium of Marine labs (LUMCON) in Houma, LA, the University of Texas' Marine Science Institutes at Port Aransas and Corpus Christi and several others.

My first significant leadership position as the Managing Director of the University of Massachusetts Boston (UMB) Nantucket Field Station came about when I was "voluntold" to serve on a committee reviewing the status and operations of the field station. At the time I was only three years out of a doctorate program and acting as the assistant to the Chair of the Environmental Coastal and Ocean Science program at UMB. Because my boss at the time did not like to go to committee meetings, he sent me to take notes for a committee doing strategic planning for the UMB Nantucket Field Station. Over the next six months, I attended every meeting, learning a lot about the position and meeting others in the university who interacted with the director.

I have often volunteered or simply done extra work throughout my life for no pay because it served me at certain points in my career. It is critical to note that I recognize this may be problematic and underscore larger issues with the expectation of "free" labor. Women and other marginalized populations are often asked to serve without any additional access to resources or compensation. Oluo (2018), a black female scholar, expresses the frustration and emotional burden placed on marginalized and disenfranchised communities, in particular, when they are constantly asked to serve on diversity committees (tokenism) or to train white peers on the issues impacting students of color. This is a significant issue that highlights larger concerns with diversity and equity in our society. For me, I deemed it beneficial at certain points in my career to trade my time for professional development, allowing me to contribute in meaningful ways to my organization while further developing my leadership skills and expanding my network.

In the case of working at UMB, I started writing articles for the campus newspaper, the *University Reporter,* to hone my writing skills and to develop relationships with people throughout the university. Every other month, I would interview a new hire or a faculty member releasing a new book for a "color" piece on diversity of programs or people. This allowed me to make friends in departments as varied as the English or History departments or at the campus radio station, WUMB, and prevented me from becoming trapped in a silo which can often happen in a university setting. When the time came to ask the current director to take early retirement, I had built up enough relationships to succeed in getting the position even in a very strong field of several dozen candidates, many of whom I met during the course of the next twelve years of my career.

Volunteering in diverse contexts played a critical role in my professional, social, and educational development throughout my career, generating transferable leadership skills and boosting my curriculum vitae. A body of literature underscores the importance of volunteering in higher education, especially for students, as these experiences allow for line items on resumes, network building, and skill development (MacNeela & Gannon, 2014; Bowman & Waite, 2003).

Q3: How did my personal life impact my experiences at FSMLs?

One of the reasons why I have always felt I could do anything in life is because my mother never gave me the impression I couldn't. She was completely supportive of anything I suggested, no matter how outlandish or unlikely. She clearly demonstrated throughout her life that education was important and critical for well-being, obtaining multiple degrees and certificates from nursing to psychology, English, computer languages, divinity, and sign language. My father also was content to do the lion's share of housekeeping although he was the primary breadwinner and a chemical engineer at Phillips Petroleum Company. My father immigrated from Turkey in 1950 and quickly got both his master's and doctoral degrees. As a Muslim Turk who married a Baptist girl in Oklahoma in the 1950s, both were obviously willing to seek out non-traditional relationship and roles.

It was not until she had passed when my very unreliable stepfather told me she regretted having children and said it kept her from doing what she wanted for a career. I dismissed that at the time as she had gotten multiple degrees and worked outside of the home since I was nine and my youngest brother was two, out of necessity of course, having lost our father. Twenty years later, while reading through her diary, I read entries that seemed to support his allegations. That was primarily a result of the time and place (1950s and 1960s Oklahoma) and was likely augmented by society's norms. This same restriction was placed on my great aunt, who was forced to get a home economics degree instead of the geology degree she desired to obtain. She co-discovered a trilobite with and spent years grading student geology papers for her husband. In high school, my high-school counselor took a look at my class roster, my grades, test scores, and aptitude tests and told me "you can do anything you want to do." At the time I was annoyed because I was seeking guidance on choosing a college or career, not a blanket "the world is your oyster, have at it" statement. In retrospect, it was a step toward building my confidence.

The literature backs up the importance of socialization processes in building confidence (Shapiro et al., 2015). Socialization early in life, with role models who are willing to challenge gender roles, has been shown to increase the likelihood that a woman will go on to a career in science and engineering (Dennehy & Dasgupta, 2017; Thomas et al., 2015). By modeling that energy and sharing a "you can do anything" perspective, my mother provided the framework for me to succeed.

Because, even early on in life, I did not feel constrained to follow a gendered "normal" path, I was able to take risks, some of which panned out (going back to school to get my doctorate), and some of which did not (a couple of marriages). A high tolerance for risk-taking behavior is a key component for leadership (Ertak & Gurdal, 2010; Jung et al., 2020). Another key component for leadership is overcoming a fear of failure and becoming willing to make mistakes, a tendency of "fear tolerant leaders" (Farson & Keyes, 2002). This often goes hand-in-hand with a risk-taking attitude. The tolerance of taking a risk and trying a new approach, even in the face of failure, can be developed over time by starting small and taking on larger risks subsequently.

Being thrust into a role as a head of household and caretaker for my brothers and mother at a young age (nine) I am sure had some bearing on my experiences at field stations. FSMLs are typically "jack and jill of all trades" type environments in which very limited staff have to perform all the tasks. There are rarely significant support systems, such as those present on the main campus, so every field station director has to be creative and "make do."

At certain points in my career, my professional and personal life intersected, creating some tension. For example, my husband worked for me at UMB-NFS as a maintenance worker, custodian, and education coordinator. A few times, repair people or faculty members would pull up when they arrived at the field station and address him first, assuming he was the director, not me. This reaffirms gender stereotypes and social norms that men are in charge and hold positions of power. When we went through the process of repairing the septic system and upgrading the facilities, it occurred a little more frequently. Interestingly, college students, high-school interns, and K-12 classes never had issues recognizing me as "the boss."

From a communication studies perspective, these are considered gendered microaggressions, "nuanced and brief everyday exchanges that communicate sexist denigration and slights toward women and are conveyed verbally and/or nonverbally through facial expression, gaze, and other gestures" (Yang & Carroll, 2018, p. 30). Over time, gendered microaggressions have the potential to result in burnout and may negatively impact organizational culture, including leadership opportunities for women (Yang & Carroll, 2018). Complicating the issue of gendered microaggressions is how to redress the behavior. Women who directly challenge a microaggression with "no, I am the boss" may face additional gender stereotyping, such as confusing directness with "bitchiness." An emerging area of research relates to defining bystander responsibilities within the context of challenging microaggressions

(Haynes-Baratz et al., 2021). Challenging these microaggressions has been a mainstay throughout my career as I worked to support other women, personally and professionally. Many women, even Supreme Court justices (Jacobi & Schweers, 2017), have experienced the frustration of speaking up in a large room of people to suggest a new idea or approach. Ten minutes later, if a man repeats the same exact idea, it is an excellent idea and everyone is willing to try it. I have seen that myself in meetings where incredibly intelligent women have presented ideas that were not picked up and engaged with until repeated later by a man. Fortunately, that has only happened to me once and in most instances, people will repeat what I have said later and attribute it to me. "Mansplaining" of course is a term used recently to describe quite well what it feels like to have basic facts explained to a woman by a man, often about their own lives or jobs.

Q4: What factors impacted my success as a leader throughout my career?

In addition to school and work life, I have been a leader in many volunteer and nonprofit organizations. I have been the president of the Nantucket Civic League, the Society of Women Geographers (an organization of extremely driven scientists, mountaineers, astronauts, and explorers), and the OBFS. Why do people give me power, in the classroom, a worksite, committee meetings, at a civic association, or in the school play? As previously noted, inherent leadership traits, such as my communication style, decisiveness, and organizational skills (Yukl, 2006; Johnson et al., 1998), may play a role, allowing me to challenge gender stereotypes (Eagly et al., 2020). However, additional factors may play a role.

I have a deep voice. Researchers have shown that both men and women prefer lower voices in their leaders and that women especially prefer lower (deeper, more baritone) voices for both male and female leaders while men mainly respond to lower voices for women leaders (Anderson & Klofstad, 2017; Tigue et al., 2012). Theories for this preference revolve around the fact that lower voices imply strength for men while they imply greater age (and more experience) for women, as women's voices tend to deepen as they get older (Anderson & Klofstad, 2017).

Moreover, I am very calm most of the time. I have been told I am imposing which is frankly, hilarious. I am super responsive and fairly organized. Most of all, I am willing to do the job, which often becomes the prime criteria. I also try to listen to everyone's opinions in a group and create an atmosphere of inclusion. As noted earlier, transformational leaders often seek to create a positive shared vision and motivate others to achieve the vision together (PSU, 2014). Furthermore, through transformational leadership, leaders may inspire a deeper level of trust and connectivity with their workforce (Bilal et al., 2021). This is the perspective with which I approach my role as a leader. When I was the managing director and eventually executive director at the UMass Boston Nantucket Field Station, I attracted a high percentage of women and LGBTQ students as interns. I asked one such person who was a year-round islander why that was the case and they told me they knew they would feel welcomed and valuable. There is extensive literature regarding the difference between men and women, their communication (and listening) styles and how that relates to the workplace and leadership (Merchant, 2012). Overall, however, creating a sense of inclusion and active listening is invaluable for gaining the respect of colleagues. Since transformational leadership is all about the imagination—imagining dreams without limits and imagining you are in another person's shoes—it can provide the opportunity to create an inclusive climate wherever you go. People do not forget those who show them kindness, respect, and validation.

Q5: What strategies have been successful in overcoming any potential barriers to leadership success?

Many of the barriers that women face are based on the social construct of womanhood (Else-Quest & Hyde, 2021). Paving your own way is a big part of leadership, but do we teach girls to do that? Is there something that happens in people's lives that makes some people better at paving their own path than others? Are there mindsets that can be avoided or reframed that enable success or at least do not present new barriers? In my reflection, two major strategies for overcoming barriers arose: (i) understanding duty and conquering the fear of failure and (ii) acquiring skills and trying things that build confidence.

1. *Understanding duty and conquering the fear of failure/learning to walk away*: It is very easy to become trapped in a situation you don't like out of a misplaced feeling of obligation or duty. This may be even more prevalent with internal bias that is applied to typical female upbringing in which women are taught to put up with things or to "not cause trouble." Some researchers have found that women have a stronger sense of duty when it comes to caregiving (Boeije & Doorne-Huiskes, 2010) and that they tend to subsume themselves in the care of ill spouses. Men in the same situations were better at drawing boundaries and implementing self-care. Although I spent a large part of my early life taking care of others and have been married most of my adult life, I eventually learned the difference between doing something because you want to versus "duty for the sake of duty." For example, I took a job in phone sales prior to earning my graduate degrees. I made it 48 hours; my sense of duty forced me to stay that long. I am a terrible telephone solicitor with way too much

empathy for the person on the other end of the phone, and I learned to overpower my sense of obligation and walk away from that bad situation. Similarly, I ended my first marriage the day I realized the marriage was irreparable with basically just the clothes on my back. It was from these experiences I was able to build confidence in myself and delineate between a sense of duty and drawing necessary boundaries. Later in life when doing jobs that I could see were "going south," I would give two weeks' notice and MOVE ON.

2. *Acquiring skills and trying things that build confidence*: In addition to building confidence in my ability to set boundaries, working to acquire skills and build confidence through experiences has been helpful to overcome any potential barriers in my personal or professional life. Below I provide three examples of experiences that helped me build confidence.
   a. Skydiving: You jump out of a plane, you live, everything else afterward seems pretty easy. Actually my brothers and I did an accelerated free fall 12-hour skydiving class together and then jumped the next day (not in tandem but solo with instructors jumping at the same time and close enough to save you if needed). Once your shoot opens and you see how easy it is to control your descent, you really feel empowered.
   b. First aid/CPR training: When I was a teenager, I taught CPR/First-aid classes with my mom; it was very empowering to me to train people in life-saving skills. Even today, I feel that safety training is not only critical but empowering. At the hard chrome-plating shop, I introduced an entire safety program and helped save limbs and eyesight for people with very serious injuries.
   c. Public speaking: What better way to tell compelling stories about first-aid classes and skydiving? Seriously, Tulsa Junior College where I got my associate's degree in science required public speaking (and logic) for all students. I participated in debate in high school, and public speaking really helped me become a confident speaker, which has served me well, especially in large groups and board room settings.

In general, these three examples helped me build confidence in myself as they pushed me to step outside of my comfort zone. I constantly seek out other opportunities to build my confidence.

Q6: What other factors have impacted my experiences and career within FSMLs?

I have always been able to remind myself that I am doing the best that I can. That has been a pillar of myself worth. Even though I remind myself of that, it has also been my experience that FSMLs are not overly judgmental places and that comradery and collaboration are more common in a remote field setting (Janovy & Major, 2009). These, in tandem, have helped to build my self-confidence and efficacy as a member and leader in the FSML community.

FSMLs, as mentioned above, also require staff and researchers to do without the backbone of support, which is present on a university campus, from plumbing repairs to purchasing and sourcing. People who do well in a FSML setting tend to be McGuyver types who are willing to try and fix what needs to be fixed themselves. This allows one to develop confidence, try out a series of roles, and operate in a way that is not typically micromanaged.

However, while FSMLs may provide an opportunity to build self-efficacy and confidence, we certainly have to address the constant elephant in the room which is the prevalence of sexual assault on women in the workplace (Clancy et al., 2014). From the reflection, I said: "I am concerned for women that are trying to be leaders or just make their way in the world. If you're always worried that someone's trying to assault you. I mean, how do you manage? How do you make your way in the world?" Establishing a safe and secure workplace is critical for allowing female leaders to develop and come up through the ranks. I was relatively fortunate and personally only experienced a few minor incidences of sexual harassment in the field, primarily on research trips in remote areas. In my career at FSMLs, I was in a leadership position which one could assume to be less vulnerable to the power imbalances that can lead to sexual harassment (Philipps, et al., 2019). In contrast, McLaughlin, et al., (2012) found that women in positions of leadership can be more frequently exposed to the threat of harassment, possibly as an "equalizer" effect or even due to "masculine overcompensation" (p. 627).

Q7: Looking forward, what changes are needed to support future leaders and sustain FSMLs?

At the end of the interview process, both of the interviewers said they felt empowered just listening to me and hearing my story. I don't think that is an unusual response. We can lean on each other and listen to each other and let ourselves be role models. The AAUW (2016) identified role modeling as a concrete method for overcoming stereotyping and bias in the workplace. By bringing up your colleagues with you, in my experience, you are building a network that will increase your own opportunities for advancement. In addition to bringing up my colleagues, I want to provide readers with three overarching recommendations for empowering women into leadership roles.

1) Freeing oneself up for failure and being willing to take risks allows one to assume a role of leadership at times that may feel out of sync or even premature.

a) Be persistent in looking for roles and opportunities. Be willing to sell the idea of creating a position in an organization if one does not exist. Returning to Eagly and Carli's (2007) description of the barriers for women leaders being a labyrinth: "Passage through a labyrinth requires persistence, awareness of one's progress, and a careful analysis of the puzzles that lie ahead (abstract)."
b) Fish or cut bait. If you feel you are failing or not challenged, be prepared to try something new.
c) Transitions without fear: Easy to say and harder to do. Realize that everyone fails; every leader has a story of failure from Greta Thunberg to Malala Yousafzai. Work on getting past a fear of failure and be prepared to walk away if you are not achieving what you need to achieve.

2) Simply taking that role or placing oneself in the position, although it can cause trepidation, rarely ends in death or the loss of a job, so it is important to remove the fear of failure and "not being good enough" through visioning, role-playing, cross supportive mentoring, a buddy system of encouragement, or other active practice.
   a) Identify colleagues who are supportive and can act as mentors for times when you need solid advice on a leadership task. In other words, find a reliable sounding board. Buzzanell et al. (2015) found that *authentic* (i.e., less formal, with personally chosen mentors) mentoring experiences were key for supporting women engineering faculty of color in the academy. Similarly, Montgomery (2017) advocates that more proactive, individual-centered mentoring provides the best model of support for mentoring relationships.
   b) Be prepared to take "stretch assignments," that is, a role or responsibility that seems to be a bit too much at the time.
3) Seeing oneself as no different from others, regardless of age, rank, gender, or experience, allows oneself to assume leadership roles without shouldering the constraints or stereotypes carried by others.

a) From an interview with Dr. Julian Barling in Minerva, "Leadership is all about the imagination—it's about imagining you are the other. So before doing anything else, put yourself in the other's shoes. Ask yourself—how would I respond if I were them?" Furthermore, Iris Bahar, professor in computer science and engineering at Brown University, when asked about how she was able to overcome imposter syndrome said, "I think having a sense of community is extremely important," she said. "Find your cohort and find your support group, and that can be really, really helpful in . . . making sure you're in a good place" (Walker, 2021, para. 10). Bahar also had a role model; her father was a scientist, similar to my background in which my father was a chemical engineer. Having early role models makes envisioning oneself in a science or engineering field more likely (Dennehy & Dasgupta, 2017). But Bahar also overcame imposter syndrome, and she actively creates and seeks out communities of like-minded women scientists in order to provide the cohort support that can build confidence.

LIMITATIONS AND FUTURE RESEARCH

Distilling the very human experience of holding a leadership position as a woman in the field sciences from one person's perspective is by definition limiting. Wall (2008) clearly described a variety of pitfalls that accompany the act of autoethnography, from the difficulty of establishing objectivity, to representing oneself clearly, to the validity of drawing conclusions from what is in actuality, a single source. Méndez (2013) evaluated the pros and cons of autoethnography including possible ethical issues that can arise and the difficulty many researchers have in providing an authentically honest evaluation of their experiences. Ultimately, Méndez (2013) falls on the side of autoethnography being a useful tool:

> Thus, the richness of autoethnography is in those realities that emerge from the interaction between the self and its own experiences that reflect the cultural and social context in which those events took place. It is through this representation that understanding of a particular phenomenon is accomplished. (p. 284)

CONCLUSION

How do we get more women into leadership positions at FSMLs? What types of barriers exist and are they physical, monetary, or mental barriers? As part of our mission we can adopt and/or share advice and resources provided by groups like the OBFS, the National Association of Marine Labs, and the American Associations of University Women, among others. *GenderInsite* (2018) identified three sets of actors that contributed to positive changes regarding gender diversity in leadership roles: (1) "individual researchers who . . . refused to accept society's restraints on women's roles"; (2) "independent advisory boards tasked with addressing gender equality and equity"; and (3) "to take advantage of opportunities presented within processes of policy formulation" (p. 93).

Overall, gaining power by sharing power and sharing our experiences in order to empower each other emerged during the interview process as a meaningful and impactful tool. Providing access to role models and being willing to act as role models and mentors for the next generations will increase the number of women in leadership positions. We as a community need to continue to work to empower the next generation of women leaders in order to create long-term change and retention for women leaders in the FSML community. We also must be willing to share the stories of our failures and our successes.

REFERENCES

Anderson, L. (2006). Analytic autoethnography. *Journal of Contemporary Ethnography, 35*(4), 373–395. https://doi.org/10.1177/0891241605280449

Anderson, R. C., & Klofstad, C. A. (2012) Preference for leaders with masculine voices holds in the case of feminine leadership roles. *PLoS One, 7*(12), e51216. https://doi.org/10.1371/journal.pone.0051216

Andrews, S. (2013). *Emotional intelligence implications on the career advancement of women in a Fortune 500 pharmaceutical company* [Master's thesis, Pepperdine University]. Pepperdine Digital Commons. https://digitalcommons.pepperdine.edu/etd/394

Andrews, S. (2018). *The power of perception: Leadership, emotional intelligence, and the gender divide.* Morgan James Publishing.

American Association of University Women (AAUW). (2016). *Barrier and bias: The status of women in leadership.* https://www.aauw.org/resources/research/barrier-bias/

Association of Women in Science [AWIS]. (2019). *AWIS member leadership survey, 2018-2019.* https://www.awis.org/awis-member-leadership-survey-2018-2019/

Barling, J. (2014). *The science of leadership: Lessons from research on organizational leaders.* Oxford University Press.

Barsh, J., & Yee, L. (2012). *Unlocking the full potential of women at work.* McKinsey & Company.

Bilal, A., Ahmad, W., Muhammad, J., Huseynov, R., & Nagy, H. (2021). How women's transformational leadership induces employees' innovative behaviour through trust and connectivity: A sequential mediation model. *Global Business Review,* 1–16. https://doi.org/10.1177/0972150920982760

Bettinger, E., & Long, B. (2005). Do faculty serve as role models? The impact of instructor gender on female students. *The American Economic Review, 95*(2), 152–157. http://www.jstor.org/stable/4132808

Bochner, A. P., & Ellis, C. (2016). *Evocative autoethnography: Writing lives and telling stories.* Left Coast Press.

Boeije, H., & Doorne-Huiskes, A. (2010). Fulfilling a sense of duty: How men and women giving care to spouses with multiple sclerosis interpret this role. *Community, Work & Family, 6*(3), 223–244. https://doi.org/10.1080/1366880032000143438

Bowman, L. L., & Waite, B. M. (2003). Volunteering in research: Student satisfaction and educational benefits. *Teaching of Psychology, 30*(2), 102–106. https://doi.org/10.1207/S15328023TOP3002_03

Buzzanell, P. M., Long, Z., Anderson, L. B., Kokini, K., & Batra, J. C. (2015). Mentoring in academe: A feminist poststructural lens on stories of women engineering faculty of color. *Management Communication Quarterly, 29*(3), 440–457. https://doi.org/10.1177/0893318915574311

Byko, M. (2005). Challenges and opportunities for women in science and engineering. *The Member Journal of The Minerals, Metals & Materials Society*. https://www.tms.org/pubs/journals/JOM/0504/Byko/Byko-0504.html

Casad, B. J., Franks, J. E., Garasky, C. E., Kittleman, M. M., Roesler, A. C., Hall, D. Y., & Petzel, Z. W. (2021). Gender inequality in academia: Problems and solutions for women faculty in STEM. *Journal of Neuroscience Research, 99*, 13–23. https://doi.org/10.1002/jnr.24631

Center for Advancing Health. (2002). Levels of testosterone during pregnancy appear to influence the gender-role behavior of preschool girls, according to a new study. *EurekAlert*. https://www.eurekalert.org/pub_releases/2002-11/cfta-sst111102.php

Clancy, K. B., Nelson, R. G., Rutherford, J. N., & Hinde, K. (2014). Survey of academic field experiences (SAFE): Trainees report harassment and assault. *PLoS One*, *9*(7), e102172. https://doi.org/10.1371/journal.pone.0102172

Daft, R. L. (2005). *The leadership experience* (3rd ed.). Cengage Learning.

Dasgupta, N., & Asgari, S. (2004). Seeing is believing: Exposure to counterstereotypic women leaders and its effect on the malleability of automatic gender stereotyping. *Journal of Experimental Social Psychology, 40*(5), 642–658. https://doi.org/10.1016/j.jesp.2004.02.003

Demery, A. J. C., & Pipkin, M. A. (2021) Safe fieldwork strategies for at-risk individuals, their supervisors and institutions. *Nature Ecology & Evolution 5*, 5–9. https://doi.org/10.1038/s41559-020-01328-5

Dennehy, T. C., & Dasgupta, N. (2017). Female peer mentors early in college increase women's positive academic experiences and retention in engineering. *Proceedings of the National Academy of Sciences of the United States of America, 114*(23), 5964–5969. https://doi.org/10.1073/pnas.1613117114

Drummond, A., Ellis, C., Hook, M., Murray, M. & Seymour, A. (2002). *NVAA: Leadership in victim services*. https://www.ojp.gov/ncjrs/virtual-library/abstracts/leadership-victim-services

Eagly, A. H., & Karau, S. J. (2002). Role congruity theory of prejudice toward female leaders. *Psychological Review, 109*(3), 573–598. https://doi.org/10.1037/0033-295x.109.3.573

Eagly, A. H., Nater, C., Miller, D. I., Kaufmann, M., & Sczesny, S. (2020). Gender stereotypes have changed: A cross-temporal meta-analysis of U.S. public opinion polls from 1946 to 2018. *American Psychologist, 75*(3), 301–315. https://doi.org/10.1037/amp0000494

Eagly, A., & Carli, L. (2007). Women and the labyrinth of leadership. *Harvard Business Review*. https://hbr.org/2007/09/women-and-the-labyrinth-of-leadership

Eagly, A., Johannesen-Schmidt, M., & van Engen, M. (2003). Transformational, transactional, and laissez-faire leadership styles: A meta-analysis comparing women and men. *Psychological Bulletin, 129*, 569–591.

Else-Quest, N. M., & Hyde, J. S. (2021). *Psychology of women and gender* (10th Ed.). Sage.

Else, H. (2019, March 20). Female scientists get less money and staff for their first labs. *Nature*. https://www.nature.com/articles/d41586-019-00933-0

Ertac, S., & Gurdal, M. Y. (2010). *Deciding to decide: Gender, leadership and risk-taking in groups* (Working Paper, No. 1028). TÜSİAD-Koç University Economic Research Forum, Istanbul.

Farson, R., & Keys, R. (2002). The fear-tolerant leader. *Harvard Business Review*. https://hbr.org/2002/08/the-failure-tolerant-leader

Fathima, F. N., Awor, P., Yen, Y. C., Gnanaselvam, N. A., & Zakham, F. (2020). Challenges and coping strategies faced by female scientists—A multicentric cross sectional study. *PLoS One, 15*(9), e0238635. https://doi.org/10.1371/journal.pone.0238635

Fitzgerald, L. F., & Ormerod, A. J. (1993). Breaking silence: The sexual harassment of women in academia and the workplace. In F. L. Denmark & M. A. Paludi (Eds.), *Psychology of women: A handbook of issues and theories* (pp. 553–581). Greenwood Press/Greenwood Publishing Group.

Folta, S. C., Seguin, R. A., Ackerman, J., & Nelson, M. E. (2012). A qualitative study of leadership characteristics among women who catalyze positive community change. *BMC Public Health, 12*, 383. https://doi.org/10.1186/1471-2458-12-383

GenderInSITE. (2018). *Pathways to success: Bringing a gender lens to the scientific leadership of global challenges*. http://hdl.handle.net/20.500.11911/113

Hartley, J. M., & Tansey, E. M. (2015). White coats and no trousers: Narrating the experiences of women technicians in medical laboratories, 1930-90. *Notes and Records of the Royal Society of London, 69*(1), 25–36. https://doi.org/10.1098/rsnr.2014.0058

Haynes-Baratz, M. C., Bond, M. A., Allen, C. T., Li, Y. L., & Metinyurt, T. (2021). Challenging gendered microaggressions in the academy: A social–ecological analysis of bystander action among faculty. *Journal of Diversity in Higher Education*. https://doi.org/10.1037/dhe0000315

Hilgenkamp, K. D., & Livingston, M. M. (2002). Tomboys, masculine characteristics, and self-ratings of confidence in career success. *Psychological reports, 90*, 743–749. https://doi.org/10.2466/pr0.2002.90.3.743

Hines, M., Golombok, S., Rust, J., Johnston, K. J., Golding, J., & Parents and Children Study Team. (2002). Testosterone during pregnancy and gender role behavior of preschool children: A longitudinal, population Study. *Child Development, 73*(6), 1678–1687. https://doi.org/10.1111/1467-8624.00498

Hyde, J. S. (2014). Gender similarities and differences. *Annual Review of Psychology, 65*, 373–398. https://doi.org/10.1146/annurev-psych-010213-115057

Hunt, V., Layton, D., & Prince, S. (2015). *Diversity Matters*. McKinsey and Company.

Hunt, V., Prince, S., Dixon-Fyle, S., & Yee, L. (2018). *Delivering through diversity.* McKinsey and Company.

Jacobi, T., & Schweers, D. (2017). Justice, interrupted: The effect of gender, ideology, and seniority at Supreme Court oral arguments. *Virginia Law Review, 103*(7), 1379–1485. http://www.jstor.org/stable/26401668

Jago, A. G. (1982). Leadership: Perspectives in theory and research. *Management Science, 28*(3), 315–336. https://doi.org/10.1287/mnsc.28.3.315

Janovy, Jr., J., & Major, K. M. (2009). Why we have field stations: Reflections on the cultivation of biologists. *BioScience*, *59*(3), 217–222. https://doi.org/10.1525/bio.2009.59.3.6

Johnson, A., Vernon, P., McCarthy, J., Molson, M., Harris, J., & Jang, K. (1998). Nature vs nurture: Are leaders born or made? A behavior genetic investigation of leadership style. *Twin Research, 1*(4), 216–223. https://doi.org/10.1375/twin.1.4.216

Jung, K., Kang, S., & Choi, S. (2020). Empowering leadership, risk-taking behavior, and employees' commitment to organizational change: The mediated moderating role of task complexity. *Sustainability, 12*(6), 2340. https://doi.org/10.3390/su12062340

Lindolf, T. R., & Taylor, B. C. (2017). *Qualitative communication research.* Sage.

MacNeela, P., & Gannon, N. (2014). Process and positive development: An interpretative phenomenological analysis of university student volunteering. *Journal of Adolescent Research*, *29*(3), 407–436. https://doi.org/10.1177/0743558413510968

Mansfield, B., Lave, R., McSweeney, K., Bonds, A., Cockburn, J., Domosh, M., Hamilton, T., Hawkins, R., Hessl, A., Munroe, D., Ojeda, D., & Radel, C. (2019). It's time to recognize how men's careers benefit from sexually harassing women in academia. *Human Geography*, *12*(1), 82–87. https://doi.org/10.1177/194277861901200110

Martinez, A., & Christnacht, C. (2021*). Women are nearly half of U.S. workforce but only 27% of STEM workers.* https://www.census.gov/library/stories/2021/01/women-making-gains-in-stem-occupations-but-still-underrepresented.html

McCollough, L. (2011). Women's leadership in science, technology, engineering & mathematics: Barriers to participation. *Forum on Public Policy, 2*, 1–11. https://eric.ed.gov/?id=EJ944199

Méndez, M. (2013). Autoethnography as a research method: Advantages, limitations and criticisms. *Colombian Applied Linguistics Journal, 15*(2), 279–287. http://www.scielo.org.co/scielo.php?script=sci_arttext&pid=S0123-46412013000200010&lng=en&tlng=en.

Merchant, K. (2012). How men and women differ: Gender differences in communication styles, influence tactics, and leadership styles (Publication No. 513) [CMC Senior Theses, Claremont McKenna]. Scholarship@Claremont. http://scholarship.claremont.edu/cmc_theses/513

Montgomery, B. L. (2017). Mapping a mentoring roadmap and developing a supportive network for strategic career advancement. *SAGE Open, 7*(2), 1–13. https://doi.org/10.1177/2158244017710288

Northouse, P. G. (2010). *Leadership: Theory and practice* (5th ed.). Sage

National Science Foundation: National Center for Science and Engineering Statistics. (2018). Survey of doctorate recipients survey year 2017. U.S. residing employed doctoral scientists and engineers in 4-year educational institutions, by field of doctorate, sex, and tenure status: 2017. https://ncsesdata.nsf.gov/doctoratework/2017/html/sdr2017_dst_20.html

Oktay, S. D., & Kloeppel, B. D. (2022). The gift relationship: How mentoring leads to success for women in field station leadership. In V. McDermott, J. Gee, & A. R. May (Eds.), *Women of the wild: Challenging gender disparities in field stations and marine laboratories* (pp. 169–197). Lexington Books.

Oluo, I. (2018). *So you want to talk about race.* Seal Press.

Pennsylvania State University World Campus. (2014). *PSYCH 485 Lesson 10: Transformational leadership.* https://courses.worldcampus.psu.edu/fa14/psych485/001/content/10_lesson/07_page.html

Phillips, S. P., Webber, J., Imbeau, S., Quaife, T., Hagan, D., Maar, M., & Abourbih, J. (2019). Sexual Harassment of Canadian Medical Students: A National Survey. *EClinicalMedicine, 7,* 15–20. https://doi.org/10.1016/j.eclinm.2019.01.008.

Rogers, E. B., & Rose, J. (2019). A critical exploration of women's gendered experiences in outdoor leadership. *Journal of Experiential Education, 42*(1), 37–50. https://doi.org/10.1177/1053825918820710

Rowe, W. G. (2007) *Cases in leadership.* Sage Publications, Inc.

Silva, D & Mendis, Kanchana. (2017). Male vs female leaders: Analysis of transformational, transactional & laissez-faire women leadership styles. *European Journal of Business and Management, 9*(9), 19–26.

Shapiro, M., Grossman, D., Carter, S., Martin, K., Deyton, P., & Hammer, D. (2015) Middle school girls and the "leaky pipeline" to leadership. *Middle School Journal, 46*(5), 3–13. https://doi.org/10.1080/00940771.2015.11461919

Simon, S., & Hoyt, C. (2013). Exploring the effect of media images on women's leadership self-perceptions and aspirations. *Group Processes & Intergroup Relations, 16,* 232–245. https://doi.org/10.1177/1368430212451176.

Taylor, Y. J., Scott, V. C., & Danielle Connor, C. (2020). Perceptions, experiences, and outcomes of lactation support in the workplace: A systematic literature review. *Journal of Human Lactation, 36*(4), 657–672. https://doi.org/10.1177/0890334420930696

Tigue, C. C., Borak, D. J., O'Connor, J. J. M., Schandl, C., & Feinberg, D. R. (2012). Voice pitch influences voting behaviour. *Evolution Human Behavior, 33,* 210–216. https://10.1016/j.evolhumbehav.2011.09.004.

Thomas, N., Bystydzienski, J., & Desai, A. (2015). Changing institutional culture through peer mentoring of women STEM faculty. *Innovative Higher Education, 40,* 143–157. https://doi.org/10.1007/s10755-014-9300-9

University of Minnesota. (2013). *Communication in the real World: An introduction to communication studies.* https://open.lib.umn.edu/communication/chapter/14-1-leadership-and-small-group-communication/

Walker, J. (2021). *Female Professors in STEM Reflect on their experience in the fields: Women in STEM on navigating male-dominated fields in academia.* https://

www.browndailyherald.com/2021/03/22/female-professors-in-stem-reflect-on-experiences-in-their-fields/

Wall, S. (2008). Easier said than done: Writing an autoethnography. *International Journal of Qualitative Methods, 7,* 38–53. https://doi.org/10.1177/160940690800700103

Woudstra, I. (2021). Role models are key in gender diversity – especially in tech & engineering. *Women in Tech.* https://shecancode.io/blog/role-models-are-key-in-gender-diversity-especially-in-tech-engineering

Yang, Y., & Carroll, D. W. (2018). Gendered microaggressions in science, technology, engineering, and mathematics. *Leadership and Research in Education, 4*(special issue), 28–45.

Yu, J., McLellan, R., & Winter, L. (2021). Which boys and which girls are falling behind? Linking adolescents' gender role profiles to motivation, engagement, and achievement. *Journal of Youth Adolescence, 50*, 336–352. https://doi.org/10.1007/s10964-020-01293-z

Yukl, G. (2006). *Leadership in organizations* (6th ed.). Pearson-Prentice Hall.

Chapter 6

From the Standpoint of Women FSML Directors

Communication, Leadership, and the Impact of Gender Norms

Victoria M. McDermott and Amy R. May

INTRODUCTION

Field stations and marine laboratories (FSMLs) play an integral role in facilitating research to enhance our understanding of ecosystems around the world (National Research Council NRC, 2014). Fieldwork, which refers to any work-related activities outside of the home institution, is often conducted at FSMLs and provides an opportunity for scholars to gain firsthand experience conducting experiments, collecting data, and gaining skills in natural history, such as how to identify species (Beltrans et al., 2020; "In the field," 2018) in environments that often cannot be reliably created under laboratory conditions. FSMLs provide basic support for scientists, such as food, accommodations, and lab space, and often share the mission of the institutions with which they are affiliated, namely to support research, teaching, and public education. The ways in which FSMLs are structured and how these values are prioritized and executed differ across stations and are often influenced by the station's director (NRC, 2014).

FSML directors, much like top management within a corporate organization, in theory play a critical role in setting the culture and social norms within a field station (Harwiki, 2016; Hu et al., 2012). In practice, directors are often in charge of enacting policies established by their home institutions, which are designed for a university campus context. These institutional policies may govern day-to-day operations, enforce rules and guidelines, control access to the facilities, and hiring of support staff to ensure maintenance of the station. Women are underrepresented in directorships, creating a gap in our understanding of this critical role (see chapter 9 by Roketenetz & Holliday in this edited volume). Thus, the present case explores women's experiences with directorships at FSMLs and how they navigate these gendered spaces.

Through the qualitative analyses of interviews with FSML directors and of FSML director job descriptions, the current study explores the following questions: *What role does gender play in the communication and leadership roles and responsibilities for FSML directors? What training opportunities are available for directors to support their career trajectories?* and *How can the standpoint theory framework help to examine possible effects of gendered experiences in directorships?* Findings indicate that gender impacts communication and leadership roles, responsibilities, and experiences of women FSML directors. In contrast to published job descriptions of FSML directors, which require years of prior experience and training, interview responses from FSML directors note a lack of training prior to or during their tenures in leadership positions. Potential barriers to job recruitment and hiring include lack of consistency, transparency, and overall support for women to move into positions of authority, providing a lens to frame the experiences of women directors within the context of feminist standpoint theory.

This chapter begins with an overview of the critical role FSMLs play in scientific discovery. Next, we explore the literature related to gender and leadership, gender disparities in STEM, and standpoint theory, and then transition into a description of the data collection and data analysis methods used for this research project. The manuscript closes with the study's findings and theoretical and practical implications for the FSML community to facilitate and better support directorship experiences for women FSML directors.

LITERATURE REVIEW

Field Station and Marine Laboratories: An Overview

FSMLs are often the only places to collect data from a rapidly declining and changing diversity of habitats. These protected lands and research facilities allow researchers to monitor particular locations and address specific research questions that extend beyond the lifetime of a single Principal Investigator's (PI) lab. Rather, study can span across hundreds of years to track individual populations and broadscale environmental changes across populations and ecoregions. The types of science and questions that FSMLs allow researchers to ask and explore, as well as the iterative process of comparing field and laboratory research, provides crucial insights into ecological functioning that would not be possible strictly within a laboratory setting (Baker, 2015; NRC, 2014; Tydeck et al., 2016). The infrastructure (e.g., accommodations, transportation, food, lab space) provided by field stations provide access to often isolated, confined, and extreme (ICE) environments (Golden et al., 2017). Furthermore, fieldwork has been known to increase student retention rates within science (Freeman et al., 2014, Zavaleta et al., 2020), and field stations have been noted to influence scientists' desire to continue in academic or scientific career paths (Baker, 2015; Tydecks et al., 2016, Zavaleta et a., 2020). Overall, FSMLs allow researchers to focus specifically on data collection and research without having to first attend to surviving in ICE environments (Organization of Biological Field Stations [OBFS], 2018; Tydecks et al., 2016).

Traditional Gender Roles and Barriers to Leadership

Although sex refers to the biological differences between males and females, gender is a socially constructed concept of roles, behaviors, expressions, and identities of girls, women, boys, men, and gender diverse people (Canadian Institutes of Health Research CIHR, 2020). It is neither binary nor static; however, gender is institutionalized by society, impacting the ways in which it is performed (Lester, 2008; CIHR, 2020). Sex stereotypes or traditional gender roles are "socially shared beliefs about what qualities can be assigned to individuals based on their membership in the female or male half of the human race" (Lips, 2020, p. 4). In other words, they are culturally shared beliefs about how men and women should act, think, and behave (Lips, 2020).

Previous research has attempted to identify socially constructed characteristics and/or traits for men and women that transcend culture. Adventurous, dominant, forceful, independent, masculine, and strong are identified as traits associated with men across 25 countries (Lips, 2020; Williams & Best, 1990). The characteristics associated with women are sentimental, submissive, charming, emotional, fussy, and weak (Lips, 2020; Williams & Bennett, 1975). Within the context of existing power structures, the traits for men may be associated with desirable leadership qualities (Hoyt et al., 2009) while the traits for women seemingly reduce them to emotional creatures too challenged to succeed in positions of leadership (see Oktay chapter 5 in this edited volume).

Due to these prescriptive traditional gender roles, gender has long been a factor in people's access to jobs and success in leadership positions (Koenig, 2018). Gender gaps in fields such as science, mathematics, and medicine that favor the masculine identity reinforce gender inequalities that fall in line with traditional Western gender roles (Tomasetto et al., 2011). For example, gender stereotypes such as "girls can't do math" create a threatening environment for women, resulting in internalized self-doubt, and consequently, poor performance (Tomasetto et al., 2011). Over time, these internalized biases can impact women as they make career choices and navigate the workforce (Janssen & Backes-Gellner, 2015).

Traditional gender roles or gender stereotypes can be damaging for women trying to obtain or when in leadership positions as stepping outside feminine identity characteristics can lead to backlash from others (Hoyt et al., 2009). For women who do obtain positions of power, they may be less likely to be supported by their colleagues (Hoyt et al., 2009). Even though gender stereotypes are highly oversimplified binary categorizations of people's abilities and behaviors, they impact the real-world experiences of women, encouraging them to hold jobs in caretaker roles, such as a nurse, teacher, or administrative support. Even in positions of leadership, women may be asked to perform social support roles based on the structure of these categorizations. Men, on the other hand, are encouraged to take on more ambitious roles, such as managers and executives, even in fields and disciplines that are typically associated with the feminine identity, that is, nursing (Newman et al., 2019).

Gender Disparities in STEM

Although there has been a collective call to close gender disparities in the sciences for decades, the STEM fields have been slow to respond (Branch, 2016). As scientific disciplines remain male-dominated, only one in four in STEM academic leadership positions are held by women (McCullough, 2020). These gender ratios are similar for field station directorships despite a lack of comprehensive data. Moreover, most FSMLs exist within cultures that retain a binary view of gender defined by biological sex. Previous research has found that within heavily gendered professions (e.g., sciences, public relations), different genders have different experiences, job responsibilities, and rewards in professional positions with identical job descriptions (Aldoory & Toth, 2009a; Wessel et al., 2014), challenging perspective-taking. For example, women report getting paid less than their male counterparts and remarked about their difficult experiences when attempting to exert authority when in positions of power (Aldoory & Toth, 2009a; Aldoory & Toth, 2009b; Schmidt et al., 2005; Wessel et al., 2014).

Women face systemic and cultural barriers in the sciences that negatively impact their ability to obtain leadership positions. Ceci and Williams (2011) found that access to resources among men and women is not equitable, impacting publishing rates, as well as access to full-time positions (Davies et al. 2021). Other barriers to success in STEM include an overload of teaching and service requirements, which negatively impact research opportunities (Toutkoushian & Bellas, 1999; Valian, 2004), inadequate mentoring and insufficient role modeling (Dunham et al., 2012; Tyson & Borman, 2010), and exclusion from informal networks and fewer opportunities for collaborations (Gaughan & Bozeman, 2016; Heilman et al., 2004; Tyson & Borman, 2010). Sattari and Sandefur (2017) explored the ways in which men perceive gender equality in STEM. Findings indicate that some men may take a gender-blind perspective in the workplace, negating the idea that women struggle "more" in STEM careers (Sattari & Sandefur, 2017). Overall, these systemic and cultural barriers negatively impact women's ability to succeed and rise into leadership positions within STEM career paths.

Gender Disparities in FSMLs

Across the diverse array of FSMLs, limited research has explored the difference in gendered experiences. In 2005, Schmidt and colleagues found that women in positions of leadership on Antarctic expeditions received less social support than other expeditioners. The lack of social support for women in leadership can be an additional source of stress for leaders, especially leaders who highly value group cohesion (Rudman & Kilianski, 2000; Schmidt et al., 2005). McGuire, Primack, and Losos (2012) conducted a survey that explored whether persistent challenges exist for women ecologists. Their results suggested that the rigorous demands of academia and fieldwork do not assist in fostering or maintaining serious relationships or supporting decisions related to parenthood and family. Finally, research conducted in 2019 indicates that women at field stations often perceive that they take on more emotional burdens while in the field (McDermott, 2019). Over time, the experiences in gendered professions, such as the lack of social support, low rates of women to attain positions of power, and high levels of emotional output can negatively impact mental health through an increase in stress, anxiety, and depression (Fouad & Singh, 2011; Germain et al., 2012; von Hippel et al., 2015).

Role of Field Station Directors

As women encounter obstacles to promotion and leadership, they do not always advance to the position of FSML directors. FSML directors, however, play an integral role at the FSMLs they direct. Onsite leadership sets the tone of the culture at the station. FSML directors, much like top management within a corporate organization, play a critical role in setting the onsite culture and social norms within a field station (Harwiki, 2016; Hu et al., 2012). Directors are often in charge of what policies are enacted, how consequences are enforced, who is permitted to conduct research at the facility, what activities are allowed, and who is hired to assist in the supporting roles of the station, including K-12 educational programming staff, volunteer coordinators, and maintenance. As a FSML director, the particular ways in which station policies and priorities are interpreted can dictate the overall organizational structure and culture of the station, as well as how the station engages with the surrounding local communities and affiliated institutions. If many of these stations are led from a traditionally masculine perspective, those who identify outside of that perspective may experience barriers to success that those in the dominant coalition cannot recognize or can identify but do not respect.

Standpoint Theory

Standpoint theory explores the relationship between knowledge and power (Hartsock, 2019). Specifically, standpoint theory argues that current structures in society inherently privilege and enable groups of people through knowledge and inevitably power (Rolin, 2009). Those in the dominant societal position (i.e., men within the context of gender) create and reinforce what norms and knowledge are valued. Standpoint theory scholars argue for research to begin with those who are "oppressed" (Harding, 1991; Hartsock, 2019), positing that those who are oppressed may be epistemologically privileged. Although women continue to gain power in society, women are still considered marginalized and underrepresented in leadership. More specifically, in institutions of hegemonic masculinity (i.e., STEM, the military), scholars have argued for the value of standpoint theory (Kronsell, 2011; McDermott, 2019). Often institutions of hegemonic masculinity, like the sciences, represent and reify specific notions of masculinity in ways that make it the norm (Landau, 2008). Therefore, by listening to the voices of women who challenge the norms of hegemonic masculinity, new perspectives can provide innovative insights into effective processes, strategies, and ways of knowing (Kronsell, 2011).

This chapter seeks to examine how gender may impact the communication styles, leadership roles, and responsibilities of FSML directors. FSML directors play a vital role in maintaining the station, setting station culture, enforcing station policies, and much more. Therefore, it is essential to know how women FSML directors make sense of the role of communication and the impact of gender on director leadership roles and responsibilities. Through the framework of standpoint theory, this study seeks to provide theoretical and practical extensions to understand how gender discrepancies over time can impact female FSML director experiences (von Hippel et al., 2015). We identify gaps in training for women pursuing careers as directors may inform future training practices and programs to better support women into positions of power in FSMLs. We call for additional scholarship through asking the following research questions:

RQ1: What role does gender play in the communication practices/styles/ behaviors and leadership roles and responsibilities for FSML directors?

RQ2: What training opportunities are available for FSMLs directors to support their career trajectories?
RQ3: *How can the standpoint theory framework show the effect of gendered experiences in FSML directorships?*

METHODS

To answer the research questions, two sets of data were collected: in-depth interviews and job descriptions. Through the use of multiple sources of data, we sought to triangulate the case study findings and expand analytic generalizations regarding standpoint theory and provide practical implications for filling gaps in directorship training (Yin, 2013). The subsequent sections outline the data collection and data analysis procedures.

Data Collection

Interviews

First, three directors of field stations were interviewed. Three directors that identified as women within the same university field station system were recruited by a contact in the field to answer a semi-structured interview protocol. Interviews with directors provided direct insights into the lived experiences of female field station directors (Alshenqeeti, 2014; Yin, 2013). Due to the niche participant criteria (Buzzanell et al., 2015; Tracy, 2020), the small sample of rich narratives provides vital insights into understanding people's leadership experiences within field station organizations.

After receiving Institutional Review Board (IRB) approval, interviews were conducted using a semi-structured interview protocol. Each interview started with an overview of the informed consent. Following an overview of the informed consent, demographic data were collected. The demographic information collected included gender identity, official title, years in the position, and the number of employees managed. Once the demographic information was collected, the interview started with rapport-building questions. The interview protocol then sought to explicate job role tasks along with communication and relationship management experiences. Sample interview questions included the following: *How would you characterize your responsibilities as the field station director? How does communication impact your role as the field station director?* and *What factors, if any, support you in your leadership/communication ability?*

Table 6.1 Participant Pseudonyms and Demographics

Participant Pseudonyms	*Participant Descriptions*
Jane	Began working at the station at a different job. Has 5+ years of experience at the station, 2+ in the director positions. Directly manages 3 employees who also manage 2–5 people.
Ella	Has 3+ years of experience managing the station. Her director role is only 20% of her employee contract (80% faculty load). Works in conjunction with site manager and cattle manager.
Marie	Has 1 year of experience managing the station. Her director role is only 10% of her employee contract (90% faculty load). Works in conjunction with an operations manager who stays on site.

Source: Author data.

Following the interviews, participants were given a pseudonym for the analysis of the dataset and results write-up to ensure anonymity. Table 6.1 provides a general description of participants' demographic breakdown.

Job Descriptions

For the second set of data, 34 FSML director job descriptions were collected. Previous research has analyzed job descriptions to understand companies' priorities during the hiring process (Bhargava & Theunissen, 2019; Blackman, 2006; Kim & Angnakoon, 2016). For example, thematic analysis of entry-level public relations practitioner jobs found that companies placed little emphasis on the work and instead focused on the elements of "fit" (Bhargava & Theunissen, 2019).

Thus, field station director job descriptions were collected and analyzed using content analysis to see if gendered language appeared within the descriptions, as well as to see if there were discrepancies between explicit and implicit job responsibilities identified in the interviews. All job descriptions were collected from the OBFS website. As stated on their website, "the mission of the Organization of Biological Field Stations (OBFS) is to help member stations increase their effectiveness in supporting critical research, education, and outreach programs" (OBFS, 2021, para. 2). With 175 affiliated stations and a strong reputation within the FSML community, OBFS was identified as a viable platform for collecting job descriptions.

Under the "News and Jobs" section of their website all job descriptions titled "Director" or "Executive Director" were collected for analysis. Job descriptions that included additional titles such as site manager/director, operations manager/director, assistant director positions, program or outreach directors were not collected as those positions were not necessarily the head director of the station. In total, 34 job descriptions ranging from 2011 to 2020 met the inclusion criteria. In addition to the job posting themselves, if posts had additional hyperlinks or PDFs that were still active and contained additional information about the job description or application process, the additional data was collected for analysis. A total of five additional documents/web pages were analyzed in conjunction with the job description posts.

Qualitative Analysis

Once all the data has been collected and interview audios were transcribed, grounded theory coding (Charmaz, 1996; Lambert, 2019; Strauss & Corbin, 1997) was used to analyze the datasets. The interviews resulted in 145 minutes of audio recording and 121 pages of transcribed data. The analysis of the website resulted in 4 pages of single-spaced data and the collected job descriptions resulted in 73 pages of single-spaced data.

The grounded theory coding approach was chosen for analysis as it uses a "systematic set of procedures to develop an inductively derived grounded theory about a phenomenon" (Strauss & Corbin, 1990, p. 24). Thus, we read through each dataset three times using open coding to analyze the dataset. The first read-through was to get a foundational understanding of the data. During the second read-through, we took notes of important quotes or ideas and recurring themes (Charmaz, 1996). As stated by Charmaz (1996), in this phase of data analysis, we created "analytic codes and categories developed from data, not from preconceived hypotheses" (p. 28). Finally, in the third phase of data analysis, we used the categories and codes developed in phase two to identify overarching themes to answer the research question (Tie et al., 2019). Quotes and written statements were extracted from the datasets to exemplify the themes within the results section.

FINDINGS

Through the analysis and synthesis of the three datasets, themes were generated to answer the three research questions posed. The themes answering RQ1 were *Gender impacts communication styles and efficiency* and *Gender impacts experiences with power*. Themes answering RQ2 were *There is no training* and *But training is required for job application.* Finally, themes answering RQ3 included *Highlighting the roles of communication* and *Illuminating barriers to women's leadership and job application.*

RQ1: What role does gender play in the communication and leadership roles and responsibilities for FSML directors?

Gender Impacts Communication Styles and Efficiency

The first theme identified to answer RQ1 affirms gender impacts communication styles and efficiency. Participants perceived that they altered their communication with all stakeholders (i.e., staff, students, other researchers, locals, university administrators) based on gender expectations. There were three main ways gender impacted communication: structures that hinder communication, traditional gender communication norms and power disparities reinforced, and the impact of remoteness on communication.

Structures that Hinder Communication

A major impact on communication style and efficiency participants mentioned was that there are often structures in place that greatly hinder communication (e.g., university hierarchy, FSML division of job duties and responsibilities). All of the field stations that were included in this study were housed under two colleges within the same university. This was one of the first structural barriers hindering communication. As Ella explained, "there's historically some tension between those colleges" and their deans. Ella went on to say, "Within academia, [there are] a lot of the structure[s] inherent in universities that create tension, you know all the bean counters want their credit for their thing, and so it breeds a lot of selfishness." Ultimately, as Ella observed, this tension made the director role "a little bit tougher than it would be otherwise."

Within the field station, there were additional structures that made communication difficult. For example, Jane explained that managing the daily operations of the field station from remote locations impacted communication across multiple levels including between onsite and offsite campus administration. As Jane explained even though she didn't have direct supervision of the maintenance and kitchen staff, "he [the kitchen and maintenance lead] is 200 miles away, so I do have a lot of like direct conversations with them [his staff] so it's a little awkward." Similarly, Marie explained the difficulty of split position responsibilities. Responsibilities being split across two positions makes communication confusing as Marie explained, "it's kind of a split position that's been really challenging honestly . . . it's often unclear who's following what." Marie continued on to say, "in these positions, it's really [important to] pay attention to what are the structures that help field campuses succeed and if those structures do or don't facilitate good communications." Bureaucracies, hierarchies, and red-tape often made it difficult for directors to communicate with others and exert their authority to keep the station functioning.

Traditional Gender Communication Norms and Power Disparities Reinforced

Traditional gender norms were often reinforced through communication. For example, one traditional gender norm that was reinforced through communicative behaviors was to avoid conflict. Jane struggled internally stating,

> You know, I go back and forth on, "Is this a way that I was trained to be like a good little girl?" That I, like, want everyone to be happy and I don't want to make waves. That I, you know, maintain relationships in a way that makes people feel good? Or is that just a survival strategy?

The internal struggle trying to decipher if decisions they made were based on previously taught gender norms or simply "wanting everyone to be happy" was mentioned throughout all participants' responses.

Additionally, gender impacted how communicative behaviors were received by others. For example, many times the women were mistaken for being employees and not the station director. The participants often questioned if their gender impacted how others interpreted their authority. As Jane explained

> I think, unfortunately, like being a woman who's willing to verbalize uncertainty, that sometimes creates space for somebody who's more, appears more confident, I don't think it's a lack of confidence, I think it's a genuine like, "not sure what's right here, seeking input," then that creates what some people will take as like a leadership vacuum and like come in and I'm just like "whoa whoa that's not what I was asking for."

Seen as a "leadership vacuum" people took uncertainty from a woman director negatively, whereas Jane openly pondered during the interview if the response from a male director might be different or perceived differently by support staff.

In addition to avoiding conflict and wanting everyone to be happy, traditional gender norms impacted communication flow and who was included/excluded. All participants remarked that they were overlooked or kept out of the loop in important conversations, even though they were their station's director. Jane stated, "I think that there are subtle gender things that play into being excluded from conversations that impact the station. It happens actually at the college leadership level fairly regularly." Although participants mentioned that they did not believe this happened on purpose, they did speculate that they might be excluded from discussions about making important decisions that might not happen as often to a male counterpart. For example, as Marie noted, "there are times when I think people speak to me in ways that they would not speak to that stereotypical masculine leadership style." Jane explained a similar situation in which a male community leader communicated important information to her male employee instead of with her, the director:

> He [a male superintendent] let this person [her male employee] know that this [potential crisis] is coming down the pike or potentially coming down the pike, so my male employee let me know. So I reached out to him [male superintendent] and he was like "Oh yeah, don't worry." Then as the situation developed the male superintendent continued to communicate with my male employee. And I was like "hey." And then it got to the point where there was like a clear miscommunication and it was actually going to impact a fairly big decision and I'm like texting and emailing him [the male superintendent] "like, hey, I need to talk to you. I need to clear this up." I was just so fired up and then it ended up like actually somebody else wrote to him and was like "hey, she's the director." And so then finally he starts communicating directly with me.

Even though Jane is the director of the station, it ultimately took a prominent outside community leader telling the male superintendent to communicate directly with Jane in order for him to treat her with respect and as an equal leader in the community. This sentiment was echoed by Marie who stated, "gender assumptions are significant at a place like that [the field station]." Marie explained how traditional gender roles played out implicitly in the following interaction at her station.

> In the last iteration of the ranch managers out there, it was assumed that [the woman staff member] was doing all the cleaning and upkeep of the place, which she did. And [the man staff member] did all the maintenance, right? But it was almost like that was expected to carry over into the next iteration. And when the maintenance plan was written, there's nothing on cleaning. Well there's nobody to clean the facility anymore, so that [maintenance] person has to do it. I think I felt like the assumption was on me, like that is that something that I'm supposed to be doing, but, you know, that's not what I signed up to do here either.

Overall, Marie stated, "if I were to summarize it, I thought I'd be in much more of a leadership role than I feel like I am. I feel like I'm more in a secretarial role, so I am not, I am not visioning and creating. I am receiving a vision and then delivering it." Finally, Ella contemplated whether her gender impacted relationships with the state cattlemen association, "I do wonder, like we haven't had as much participation from the [state] cattlemen association, as we would like who's a very important stakeholder for this, and I wonder to what extent that is because we [director and station manager] are both women."

Impact of Remoteness on Communication

Remoteness impacted communication in two main ways, accessibility and reinforcing gender norms. At the most basic level, remoteness made communication difficult. For example, many locations surrounding remote locations do not have internet, and it is easy for internet to go down in a remote FSML. Marie jokingly said that you could see hikers stop on the bridge near the field station to check cell phone messages and call loved ones as it was the only spot with internet connection within 30 miles. For stations that are extremely remote like Marie's, which are only accessible by plane for part of the year, losing internet meant the loss of communication entirely with the outside world. Ella had a similar experience as her staffer frequently went out into fields with little to no cell reception. As Ella explained about one of the FSML workers:

> He's like this kind of person, if you run into them out on the road, then you'll have this great exchange and you're like, "Oh man, I'm so glad I saw you." But getting him otherwise can be a little challenging; he's usually fairly good with phone calls. But sometimes, you know, he's just in the middle of nowhere and he's not always getting his messages and stuff. So that part's been a little bit more challenging.

In addition to the basic need for communication, the impact of traditional gender norms seemed to be compounded by the remoteness. As Marie stated, "it [gender disparities] does seem, like, significant in the wilderness." All the participants commented that the outdoors workplace amplifies a specific stigma related to gender. Not only did gender impact communication of directors. When at the station, the remoteness impacted staff. As Jane explained:

> We joke that people know the spaces on campus that you can go cry in. And, like, I know that there's a network of like, three of our female staff in particular they know the deep freezer next to the walk-in has a loud motor, so that's a good place to go cry.

The remoteness of the field station may have had a compounding effect on barriers to communication and increased emotional vulnerability. Furthermore, the confinements of camp meant that people had to get creative in order to express their emotions in secret. Unlike a 9-to-5 job where someone could go home at the end of the day to decompress and communicate their workday with close friends and family, the nature of field station life can be exacerbated by the expectation without compensation of living and working in the same location and the remoteness 24/7.

RQ2: What training opportunities are available for FSMLs directors to support their career trajectories?

There Is No Training

Overall when asked about training, all participants mentioned how they had no official leadership or communication training prior to or during their directorship. We underscore that there is a large gap in training. The only training in communication or leadership participants had was from previous work experiences. As Jane noted, her background in wilderness education provided a helpful framework for understanding communication and leadership dynamics within the workplace, "none of that [communication/leadership training] was part of this work. It was just all things that I have sought out, either that were part of my former work in environmental education or things that I've sought out personally." Marie also mentioned having previous training in science communication; however, she received no training related to what it means to be a director, an effective communicator, or manager and director that is specific to her current position.

All participants pointed to the fact that although their university leadership encouraged continuing professional development, there was no time allotted during the work week to participate in training. For example, Ella explained that her Dean signed her up for a grant writing training, but due to time constraints, Ella had to decide between doing the training or just spending the time on writing the grant. As noted by Ella, "I ended up having to withdraw because I didn't have time. I was like I don't even have time, I can either write a proposal or I can take this [training] . . . I would rather just write the proposal." The lack of time among participants meant that they often had to prioritize completing tasks to keep the station running over cultivating their own professional development.

Ultimately, participants commented that the lack of training, however, was not specific to FSMLs, but plagues all of academia. As Ella stated, "But that's not unusual in academia, I mean we don't really get much training on teaching but we're expected to do that and do it well, right?" Occasionally when they did attend a training, participants mentioned it did not meet their expectations or improve their leadership abilities. Jane stated, "I did a university leadership academy, but that was more like 'here are the parts of the university.' Yeah it's not what I thought it was gonna be." Even though participants had little time and opportunities for engaging in professional development, they mentioned being open to and wanting effective leadership and communication training. As stated by Marie, "I would love more leadership training."

But Training Is Required for Job Applications

In contrast to the lack of training identified by participants, the job descriptions of director positions that we collected and analyzed often had strict requirements in regards to previous training and certifications. Some job descriptions required or preferred that applicants had received training requirements related to leadership or management experience. Other positions required training and certifications for things such as "facilitating infrastructure and facilities maintenance," knowledge of a university's specific policies before employment, and even a "U.S. Coast Guard boating certificate or a State of California Boater Card possessed or obtained before appointment." These data confirm there are significant disparities between professional development opportunities, assigned time to engage in professional development, and the requirements to successfully compete for directorship positions.

RQ3: How the standpoint theory framework can teach us about the effects of gendered experiences in FSML directorships?

Highlighting the Role of Communication

The first theme that emerged to answer RQ3 was the use of standpoint theory to allow the role of communication in women director's lives to emerge from the dataset. Findings indicate that women directors communicate in a variety of ways: communication coping strategies, communication for managing relationships, and building communication networks of support.

Communication Coping Strategies

By beginning with the lives of women FSML directors, the theme of communication coping strategies emerged. All participants touched upon how they had to adopt specific communication strategies in order to succeed as a leader and director. These coping strategies ranged from trying not to be "negative" about their work life, to enlisting men as advocates to get approval to complete tasks.

Using the first coping strategy participants tried to focus on the positive aspects of the job. Marie mentioned trying not to "fixate too much on all of the things that don't work." Marie also often tried to focus on the important role the station played in the lives of her students. As Marie put it, "I believe in what I do, I believe it has an impact and sometimes that has to be enough." Similarly, Jane laughed as she explained:

> What's It's like in? the movie *The Devil Wears Prada*, yeah right, where they do that thing like anytime they start saying something negative about their employer they switch it, like, "but anyway, it's actually really great here, I feel really blessed to have this job."

Along those lines, Marie mentioned the role of "grit" in her leadership success, "I'm not sure that any of us would be here unless we had grit, so we've got some tools that we've developed along the way."

Some of the more specific communication coping strategies the women directors used to navigate their roles were to defer to higher leadership decisions and strategically use colleague support. Being split between two colleges, Ella explained that her communication coping strategy was to defer to her Dean's decision at all times. Ella stated, I try to "not cross [my] college." Jane noted how she used the practical coping strategy of strategic alliances to communicate through barriers. Jane explained:

> He and I are in a lot of meetings together and I'll be like "hey, this is what I need from you, I need you to like back up everything that I say and whatever I'm going to say I need you to be on my team." Actually there's two people that I do that to, two men, that I'm just like "what I need from you in this meeting is blank. I'm going to lead and I need you to be my backup."

Ultimately, getting male colleagues to support her decisions was a strategic communication decision that Jane used to succeed at her job. Jane ultimately ended the example with, "So that's a strategy that I wish I didn't have to use." From intra-communication strategies of staying positive to practical interpersonal communication strategies, such as relying on the support of male colleagues, the experiences women had in these leadership positions lead them to develop communication coping strategies for success.

Communication for Managing Relationships

Another theme that emerged under the role of communication was how key communication was to manage relationships. Directors often had to manage relationships among a variety of constituents and stakeholders. From students to local communities to university leadership, communication was the main factor in maintaining relationships with the public. Marie stated, "Our whole world is communication." Communication was a cornerstone in building important relationships, especially with the local community." As Ella stated, "we do have regularly held outreach events where we invite the public." Ella went on to explain that these events allowed the station to share scientists' research with the local community and build important connections with the public. Interestingly, Jane noted that due to working frequently with schools they often served as a mediator between the local school administration and teachers. As Jane stated, "sometimes, like, we are the intermediary between those groups [principals and teachers] . . . I have a lot of friends who are teachers and I ask 'Should I talk to your principal about this, or should I talk to the teachers' and they're, like, 'Both.'"

Not only do directors have to manage relationships with outside communities, communication was valued as a way to manage relationships with their affiliated university leadership and among their field station employees. Marie's statement summarizes the role of communication in field stations as the following, "Our worth is based on, like, what do we do as a field campus, why are we here. We have to communicate that to the forest service, we have to make a case for that to the American public to the State, all of that."

Building Communication Networks of Female Support

All participants highlighted that they had to build networks of support for themselves in order to succeed in their directorship. For example, as Marie stated, "I kind of built, I think, support around the networks that I already have and definitely reached out to my women colleagues for support." Jane also mentioned the need for female support. When explaining a tense conversation with a male colleague, Jane explained how a female employee verbally supported her decision to launch a new program:

> A colleague went off in a snarky rant, he's like "I mean, why are we doing this," and my female employee was like "because this is the kind of programming and the kind of group that we really want to serve and it furthers our mission," and I was like, "Okay, good work."

As women in leadership positions, it was important to surround themselves with female support networks. These support networks, both within and without of the station and their supporting institutional systems, provided an outlet for the participants to make sense of their experiences and find mental and emotional support.

Illuminating Barriers to Leadership and Job Application

Barriers to leadership and job application were identified in both the interviews and the job descriptions. Some of the barriers to leadership and job application within the interviews included gendered history and funding, value in the university's eyes, and gender ratios. Barriers within the job descriptions (JD) included lack of consistency, lack of transparency, logistical barriers, and binary language and equity statements.

Within the Interviews

According to participants, one of the biggest obstacles to leadership and to acquiring FSML jobs was that many FSMLs do not have a history of female directorship. This male leadership legacy could present a barrier for those outside of the traditional white, male identity to see themselves in a directorship position. For example, even though Jane was the third director in the station's history, she was the first woman in the director position. Moreover, for well-established FSMLs with a history of male directorship, previous relationships with local communities, university leadership, researchers, and FSML staff could impact a hiring committee's decision to continue or disrupt a gendered leadership legacy.

In addition to a history of male leadership, the chronic underfunding and undervaluing of community-based research completed at FSMLs makes it difficult for directors. This undervaluing of some FSML research led all the participants to feel on edge about job security. For example, Ella stated, "ultimately nobody is gonna watch out for you, except you, unfortunately, so you know you kind of have to keep that in mind. I do." This was echoed by Marie who explained how two women FSML directors had recently been passed up for a secure tenure-track position for a white male colleague who was not a station director, "[at] what point do I walk into a room and it's not three quarters, and being generous here, men and a quarter woman and the women are on research tracks, instead of tenure track lines." The impact of long-term insecurity and challenges to leadership due to gender lead to disillusionment among participants. Both Jane and Marie mentioned how negative experiences based on gender were exhausting overtime. As Marie stated, "over time, that [lack of women in leadership] gets real demoralizing."

Within the Job Descriptions (JDs)

A major finding of the JD analysis is that there are several interacting potential barriers that impact the recruitment and successful application of not only women but other minoritized individuals for director positions at FSMLs. These barriers included a lack of consistency across JD requirements, a lack of transparency, logistical barriers, and binary language and equity statements.

Lack of consistency. To start, the directorship JDs severely lacked consistency ranging from the tasks a potential director would be required to do in their position to the qualifications needed to apply. For example, some JDs included information about the university culture and values that the station was affiliated with, whereas other JDs simply contained bullet points explaining the roles and responsibilities of the job. Some JDs had multiple sections outlining preferred qualifications and job role and responsibilities, while other JDs had a few sentences about the roles and responsibilities with little to no information about preferred applicant qualifications. In addition to the lack of consistency in language describing job roles and responsibilities, there was a lack of consistency in reporting structure. For example, some jobs had directors reporting to an executive director, some reported to a faculty director, and some reported to an advisory board. The lack of consistency among the hierarchies at stations could later impact the power and authority a director is able to exert in their position.

Although not all JDs mentioned a degree, and the ones that did ranged from requiring a bachelor's to a PhD. Eighteen JDs required a PhD, five required a minimum of a master's degree, and four required a minimum of a bachelor's degree. Of the JDs that require a PhD, only ten mentioned the potential for a tenure track based on funding availability. Similar to the broad range of educational requirements, the experience requirements varied from requesting a minimum of 3 years of field station directorship experience to a minimum of 10+ years of field station directorship experience. Overall, the lack of consistency among JDs could ultimately impact what it means to be the "director" at different field stations.

Lack of transparency. Another barrier to recruitment may be the lack of transparency within the JDs. For example, a total of 9 out of 34 JDs included a potential salary. Even more importantly, the potential salaries for the same position ranged greatly from one JD to the next, "monthly stipend (between $1,000 and $1,200) with lodging and food provided" to "$63,000–$72,000" to "$90,684.00–$115,728.00 annually." The large discrepancies within potential salary for those JDs that did include a salary could be seen as a lack of transparency for potential applicants.

Additionally, many JDs hinted at additional role requirements without providing specific timing or percentage breakdown and one even mentioned having to step into a completely different role as needed. As stated in the description, "The Director is expected to step into the Environmental Education Intern's role if needed" and went on to explain the job expectations of the education intern. Other additional role requirements included having to manage a professorship and international publishing on top of the administrative and leadership tasks associated with the directorship. Aside from two JDs, these JDs did not mention how much "time" a person would be given to devote to each role. As noted in the interviews, although directorships were only 10% and 20% of their job roles, respectively, Ella and Marie spent more than half of their time directing the station.

Logistical barriers. JDs often presented logistical barriers that might hinder a minoritized person from applying. These barriers included things such as extensive previous outdoor field experiences, physical requirements, that is, lifting requirements, "physical and mental standards," and having to commit to a position for a specific period of time. Even though many FSMLs require directors to live on site or visit frequently, there was no mention of family accommodations in 33 out of the 34 JDs.

Only two applications mentioned providing support to overcome potential logistical barriers. One JD allowed applicants to mail in their application if they did not have access to the internet. The only other JD acknowledging logistical barriers mentioned family accommodations stating:

> We recognize that recruiting and retaining faculty may involve considerations of spouses and domestic partners. To that end, where possible, the College will attempt to accommodate and respond creatively to the needs of spouses and partners of members of the faculty.

The barriers presented in these JDs are significant as only one JD acknowledged the digital divide that many low-income and minoritized groups face and only one JD acknowledged that family could impact job application and acceptance.

Binary language and equity statements. Finally, binary gendered language was found within three JDs "he/she is expected" and "S/he will." Although limited, this is a significant barrier for application if the gender spectrum is not recognized prior to even submitting an application. Furthermore, not all JDs include a statement of diversity, equity, and inclusion. A total of 14 out of 34 JDs did not have a diversity statement. While these statements are often boilerplate templates, they are important for showcasing that an organization does value and understand diversity, equity, and inclusion issues exist in the workplace.

DISCUSSION

By documenting the voices and experiences of three women FSML directors (Harding, 1991; Hartsock, 2019), in conjunction with the JDs (Bhargava & Theunissen, 2019), this study uncovered a variety of gendered experiences that women may encounter when attempting to obtain or progress in a FSML directorship. Findings indicate that women FSML directors often face unexpected job roles and responsibilities, as well as barriers to effective communication. Overall, lack of communication was found to play a large role in women FSML directors' experiences. Most importantly, the lack of training before entering into and while occupying leadership positions, as well as the gendered language within JDs and lack of family support may present barriers to position application and retention rates. Ultimately, findings from our case study reinforce previous literature and add theoretical extensions and practical implications for improving women FSML directors' communication and leadership experiences. The subsequent sections will overview the theoretical and practical extensions derived from this study's findings.

Theoretical

Using standpoint theory, we posit the value of analyzing the role of communication in power and knowledge transfer. Standpoint theory examines the relationship between those with power and knowledge and those who may or may not have access to power and knowledge (Harding, 1991; Hartsock, 2019; Rolin, 2009). This study seeks to expand the application of standpoint theory by examining the mechanistic role that communication plays in the relationship between power and knowledge. Findings from this case study suggest that through communication, the differential of power and knowledge can be lessened or expanded. Communication is a way women FSML directors can learn the unwritten cultural norms of a university system and history of FSML stakeholder relationships. However, communication can also be used to increase power and knowledge gaps and disparities. Previous research supports exclusion from informal professional networks and fewer opportunities for collaborations negatively impact women's success in STEM (Gaughan & Bozeman, 2016; Heilman et al., 2004; Tyson & Borman, 2010). Thus, when women directors are left out of important conversations, power gaps widen (Harding, 1991; Hartsock, 2019). Therefore, the results from this study support the argument in favor of evaluating the role of communication in the transfer of knowledge and power. Exploring how organizational communication practices can reify oppression may expand the application of standpoint theory within the communication discipline.

Practical

Practically, findings from this study provide two overarching suggestions for FSMLs. These suggestions seek to improve the experiences of and increase the recruitment of minoritized individuals for leadership positions.

First, using less gendered language in JDs and more transparency surrounding implicit/explicit job responsibilities may increase the potential applicant pools for leadership positions. For example, the lack of consistency throughout JDs could negatively impact the field as a whole if some directors are expected to do more with less. The lack of consistency in preferred qualifications could also hinder someone from applying due to the large range of educational and certificate requirements. As argued by Nickel and colleagues (2018), creating more standardized JDs may allow for the successful recruitment and retention of diverse, capable leaders. Furthermore, institutions are encouraged to portray realistic time breakdowns in JDs. Through the standardization of JDs and realistic job time breakdowns, FSML directors will be able to argue for the re-allocation of job roles and responsibilities, as well as salary increases with university administrators. Allowing directors to invest adequate time and effort into their stations without being stretched thin would allow all directors, especially women to exercise leadership and authority more successfully. In both the JDs and in practice, taking on additional, unforeseen responsibilities negatively impacted women's directorship experiences (Toutkoushian & Bellas, 1999; Valian, 2004).

Second, all participants in this study mentioned having no applicable/appropriate training to prepare them for director communication and leadership. Therefore, providing effective training to facilitate the growth of communication and leadership skills may benefit people who are interested in and currently acting in directorship positions. The investment will pay off for their home institutions and perhaps lead the way to a more equitable and inclusive model of leadership. In relatively small, outlying and isolated communities, FSML directors could be allowed to play such a crucial role in transforming the climate of the FSMLs, STEM, and larger parent organizations (Harwiki, 2016; Hu et al., 2012). Leadership training has been shown to positively impact organizational effectiveness and culture (Jacobsen et al., 2021; Koohang et al., 2016; Lacerenza et al., 2017). Therefore, training should be provided to directors throughout their career to refine and cultivate their leadership skills. Institutions should support women's authority and positions of leadership by providing the time and resources necessary to engage in professional development training (McGuire et al., 2012; Schmidt et al., 2005). Moreover, we need to rethink how to appeal to a diversity of candidates; if we expect people to apply to jobs with specific, expensive scientific training, and previous strong place-based outdoor knowledge, we may be reinforcing application biases. For example, requiring a boating or SCUBA license or a minimum 50-lb. lifting capability prior to directorship appointment privileges those who have access to additional resources when in fact other candidates may be much stronger applicants in every other aspect of the JD, especially in most positions where there are others onsite who have these skill sets and areas of expertise. As previous research has found, access to resources among men and women in STEM is not equitable (Ceci & Williams, 2011). Therefore, limiting the "required" aspects of JDs may result in larger and more diverse candidate pools. From there, institutions are encouraged to critically evaluate their subsequent interview and hiring processes to identify additional barriers.

LIMITATIONS AND FUTURE RESEARCH

Although this case study provides important theoretical and practical implications, there were some limitations. The number of interviews was small. We have just begun to identify questions for further research. We choose to analyze 34 JDs from one FSML professional organization. The FSML community is broken into a variety of organizations and networks such as the Long-Term Ecological Research (LTER) community, OBFS, Ecological Society of America (ESA), and Undergraduate Field Experiences Research Network (UFERN), so expanding the job posting data collection could provide additional insights into the discrepancies between JDs and directors' lived experiences. Finally, the present case study only evaluated one university system FSML network. Evaluating multiple university system field stations, as well as FSMLs not affiliated with a university may provide further insights into the experiences of directors (and to have enough of a sample size to group across all field facilities as well as to split them by agency, R1 University, SLAs, federal and state agencies, etc.). Overall, more research is needed to understand the gendered leadership experiences at FSMLs. Finally, the researchers identify as white women working in higher education; moreover, the researchers actively work with women affiliated with FSMLs. This introduced multiple layers of potential bias and privilege that may have impacted data analysis.

CONCLUSION

FSML directors play a fundamental role in the functioning and success of FSMLs, but it is a role that is constrained by institutional culture, status, and bureaucracy. Understanding the effect of gender on directors' experiences provides insights into systemic barriers to success that may not be seen by the dominant coalition. Universities and FSMLs are challenged to critically evaluate their steadfast structures (i.e., hiring practices, job roles and responsibilities, hierarchy structures) to identify barriers to success for women and other minoritized groups. This study highlights the value and role of communication in exploring standpoint theory, as well as suggests two tangible recommendations for university administrators to better support their women FSML directors. By beginning with the lives of the marginalized, we are able to identify factors that hinder the leadership success of diverse voices who promise to propel the growth of and innovation in our disciplines (Zavaleta et al. 2020).

REFERENCES

Aldoory, L., & Toth, E. (2009a). Gender discrepancies in a gendered profession: A developing theory for public relations. *Journal of Public Relations Research, 14*(2), 103–126. https://doi.org/10.1207/S1532754XJPRR1402_2

Aldoory, L., & Toth, E. (2009b). Leadership and gender in public relations: Perceived effectiveness of transformational and transactional leadership styles. *Journal of Public Relations Research, 16*(2), 157–183. https://doi.org/10.1207/s1532754xjprr1602_2

Alshenqeeti, H. (2014). Interviewing as a data collection method: A critical review. *English Linguistics Research, 3*(1), 39–45. http://dx.doi.org/10.5430/elr.v3n1p39

Baker, B. (2015). The way forward for biological field stations: Change needed to ensure survival and scientific relevance. *BioScience, 65*(2), 123–129.

Beltran, R. S., Marnocha, E., Race, A., Croll, D. A., Dayton, G. H., & Zavaleta, E. S. (2020). Field courses narrow demographic achievement gaps in ecology and evolutionary biology. *Ecology and Evolution, 10*(12), 5184–5196. https://doi.org/10.1002/ece3.6300

Bhargava, D., & Theunissen, P. (2019). The future of PR is 'fantastic', 'friendly' and 'funny': Occupational stereotypes and symbolic capital in entry-level job advertisements. *Public Relations Review, 45*, 1–12. https://doi.org/10.1016/j.pubrev.2019.101822.

Blackman, A. (2006). Graduating students' responses to recruitment advertisements. *Journal of Business Communication, 43*(4), 367–388.https://doi.org/10.1177/0021943606291705.

Branch, E. H. (2016). *Pathways, potholes, and the persistence of women in science.* Lexington Books.

Buzzanell, P. M, Long, Z., Anderson, L. B., Kokini, K., & Batra, J. C. (2015). Mentoring in academe: A feminist poststructural lens on stories of women engineering faculty of color. *Management Communication Quarterly*, 1–18. http://doi.10.1177/0893318915574311

Canadian Institutes of Health Research. (2020, April 28). *What is gender? What is sex?* https://cihr-irsc.gc.ca/e/48642.html

Charmaz, K. (1996). The search for meanings - grounded theory. In J. A. Smith, R. Harre, & L. Van Langenhove (Eds.). *Rethinking methods in psychology* (pp. 27–49). SAGE.

Davies, S. W., Putnam, H. M., Ainsworth, T., Baum, J. K., Bove, C. B., Crosby SC, . . . Bates, A. E. (2021) Promoting inclusive metrics of success and impact to dismantle a discriminatory reward system in science. *PLoS Biology, 19*(6), e3001282. https://doi.org/10.1371/journal.pbio.3001282

Dunham, C. C., Weathers, L. H., Hoo, K., & Heintz, C. (2012). I just need someone who knows the ropes: Mentoring and female faculty in science and engineering. *Journal of Women and Minorities in Science and Engineering, 18*, 79–96.

Flyvbjerg, B. (2006). Five misunderstandings about case-study research. *Qualitative Inquiry, 12*(2), 219–245.

Fouad, N. A., & Singh, R. (2011). *Stemming the tide: Why women leave engineering.* University of Wisconsin.

Freeman, S., Eddy, S. L., McDonough, M., Smith, M. K., Okoroafor, N., Jordt, H., & Wenderoth, M. P. (2014). Active learning increases student performance in science, engineering, and mathematics. *Proceedings of the National Academy of Sciences of the United States of America, 111*(23), 8410–8415. https://doi.org.10.1073/pnas.1319030111

Garger, J. (2013). Using the case study method in PhD research. *Brighthub.* http://www.brighthub.com/education/postgraduate/articles/77789.aspx

Gaughan, M., & Bozeman, B. (2016). Using the prisms of gender and rank to interpret research collaboration power dynamics. *Social Studies of Science, 46*, 536–558.

Germain, M., Herzog, M. J. R., & Hamilton, P. R. (2012). Women employed in male-dominated industries: lessons learned from female aircraft pilots, pilots-in-training and mixed gender flight instructors. *Human Resource Development International, 15*(4), 435–453.

Golden, S. J., Chang, C., & Kozlowski, S. W. J. (2017). Teams in isolated, confined, and extreme (ICE) environments: Review and integration. *Journal of Organizational Behavior, 39*, 701–715.

Harding, S. (1991). *Whose science/ whose knowledge?.* Cornell University Press.

Hartsock, N. C. M. (2019). *The feminist standpoint revisited and other essays.* Routledge.

Harwiki, W. (2016). The impact of servant leadership on organization culture, organizational commitment, organizational citizenship behaviour (OCB) and employee performance in women cooperatives. *Procedia-Social and Behavioral Sciences, 219*, 283-290.

Hasim, M. S., Hashim, A. E., Ariff, N. R. M., Sapeciay, Z., & Abdullah, A. S. (2018). Commitment to sustainability: A content analysis of websites for university organisations. *IOP conference series: Earth and Environmental Science, 117*(1), 012046.

Heilman, M. E., Wallen, A. S., Fuchs, D., & Tamkins, M. M. (2004). Penalties for success: Reactions to women who succeed at male gender-typed tasks. *Journal of Applied Psychology, 89*, 416–427.

Hoyt, C. L., Simon, S., & Reid, L. (2009). Choosing the best (wo) man for the job: The effects of mortality salience, sex, and gender stereotypes on leader evaluations. *The Leadership Quarterly, 20*(2), 233–246.

Hu, Q., Dinev, T., Hart, P., & Cooke, D. (2012). Managing employee compliance with information security policies: The critical role of top management and organizational culture. *Decision Sciences, 43*(4), 615–660.

In the field. (2018, September 25). *AdvanceGeo*. https://serc.carleton.edu/advancegeo/resources/field_work.html

Jacobsen, C. B., Andersen, L. B., Bøllingtoft, A., & Eriksen, T. L. M. (2021). Can leadership training improve organizational effectiveness? Evidence from a randomized field experiment on transformational and transactional leadership. *Public Administration Review*, 1–15. https://doi.org.10.1111/puar.13356.

Janssen, S., & Backes-Gellner, U. (2016). Occupational stereotypes and gender-specific job satisfaction. *Industrial Relations: A Journal of Economy and Society*, *55*(1), 71–91.

Jose, A., & Lee, S. M. (2007). Environmental reporting of global corporations: A content analysis based on website disclosures. *Journal of Business Ethics*, *72*(4), 307–321.

Kim, J., & Angnakoon, P. (2016). Research using job advertisements: A methodological assessment. *Library & Information Science Research, 38*(4), 327–335. https://doi.org/10.1016/j.lisr.2016.11.006.

Koenig, A. M. (2018). Comparing prescriptive and descriptive gender stereotypes about children, adults, and the elderly. *Frontiers in psychology*, *9*, 1086.

Koohang, A., Paliszkiewicz, J., & Goluchowski, J. (2017). The impact of leadership on trust, knowledge management, and organizational performance: A research model. *Industrial Management & Data Systems, 117*(3), 521–537. https://doi.org/10.1108/IMDS-02-2016-0072

Kronsell, A. (2011). Gendered practices in institutions of hegemonic masculinity. *International Feminist Journal of Politics, 7*(2), 280–298. https://doi.org/10.1080/1461674050006517O

Krusenvik, L. (2016). *Using case studies as a scientific method: Advantages and disadvantages*. Unpublished paper, Halmstad University.

Lacerenza, C. N., Reyes, D. L., Marlow, S. L., Joseph, D. L., & Salas, E. (2017). Leadership training design, delivery, and implementation: A meta-analysis. *Journal of Applied Psychology*, *102*(12), 1–33. http://doi.org/10.1037/apl0000241

Lambert, M. (2019). *Practical research methods in education: An early researcher's critical guide*. Routledge.

Landau, I. (2008). Problems with feminist standpoint theory in science education. *Science & Education, 17*, 1081–1088.https://doi.org/10.1007/s11191-007-9131-5

Lips, H. (2020). *Sex and gender: An introduction, seventh edition.* Waveland Press, Inc.

Lester, J. (2008). Performing gender in the workplace: Gender socialization, power, and identity among women faculty members. *Community College Review*, *35*(4), 277–305.

McCullough, L. (2020). Proportions of women in STEM leadership in the academy in the USA. *Education Sciences, 10*(1), 1. https://doi.org/10.3390/educsci10010001

McDermott, V. (2019). *'It's a magnifying glass': the communication of power in a remote field station* [Unpublished Master's thesis]. University of Alaska Fairbanks, Scholarworks.

National Research Council [NRC]. (2014). *Enhancing the value and sustainability of field stations and marine laboratories in the twenty-first century*. National Academies Press.

Newman, C., Stilwell, B., Rick, S., & Peterson, K. (2019). Investing in the power of nurse leadership: What will it take? https://www.intrahealth.org/sites/ihweb/files/attachment-files/investing-nurse-leadershipreport.pdf

Nickel, B. L., Roof, J., Dolejs, S., Choi, J. N., & Torbeck, L. (2018). Identifying managerial roles of general surgery coordinators: making the case for utilization of a standardized job description framework. *Journal of Surgical Education*, *75*(6), e38–e46.

OBFS. (2018). What are field stations. https://www.obfs.org/what-s-a-fieldstation-

OBFS. (2021). Home. https://www.obfs.org/

Oktay, S. D. (2022). Experiences of a female leader in FSMLs. In V. McDermott, J. Gee, & A. R. May (Eds.), *Women of the wild: Challenging gender disparities in field stations and marine laboratories* (p. 89–114). Lexington Books.

Roketenetz, L. D., & Holliday, G. M. (2022). Are field stations and nature centers gendered work spaces?. In V. McDermott, J. Gee, & A. R. May (Eds.), *Women of the wild: Challenging gender disparities in field stations and marine laboratories* (p. 199–224). Lexington Books.

Rolin, K. (2009). Standpoint theory as a methodology for the study of power relations. *Hypatia, 24*(4), 218–226. https://www.jstor.org/stable/20618192

Rudman, L. A., & Kilianski, S. E. (2000). Implicit and explicit attitudes toward female authority. *Personality and Social Psychology Bulletin, 26*, 1315–1328.

Sattari, N., & Sandefur, R. L. (2019). Gender in academic STEM: A focus on men faculty. *Gender Work Organization, 26*,158–179. https://doi.org/10.1111/gwao.12249

Schmidt, L. L., Wood, J., & Lugg, D. J. (2005a). Gender differences in leader and follower perceptions of social support in Antarctica. *Acta Astronnautica, 56*, 923–931.

Soy, S (1997). *The case study as a research method.* Unpublished paper, University of Texas at Austin.

Strauss, A., & Corbin, J. (1990). *Basics of qualitative research: Grounded theory procedures and techniques.* Sage.

Strauss, A., & Corbin, J. M. (1997). *Grounded theory in practice*. SAGE.

Tie, Y. C., Birks, M., & Francis, K. (2019). Grounded theory research: A design for movie researchers. *SAGE Open Medicine, 7*, 1–8. https://doi.org.10.1177/2050312118822927

Tomasetto, C., Alparone, F. R., & Cadinu, M. (2011). Girls' math performance under stereotype threat: The moderating role of mothers' gender stereotypes. *Developmental Psychology*, *47*(4), 943.

Toutkoushian, R. K., & Bellas, M. L. (1999). Faculty time allocations and research productivity: Gender, race and family effects. *The Review of Higher Education, 22*, 367–390.

Tracy, S. J. (2019). *Qualitative research methods: Collecting evidence, crafting analysis, communicating impact.* Wiley-Blackwell.

Tydecks, L., Bremerich, V., Jentschke, I., Likens, G. E., & Tockner, K. (2016). Biological field stations: A global infrastructure for research, education, and public engagement. *BioScience, 66,* 164–171.

Tyson, W., & Borman, K. M. (2010).'We've all learned a lot of ways not to solve the problem': Perceptions of science and engineering pathways among tenured women faculty. *Journal of Women and Minorities in Science and Engineering, 16,* 275–291.

Valian, V. (2004). Beyond gender schemas: Improving the advancement of women in academia. *NWSA Journal, 16*(1), 207–220.

von Hippel, C., Sekaquaptewa, D., & McFarlane, M. (2015). Stereotype threat among women in finance: Negative effects on identity, workplace well-being, and recruiting. *Psychology of Women Quarterly, 39*(3), 405–414. DOI: 10.1177/0361684315574501

Wessel, J. L., Hagiwara, N., Ryan, A. M., & Kermond, C. M. (2015). Should women applicants "man up" for traditionally masculine fields? Effectiveness of two verbal identity management strategies. *Psychology of Women Quarterly, 39*(2), 243–255. https://doi.org/10.1177/0361684314543265

Williams, J. E., & Bennett, S. M. (1975). The definition of sex stereotypes via the adjective check list. *Sex Roles, 1*(4), 327–337.

Williams, J. E., & Best, D. L. (1990). *Measuring sex stereotypes: A multination study, Rev.* Sage Publications, Inc.

Zavaleta, E. S., Beltran, R. S., & Borker, A. L. (2020). How field courses propel inclusion and collective excellence. *Scientific Life, 35*(11), 953–956. https://doi.org/10.1016/j.tree.2020.08.005

Chapter 7

Identifying Factors that Contribute to Positive and Negative Student Experiences at Field-Based Institutions

Danielle M. Becker, Jessica E. Griffin, and Cassandra M. L. Miller[1]

INTRODUCTION

Our natural world is enduring dramatic environmental changes associated with the global climate crisis, including but not limited to rising sea surface temperatures and levels, fires, droughts, and floods. The devastating effects of climate change threaten both the well-being of humans and the natural world, with a significant burden placed on already vulnerable communities and fragile ecosystems. Thus, the need to understand, predict, and sustain natural ecosystems in the face of climate change, biodiversity loss, natural resource extraction, and pollution is increasingly important (IPCC, 2017; Shukla et al., 2019). Innovation and collaboration are necessary to achieve strides in policy, conservation, research, and education that will protect valuable ecosystems and threatened communities (IPCC, 2017).

Scientific research, particularly that which is conducted at field stations and marine labs (FSMLs), enables us to engage with the natural world and seek solutions to the climate crisis. FSMLs, often home to crucial long-term ecological monitoring projects, allow scientists to gain hands-on experience conducting scientific research related to the global climate crisis (Janovy & Major, 2009; National Research Council NRC, 2014). Moreover, student experiences at FSMLs are important for building scientific self-efficacy and long-term retention in science, technology, engineering, and math (STEM) career paths (Zavaleta et al., 2020). Unfortunately, however, there are barriers for students to engage in fieldwork (Fournier et al., 2015; Jensen et al., 2021) and research and popular press articles have noted that some students may have negative experiences when in the field, being subject to sexual harassment, bullying, and other forms of traumatizing behaviors (Clancy et al., 2014; Gluckman, 2018). Currently, there is little research exploring the factors that create positive or negative field experiences for students and the potential lasting impacts of these positive and negative experiences.

This chapter seeks to contribute to a better understanding of the student experience at FSMLs. We begin this chapter with a brief overview of relevant literature. Following our review of literature, we explain our process for developing, piloting, and releasing a qualitative survey to the FSML community to collect data regarding students' experiences at FSMLs. Using thematic coding we analyzed 402 survey responses. Analysis of our data suggests five emergent themes that survey respondents referred to as influencing their positive and negative FSML experiences including: workplace culture, inequity, communication, relationships, and support. From this analysis, we provide recommendations for developing more inclusive, accessible, and equitable FSML experiences for students and specifically for students who identify in the feminine or in a minoritized gender, sexual orientation, race, and/or ethnicity.

LITERATURE REVIEW

Field Stations and Marine Laboratories (FSMLs)

The foundation of a STEM career is built upon a supportive FSML community that fosters opportunities for engagement, education, and inspiration (Janovy & Major, 2009; NRC, 2014; Zavaleta et al., 2020). FSMLs are invaluable sources of ecological knowledge that facilitate an environment for training the next generation of scientists and are at the center of cutting-edge research (see chapter 1 by McDermott, Gee, & May of this edited volume for more information; Tydecks et al., 2016). For many scientists, experiences at FSMLs provide important training and learning opportunities that inspire their future research and launch their careers (Janovy & Major, 2009). More than 90% of FSMLs offer undergraduate training, including formal courses, research and service internships, and field trips (OBFS, n.d.). Furthermore, of the 72% of FSMLs that run undergraduate research programs, half of them reported an increase in undergraduate enrollment over the previous ten years (Hodder, 2009). As undergraduate enrollment in field courses continues to increase, positive experiences at FSMLs have the opportunity to be "catalysts" (Zavaleta et al., 2020, p. 953) for STEM careers building scientific self-efficacy, enhancing a students' sense of belonging in the scientific community, and strongly shaping students' major choice and interest in graduate school (O'Brien et al., 2020; Zavaleta et al., 2020).

Although positive experiences have the opportunity to be transformative for students, negative experiences at FSMLs may have similarly strong adverse effects on the trajectory of early-career researchers, especially students. Individual FSML practices may lead to a toxic workplace culture due to factors like isolated environments, lack of resources, and legacies of historic exclusion (see McDermott, Gee, & May, chapter 1). For instance, due to the isolated nature of many FSMLs, researchers may be more vulnerable to becoming the target of harassment or violence (Gluckman, 2018). Recent surveys of biological anthropologists indicate that harassment is commonly experienced in field-based settings (Clancy et al., 2014). Moreover, major news outlets have reported that women in the U.S. National Parks system experience rampant sexual harassment (Gilpin, 2016). Many women in this setting found that the combination of isolation within the park and a lack of willingness by management to address the problem created a hostile workplace environment. Furthermore, the Department of the Interior filed a report in 2016 demonstrating that administrators in the River District of the Grand Canyon had been aware of harassment targeting women employees and had done nothing to address it (Gilpin, 2016).

Similarly, people from minoritized backgrounds and women have historically been excluded from participating in the field of science (O'Brien et al., 2020). This has led to an underrepresentation of women and people of color in positions of power and leadership within the sciences and specifically at FSMLs (Anadu et al., 2020; Jensen et al., 2021). The result of this underrepresentation has been bullying, feelings of exclusion, and physical and sexual harassment (Demery & Pipkin, 2021; Halsey et al., 2020; Jensen et al., 2021). People who are already subject to discrimination based on their identity may be more likely to be targeted by these behaviors in isolated environments (Cech & Waidzunas, 2021). Non-white scientists routinely experience racial discrimination in field settings, both from coworkers and from local communities encountered when working in remote areas (Halsey et al., 2020; Viglione, 2020).

However, diversity (e.g., gender, sexual orientation, race, ethnicity) in science is invaluable. Cutting-edge research and scientific success have been found to increase when diversity increases. More diverse teams outperform homogeneous teams, even when the homogeneous teams are composed of individuals that have a relatively greater ability than the more diverse team (Swartz et al., 2019). Diverse teams have unique backgrounds and experiences that influence how they view and tackle problems which result in creative solutions to interdisciplinary societal challenges, like climate change adaptation. Therefore, the exclusion of historically minoritized groups may hinder innovation in STEM going forward.

While experiences at FSMLs may improve careers, the toxic atmospheres at some of these workplaces may exacerbate existing inequalities in the

STEM workforce. And, although negative experiences at FSMLs are becoming increasingly recognized (Demery & Pipkin, 2021; Flowers et al., 2021; Halsey et al., 2020; Jensen et al., 2021), less is known about how these experiences affect the career trajectories of early-career professionals or retention of professionals from diverse backgrounds in STEM. Understanding how experiences at FSMLs affect career trajectories is crucial for building a more inclusive community of field researchers and creating an inclusive community in which *all* field researchers feel valued and respected improves the likelihood of scientific success.

Weick's Sensemaking

One way in which communication scholars have sought to understand workplace culture is through Weick's (1995) sensemaking theory. Previous research has argued that sensemaking and culture are intertwined on multiple levels (Dougherty & Smythe, 2004; Weick, 2001). Weick posits that shared experiences through processes of sensemaking create a shared understanding of organizational culture. Through the telling and processing of stories and experiences, people create and sustain an organization's culture.

In regards to FSMLs, there may be two layers of organizational culture impacting students' experiences: the culture of the individual field station and the greater national/international field-based research community. Both may have significant impacts on students' experiences and subsequent trajectories. Thus, Weick's (1995) sensemaking provides a useful framework for understanding cultures that foster positive versus negative experiences for students. Weick (1995) argues that there are seven properties to sensemaking: identity, retrospection, ongoing, extracted cues, enactment, social, and plausibility. *Identity* "suggests that organizational actors come to know themselves based on their interactions with others" (Dougherty & Smythe, 2004, p. 965). The second property, *retrospection*, explains that people make sense of events after they occur. Sensemaking is an *ongoing* process with history and past experiences influencing present and future understanding of events and is based on extracted cues from the surrounding environment. *Enactment* "suggests that organizational actors not only act within an environment but also that they are a part of that environment" (Dougherty & Smythe, 2004, p. 965). Finally, sensemaking is based on *plausibility*. In other words, an event or experience must seem reasonable within the historical and contemporary context of the organization and the organization's culture. Overall, sensemaking provides a useful framework for understanding how organizational culture within FSMLs can result in positive or negative experiences. Previous research has used Weick's sensemaking to understand how organizational cultures can perpetuate sexual harassment (Doughtery & Smythe, 2004) and the reinforcement of power and gender structures (Long & Mills, 2010; Mills & Mills, 2000, 2017).

Current Issue

As scholarly research (Demery & Pipkin, 2021; Flowers et al., 2021; Halsey et al., 2020; Jensen et al., 2021) and popular press (Alcalde & Subramaniam, 2020; Barber et al., 2020) bring to light the systemic issues faced inside and outside of academia, it becomes even more important to understand the experiences of students in field-based institutions. Therefore, through the lens of Weick's (1995) sensemaking, we sought to understand the factors that impact positive and negative student experiences at FSMLs guided by the research questions: *What are the experiences of students at FSMLs? What factors contribute to negative versus positive experiences for these students?*

METHODS

Recruitment, Population, and Protocol

The data analyzed for this study was collected via an anonymous Institutional Review Board (IRB) approved survey distributed internationally to ecological professionals (students, federal employees, technicians, professors, etc.) who had been or are still a part of the field-based STEM community. The survey was distributed broadly to ecological professionals through individual social media networks (i.e., Facebook, Instagram, and Twitter), direct postings to broad scientific listservs, universities, NGOs, email invitations to colleagues and department chairs of FSMLs, and requests sent to organizations and societies that focused on diversity and inclusion practices in field-based STEM fields (n = 60 organizations/listservs/emails contact in total).

We used the Qualtrics survey software to compose and distribute our survey. The survey was piloted before being released in two phases. The first release phase was open from January 21, 2021, until February 16, 2021, and was open to anyone that previously or currently self-identified as a member of the field-based STEM community and/or FSMLs. The survey was re-released from April 19, 2021, until May 3, 2021, and was sent to a new set of professional organizations in an attempt to receive a diverse sample of responses. No compensation or incentives were offered for participation in the survey. All respondents were required to read the informed consent statement before beginning the survey and participants were able to exit the survey at any point in time with no consequences.

Our survey included a mix of open-ended, sliding scale, multiple-choice, and choose-all-that-apply style questions. The survey opened by collecting information on the participant's career stage, field of specialization, and their relationship to FSMLs. We then asked participants to reflect on and describe their best and worst experiences at field-based institutions and whether these experiences affected their career trajectory. With regard to positive and negative experiences at FSMLs, we asked respondents to identify the role of workplace culture, support in different forms, and characteristics of the field-based setting in the quality of their experiences. The survey closed by asking participants to provide general demographic information, such as gender identity, level of education, country of residence, racial and/or ethnic identities. For all responses, a "*I prefer not to say*" or leave blank option was available for an opt-out in case respondents did not want to share this information.

Qualitative Analysis

Once data collection had closed, we coded the data using qualitative thematic coding (Miles et al., 2013). We only analyzed responses in which the respondent agreed to the informed consent and completed the survey, which totaled 402. Due to the high volume of responses and the number of questions asked in the survey, data that did not answer the research questions posed in this chapter were left out of the manuscript. We read through responses to the following survey questions, as well as the demographic data collected: "*What factors do you perceive as contributing to incidents of an unhealthy, unsupportive, or otherwise negative workplace culture?*" and "*If you experienced a healthy, supportive or otherwise positive workplace culture and chose to continue pursuing your career in sciences, what factors contributed to your positive experience?*" We individually coded the open-ended responses assigning "symbolic meaning to the descriptive information compiled" (Miles et al., 2013, p. 71-72). We created as many categories to characterize the data as possible before moving to a second level of coding, where we each generated and identified overarching patterns to describe the data (Miles et al., 2013), and finally met to discuss our findings. We engaged in collaborative sensemaking, to establish the main themes that described participant responses. Once the themes were identified, representative quotes from participants were chosen to exemplify each theme.

RESULTS

A total of 402 individuals completed the informed consent and the survey. Demographic data including gender identity, age, and racial identity can be found in tables 7.1–7.3 in appendix A. To answer the research question, we generated five main themes from the dataset. With these themes, we sought to highlight the positive and negative experiences of students who visit, volunteer, or are employed at FSMLs and to understand how these experiences affected them. In this section, we address each theme: Workplace culture, Inequity, Communication, Relationships, and Support.

WHAT ARE THE EXPERIENCES OF STUDENTS AT FSMLS? WHAT FACTORS CONTRIBUTE TO NEGATIVE VERSUS POSITIVE EXPERIENCES FOR THESE STUDENTS?

Workplace Culture

We define workplace culture as the culmination of attitudes, beliefs, and behaviors that contribute to the atmosphere in a workplace. The main components of workplace culture are leadership, communication, management, workplace practices, policies, philosophies, and people. The mission, values, and vision of a workplace also contribute to the workplace culture.

In a healthy workplace culture, employee insight is valued, and employee behaviors and organizational policies are aligned with the overall goals of the organization while considering the well-being of individuals. Workplace culture can impact individual attitudes, work-life balance, health, growth opportunities, and overall job satisfaction. Unfortunately, aspects of culture that can lead to negative experiences, such as bullying, peer pressure, and information hoarding occur in many workplaces. From participant responses, two subthemes emerged related to workplace culture that contributed to positive and negative experiences at FSMLs, most of which were related to unspoken norms and workplace practices and values.

Unspoken Norms

Unspoken norms refer to unofficial rules of conduct that members of the community are expected to know without being told. Often, unspoken norms and participants' experiences were intertwined with expectations surrounding alcohol. For example, one of the unspoken norms participants frequently mentioned was the expectation that members of the field station will engage in alcohol consumption among colleagues, often to excess. Respondents noted feeling negatively affected by "heavy drinking culture," "alcohol/partying culture," "unsafe alcohol practices," and one person said that "in general those in charge had an unstated but widely known 'don't ask, don't tell' attitude especially toward alcohol consumption." Conversely, those with positive experiences enjoyed a culture in which "no drinking means no drinking," and the FSMLs that "ha[d] socializing [opportunities] not centered around drinking." Unspoken norms had the ability to significantly impact a student's experience for better or worse.

Another unspoken norm is the celebration of overwork, and the idea that resting or taking time off should be discouraged. Participants in our survey said they were negatively affected by "the idea that overworking oneself should be applauded." In a workplace with this sort of culture, people who overwork themselves are rewarded, even when they harm themselves in the process by not taking the time they need to rest. Similarly, another unspoken norm that was mentioned by participants was the idea that people should quietly endure bullying or other abusive behaviors. Participants noted that in these workplace cultures, bullying and other abusive behavior were thought to be something that everyone has had to go through, and therefore no one should complain about it. We often call this "hazing." For example, one participant said, "Hurt people, hurt people. I imagine that P.I.s [principal investigators] who have not received help in their past probably think harmful behaviors toward students is normal and thus perpetuate it." Supervisors who were hazed early in their careers perpetuated the cycle of abuse, and the idea that hazing is something everyone must endure becomes an unspoken norm. This behavior may often lead to negative workplace experiences.

Workplace Practices/Values

Under workplace practices and values, participants identified two distinct factors that impacted their experiences: (i) treatment of staff, visitors, and junior employees and (ii) safety and accountability.

Treatment of staff, visitors, and junior employees. Many field-based work environments employ a number of seasonal staff. For example, at Rocky Mountain Biological Laboratory in Gothic, Colorado, almost all employees only work in the summer months, as the laboratory is very difficult to access during the snowy winter months (RMBL, 2021). This is an extreme example; at many field stations, there is a core staff who work at the facility year-round, and a larger group of seasonal employees who change year-to-year.

Respondents identified the treatment of seasonal and junior staff as an element of workplace culture that affected the quality of their experience. For example, some respondents noted that they were discouraged by being treated as "just an undergraduate" or "just seasonals [*sic*]." Seeing year-round staff treat the "visiting" scientists as if they are the "other" often negatively impacted their FSML experience. Another respondent noted that "people not from the main institution were treated as outsiders." Employees felt that they were not valued and had negative experiences as a result. Similarly, participants reported that high turnover in staff indicated a potentially negative workplace culture. How staff and early-career scholars are treated in the workplace goes a long way toward creating a positive or negative culture.

In addition to the way FSML employees were treated, the treatment from researchers in leadership roles had a large impact on students' experiences. For example, one respondent noted, "some P.I.s looked down on facilities staff and some facilities staff would lash out or otherwise mistreat/belittle researchers." FSMLs, like other scientific workplaces, tend to have a hierarchical structure, with the PI being the head of the research group and having a great deal of influence over the culture of the group. Another respondent said, "The leaders of the field station, PI or otherwise, have a huge impact on this [workplace culture]. They set the tone of respect or disrespect for the rest of the people there." As PIs and year-round staff often act as role models for incoming researchers and community members, it is vital that everyone from undergraduates to seasonal staff to directors be treated with respect. Participants noted that a FSML's attention to facilitating a respectful workplace for all community members (i.e., supporting staff, visitors, researchers, students, etc.) was crucial for a positive experience. Although there may be many staff and researchers transitioning in and out of a FSML, participants mentioned that how these transitions were handled was important for cultivating a sense of respect within the community. Participants noted how one person can make a significant difference in the climate and culture of a FSML and that the treatment of community members, in general, tended to affect how open or closed, productive or destructive, a FSML culture could be.

Safety and accountability. Second, the level of emphasis on safety and accountability in a FSML's culture played a large role in participants' experiences at the station. Personal safety in a field-based setting ranges from direct, physical safety from injury on the job, and mental and emotional safety from harassment or other potential harms by FSML employees, other FSML visitors, or members of the local community. A lack of safety for employees, or a lack of prioritizing safety, can contribute to negative workplace experiences. One respondent described the following situation:

> I have had incidents where I had to stay alone overnight in a trailer, working in a site where police found a dead body, encountering creepy men with guns, watching a car fall off a cliff adjacent to my field site, etc. Part of these issues arise from feeling unsafe when doing fieldwork alone in remote areas.

This quote describes the physical, psychological, and emotional toll that a lack of safety prioritization can take on staff. Especially in remote locations, feelings of unease may be amplified resulting in long-term negative impacts for staff, students, and researchers.

Furthermore, when problems arise that affect the safety of FSML members, how these problems are addressed by management can have a major effect on the community. When complaints are ignored or mishandled, community members perceive that their safety is not a priority to leadership. As one respondent wrote, "[The] university being unsupportive of student complaints and ignoring harassment" led to negative FSML experiences and not feeling valued by the university or FSML leadership. Other respondents wrote, a "lack of infrastructure to handle complaints of harassment," being "generally dismissive in response to complaints [of] misconduct," and "no safety protocols" all contributed to an unhealthy workplace environment.

Alternatively, when safety and accountability are prioritized, respondents stated that it contributed to positive workplace experiences. As one participant wrote, "In terms of safety, the field station had a zero tolerance policy for harassement [*sic*]" and "safety was a high priority in action as well as in words." This was echoed by another participant who noted the value of "open and clear communication about safety" in creating a positive FSML experience.

Inequity

An important and widely encompassing topic, we define inequity to be the actual or perceived unfair treatment, access, opportunity, and advancement based on identities such as gender, racial identity, sexual orientation, religious beliefs, and more. This includes the structural barriers, microaggressions, discrimination, harassment, and implicit biases that prevent the full participation of underrepresented and historically marginalized groups in STEM. Here we use the term underrepresented to refer to minoritized groups that include Black, Indigenous, and People of Color (BIPOC), Lesbian, Gay, Bisexual, Transgender, Queer/or Questioning, Intersex, and Asexual/Ally (LGBTQIA+), and all people discriminated against based on ethnicity, gender, sexual orientation, economic class, disability status, religion, and/or those that are at the intersection of any of these identities. Relative to the U.S. population, individuals from these backgrounds are underrepresented in STEM at all career stages (Bernard & Cooperdock, 2018; National Science Foundation NSF, 2019). From our dataset, we identified three important subthemes of inequity: discrimination, harassment, and bias.

Discrimination

Minoritized students at FSMLs can often face discrimination and "othering" that can affect their personal safety, mental health, and professional development (Demery & Pipkin, 2020). In the context of our results, discrimination encompasses the inequitable treatment of different categories of people based on race, age, sexual orientation, etc. Results from our survey indicate that the prevalence of discrimination at FSMLs contributes to negative student experiences. For example, one respondent noted that the "willful ignorance [to] confront the racism, sexism, and homophobia present" negatively affected their experience. Multiple respondents noted that "PIs show favoritism" and this could lead to "unequal pay for equal jobs." Similarly, participants felt that coworkers were treated differently for the same actions, highlighting favoritism, as well as "sexism and ageism for younger women in workplace culture." Some FSMLs still feel like an "old boys club, [where] women [are] less (or not) welcome." Overall, outward discrimination occurred as "transphobia, homophobia, [and] ableism" and "derogatory remarks and subtly expressed negative attitudes towards people on the basis of race, gender, ethnicity, low SES [socio-economic status]."

In addition to outward discrimination, participants noted that there were also less intentional, systematic discrimination that occurred. Participants described a "general lack of acknowledgement [*sic*] of equity and inclusion issues," which led to instances of exclusion. One participant explained, "[My] supervisor did not consider me for a promotion because I was perceived to be 'too this or that' but I think it was due to ingrained racism and perceptions of professionalism in a field-based position." This was reiterated by another participant who stated, "in retrospect I can recall instances when I observed the one student of color excluded or slighted by peers." Other systematic discrimination included a "lack of diversity in PIs/other leadership roles" and "poor planning and organization, issues with accessibility for disabled individuals." Overall, these instances led to a perception of discrimination against anyone outside of a cis-gender, white, male, middle-class identity, fostering "a community that does not support women, gender minorities, and BIPOC in their respective fields."

In contrast, a "workplace culture that values identities and celebrates contributions by diverse staff," exhibits "cultural competency," and has "women in leadership positions" contributed to positive experiences at FSMLs. Moreover, "the ability to participate as an equal" stood out as a way to promote a "sense of belonging" and inclusion within the FSML community. Feeling a sense of belonging in Ecology and Evolutionary Biology (EEB) has been shown to have a large impact on minoritized and underrepresented students' postgraduate pursuits (O'Brien et al., 2020).

Harassment

A diverse scientific community provides value to the wider research community as a whole, yet barriers to success still unintentionally and intentionally exist, like harassment. We define harassment as all the repeated unwelcome conduct that evolves from discriminatory behaviors, which are detrimental to an individual's well-being. Similar to discrimination, harassment, especially sexual harassment, had negative impacts on students' experiences in FSMLs. For example, as one participant stated, "the Chief scientist sexually harassed most of the female students and there is no way to deal with that since he is the person you are supposed to bring issues to . . . no way to look up resources." Unfortunately, this experience was not unique nor isolated, as many other respondents echoed these sentiments stating that "I was harassed and then felt trapped by the very remote nature of the place" and "I was harassed by one of the students and had no one to report it to. When I did report it to the general administrator at the lab, I was ignored and told to suck it up."

Participants felt that factors such as isolation, lack of reporting structures, living and working with their harasser, and a lack of community support exacerbated the incidents of harassment. Participants frequently noted that the remoteness of many FSMLs, as well as the current leadership "as perpetrators of harassment, lack of recognition or consequences for harassers" and "universit[ies] being unsupportive of student complaints and ignoring harassment" intensified the negative impacts of harassment. Furthermore, one participant wrote that they experienced "harassment outside of the workplace by someone from the workplace and having to live and work with them in an environment where everyone is around each other all of the time" was difficult and contributed to a negative field experience. One quote in particular sums up participants' stark experiences with harassment: "We were typically pretty good about not going out by ourselves during the night, but we did not anticipate it during the day. I think I would have personally appreciated a heads up about this safety concern." Here, the participant makes it clear they did everything you are *supposed* to do to avoid being sexually harassed.

In cases where FSMLs defined expectations and boundaries for the community, participants noticed and remembered these initiatives for the positive contributions it had on their experiences. For example, factors that contributed to positive student experience included "clearly set expectations and goals" and "leadership setting clear and safe boundaries for everyone and then sticking to those boundaries." Additionally, multiple stations made it known that there was "a zero tolerance policy for harassment." Participants also noted that the ability to "receiv[e] support from station managers when having a negative experience" contributed to a healthy, supportive experience. One participant also highlighted that leadership "ma[de] a special effort to champion people from underrepresented (historically excluded) groups." Creating a safe environment to support and "celebrat[e] successes" together as a community fostered a positive atmosphere. Finally, positive experiences encompassed a myriad of these factors best summed up through one response,

> We were all mandated to complete a sexual harassment training prior to arriving at the field station. Additionally, we were briefed on who the Title IX officer was. There was also a diversity committee that worked to ensure there was an inclusive environment at the station.

Bias

Finally, bias played a major role in participants' feelings of otherness and greatly impacted their experiences at FSMLs. In our analysis, bias is the prejudice or inclination for or against something or someone. Biases, whether explicit or implicit, can be either positive or negative but regardless of mental shortcuts can result in prejudgments that lead to impulsive decisions or even escalate to discriminatory practices. Some participants encountered gender-based, age-based, and race-based biases. For those with intersectional identities, the effects of multiple biases may intensify the negative experiences they encounter.

As one participant wrote, "macho attitudes of technicians & vessel crews can be toxic toward female students." Another shared, "They disrespect me because I am (relatively) young, I am a woman, and I am a student (even as a PhD student)." In addition to macho attitudes, another participant stated that a "lack of diversity and cultural literacy on the part of fellow interns and some staff members" contributed to bias in the workplace and negative FSML experiences. This lack of diversity and cultural literacy was echoed by two other participants who stated, "They [FSML leadership] made it extremely difficult to work due to my immigration status," and "culturally tone-deaf authority figures" contributed heavily to a negative FSML experience. Furthermore, behavior at some FSMLs creates an environment in which underrepresented groups in the sciences are "othered" or "tokenized." Conscious and unconscious biases permeate FSML environments and compound negative experiences.

Communication

The third overarching theme that emerged from the dataset was communication. We define communication as the process of exchanging information, verbally or nonverbally, between people, groups, and/or institutions. Open and effective communication is a vital component of healthy workplace environments, and the results of our survey further support this idea. Many respondents referred to communication and its role in defining their experiences. For example, many participants identified a lack of communication as detrimental to their experience, stating a "lack of communication and lack of management with clear goals, expectations, resource management" and "not being open about expected number of hours/pay prior to job" led to confusion and tension between staff and management. In general, unclear expectations, whether to do with pay, working hours, the purpose of the research, or the tasks that the person was expected to complete, contributed to negative workplace experiences.

In addition to a lack of clear communication with leadership, participants also noted that unclear communication and policies from the university, as well as the FSML, added to negative experiences. For example, a respondent identified a "lack of communication and planning, no emergency plan in place . . . exploit[ation] of the personnel and making them work unpaid overtime" contributed most significantly to their negative experience. The most commonly noted negative experiences were due to "absent PI," "unresponsive PI," and overall a "lack of guidance with research and unresponsive administration." Finally, "not acknowledging their [students'] efforts and passion" led to a lack of support and feelings of burnout.

In contrast, positive experiences were often connected to "open communication." One respondent stated that the PI's "genuine interest in my goals and life plans" contributed positively to their research experience. This sentiment was echoed through many of the responses. Furthermore, "good communication between all staff levels" and "clear communication . . . clear goals and expectations" highlight the value of open communication in the FSML workplace. Fostering an environment that allows for open communication ensures that students "fe[el] comfortable asking questions" and "admitting mistakes" creates a positive experience and a safe workplace environment. These environments also present opportunities for professional development as students learn from mistakes in a welcoming setting.

Relationships

The fourth overarching theme that emerged from the survey responses was the impact of relationships on experiences. Relationships are interpersonal connections that have important implications for not only the individuals but also for the organizations where they are developed. Relationships can be multifaceted and complex. They can be both positive and negative and exist inside or outside of the organization and can directly affect productivity, efficiency, creativity, and decision-making. They can also affect the retention of early-career professionals, who may be more likely to stay on a STEM career path if they have strong interpersonal relationships to support them on this path. Quality relationships lead to better experiences for students at FSMLs. For example, one respondent noted that "my advisor has provided very excellent mentoring to me" at a place where they had a positive FSML experience. In addition to positive experiences with advisors and mentors, relationships among peers at FSMLs can contribute to positive outcomes of student experiences. For example, participants noted that peers who were open to collaboration and helping each other greatly enhanced their FSML experience.

Although relationships can have long-term positive impacts on student retention in STEM, toxic relationships can have the inverse effect. A common theme that respondents referred to when describing negative relationship experiences was that a supervisor or PI was absent, physically or in terms of mentorship, during their time working at a FSML. This often left students feeling abandoned and unappreciated. Additionally, respondents identified inappropriate behaviors that occurred between students or employees and supervisors, which contributed to negative workplace experiences and relationships. At one FSML, "It is accepted that on occasion some senior researcher would skinny dip with students or harass them." Similarly, another respondent spoke of "general knowledge of specific people (faculty, postdoc) known to have sex with undergrads at the field station." The role of a PI, manager, or mentor is extremely important in many students' careers, from providing research opportunities to giving career advice. When these relationships were taken advantage of, students reported negative FSML experiences. Furthermore, in some FSMLs, students found that their peers were competitive and did not help each other with research. Competitive atmospheres tended to contribute to negative environments, as these environments tended to foster less peer-to-peer support.

Boundaries are important for healthy relationships, and a lack of respect for others' boundaries can contribute to a hostile workplace environment and relationships, while clear, respected boundaries help students and workers feel comfortable conducting their research and connecting with community members. In our survey, in response to our question asking about positive experiences, one respondent said, "Openness, trust, and someone in leadership setting clear and safe boundaries for everyone and then sticking to those boundaries" was a vital part of cultivating their positive experience at a FSML. Conversely, having "no physical or emotional privacy" contributed to negative experiences. In addition, all FSMLs are embedded in local communities, and sometimes, whether due to previous grievances, lack of mutual respect or other factors, there may be hostility between the local community and the community at the FSML. One respondent stated that "the relationship between the field station and the surrounding community was unhealthy/not well built," which contributed to their negative experience. Relationships of all kinds, not just interpersonal relationships, can impact the culture and climate fostered at a FSML. In general, boundaries must be used to cultivate positive relationships among peers, with mentors/leadership and with local communities.

Support

The final theme we identified from our survey was the importance of support. Support is the perception that one is cared for, respected, and valued. Social support consists of three main categories: (1) instrumental support (financial, infrastructure), (2) emotional support (nurture), and (3) informational support (advice). Social support can be measured by the difference between perceived and actual assistance received within a social network. Participants emphasized that the level of support they perceived to receive was crucial in determining if they had a positive or negative experience at a FSML. Overall, the most supportive and positive workplace experiences occurred when all three forms of support were met for students. No one form of support may be more important than another as students' experiences at FSMLs are very diverse and complex.

Instrumental Support

Under the category of instrumental support, participants mentioned that sufficient pay and adequate facilities were key elements that respondents said contributed to positive and negative workplace experiences. One respondent said that "exploiting the personnel and making them work unpaid overtime, but not acknowledging their efforts and passion" contributed to a negative workplace environment. When staff are not paid appropriately, the lack of support leads to both resentment and struggles to remain financially solvent, which retracts from students' ability to have positive outcomes as a result of their experience. However, when staff are paid adequately for their time and receive fair time off, they feel appreciated and valued by FSML leadership and the larger community.

Emotional and Mental Support

Emotional support from supervisors and other students can be just as important as monetary and instrumental support. Many respondents who reported positive workplace experiences described receiving emotional support, such as "Supportive mentorship that allows for mistakes to be made while providing the resources to succeed." A respondent went into great detail to say that FSMLs that show "support for all students" and that "recogn[ize] that 'success' and 'struggle' are mutli-faceted [*sic*] and everyone has some successes and some struggles, and supporting people in their struggles and celebrating their success" contributed to their positive FSML experience. An environment that supports students through highs and lows helps foster a sense of community and deepens positive experiences.

Informational Support

For students and early-career professionals working at FSMLs, the ability to gain new skills and learn new scientific concepts can be key for the development of their careers moving forward. For some students at FSMLs, they are expected to complete tasks without being given much context or opportunity to learn new concepts; they are essentially treated as a source of labor. In better workplace experiences, however, students have the opportunity to learn and grow professionally, whether through learning from their supervisor, helping with a variety of research projects, or by being given the opportunity to develop a research project from scratch. For example, respondents with positive workplace experiences described "freedom to conduct experiments how I see fit." Additionally, career support was often an element of positive workplace experiences; respondents described mentors who invested in furthering their students' careers. For example, "they constantly provided information about outside opportunities in the field and other events that would help booster [*sic*] our networking and education, such as conferences, meetings, etc."

DISCUSSION

Through the use of Weick's sensemaking (1995), we were able to ask participants to reflect on the factors that contributed to positive and negative experiences while at FSMLs. Our findings indicate that there are stark differences in student experiences from one FSML to another. Although field-based experiences have been shown to increase scientific self-efficacy and retention (Hodder, 2009; Zavaleta et al., 2020), some of the experiences collected in this study show that negative field-based experiences can have detrimental consequences. From identity-based discrimination and sexual harassment to unequal pay and a lack of mentorship, the remote and isolating nature of FSMLs has the potential to exacerbate negative student experiences. Therefore, from this data we suggest two practical implications/recommendations for improving student experiences at FSMLs: (1) the role of communication in the culture cultivated by leadership and colleagues and (2) student awareness of rights and resources.

The Role of Communication in the Culture Cultivated by Leadership

Findings from this study indicate that communication, verbal, nonverbal, and unspoken, plays a large role in the culture and climate cultivated at FSMLs.

Furthermore, the community members present at a FSML can dramatically change people's perceptions of safety and comfort. Similar to the findings of Doughtery and Smythe (2004) and Long and Mills (2010), this study used Weick's (1995) sensemaking to understand how the reinforcement of inequitable structures of power, gender, and race was perpetuated in negative organizational climates. Participants noted that factors such as biased comments and discrimination based on ableism and sexual orientation that were allowed to occur in an organizational climate often lead to very negative workplace experiences. Seemingly small instances of discrimination over time lead to cumulative escalations in inequitable practices and have the potential to foster hostile, harassment-filled climates. Findings from this research indicate that in toxic FSML climates students often experienced all three levels of inequity: discrimination, harassment, and bias. This can lead to student burnout and contribute to the "leaky pipeline" of women and underrepresented peoples leaving STEM careers (Agee & Li, 2018; Blickenstaff, 2006; Hu et al., 2019).

Overall, FSMLs that do not actively prioritize abolishing inequitable policies and attitudes contribute to student disengagement in STEM, disproportionately impacting students from historically marginalized and minoritized backgrounds (Riegle-Crumb et al., 2019). An inclusive FSML will strive to eliminate instances of inequity, discrimination, harassment, and bias and instead foster a community that promotes a sense of belonging (Chaudhary & Berhe, 2020). As we move forward and address pressing societal issues, creating equitable and inclusive FSML experiences that are truly welcoming to a diversity of people in STEM is critical and will allow for diverse ideas and perspectives to flourish (Hofstra et al., 2020).

Therefore, our findings indicate that communication can play a crucial role in fostering more equitable, inclusive, and accessible FSML communities and in their overall functioning. Whether communication is used to perpetuate harassment or to facilitate effective mentorship, it is often the biggest factor influencing a student's positive or negative experiences at FSMLs and in STEM in general (Kisselburgh et al., 2009). From this knowledge, the FSML community is then challenged to engage with communication researchers, educators, and scholars to create community structures that facilitate clear, respectful communication with all community members.

Student Awareness of Rights and Resources

When in the field, students, staff, researchers, and faculty may not be aware of their rights and resources. As noted in chapter 1 of this volume

(McDermott et al., 2022), FSMLs can often function as places in-between with unclear policies and less formal interactions among peers, leadership, and staff. However, students have rights even in these untamed spaces. One way we can prepare students for the field is by communicating the rights and resources all students are entitled to. Borrowing from the field of human rights education (HRE),[2] we can engage in the "training, dissemination and information efforts aimed at the building of a universal culture of human rights through the imparting of knowledge and skills and the molding of attitudes directed [at] the strengthening of respect for human rights and fundamental freedoms" (United Nations, Office of the High Commissioner for Human Rights, 1997, p. 5). Similarly, making sure students have access to FSML-specific resources is vital for reporting structures and accountability. Before arriving on-site, students should be aware of the FSML leadership hierarchy, structures for reporting harassment, and should create plans for getting assistance in worst-case scenarios (i.e., a person in a position of power is the bully).

Moreover, another resource we can give students going into the field is to use boundaries to manage up and manage down their relationships with all FSML community members (Herman, 2008; Kras et al., 2015; Welsh et al., 2019). Managing up is the "process of consciously working with a supervisor to obtain the best possible results for you, your supervisor and your organization" and is "a deliberate effort to bring understanding and cooperation to a relationship between individuals who often have very different perspectives" (Herman, 2008, p. 46). In other words, managing up is the communicative process of setting boundaries with supervisors and mentors to maintain health working relationships. Oftentimes those in positions of power are expected to set the boundaries and tone for the relationship with subordinates, that is, managing down (Welsh et al., 2019). Managing up gives power back to subordinates (or students) by setting foundational relationship boundaries and expectations. Boundaries are important for healthy relationships, and a lack of respect for others' boundaries can contribute to a hostile workplace environment. In general, clear, respected boundaries help students and workers feel comfortable conducting their research (Welsh et al., 2019). Boundaries, established through clear communication, can greatly enhance the FSML work environment for students if they are aware of their rights and abilities to enact them (Bulger et al., 2007; Ezzedeen & Zikic, 2017; Kirby et al., 2003). Furthermore, as argued by Mitra & Buzzanell (2017), the ongoing negotiation of the tension between meaningful work and boundaries can lead to greater work satisfaction, especially in a positive workplace environment, in the long run.

LIMITATIONS AND FUTURE RESEARCH

Over the course of both survey releases we contacted ~60 FSML-related organizations representing a wide array of communities of students and professionals; however, this does not cover every FSML subdiscipline, community, and individual experience. Our sample also included only those FSML researchers who are members of their professional societies, participate in organizational listservs, or are active on social media, as well as those who volunteered to take the survey. Second, while our survey aims to understand factors that may cause professionals to leave the field, unfortunately, our survey may not have reached many professionals who left the field due to negative experiences. It remains a challenge to identify and contact professionally trained STEM individuals who have chosen or been forced to leave their fields. Additionally, we had a disproportionately large number of respondents who identify as white women, though our demographic data remains in balance with NSF statistics (NSF, 2019). While many groups are traditionally excluded from ecological research, our responses still included a disproportionate number of white respondents (appendix A, table 7.2).

Despite these limitations, our analysis is essential for moving the FSML and communication fields forward. Our results shed light on factors that contribute to positive student experiences at FSMLs, to increased student retention, and provide a guide for creating a welcoming, inclusive FSML culture. We encourage future research to expand on this topic, with a focus on the impacts of implemented strategies on student retention.

CONCLUSION

Field-based science has the potential to positively impact the long-term success of early-career professionals and students in STEM. Findings from this survey indicate that FSMLs can be transformative places in which collaboration, mentorship, and science flourish. FSMLs that do not seek out ways to increase equity, inclusion, accessibility, and diversity, however, may foster negative cultural climates that can lead to detrimental field experiences for students. Therefore, it is imperative that FSMLs seek to create structures that facilitate positive FSML experiences, especially for women and underrepresented communities such as BIPOC and LGBTQIA+ members. Communication provides a stepping-stone for improving the cultural climate at FSMLs. By engaging in reflective practices, such as sensemaking, we can provide the tools necessary to begin acknowledging, educating, and holding FSMLs and those perpetuating negative behavior accountable for workplace discrimination, harassment, and bias.

APPENDIX A: PARTICIPANT DEMOGRAPHICS

Table 7.1 Gender Identities of Survey Respondents

Gender Identity	*Number of Respondents*	*Percentage of Respondents*
Woman	245	62.98
Man	125	32.13
Non-binary/non-conforming	11	2.83
Prefer not to respond	4	1.03
Not listed	4	1.03

Note. Out of 402 respondents, 389 answered this question, including those who chose "prefer not to respond." We assume the remaining survey respondents skipped the question either purposefully or accidentally. Percentages indicate percent of responses, not including those who skipped the question.
Source: Author data.

Table 7.2 Racial Identities of Survey Respondents

Racial Identity	*Number of Respondents*	*Percentage of Respondents*
White	281	81.69
Latinx/Hispanic	25	7.27
Mixed race	10	2.91
Black or African American	3	0.87
Asian or Pacific Islander	12	3.49
Indigenous	2	0.58
Prefer not to respond	8	2.33
Other	3	0.87

Note. Out of 402 respondents, 344 answered this question, including those who chose "prefer not to respond." We assume the remaining survey respondents skipped the question either purposefully or accidentally. Percentages indicate percent of responses, not including those who skipped the question.
Source: Author data.

Table 7.3 Ages of Survey Respondents

Age (Years)	*Number of Respondents*	*Percentage of Respondents*
18–24	53	14.02
24–34	171	45.24
35–44	66	17.46
45–54	32	8.47
55–64	23	6.08
65–74	24	6.35
75 or older	9	2.38

Note. Out of 402 respondents, 378 answered this question. We assume the remaining survey respondents skipped the question either purposefully or accidentally. Percentages indicate percent of responses, not including those who skipped the question.
Source: Author data.

NOTES

1. Listed alphabetically, the authors share equal primary authorship of this research and manuscript.
2. See Tibbitts & Fernekes (2011) for more information on Human Rights Education.

REFERENCES

Agee, E. A., & Li. Y. (2018). Fighting the leaky pipeline: Developing peer support for women in the earth and environmental sciences. *Michigan Journal of Sustainability, 6*(1), 67–76. http://dx.doi.org/10.3998/mjs.12333712.0006.107

Alcalde, C., & Subramaniam M. (2020, July 17). Women in leadership: Challenges and recommendations. *Inside HigherEd.* https://www.insidehighered.com/views/2020/07/17/women-leadership-academe-still-face-challenges-structures-systems-and-mind-sets

Anadu, J., Ali, H., & Jackson, C. (2020). Ten steps to protect BIPOC scholars in the field. *Eos*. https://doi.org/10.1029/2020eo150525

Barber, P. H., Hayes, T. B., Johnson, T. L., Márques-Magaña, L., & 10,231 signatories. (2020). Systemic racism in higher education. *Science, 369*(6510), 1140–1441. https://doi.org/10.1126/science.abd7140

Bernard, R. E., & Cooperdock, E. H. G. (2018). No progress on diversity in 40 years. *Nature Geoscience,* 11, 292–295. https://doi.org/10.1038/s41561-018-0116-6

Blickenstaff, J. C. (2006). Women and science careers: Leaky pipeline or gender filter. *Gender and Education, 17*(5), 369–386. https://doi.org/10.1080/09540250500145072

Bulger, C. A., Matthews, R. A., & Hoffman, M. E. (2007). Work and personal life boundary management: Boundary strength, work/personal life balance, and the segmentation-integration continuum. *Journal of Occupational Health Psychology, 12*(4), 365–375. https://doi.org/10.1037/1076-8998.12.4.365

Cech, E. A., & Waidzunas, T. J. (2021). Systemic inequalities for LGBTQ professionals in STEM. *Science Advances, 7*(3), eabe0933. https://doi.org/10.1126/sciadv.abe0933

Chaudhary, V. B., & Berhe, A. A. (2020). Ten simple rules for building an antiracist lab. *PLoS Computational Biology, 16*(10), e1008210. https://doi.org/10.1371/journal.pcbi.1008210

Clancy, K. B., Nelson, R. G., Rutherford, J. N., & Hinde, K. (2014). Survey of academic field experiences (SAFE): Trainees report harassment and assault. *PLoS One*, *9*(7), e102172. https://doi.org/10.1371/journal.pone.0102172

Demery, A. J. C., & Pipkin, M. A. (2021). Safe fieldwork strategies for at-risk individuals, their supervisors and institutions. *Nature Ecology & Evolution, 5*, 5–9. https://doi.org/10.1038/s41559-020-01328-5

Dougherty, D., & Smythe, M. J. (2004). Sensemaking, organization culture, and sexual harassment. *Journal of Applied Communication Research, 32*(4), 293–317. https://doi.org/10.1080/0090988042000275998

Ezzedeen, S. R., & Zikic, J. (2017). Finding balance amid boundarylessness: An interpretive study of entrepreneurial work-life balance and boundary management. *Journal of Family Issues, 38*(11), 1546–1576. https://doi.org/10.1177/0192513X15600731

Flowers, S. K., O'Connell, K., & McDermott, V. M. (2021). Crafting Field Station and Marine Lab Communities for Undergraduate Diversity, Equity, and Inclusion. *The Bulletin of the Ecological Society of America*, e01908. https://doi.org/10.1002/bes2.1908

Fournier, A. M. V., Holford, A. J., Bond, A. L., & Leighton, M. A. (2015). Unpaid work and access to science professions. *PLoS One, 14*(6), e0217032. https://doi.org/10.1371/journal.pone.0217032

Gilpin, L. (2016, December 15). The National Park service has a big sexual harassment problem. *The Atlantic*. https://www.theatlantic.com/science/archive/2016/12/park-service- harassment/510680/

Gluckman, N. (2018, July 15). Field sites are harassment hell. Here's how to improve them. *The Chronicle of Higher Education*. https://www.chronicle.com/article/field-sites-are-harassment-hell-heres-how-to-improve-them/

Halsey, S. J., Strickland, L. R., Scott-Richardson, M., Perrin-Stowe, T., & Massenberg, L. (2020). Elevate, don't assimilate, to revolutionize the experience of scientists who are Black, Indigenous and people of colour. *Nature Ecology & Evolution, 4*, 1291–1293. https://doi/org/10.1038/s41559-020-01297-9

Herman, B. K. (2008). Managing up: Dynamic following in an organizational setting. *The Physician Executive, 34*(1), 46–49.

Hodder, J. (2009). What are undergraduates doing at biological field stations and marine laboratories?. *BioScience, 59*, 666–672. https://doi.org/10.1525/bio.2009.59.8.8

Hofstra, B., Kulkarni, V. V., Munoz-Najar Galvez, S., H., B., Jurafsky, D., & McFarland, D. A. (2020). The diversity–innovation paradox in science. *Proceedings of the National Academy of Sciences, 117*(17), 9284–9291. https://doi.org/10.1073/pnas.1915378117.

Hu, Y., Ellis, R. J., Hewitt, B., Yang, A. D., Cheung, E. O., Moskowitz, J. T., Potts, J. R., Buyske, J., Hoyt, D. B., Nasca, T. J., & Bilimoria, K. Y. (2019). Discrimination, abuse, harassment, and burnout in surgical resident training. *The New England Journal of Medicine, 381*, 1741–1752. https://doi.org/10.1056/NEJMsa1903759

IPPC. (2017). Special Report on climate change, desertification, land degradation, sustainable land management, food security, and greenhouse gas fluxes in terrestrial Ecosystems (SR2). https://www.ipcc.ch/site/assets/uploads/2018/07/sr2_background_report_final.pdf

Janovy, J., & Major, K. M. (2009). Why we have field stations: Reflections on the cultivation of biologists. *BioScience, 59*(3), 217–222. https://doi.org/10.1525/bio.2009.59.3.6

Jensen, A. J., Bombaci, S. P., Gigliotti, L. C., Harris, S. N., Marneweck, C. J., Muthersbaugh, M. S., Newman, B. A., Rodriguez, S. L., Saldo, E. A., Shute, K. E., Titus, K. L., Williams, A. L., Yu, Z. W., & Jachowski, D. S. (2021). Attracting diverse students to field experiences requires adequate pate, flexibility, and inclusion. *BioScience, 71*(7), 757–700. https://doi.org/10.1093/biosci/biab039

Kirby, E. L., Golden, A. G., Medved, C. E., Jorgenson, J., & Buzzanell, P. M. (2003). An organizational communication challenge to the discourse of work and family research: From problematics to empowerment. In P. J. Kalbfleisch (Eds.), *Communication yearbook: 27* (pp. 1–43). Lawrence Erlbaum.

Kisselburgh, L. G., Berkelaar, B. L., & Buzzanell, P. M. (2009). Discourse, gender, and the meaning of work: Rearticulating science, technology, and engineering careers through communicative lenses. *Annals of the International Communication Association, 33*(1), 385–414. https://doi.org/10.1080/23808985.2009.11679089

Kras, K. R., Rudes, D. S., & Taxman, F. S. (2015). Managing up and down: Community corrections middle managers' role conflict ambiguity during organizational change. *Journal of Crime and Justice, 40*(2), 173–187. https://doi.org/10.1080/0735648X.2015.1085889

Long, B. S., & Mills, J. H. (2010). Workplace spirituality, contested meaning, and the culture of organization: A critical sensemaking account. *Journal of Organizational Change Management, 23*(3), 325–341. https://doi.org/10.1108/09534811011049635

McDermott, V., Gee, J., & May, A. (2022). Defining the role and value of FMSLs. In V. McDermott, J. Gee, & A. R. May (Eds.), *Women of the wild: Challenging gender disparities in field stations and marine laboratories* (pp. 3–15). Lexington Books.

Miles, M. B., Huberman, A. M., & Saldaña, J. (2013). *Qualitative data analysis: A methods sourcebook* (3rd ed.). SAGE.

Mills, J. H., & Mills, A. J. (2000). *Sensemaking and the gendering of organizational culture.* Proceedings at the ASAC-IFSAM Conference, Montreal, Quebec.

Mills, J. H., & Mills, A. J. (2017). Rules, sensemaking, formative contexts, and discourse in the gendering of organizational culture. In A. J. Mills (Eds.) *Insights and research on the study of gender and intersectionality in international airline cultures* (pp. 49–69). Emerald Publishing Limited.

Mitra, R., & Buzzanell, P. M. (2017). Communicative tensions of meaningful work: The case of sustainability practitioners. *Human Relations, 70*(5), 594–615. https://doi.org/10.1177/0018726716663288

National Research Council. (2014). Enhancing the value and sustainability of field stations and marine laboratories in the 21st century. *The National Academies Press.* https://doi.org/10.17226/18806

National Science Foundation, National Center for Science and Engineering Statistics. (2019). *Women, Minorities, and Persons with Disabilities in Science and Engineering: 2019* (NSF Special Report NSF 19-304). https://www.nsf.gov/statistics/wmpd.

O'Brien, L. T., Bart, H. L., & Garcia, D. M. (2020). Why are there so few ethnic minorities in ecology and evolutionary biology? Challenges to inclusion and the role of sense of belonging. *Social Psychology of Education, 23*(2), 449–447. https://doi.org/10.1007/s11218-019-09538-x

OBFS. (n.d.). *Field station and marine laboratories of the future: A strategic vision.* https://www.obfs.org/assets/docs/fsml_final_report.pdf

Riegle-Crumb, C., King, B., & Irizarry, Y. (2019) Does STEM stand out? Examining racial/ethnic gaps in persistence across postsecondary fields. *Educational Researcher, 48*(3), 133–144. https://doi.org/10.3102/0013189X19831006

RMBL. (2021). *Rates & fees*. https://www.rmbl.org/field-station-info/rates-and-fees/

Shukla, P. R., Skea, J., Calvo Buendia, E., Masson-Delmotte, V., Pörtner, H. O., Roberts, D. C., ... & Malley, J. (2019). *IPCC, 2019: Climate Change and Land: an IPCC special report on climate change, desertification, land degradation, sustainable land management, food security, and greenhouse gas fluxes in terrestrial ecosystems*.

Swartz, T. H., Palermo, A. S., Masur, S. K., & Aberg, J. A. (2019). The science of value of diversity: Closing the gaps in our understanding of inclusion and diversity. *Journal of Infectious Diseases, 220*, S33–S41. https://doi.org/10.1093/infdis/jiz174

Tibbitts, F., & Fernekes, W. (2011). Human Rights Education. In S. Totten, & J. E. Pederson (Eds.), *Teaching and studying social issues: Major programs and approaches* (pp. 87–117). Information Age Publishing.

Tydecks, L., Bremerich, V., Jentschke, I., Likens, G. E., & Tockner, K. (2016). Biological field stations: A global infrastructure for research, education, and public engagement. *BioScience, 66*(2), 164–171. https://doi.org/10.1093/biosci/biv174

United Nations, Office of the High Commissioner for Human Rights. (1997). *International plan of action for the decade of human rights education*. United Nations.

Viglione, G. (2020, August 24). Racism and harassment are common in field research – scientists are speaking up. *Nature*. https://www.nature.com/articles/d41586-020-02328-y

Welsh, E. T., Henderson, K. E., & Diehn, E. W. (2019). "Aren't bosses supposed to manage you?" A qualitative study managing your boss. *Journal of Managerial Issues, 31*(1), 65–84.

Weick, K. E. (1995). *Sensemaking in organisations*. Sage.

Weick, K. E. (2001). *Making sense of the organization*. Blackwell Publishers.

Zavaleta, E. S., Beltran, R. S., & Borker, A. L. (2020). How field courses propel inclusion and collective excellence. *Scientific Life, 35*(11), 953–956. https://doi.org/10.1016/j.tree.2020.08.005

Chapter 8

The Gift Relationship

How Mentoring Results in Success for Women in Field Station Leadership Roles

Sarah D. Oktay and Brian D. Kloeppel

INTRODUCTION

You can pick your ancestors, they don't all have to be the people related to you.

Leaders at field stations and marine labs (FSMLs) require a wide range of skills to successfully navigate the labyrinth of scientific, educational, operational, strategic, and political challenges needed for success in their job. These skills are rarely acquired via professional training, but rather gained over time through experience, reflection, and discussion. One critical type of relationship-building for leadership development is bi-directional mentor-mentee relationships. Mentees often have complex needs that evolve over the lifetime of their career. As such, some models of mentorship advocate going beyond a single mentor and instead emphasize the importance of mentor networks or webs, with mentorship evolving as the needs and aspirations of mentees change through career stages (Davies et al., 2021; Fogel, 2020; Montgomery, 2017). Additionally, some work environments are so niche that finding a representative mentor is "the professional equivalent of waiting for Prince Charming" (Sandberg, 2015, as cited by Scheinert, 2015, p. 7). Furthermore, women working in FSMLs may experience additional challenges due to remote locations, heavy workloads, and lack of representation, limiting access to and the availability of mentors.

FSMLs are small and circumscribed communities, often operating relatively independently and many times located in remote areas. As a result, access to representative mentorship opportunities can be limited. In addition, until recently, opportunities for women in leadership positions in field science were rare, impeded by the disparate ratio of women to men in natural science faculty and leadership positions (Makarova et al., 2019). Due to the complexities inherent within FSMLs, little is known about the role of mentorship in field station leadership development. Therefore, we sought to provide a better understanding and explore the access to and role of mentorship in the lives of women FSML community members.

We interviewed sixteen women in leadership positions across a variety of FSMLs in the United States, Mexico, and Costa Rica to determine how mentorship impacted their careers and what suggestions they had to facilitate success for the next generation of field station leaders. The interviewees identified the following as critical aspects of mentorships: (1) for career advancement and acquiring new skills in STEM; (2) access to female and Black, Indigenous, and People of Color (BIPOC) mentors provide more relevant support to women and underrepresented scientists; and (3) a combination of formal and informal networks and programs is needed to alleviate the lack of diversity in mentorship pools and capitalize on the unique skill sets of peers within FSMLs (Davies et al., 2021; Dennehy & Dasjuptor, 2017; Huang et al., 2000; Montgomery, 2017). From these findings and participants' suggestions, we provide recommendations for addressing the gender gap through formal and informal engagement using networks such as the Organization of Biological Field Stations (OBFS).

LITERATURE REVIEW

Structure of Mentorship

Mentorship as a construct is constantly evolving. From the structure of the mentor-mentee relationship to the functions it serves to support personal and professional development, mentorship is dynamic and impacted by many different internal and external forces. In this section, we review the relevant literature, highlighting the structure of mentor-mentee relationships, the functions it serves within a variety of different contexts, and the challenges women in STEM may encounter while working to build meaningful relationships with mentors.

Mentorship relationships are defined by four structural categories: dyads, triads, collectives, and networks. Dyads are the simplest and most traditional concept of mentorship between two people (Wanberg et al., 2006). This mentorship structure is still common practice in some STEM learning environments, such as undergraduate and graduate research and in clinical internships and residencies. However, this standard is changing (Buzzanell et al., 2015; Long et al., 2018; Montgomery, 2017). Mentoring is becoming more recognized in the academic realm, and often several mentors are necessary to guide scientific careers at all stages (Long et al., 2018; Fogel, 2021). With triads, the mentee is co-mentored by two people, introducing an additional resource for personal or professional development as a single mentor might not have the skillset or expertise to help the mentee with a particular project, relationship, or other areas of interest (Yun et al., 2016). Collective or group mentorship is similar to a lab group with more than one mentee, peer mentorship, and at least one mentor (Greco 2014). Finally, network mentorship is a mix-and-match of mentors, including peer mentors that do not necessarily interact directly with each other, but all work with the same mentee on various aspects of the mentee's career and life (DeCastro et al., 2013; Halvorson et al., 2015; Long et al., 2018).

Definition of Mentorship

There are many definitions of mentor and mentorship, adding layers of complexity to the mentor-mentee relationship and the important role it plays in leadership development. A quick Google search of "definition of mentorship" resulted in 8,960,000 results. Results reveal a complicated study area where academics, practitioners, and mentors/mentees not only challenge how mentorship is defined but how it is implemented in a variety of disciplines. While the researchers acknowledge these complexities, the goal of this research is to contribute a deeper understanding of how mentorship (dis)functions within the context of FSMLs, especially for women. As such, the researchers open this discussion with a broad definition of mentorship. Dumas (2020) defined mentorship in a traditional manner as "a reciprocal relationship between an advanced career professional and a protégé aimed at promoting the career development and fulfillment of both" (p. 167). This definition underscores the importance of the mentor(s), the mentee, and the relationship between the two or more. Although mentors and mentees may negotiate goals for the relationship, the focus is often on career development, which may include promotion, tenure, and leadership. Emerging in the mentorship literature is a growing debate related to role definitions: mentor vs. role model. Méndez-Morse (2004) expanded on the mentor versus role model definitions, noting the following:

> A role model was defined as someone whose characteristics or traits another person would want to emulate; a mentor was defined as someone who actively helps, supports, or teaches someone else how to do a job so that she will succeed. (p. 565)

Whether defined as a role model or mentor or whether a mentor serves as a role model, these strategic relationships play a critical role in professional development.

Research on the Role of Mentorship

Mentorship may serve a variety of different functions or roles for both the mentor and the mentee. In a professional context, mentors often provide career advice, access to networks, and strategic insights into how to achieve career goals with a specific organizational context. The mentor also may care for the other aspects of a mentee beyond their career, such as providing psychological and emotional support to help resolve personal challenges that may negatively impact the life and/or career of a mentee. In a more comprehensive sense, the mentor can serve as a "silent" partner (Fogel 2019), offering "behind-the-scenes" sort of advice, supporting a mentee who shares a similar identity and values.

A large body of literature demonstrates mentorship plays an important role in building people's career identities, self-efficacy, and retention within their field (Davies et. al, 2021; Eby & Allen, 2008; Méndez-Morse, 2004). Eby et al. (2008) performed a large meta-analysis of 106 studies to determine quantitatively if mentorship resulted in positive outcomes. They found a wide range of favorable behavioral, attitudinal, health-related, relational, motivational, and career outcomes for quality mentor-mentee relationships. Although the effect size was generally small, the most significant outcomes were observed in academic settings. Similar to Eby and Allen (2008), Estrada et al. (2018) found that quality mentorship and research experience occurring in the junior and senior years positively impacted students' science efficiency, identity, and values and led to an upward career trajectory for up to four years after graduation.

STEM Lagging Behind

Although mentorship has been shown to positively impact the recruitment and retention of diverse individuals, some disciplines and professional fields are still working to build positive mentoring programs and organizational cultures. A body of STEM-related research has long identified the "leaky pipeline" in which the number of doctoral receiving students is much greater than the number in academic positions which acts as a gender filter of sorts, sustaining the lack of representation for women across scientific disciplines (Blickenstaff, 2005). For example, Bernard and Cooperdock (2018) found that there was no progress in diverse doctoral graduates in geosciences from 1973 to 2016. In higher education, diversity decreases from undergraduate to graduate to faculty levels (Bernard & Cooperdock, 2018). Diversity in this context includes race, ethnicity, and gender (Ford et al., 2019). This "leaky pipeline" is not unique to geosciences and negatively impacts a majority of academic disciplines in the sciences. More starkly, however, this gap in diversity, leadership, and opportunity can be seen in the STEM fields. Collectively, the literature suggests:

> The current state of affairs suggests that once women enter STEM, they are faced with highly challenging and difficult circumstances that create uneven and extremely difficult conditions that may prevent them from succeeding and having healthy and positive work experiences. (Saxena et al., 2019, p. 509)

One solution may be an increased emphasis on and opportunity for mentorship. Research suggests women working in STEM who do not have an opportunity to connect with mentors receive fewer promotions and experience stalled organizational growth; conversely, the retention rate of women in STEM is higher in mentors who invest in long-term career goals of mentees (Saxena et al., 2019; Higgins & Constellations, 2001).

Mentoring Challenges at Field Stations

Research exploring the barriers for women in STEM and the opportunities afforded by mentorship often focuses on academic settings (Boag & Chardon, 2021; Dennehy & Dasgupta, 2017; Dumas, 2020; Hermann et al., 2016). Academic settings are the closest parallel for FSMLs, as some FSMLs are sponsored by and funded through institutions of higher learning; however, FSMLs as workplaces are unique and underresearched in the academic/scholarly literature, underscoring the importance of this research and further defining the role mentorship plays for women working in these environments. For instance, most field stations are isolated with proscribed and small communities, from one to a few employees (see chapter 1 by McDermott, Gee, & May in this edited volume for more information). Consequently, FSML cultures are driven by the demographics of the resident staff, and the representation of scientists from different backgrounds is often limited relative to other academic settings and STEM fields.

Field station environments present both advantages and challenges for mentorship. The relaxed environment and variety of incoming scientists and educators present opportunities for informal exchanges that are less available in academic or lab settings (see chapters 1 McDermott, Gee, & May, 4 Debinski, and 10 Struminger, Adame, & Shannan in this edited volume). Conversely, the separation of many field stations from the host institute or university can limit the availability of more formal networking and mentorship opportunities, such as professional society workshops or gatherings. Additionally, the workload, especially during peak field seasons or during accelerated field classes, can be exceptionally high, up to twelve hours or more per day which reduces the time available to network or build mentor relationships.

Current Issue

The professional practice of mentoring has progressed rapidly, and research has established the benefits of mentorships for success and job satisfaction from medicine to business to academia (Eby & Allen 2008; Eby et al. 2013). Although research has found that mentoring increases retention rates, little is known about the role of mentoring on leadership and career opportunity trajectory. Even less is known about the role of mentoring for women, especially women working in field-based STEM environments. Although advocacy groups, such as *The Association for Women in Science,* work to promote the full participation of women across all scientific fields through mentoring, education, and job opportunities (Fridkis-Hareli, 2011), FSMLs have additional layers of complexity that are not encountered in traditional academic settings or within laboratories. The need for more research is evident as women continue to be underrepresented, especially BIPOC in FSMLs (Davies et al., 2021). Gaensler (2018) found that setting objective goals to measure and implement diversity, equity, accessibility, and inclusion to attract and retain top talent is a critical trait to attract women and underrepresented individuals to field stations and marine laboratories, underscoring the urgency.

To address the gap in the literature and identify opportunities for mentorship for women working in FSMLs, the researchers were guided by the following research questions:

RQ1: How does mentorship facilitate career development (specifically for those in a FSML position)?
RQ2: What factors do women at field stations use or have used in the past to select mentors?
RQ3: How can we create mentorship roles/programs formally and informally (i.e., best practices) to support diversity and inclusion at field stations?

METHODS

Population and Sampling

To answer the research questions, qualitative research methods were used. A meta-literature review and sixteen interviews were conducted to answer the research questions and explore the influence of mentorship in women's careers at FSMLs. To be included in the sample, interviewees had to self-identify as women, be at least 18 years old, and have two or more years of experience working at FSMLs in roles that required some amount of supervisory duties (e.g., overseeing researchers, educators, interns, etc.).

We used our own personal networks to recruit participants. Specifically, we chose women in various stages of their careers at field stations ranging from those just starting out (minimum of two years) to women with decades of experience. We also specifically selected women of various ages at institutions that varied in size and were distributed throughout the United States, Mexico, and Costa Rica. A variety of FSMLs were selected, from large private foundations to FSMLs associated with research universities to smaller organizations associated with four-year colleges or stand-alone nonprofits. Using these selection criteria, we collected a diverse range of experiences.

Instrument

Data were collected using semi-structured interviews with a set of open-ended questions facilitated and recorded via Zoom calls. Semi-structured interviews allowed the subjects to more fully express themselves in a discussion format with the interviewer rather than a straightforward question and answer format. The informed consent document was shared with the subjects several weeks before the interview via email. All subjects agreed to be interviewed. After obtaining informed consent, we opened the interview with a rapport-building question to ease the participants into the interview process and establish open communication (Guillemin & Heggen, 2009). Each participant was asked to tell us a little bit about themselves as if they were explaining their position in a few sentences to a young scholar. All interviewees had previously met the interviewer (Sarah Oktay). Each interview subject was asked to provide their definition of mentorship to provide a shared context between the interviewer and the interviewee. The interview protocol included a total of 22 questions (Appendix A) designed to help each interviewee describe their experiences as mentors and as mentees. About 60% of the interviews extended 10 to 25 minutes beyond the allotted interview time of 45 minutes. Consequently, some interview questions were unaddressed, including how often to meet, for how long, and what type of settings worked best (Questions 12 and 13). No demographic data were collected to help avoid any discomfort associated with sharing personal aspects of identity to help promote disclosure (Bradimarte et al., 2010).

Qualitative Analysis

After all of the interviews had been conducted, the audio recording was transcribed using Zoom's transcription feature. The interviews resulted in approximately 1,600 minutes of audio and 231,850 words (approximately 925 pages double-spaced) of transcribed data. The sixteen interviews provided theoretical saturation to engage in qualitative analysis. Thematic coding was used to identify common themes shared by participants. The researchers coded for value themes and themes in verbal discourse (Lindlof & Taylor, 2017; Saldana, 2013). First, we coded the data into as many categories as possible using open coding. After the data had been coded into different categories, we compared key ideas within the data to organize the findings into larger, overarching categories. Using grounded theory and thematic framework provided by Corbin and Strauss (1990), these categories were reconfigured using axial coding to create new encompassing themes and answer the research questions. The researchers kept and discarded themes throughout the process, using thematic analysis and the research question to guide discovery. Quotes were pulled from the interview transcripts to exemplify the themes identified.

RESULTS AND DISCUSSION

Three research questions were addressed during the course of this study. The results showed that it was important to contextualize the characteristics and activities that delineated mentorship for each interviewee. The research questions elicited introspection, direct observations, specific advice, and recommendations for improving and expanding mentorship opportunities for women at FSMLs. A variety of themes were repeated by participants eventually reaching almost consensus-level agreement. Respondents identified the following themes as critical to facilitating career development: timing, altruism, and imposter syndrome. In addition, respondents identified the following selection criteria and traits to be considered when seeking out mentorship: integrity, trust, and respect; role models; and good vs. bad mentorship experiences. Lastly, respondents identified the following themes as critical to creating more opportunities for women working in FSMLs to access and benefit from mentorship: networking, tools, formal vs. informal, explicating barriers, and representation.

Definitions: What Is a Mentor?

The literature provides a spectrum of definitions for mentors from active to passive and peer-related to supervisor/supervisee (Dumas, 2020; Méndez-Morse, 2004); however, for the participants in the sample, the exercise of defining what a mentor is proved to be thought-provoking and elicited a wide range of responses from descriptions of formal mentor-mentee relations to stories of peer-to-peer or very informal mentoring/advice sessions. For example, several respondents mentioned receiving assistance "out of the blue" from unexpected mentors, for example, a "mentor can be hiding in the wings." Similarly, several people mentioned mentors that noticed when they were having difficulties, such as in writing proposals, finishing a thesis, or delegating duties. All respondents felt that a mentor should not be a mirror of who you are, but complement the abilities and teach skills that the mentee does not have or could not gain easily on her/their own. Interestingly, the simple act of asking these questions caused much reflection with many participants stating that they would be contacting their mentors to thank them and that they would be more mindful of their current mentoring relationships. The act of defining mentorship also was quite reflective as they realized many people served in a crucial mentorship-type service throughout their careers without being official mentors.

The definitions of mentorship the respondents shared included, "Providing other people with opportunities for growth in whatever way they want to grow." A "guide on the side rather than [a] sage on the stage." Several respondents felt mentors worked best as sounding boards. For example, one respondent said, "I think mentors are there to show the mentees options, to discuss the pros and cons of those options, and to provide pathways and discuss the implications of certain pathways." Mentors can be "someone who has looked out for you, supported you, maybe found money for you and presented opportunities to you; someone who clicks with you."

Many respondents were looking for deeply experienced individuals for mentors, for example, someone who "has been around the block . . . and can leave those breadcrumbs of hints on how to navigate specific situations." Although respondents said they had multiple lifetime mentors in supervisor or advisor roles, they preferred mentors who were "outside of a hierarchical relationship [not supervisors]," and they also looked for "people who do things you don't do well." In the end, the participants added to the over 8 million "hits" for mentorship, underscoring its complexity and value as both unique to the individual participants and relationship-based.

RQ1: How does mentorship facilitate career development (specifically for those in a FSML position)?

Mentorship is one of the most important factors in determining success and in learning about and taking advantage of new opportunities and advancing into leadership positions for the participants in the study. Specifically, respondents identified the following themes as critical to facilitating career development: timing, altruism, and imposter syndrome.

Timing

Each respondent felt very strongly that early mentoring and mentoring that occurred at critical times during their career made a significant impact, contributing to their success and ability to obtain a certain position or advance in current ones. This is evidenced by one respondent who noted, "I wouldn't be where I am today without the support of mentors." Time and time again, respondents stated that their career success was directly linked to well-timed and in some cases fortuitous mentorship and guidance. From encouraging participants to continue their education, for example, "Without that strong mentorship from him, I don't think I would have gone to do a Ph.D.," to how they practiced leadership, mentorship played a critical role. Specific statements included, "[mentorship] completely transformed me from a manager to a director" and "[the] best mentors are the people who made such an impact on your life that you know you wouldn't be where you are today without that person."

Altruism

These reflections on past mentorship relationships evoked strong feelings of gratitude and "luck" that permeated their need to participate in providing quality mentorship to students and colleagues. That desire to repay the kindness from their mentors was very prevalent and discussed by the majority of respondents, "You know, it helps you feel a sense of purpose in your job . . . helping see these folks succeed . . . wherever their path takes them . . . it's just really gratifying." Almost all respondents stated that it was important to "pay it forward" to create a legacy by sharing their hard-earned knowledge with others.

In some cases, negative experiences or major barriers to access mentors also drove this altruistic tendency, "That's a role (mentoring) that I want to fill for other young women coming up in the sciences because I feel like it was lacking for me" and "I have had so many bad/shitty mentors that I want to make up for them." In some cases, it was easier for respondents to give than receive advice "I give other people better advice than I give to myself."

In addition, the gift of an altruistic mentor was mentioned by many of the respondents as a trait they desired. Straus et al. (2013) identified the most valued personal characteristics of successful mentors. The most frequently mentioned trait desired by mentees in their medical-based academic setting was an altruistic mentor. Mentees need someone who gives freely of their time, attention, and advice.

Altruism was also demonstrated by mentors who expressed the desire to support emerging scientists and women; however, they also expressed benefiting from these relationships. For these mentors, mentorship is seen as a reciprocal relationship vs. a one-way flow of support. Specifically, one respondent highly valued the connection with younger people,

> I think the biggest and the best thing I got from being a mentor is the connection with younger people. . . . people that I've been mentoring are getting positions and doing things and being successful in their own lives [and] that helps me make new connections with new people. I have access now to new information and all of the things that they're learning.

Another respondent felt that the act of mentoring allowed one to evaluate their own progress and job satisfaction, "One of the things I like about being a mentor is it helps me define what I like about my job and what it takes to do my job." Another respondent emphasized that mentoring should illuminate the positive aspects of their career, "I don't want to turn off mentees by only talking about the hard stuff; pass along why you love your job." Another respondent said regarding "the benefits of being a mentor to younger women coming up in the field" is that, "I think that it has made me more empathetic." Some of these benefits are directly related to the need to develop connections, create a network, and think about one's own career over time. For example, members of the OBFS who attend annual meetings list the primary benefits of those meetings to be the networking and peer-to-peer mentoring opportunities which enable them to crowdsource solutions for the problems encountered in field station leadership roles.

Imposter Syndrome

Impostor phenomenon (IP) or syndrome is the "psychological experience of believing one's accomplishments came about not through genuine ability, but as a result of having been lucky, having worked harder than others, or having manipulated other's impressions" (Langford & Clancy, 1993, p. 495). While many people experience IP at various stages of their personal and professional lives, a body of literature explicates high levels of IP in women, especially for women in academic contexts (Langford & Clancy, 1993). For women experiencing IP, there is a tendency to downgrade or dismiss accomplishments as they constantly assess their performance based on an "internal set of standards which are never perceived to be met" (Chandra et al., 2019, p. 27). Within the context of mentorship, IP may pose a barrier for mentees, as there is a significant fear of being perceived as incompetent (Boag & Chardon, 2021; Chandra et al., 2019).

During the interviews, several respondents used the word "luck" to describe how they happened upon a positive mentorship opportunity or jumped into a new career they had not previously considered. In some cases, this was a result of a mentor waiting in the wings looking out for them and keeping an eye on likely opportunities they felt would match the person's skill set (which is a sign of both a good mentor and a good leader). Upon reflection, many of the interviewees realized that what they perceived as "luck" was actually earned respect and altruism on the part of formal or informal mentors. One person stated, "I like to mentor students who are insecure about their roles. I can identify as I experienced imposter syndrome."

Participants underscored the importance of mentorship as a mechanism to manage IP. By providing "psychosocial support" and sharing their own experiences with IP, mentors can enhance a mentee's perceived competence, identity, and effectiveness, thereby alleviating feelings of IP (Estrada et al., 2018). Specifically, "good" mentorship appears to be helpful in reducing the feeling of impostorism by focusing on a mentee's potential and providing concrete skill-based assistance and advice. Impostorism was closely related to their likelihood of asking for mentorship; however, mentees may work around IP by focusing on needed skills vs. the need for IP-specific support. For example, respondents frequently noted they used mentorship as a touchstone and to help them acquire skills they needed. More than half the respondents used mentoring sessions with a variety of people to help them learn key aspects of their jobs, such as hiring, budgeting, writing proposals, and working with employees.

RQ2: What factors do women at field stations use or have used in the past to select mentors?

In response to RQ2, respondents identified the following selection criteria and traits when seeking out mentorship: integrity, trust, and respect; role models; and good vs. bad mentorship experiences.

Integrity, Trust, and Respect

According to interview respondents, integrity, trust, and respect are critical requirements for a successful mentee/mentor relationship. Every respondent mentioned at least one of these characteristics, and typically all three of those specific words were used to describe effective mentoring relationships. Participants used the following descriptors to characterize these traits: "trustworthy, honest, [having] good listening skills, available (physically and emotionally), empathetic, objective, non-judgmental." One participant underscored the vulnerability of mentees in seeking support, noting trusted mentors do "not [make] fun of a mentee when a mentee does not know something." Another described the ideal mentorship as something that "requires trust and respect between mentor and mentee; [you] count on that mentor for advice and being able to trust the mentor that they will have your back and be there for you." Some respondents said that without deep trust between them and their mentor, they would feel uneasy about asking questions and exposing their incompetence (Boag & Chardon, 2021).

Similarly, research underscores the importance of integrity, trust, and respect in the mentor-mentee relationship. For example, Straus et al. (2013) identified these traits in their very similar study of faculty in medical schools. Additionally, feelings of trust, empathy, respect, and connectedness are often used by mentors when qualifying relationship quality (Ragins, 2010). In the literature, respect is highlighted as critically important for intercultural, intergenerational, and intergender mentor-mentee relationships. Specifically, perceived mutual respect for differences must be situated within the context of the relationship for both parties to feel valued and validated (Merriweather & Morgan, 2013). Finally, within the context of STEM, FSMLs, and academic/researched-based contexts, mentors and mentees are expected to behave in ways that meet the standards for ethical practice as defined by their disciplines with mentors often serving as exemplars (Gray & Jordan, 2012).

Role Models

Participants did not clearly distinguish between "role models" and "mentors" when seeking out sources of support, a distinction previously cited in the literature (Méndez-Morse, 2004). In certain cases, mentor and role model were used interchangeably, while at other times, distinctions were noted. For example, respondents broadly described people who had succeeded or achieved a leadership position as excellent mentors or role models. The word role model was used specifically; however, when reflecting on their responsibility to guide and support younger women, especially as it relates to parenthood and family, one interview subject stated they "also had mentors who did not know they were mentors [who were] mentoring by example," leaning more toward the definition of role model (Méndez-Morse, 2004).

"Good" vs. Bad Mentorship

Respondents often reflected on "good" mentorship and how it impacted their career trajectory. Several respondents said that good mentors "found the best in them and brought it out." These mentors boosted their confidence and gave them a safe and trusting avenue to ask questions that may have been difficult or embarrassing to ask (figure 8.1). Other respondents were not aware that mentors were "looking out" for them, in many cases making jobs available and bringing up opportunities that greatly expanded their horizons and opportunities. From the respondents interviewed, it appeared that "good," in this case "effective," mentorship provided the support to attain leadership positions and leadership opportunities. Good mentorship may change over time, however; three respondents mentioned that initially they mentored as they had been mentored but as they evolved in their careers, their definition of a mentor also evolved, for example, "I think early on your definition of mentorship is the way you were mentored; as you progress in life you start to pull in other people" and redefine what "good" mentorship looks and feels like.

What Does "Good" Mentoring Look Like? What Is the Result or Impact on People? We asked the respondents what they thought of when they thought of "good" mentoring. They mentioned the following traits and characteristics: "great listener"; successful and admirable; "inclusive of a wide range of people, values, and traits"; reflective and self-aware; "knowing where they succeeded and where they failed"; "observational and offering support to others"; "generous with their time, energy, and knowledge"; and "caring, honest, and approachable." Whether they preferred extensive one-on-one mentoring or a more hands-off approach varied throughout the careers and between respondents.

Additionally, "good" mentorship came from a variety of sources and often played a role in building self-confidence and self-efficacy. From the interviews that we conducted, we found that mentorship from parents and college and graduate school experiences shaped how women developed their confidence and navigated through a diverse array of career opportunities. Confidence in their abilities seemed to determine a potential leader's success during graduate school careers when interacting with mentors, such as faculty, thesis/dissertation committee members, and colleagues. Women tended to seek a variety of mentors who possessed the expertise they needed to advance in their career trajectory. In spite of the difficulties that could have held them back in their early careers, the majority of women interviewed felt that they were supported in their career path by mentors.

Personality and style were also explored by interview participants in relation to "good" mentoring. Respondent answers diverged regarding the type of personality that made the best mentor and how closely that should mesh with the mentee's personality. Some people expressed they worked better with people who thought more like them and others preferred mentors that were relatively different in approach and personality (Davies et al., 2021). Respondents wanted their mentors or mentees to "jive with them." One respondent stated, "Having a mentor that you don't necessarily agree with on everything allows you to balance out your perspectives. I enjoy having relationships with people who don't think the same way that I do."

Although having differing opinions was considered an asset for some, being able to get along and communicate well was critical for all respondents. Descriptions of ideal mentors landed squarely on words like warmth, caring, nurturing, and trusting. Honesty and openness were also highly valued and cited by most respondents. Respondents unequivocally stated that a personality match was instrumental in having a productive relationship; for example, "I would say personality is a big factor; getting along on a personal level. You need to feel comfortable with each other. There needs to be [like] a bond."

Specific comments and quotes from the respondents regarding "good" mentorship/mentors are diverse and included the following:

- "The best mentors . . . feel like part of 'her entourage.'" Many respondents mentioned that they kept in touch for many years with long-term mentors who became fixtures and/or touchstones in their lives.
- "True mentorship is a selfless act. Listening is so important and it is better if one can be truly objective with the mentee."
- "It'd be someone who can see your capabilities and our tangible potential; what you're capable of. Even if you're not willing to admit it."
- "A true rare mentor is that person that you know will always give you the straight answer, but also when you come away from that conversation, you're like, 'Okay, I can do this.'"
- "But I think that people saw something in me that I didn't necessarily recognize and he brought it to my attention and they made me feel like I could actually do that job."
- "[An] ideal mentor is somebody that you respect, somebody that you hope to emulate."
- "[Good mentoring is] being selfless and really like thinking strategically or ahead about [what] the next steps for this person might be and also just thinking carefully about what you say; make sure in longer relations to check-in over time [and] ask them if there's things that they could use that we're not doing or covering."
- "I'm looking for women who I think are well-rounded, who are welcoming or easy to talk to, who I think care about equity."
- "Somebody is taking a broader look at your skillset and helping you build your skills."
- "Helpful to keep you humble and point out things you still need to learn in a less stressful manner"
- "I look for mentors who are successful and not exactly like me. Works if they are older with more experience and I prefer talking to women not in academia."

As mentioned above, "good" mentoring not only helps people see themselves as capable of doing new jobs, but it also increases confidence, builds relationships, and develops personal skills that transcend the relationship (figure 8.1).

What Does "Bad" Mentoring Look Like? What Is the Result or Impact on People? "Bad" or poor or ineffective mentoring can set back a person's career and even cause them to leave the field. Several respondents told stories where they observed other women leaving the field or changing jobs based on a lack of support or even active discouragement from mentors.

Respondents typically stated that poor mentors either did not have the time or did not have the desire to help them succeed. In a few instances, poor mentors felt competitive with their mentees. Three respondents mentioned that some mentors were interested in a romantic relationship only, and when that was not part of the equation, those mentors quickly lost interest. One interviewee said that her poor mentors were field station users who simply wanted to have access to the field station or preferential treatment.

One respondent mentioned that she had "so-so mentors who were not looking out for her best interest and not very invested." Another stated that one of her bad mentors had adopted a "mean dad" model of mentorship. She speculated that the person demonstrating bad mentor characteristics was likely unaware that he was not helpful. One respondent noted that a

> big part of mentorship is sometimes you're just learning it together. And sometimes if you know too much about something you're not really a very effective mentor, because you skip all the parts of it that you got hung up on before.

Another respondent emphasized that the time invested was a critical factor,

> If someone hasn't taken the time to get to know you [and] to figure out how to bring the best out of you, then it's not going to really help you grow in a way that gives you that confidence that you need at every stage of our lives.

A few respondents mentioned that in the case of bad mentors, especially those in a supervisory or hierarchical role like a graduate advisor, that students did not have any training on which traits to look out for in a mentor and how to extract themselves from these situations, that is, "an eject button." Some respondents described instances of substandard mentorship that arose from supervisors who were de facto mentors and responsible for providing professional development advice when they were rarely properly prepared: "Often mentors tend to be our bosses, and we don't get a chance to choose them."

RQ3: How can we create mentorship roles/programs formally and informally (i.e., best practices) to support diversity and inclusion at field stations?
In response to RQ3, respondents identified the following as critical to creating more opportunities for women working in FSMLs to access and benefit from mentorship: networking, tools, formal vs. informal, explicating barriers, and representation.

Networking

Increasing formal and informal networks can be extremely effective at creating mentorship opportunities. Networking benefits both the mentor and the mentee: "Connections and knowledge from people I mentor benefit me over time," and "you never know when that person will be in a position to help you." Several respondents mentioned that their mentors became part of their long-term network and that they follow the students, employees, and interns they mentored for years. The desire to provide mentorship in order to carefully and methodically develop a network of future colleagues was an unexpected benefit listed by about a third of the respondents.

Tools

Three tools identified by participants as critical to the mentor-mentee relationship include meetings, contracts, and reflection. First, the majority of participants underscored the importance of meeting regularly and adapting to different communication channels when needed. Almost universally, respondents preferred one-on-one, in-person, relatively frequent (weekly to monthly) meetings with their mentor or mentees. While different mentors and mentees have different needs, expectations, and desires regarding how frequently they should meet, regular meetings or check-ins allow for relationship development and help build trust (Eby et al., 2007), a desired trait defined by the participants in the study. All of the participants had adapted to distance meetings as a result of the pandemic, and some preferred to use Zoom or other interfaces because of the convenience factor. Interestingly, three of the younger mentors even provided mentorship to their students and assistants via text. The experiences of the participants, while not fully developed, points to the growing significance of e-mentoring not only to meet the needs of learners coming of age in the digital era but also to promote more inclusive practices and global perspectives (Neely et al., 2017; Packard, 2003).

Contracts or some set of defined expectations were also considered as important by some interview participants. For example, one respondent provides a list of six to eight expectations to her mentees, which include items, such as "I will always listen and hear you" and "I will be honest" that was passed down to her from her advisor. Providing clear expectations may serve to promote relationship development and disclosure. Another respondent had a packet of material they provided to new mentees. Although the details of thc packet were not defined, general information regarding resources, "how-tos," or other workplace-specific information may be useful. Having some type of implicit or explicit "contract" outlining expectations was mentioned by about a quarter of the respondents and supported as a useful tool for some mentor-mentee relationships. Steele (2013) argues these contracts set "the expectations for each party, provide a context for specific interaction," and reify the definition of mentorship "for each protégé–mentor pair as they shape and are shaped by their experiences in the relationship" (p. 128).

Finally, several respondents felt that the act of talking about mentorship and reflecting on how their careers have benefited from mentorship helped them develop best practices to more mindfully conduct their own mentor-mentee relationships. One person suggested holding frequent workshops to share experiences in an informal but regularly held venue, perhaps through OBFS, as a way to develop mindfulness about mentorship capacity and capabilities. Many respondents felt that training could be helpful for mentors although others felt that some good mentors were just "born that way" and naturally good at advising others.

Informal vs Formal Mentorship

The literature distinguishes between informal and formal mentorship as did the participants in our study. Informal mentorship is considered a "natural component" of many relationships that emerges in a variety of different contexts (Izner & Crawford, 2005, p. 35). Formal mentorship, on the other hand, tends to be more structured, outcome-driven, and may or may not be a "natural" coming together of the mentor or mentee based on similar interests, values, or other aspects of self (Buzzanell et al., 2015; Izner & Crawford, 2005). Interview participants provided less "literature-based" definitions and focused more on the structure of the meetings, use of contracts, and other more subtle distinctions between informal and formal. Some participants, for example, advocated for regularly scheduled meetings with employees or students to check in both with and without an agenda. Ninety percent of the respondents felt that the frequency and meeting length for mentorship sessions often depended on the goals, length of time in the relationship, hierarchical relationship (e.g., for younger students or new employees, more frequent sessions). There was also a heavy emphasis on time and commitment. Both the mentor and mentee need to value each other's time and success and be capable of committing to an active relationship with give and take. A majority of respondents said that both mentors and mentees should "share expectations early and often," referencing the importance of some formal agreement between the pair. Many interview subjects mentioned it was critical for the mentee to be aware of their goals and to communicate that to the mentor whether in a formal document that is signed by both parties or loosely discussed periodically over the course of the mentor-mentee relationship. Mentees also expressed the need to have a plan for the goals they wished to accomplish, as one respondent succinctly described it: "What's your mission statement? What's your vision for yourself?"

Others described informal outreach to a variety of mentors based on the question one has or the skill one needs to attain at that moment in time, describing a more informal relationship. As noted by one interviewee: "I usually would send an email or call and say, here's my situation. What do you think is the best way to approach this?" The location also contributed to the informal nature of the relationship. At least seven respondents mentioned that mentoring while hiking or doing fieldwork or watching the ocean or otherwise occupied was more productive and less stressful for both parties. They enjoyed mentoring on the side while doing tasks to allow for natural dialogue and deeper conversations. The locations of field stations in remote and beautiful settings became an advantage for these conversation spaces. At least two respondents mentioned that they took their mentees somewhere significant to foster a sense of relaxation and "specialness."

Barriers

Field stations breed resilience and a "can do" attitude, but they can also be far removed from population centers, host institutes, or college campuses (Billick et al., 2013; Struminger et al., 2018). This distance led many of the respondents to list "lack of access" to mentors as a barrier: "Really one of the main ones [barriers] was just [being] a little bit isolated at a field station and I think that's a classic one for field stations. It's really easy to feel isolated." Thus, working at remote field stations proved to be a barrier for many of the interviewees who had to be more creative and reach out proactively for mentorship. Others had trouble finding good mentors in their field or for their unique job positions (e.g., GIS, computers, sensor networks, etc.). Specifically, leadership positions at FSMLs are a "very unique job [that] creates a barrier [where it is] harder to find mentors although OBFS colleagues have been helpful; maybe set up on the website a way to share time and advice sessions." Availability and time for mentorship were also listed as barriers.

Representation

As it relates to representation, approximately 85% of the respondents noted that having female mentors is important. Interview participants noted "it's absolutely critical to have BIPOC mentors and students"; "I wish that I would have had more female mentors. Diversity of voices is tremendously important. For me, that was lacking." Other representative responses include the following:

- "[It is] critical there are mentors out there that represent the full diversity of people that we have in our world; [It is] huge for her having a very strong female scientist as a mentor early in her career made her feel she could do science [and could be a leader]; resilience is really important."

- One respondent shared that she had noticed many BIPOC role models who were called to fill multiple roles, and consequently would be stretched thin as one of a small handful of people who could mentor upcoming BIPOC students or scientists. To make matters worse, "in some programs BIPOC students are poached by the government [who can offer higher starting salaries] after they get their master's degree."
- "It's incredibly important because there's a lot of nuances that come with being a woman or a Person of Color and not having mentors that are similar to you [is a barrier]. It will never be adequate, there's a lot that goes along with those identities."
- "Students need a diverse set of mentors to choose from, including [people from a diversity of] sexual orientations when possible."
- "BIPOC students [in her example overseas: African students and here: Native American/Indigenous] need each other, too, not just the mentors; they need a cohort." In her experience of one program, "they have too many gringo mentors; maybe an exchange program would fix that!"

Two additional considerations related to representation were mentioned by participants. Not all representative mentorship relationships were deemed supportive by interview participants. One interviewee shared that her Black friend had a bad experience with a Black female boss. "There's such a paucity of us in the field that it is instant competition" and that "she should have had my back the most but had my back the least." Regarding gender representations, many of the participants noted they had perfectly good and useful mentorships with men throughout their careers (Drury et al., 2011; Eby et al., 2008).

FINAL RECOMMENDATIONS

Field station personnel tend to be problem solvers as a normal extension of their duties, and this interview process elicited many direct recommendations regarding the ways to promote and improve mentorship practices at FSMLs. We provide five recommendations below: develop formal and informal opportunities for networking; develop a blueprint/best practices document; training for mentors; create a field station leadership mentorship team; and reward systems.

Develop Formal and Informal Opportunities for Networking

The majority of respondents felt that frequent informal and/or formal scheduled sessions with peers in the OBFS network would be an excellent tool for bridging the gap in access to peer mentoring. Many respondents shared some of the mentoring networks opportunities they had been using. Some comments: "OBFS has been a huge source of mentorship"; "I would like more formal opportunities to be mentored or provide mentorship [from my career stage, mid-career]"; "[I] would like more opportunities to be mentored, [and it is] harder to find [mentorship] in leadership positions"; and "if we set up an OBFS mentorship panel [and] break it down into segments of topics so it does not feel like a life commitment, topics like fundraising, finance, science communication, etc. [would be helpful for building formal mentorship networks]."

A majority of respondents felt that FSMLs are so unusual that peer-to-peer mentoring is one of the better solutions/tools. Several respondents stated that they had a cadre of informal "one-off" mentors that they could reach out to for very specific needs. Getting targeted advice on things such as leadership, budgeting, running a business, science communication, grant writing, human resources, project management, and operations was listed as important for success in the "jill of all trades" world of field station management.

Develop a Blueprint/Best Practices Document

Several respondents mentioned examples of ongoing programs using best practices for resources such as written mentor-mentee contracts and "mentorship start-up packages." In general, these resources were used to establish baseline expectations for both parties in the mentoring relationships. As mentioned previously, these best practices documents can set the tone and structure for the mentor-mentee relationship so that everyone is held accountable.

Training for Mentors

Mentorship training was brought up by approximately 60% of the respondents as needed. Most good mentors became that way either through having guidance from other good role models, from learning what *not* to do from bad mentors, or as a result of formal or informal training. Several respondents also mentioned their role in being a boss automatically included some mentorship responsibilities. As noted by one interviewee: "Manager versus mentor, like, what's the difference between those two? And how can you fill both of those roles?"

The ability to obtain training throughout one's career to provide good mentorship is seen as a professional development need that underscores the changing needs of mentees as their career progresses (see chapter 6 by McDermott & May in this edited volume). Mentoring grows and

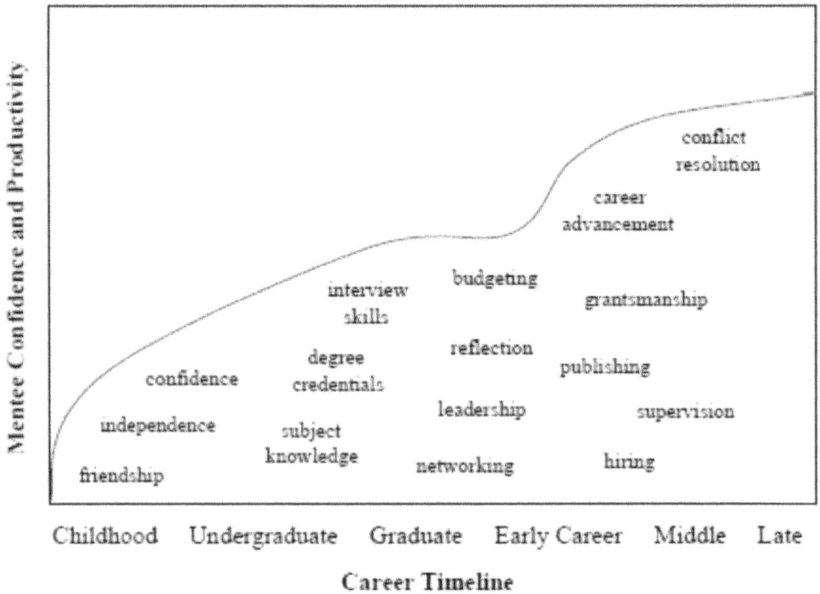

Figure 8.1 Skills and Attributes Accumulated from Mentoring Build Increased Menteee Confidence and Productivity along a Career Trajectory. *Source:* Author data.

strengthens mentee's skills throughout their career from the accumulation of knowledge and independence early in their development to interview skills, grantsmanship, and conflict resolution during their career. These attributes build mentee confidence and the skills to successfully navigate challenging personnel, budgetary, and competitive situations needed in leadership positions (figure 8.1).

Create a Field Station Leadership Mentorship Team

In addition to the formal and informal networking, participants mentioned having a mentorship team within professional societies to provide additional professional support and development. For example, as one participant stated, "Hav[ing] a set of worker bees in OBFS with lots of experience willing to mentor new field station directors by conducting a site visit like a planning grant" may be helpful. Five senior people and five younger people could do a road tour of some field stations to share what has worked well and what has not worked for directors in the past. The participant went on to suggest that the mentorship team could be part of the "FSML Planning grant process" and could even be written into a planning grant to formalize the potential program.

Reward Systems

FSMLs are challenged to consider how to "compensate" mentors for their time, energy, and overall contribution to employee development and retention. Most interviewees said *emphatically* that mentors *should not be paid* and that an exchange of money would alter the dynamic too much. In fact, one or two respondents felt paying mentors would incentivize them to take on more mentees than they could handle. Although payment between mentees and mentors was discouraged, most interviewees verbalized that mentoring should be officially recognized as part of their job duties and that time should be carved out for successful mentorship. The establishment of a certification program or training module that could indicate externally both to employers and potential mentees that one had sought out and received training in mentorship was listed by some respondents as not only a useful tool but also as a way to be recognized. OBFS or other organizations could provide that training to build a community of effective mentors and mentees.

Several respondents mentioned that they tended to be mentors for young students coming to the field stations, for faculty setting up experiments, and generally for anyone trying to do science at field stations. One respondent said, "It would be nice if it [mentorship] was recognized as a job component; especially when it comes to writing recommendations which can take a lot of time. [It should be] recognized that is actually a valuable role that they play." What are other institutional ways to recognize mentoring? Universities are beginning to recognize that mentorship is critical to student success, and as a result, they are creating paid mentorship coordinating jobs (e.g., the Center for Coastal and Marine Science in California Lead Mentor) and official recognition of outstanding service in mentoring. One example is the *Curtis Wood Mentoring Award* at Western Carolina University that recognizes graduate student mentoring by faculty members. One respondent mentioned the mentorship program run by the Association of Nature Center Administrators as an excellent program that should be explored, "They have an official mentor-mentee program. Great model."

LIMITATIONS AND FUTURE RESEARCH

Although this research provides valuable insight into the role and value of mentorship in women's careers and experiences at FSMLs, there were some limitations. The instrument created and the working pool of interview subjects can introduce bias into a research process. In this case, the interviewer knew all the respondents, which made it possible to have rapport but could have easily introduced bias, even a positive bias. The size of the pool (16) is adequate but it only represented a small portion of U.S. and international field station leaders. Finally, the lead-off question took up a lot of time that was then not available for exploring tactics in mentoring.

Therefore, in light of the research limitations, future research should be explored to continue this line of inquiry. Research could be conducted before, during, and after informal or formal group mentoring or mentoring training sessions. The introduction of both formal and informal opportunities for mentorship and training should be accompanied by informal or formal assessment tools from surveys to interviews. Future work should curate and collate the many programs in existence that provide mentorship training and opportunities and more clearly identify gaps and barriers to participation. Federal, state, and private funding is beginning to address the need for people of all backgrounds and gender identities to have access to mentorship opportunities; however, an evaluation of the success of these programs and the creation of a community of practice may be effective next steps.

CONCLUSIONS AND NEXT STEPS

The quote that best summarizes the participants' responses to the value of mentoring was, *"You can pick your ancestors, they don't all have to be the people related to you."* We all need mentors, and in many cases, our success is incredibly dependent on finding the right people at the right time in our careers. Fortunately, some people are able to find mentors and act as mentors without too much difficulty. But that is not the case for all people. Barriers exist, especially for women and doubly so for BIPOC women (Grogan et al., 2021). In the world of field science, remoteness, limited staff, and a busy and varied workload all create obstacles for obtaining mentorship opportunities. Fortunately, the strong peer-to-peer network nurtured by the OBFS, within the science community, and through other professional organizations may remove some of these obstacles.

Appendix: Interview Questions

1. Tell me a little bit about yourself: How would you describe yourself to the young daughter of a colleague?
2. What is your definition of mentorship?
3. What are the defining characteristics of a meaningful mentorship from the perspective of the mentor and mentee? What are the key things in your mind that define a "good" or effective mentorship?
4. Reflecting on your experiences with mentorship, how have you benefited as a mentor and mentee? If they struggle here, encourage them to share a meaningful mentor relationship and how it impacted them.

5. How has mentorship impacted your career from degree completion to where you are now?
6. How has your need for mentorship changed over the duration of your career? Examples: starting a career, mid-way through degree, starting teaching, starting a new job, toward the end of the degree path (when burnout might be more common)?
7. How available have mentors been throughout your career? Have there been times where you needed mentorship and could not find a mentor or did not have that option?
8. What do you look for in a mentor?
9. Can you describe a time when a good mentor really helped you?
10. Have you encountered a bad mentor? What traits or actions made them a bad fit for you?
11. Have you experienced a difficult time mentoring someone? What traits or actions made that the case?
12. Your Mentorship styles:
    a. How often do you meet?
    b. How long are your mentoring sessions?
    c. How long do you maintain a mentor-mentee relationship?
    d. How do you communicate your willingness to mentor?
    e. Have you ever turned down a mentorship opportunity? Why?
13. What tools or technologies do you utilize to initiate and to maintain a mentor-mentee relationship? How much has this changed post-COVID?
14. What tips would you give someone starting in a mentorship (either as the mentor or mentee)?
15. Would you like more formal opportunities to be a mentor or be mentored?
16. What barriers have you experienced in the past regarding mentorship?
17. Do you feel mentors should be paid?
18. Does your institution reward mentorship service?
19. Do you tend to mentor the same way you have been mentored?
20. Do you seek out people like you as mentors?
21. How important is representation in mentorship, that is, women mentoring other women, people of color mentoring people of color, etc.?
22. What else would you like to add about your mentorship experiences?

REFERENCES

Bernard, R. E., & Cooperdock, E. H. G. (2018). No progress on diversity in 40 years. *Nature Geoscience, 11*(5), 292–295. https://doi.org/10.1038/s41561-018-0116-6

Billick, I., Babb, I., Kloeppel, B., Leong, J., Hodder, J., Sanders, J., & Swain, H. (2013). *Field stations and marine laboratories of the future: A strategic vision.* https://www.obfs.org/assets/docs/fsml_final_report.pdf

Blickenstaff, J. C. (2005) Women and science careers: Leaky pipeline or gender filter? *Gender and Education, 17*(4), 369–386. https://doi.org/10.1080/09540250500145072

Boag, A. E., & Chardon, N. I. (2021, February 1). Improving the advisor/advisee relationship academic mentors are not necessarily natural managers. Their graduate students often bear the brunt of this shortcoming. *The Scientist.* https://www.the-scientist.com/critic-at-large/improving-the-advisor-advisee-relationship-68352

Brandimarte, L., Acquisti, A., & Loewenstein, G. (2010, June). *Misplaced confidences: Privacy and the control* [Symposium]. Ninth Annual Workshop on the Economics of Information Security, Harvard University, Cambridge, MA.

Buzzanell, P. M., Long, Z., Anderson, L. B., Kokini, K., & Batra, J. C. (2015). Mentoring in academe: A feminist poststructural lens on stories of women engineering faculty of color. *Management Communication Quarterly, 29*(3), 440–457. https://doi.org/10.1177/0893318915574311

Chandra, S., Candace, C. A., Huebert, A., Crowley, E. C., & Das, A. M. (2019). Impostor syndrome: Could it be holding you or your mentees back? *CHEST, 156*(1), 26–32. https://journal.chestnet.org/article/S0012-3692(19)30607-5/pdf

Corbin, J., & Strauss, A. (1990). Grounded theory research: Procedures, canons, and evaluative criteria. *Qualitative Sociology, 13*(1), 3–21. https://doi.org/10.1007/BF00988593

Davies, S. W., Putnam, H. M., Ainsworth, T., Baum, J. K., Bove, C. B., Crosby, S. C., Côté, I. M., Duplouy, A., Fulweiler, R. W., Griffin, A. J., Hanley, T. C., Hill, T., Humanes, A., Mangubhai, S., Metaxas, A., Parker, L. M., Rivera, H. E., Silbiger, N. S., Smith, N. S., ... Bates, A. E. (2021). Promoting inclusive metrics of success and impact to dismantle a discriminatory reward system in science. *PLoS Biology, 19*(6), e3001282. https://doi.org/10.1371/journal.pbio.3001282

Debinski, D. (2022). Make the approach and get the data: Challenges, teamwork, and culture of support for women who are scientists and parents at field stations and marine labs. In V. McDermott, J. Gee, & A. R. May (Eds.), *Women of the wild: Challenging gender disparities in field stations and marine laboratories* (pp. 53–88). Lexington Books.

DeCastro, R., Sambuco, D., Ubel, P., Stewart, A., & Jagsi, R. (2013). Mentor networks in academic medicine: Moving beyond a dyadic conception of mentoring for junior faculty researchers. *Academic Medicine, 88*(4), 488–496. https://doi.org/10.1097/ACM.0b013e318285d302

Dennehy, T. C., & Dasgupta, N. (2017). Female peer mentors early in college increase women's positive academic experiences and retention in engineering. *Proceedings of the National Academy of Sciences of the United States of America, 114*(23), 5964–5969. https://doi.org/10.1073/pnas.1613117114

Drury, B. J., Siy, J. O., & Cheryan, S. (2011). When do female role models benefit women? The importance of differentiating recruitment from retention in STEM.

Psychological Inquiry, 22(4), 265–269. https://doi.org/10.1080/1047840X.2011.620935

Dumas, T. N. (2020). Effective mentoring for diverse leaders. In D. S. Chapman & A. Wilkerson (Eds.), *From student to scholar: Mentoring underrepresented scholars in the academy* (pp. 167–180). Palgrave Macmillan.

Eby, L. T., & Allen, T. D. (2008). Moving toward interdisciplinary dialogue in mentoring scholarship: An introduction to the special issue. *Journal of Vocational Behavior, 72*(2), 159–167.

Eby, L. T., Allen, T. D., Hoffman, B. J., Baranik, L. E., Sauer, J. B., Baldwin, S., Morrison, M. A., Kinkade, K. M., Maher, C. P., Curtis, S., & Evans, S. C. (2013). An interdisciplinary meta-analysis of the potential antecedents, correlates, and consequences of protégé perceptions of mentoring. *Psychological Bulletin, 139*(2), 441–476. https://doi.org/10.1037/a0029279

Eby, L. T., Allen, T. D., Evans, S. C., Ng, T., & Dubois, D. (2008). Does mentoring matter? A multidisciplinary meta-analysis comparing mentored and non-mentored individuals. *Journal of Vocational Behavior, 72*(2), 254–267. https://doi.org/10.1016/j.jvb.2007.04.005

Eby, L. T., Rhodes, J. E., & Allen, T. D. (2007). Definition and evolution of mentoring. In Allen, T. D., & Eby, L. T. (Eds.), *The Blackwell handbook of mentoring: A multiple perspectives approach* (pp. 7–20). Blackwell.

Estrada, M., Hernandez, P. R., & Schultz, P. W. (2018). A longitudinal study of how quality mentorship and research experience integrate underrepresented minorities into STEM careers. *CBE - Life Sciences Education, 17*, 1–13. https://doi.org/10.1187/cbe.17-04-0066

Fogel, M. L. (2020). *Advice from the Isotope Queen: Building a meaningful career while enjoying a full life*. Yaqui Gulch Press.

Ford, H. L., Brick, C., Azmitia, M., Blaufuss, K., & Dekens, P. (2019). Women from some minorities get too few talks. *Nature, 576,* 32–35. https://doi.org/10.1038/d41586-019-03688-w

Fridkis-Hareli, M. (2011). A mentoring program for women scientists meets a pressing need. *Nature Biotechnology, 29*, 287–288. https://doi.org/10.1038/nbt.1799

Gaensler, B. (2018). It takes more than a vow. *Nature, 558*, 149–151. https://media.nature.com/original/magazine-assets/d41586-018-05317-4/d41586-018-05317-4.pdf

Gray, P. W., & Jordan, S. R. (2012). Supervisors and academic integrity: Supervisors as exemplars and mentors. *Journal of Academic Ethics, 10,* 299–311. https://doi.org/10.1007/s10805-012-9155-6

Greco, V. (2014). Establishing an academic laboratory: Mentoring as a business model. *Molecular Biology of the Cell, 25*(21), 3251–3253. https://doi.org/10.1091/mbc.E14-06-1079

Grogan, P., Eviner, V., & Hobby, S. (2021). Keeping up with the times: Equity issue is now added to our self-reflection worksheet for improving scientific mentoring. *Bulletin of the Ecological Society of America,* e01841. https://doi.org/10.1002/bes2.1841

Guillemin, M., & Heggen, K. (2009). Rapport and respect: Negotiating ethical relations between researcher and participant. *Medicine, Health Care, and Philosophy, 12*(3), 291–299. http://dx.doi.org/10.1007/s11019-008-9165-8

Halvorson, M. A., Finney, J. W., Bi, X., Maisel, N. C., Hayashi, K. P., Weitlauf, J. C., & Cronkite, R. C. (2015). The changing faces of mentorship: Application of a developmental network framework in a health services research career development program. *Clinical and Translational Science, 8*(6), 824–829. https://doi.org/10.1111/cts.12355

Herrmann, S. D., Adelman, R. M., Bodford, J. E., Graudejus, O., Okun, M. A., & Kwan, V. S. Y. (2016). The effects of a female role model on academic performance and persistence of women in STEM courses. *Basic and Applied Social Psychology,* 38, 258–268. https://doi.org/10.1080/01973533.2016.1209757

Higgins, M. C., & Thomas, D. A. (2001). Constellations and careers: Toward understanding the effects of multiple developmental relationships. *Journal of Organizational Behavior*, *22*, 223–247. https://doi.org/10.1002/job.66

Huang, G., Taddese, N., & Walter, E. (2000). *Entry and persistence of women and minorities in college science and engineering education.* National Center for Education Statistics, U.S. Department of Education. https://files.eric.ed.gov/fulltext/ED444872.pdf

Inzer, L. D., & Crawford, C. B. (2005). A review of formal and informal mentoring: Processes, problems, and design. *Journal of Leadership Education, 4*(1), 31–50.

Langford, J., & Clance, P. R. (1993). The impostor phenomenon: recent research findings regarding dynamics, personality and family patterns and their implications for treatment. *Psychotherapy: Theory, Research, Practice, Training, 30*(3), 495–501. https://doi.org/10.1037/0033-3204.30.3.495.

Lindlof, T. R., & Taylor, B. C. (2017). *Qualitative communication research methods.* Sage publications.

Long, Z., Buzzanell, P. M., Kokini, K., Wilson, R. F., Batra, J. C., & Anderson, L. B. (2018). Mentoring women and minority faculty in engineering: A multidimensional mentoring network approach. *Journal of Women and Minorities in Science and Engineering, 24*(2), 121–145. https://doi.org/ 10.1615/JWomenMinorScienEng.2017019277

Makarova, E., Aeschlimann, B., & Herzog, W. (2019). The gender gap in STEM fields: The impact of the gender stereotype of math and science on secondary students' career aspirations. *Frontiers in Education, 4.* https://doi/org/10.3389/feduc.2019.00060

McDermott, V., & May, A. (2022). From the standpoint of women FSML directors: Communication, leadership, and the impact of gender norms. In V. McDermott, J. Gee, & A. R. May (Eds.), *Women of the wild: Challenging gender disparities in field stations and marine laboratories* (pp. 115–142). Lexington Books.

Méndez-Morse, S. (2004). Constructing mentors: Latina educational leaders' role models and mentors. *Educational Administration Quarterly*, 40(4), 561–590. https://doi.org/10.1177/0013161X04267112

Merriweather, L. R., & Morgan, A. J. (2013). Two cultures collide: Bridging the generation gap in a non-traditional mentorship. *Qualitative Report, 18*(12), 1–16. https://files.eric.ed.gov/fulltext/EJ1005008.pdf

Montgomery, B. L. (2017). Mapping a mentoring roadmap and developing a supportive network for strategic career advancement. *SAGE Open, 7*(2), 1–13. https://doi.org/10.1177/2158244017710288

Neely, A. R., Cotton, J., & Neely, A. D. (2017). E-mentoring: A model and review of the literature. *AIS Transactions on Human-Computer Interaction, 9*(3), 220–242. https://aisel.aisnet.org/thci/vol9/iss3/3

Packard, B. W. (2003). Web-based mentoring: Challenging traditional models to increase women's access. *Mentoring and Tutoring, 11*(1), 53–65. https://doi.org/10.1080/1361126032000054808

Ragins, B. R. (2010). Relational mentoring: A positive approach to mentoring at work. In K. S., Cameron, & G. M., Spreitzer (Eds.), *The handbook of positive organizational scholarship* (pp. 519–536). Oxford University Press.

Saldaña, J. (2013). *The coding manual for qualitative researchers.* Sage.

Saxena, M., Geiselman, T. A., & Zhang, S. (2019). Workplace incivility against women in STEM: Insights and best practices. *Business Horizons, 62*(5), 589–594. https://doi.org/10.1016/j.bushor.2019.05.005.

Scheinert, R. (2015). The science of mentoring women in science. *The NIH Catalyst, 23*(2), 6–7. https://irp.nih.gov/sites/default/files/catalyst/catalyst_v23i2.pdf

Steele, R. G. (2013). The social construction of professional mentorship, *Journal of Pediatric Psychology, 38*(2), 126–131. https://doi.org/10.1093/jpepsy/jss177

Straus, S. E., Johnson, M. O., Marquez, C., & Feldman, M. D. (2013). Characteristics of successful and failed mentoring relationships: A qualitative study across two academic health centers. *Academic Medicine: Journal of the Association of American Medical Colleges, 88*(1), 82–89. https://doi.org/10.1097/ACM.0b013e31827647a0

Struminger, R., Adame, G. M. V., & Shannan, Y. H. (2022). Women's perspective on building international community-field station partnerships. In V. McDermott, J. Gee, & A. R. May (Eds.), *Women of the wild: Challenging gender disparities in field stations and marine laboratories* (pp. 225–254). Lexington Books.

Struminger, R., Zarestky, J., Short, R. A., & Lawing, A. M. (2018). A framework for informal STEM education outreach at field stations. *BioScience, 68*(12), 969–978. https://doi.org/10.1093/biosci/biy108

Wanberg, C. R., Kammeyer-Mueller, J., & Marchese, M. (2006). Mentor and protégé predictors and outcomes of mentoring in a formal mentoring program. *Journal of Vocational Behavior, 69*(3), 410–423. https://doi.org/10.1016/j.jvb.2006.05.010

Yun, J., Baldi, B., & Sorcinelli, M. (2016). Mutual mentoring for early-career and underrepresented faculty: Model, research, and practice. *Innovative Higher Education, 41*(5), 441–451. https://doi.org/10.1007/s10755-016-9359-6

Chapter 9

Are Field Stations and Nature Centers Gendered Work Spaces?

Lara D. Roketenetz and Gary M. Holliday

INTRODUCTION

In the modern workplace, there have been innumerable gains in equalizing gender demographics among workers. For example, females now make up 46.8% of the total workforce of persons over the age of 16 in the United States (U.S. Bureau of Labor Statistics, 2021) which is a significant increase from the approximately 30% of the workforce that they comprised in 1950 (Toosi, 2012). Although statistics show that males and females are fairly evenly represented across many occupations, there are still notable exceptions in terms of staffing makeup (U.S. Bureau of Labor Statistics, 2021).

In fact, if asked, most people would and could (unconsciously) assign gender to certain jobs (feel free to try this at home!). Who do you think of if someone asks you to picture a construction worker, a firefighter, or a scientist? How about a floral designer, a nurse, or a teacher? Did you assign gender according to societal or stereotypical perceptions? If so, you might have said all three of the first jobs were more likely held by men, and all three of the second jobs were likely held by women. These perceptions in some ways are indeed supported by the current demographic data which demonstrate a clear gender discrepancy for some occupations (i.e., more likely represented by men or vice versa). For example, only 4.4% of firefighters are female while 81.5% of floral designers are women, according to the U.S. Bureau of Labor Statistics (2021). What characteristics make one gender more or less interested in working in a particular occupation? Konrad et al. (2000) reported that many job attribute preferences generally align with stereotypical gender roles. For women, some of these attributes might include a nurturing role and an opportunity to bond with coworkers, while for men some of these attributes may include earning potential and competition (Konrad et al., 2000). If you didn't automatically assign the stereotypical gender to a career, why not (and good for you—we should be working toward not automatically assuming gender based on occupation!)? Our past experiences with one or more of these occupations may change our perceptions of who can do these jobs and who actually does them (Kossek et al., 2017). Although we prefer to think that most jobs are "genderless" (Britton, 2017; Ridgeway, 2011) and that gender does not impact hiring practices, pay scales, promotions to leadership positions, etc., common sense and research tells us that there is still a long way to go toward gender equity in many careers (England, 2010; Jacobs, 2003).

Gender disparity in science, technology, engineering, and math (STEM) is even more pronounced, especially in specific fields like engineering and computer technology and has been intensively studied as it has been widely recognized as problematic (Blackburn 2017; Botella et al., 2019; Wegemer & Eccles, 2018). In general, the widespread conclusion in these studies is that women are underrepresented in most subfields of STEM. The reasons for gender disparities in certain occupations are varied, complex, and beyond the scope of this particular chapter. To frame the discussion, however, it is important to note that some of these disparities can result from fixed perceptions and stereotyping, lack of mentors and role models who reflect our identities, gender bias and discrimination, unequal opportunities, and significant pay gaps for equal work (Botella et al., 2019; Hill et al., 2010; Martinez & Christnacht, 2021; Shauman, 2017).

Diving a bit deeper into the social perceptions and stereotypes surrounding some STEM careers, Miller et al. (2018) looked at five decades of "Draw-a-Scientist" studies in the United States and predicted that as more women enter the scientific fields, and correlational representation for females scientists becomes more common in mass media (i.e., television shows, books, magazines, etc.), gender stereotypes of scientists would weaken over time. Those researchers found this to be true longitudinally across decades, that is, overall, children in more recent studies were less likely to draw the scientist as a male than in previous studies (Miller et al., 2018). However, there were interesting differences in the cumulative data. Girls were more likely to draw a female scientist than boys, but as children aged, both girls and boys increasingly drew the male scientist (Miller et al., 2018). This implies that young girls can more easily picture themselves as scientists (thanks, Dora the Explorer!) than older girls and that there are likely a variety of external environmental influences (academic, familial, societal, etc.) that cause this attitude shift over time. A 2013 study by Cundiff et al. surveyed undergraduate students and found that women who expressed stronger gender-science stereotypes (i.e., science = male association) ranked both their own science identity and intent to persist in science as weaker than their male counterparts. These social perceptions, or stereotypes, of who can and who will become a professional scientist likely contribute to the ongoing persistence of gender disparities in certain scientific occupations, although they certainly are not the only driving influence.

The authors of this chapter were specifically interested in examining gender dynamics in staffing roles at two types of organizations: field stations and marine labs (FSMLs) and nature centers (NCs). In addition to personal reasons as described by the authors below, these types of organizations were chosen because they share some important similarities while differing in meaningful ways. We describe both of these organization types as "nature-based." FSMLs and NCs have a lot of overlap in the terms used in their missions (e.g., research, education, community outreach, conservation), and therefore we would expect that they might attract and employ a similar staffing demographic in terms of gender.

LITERATURE REVIEW

FSMLs and NCs have a long history of providing a space for place-based nature study and experiential learning. According to Arvey and Riemer (1966), FSMLs began more than 100 years ago primarily as places for students to conduct in-situ field study and out-of-classroom learning spaces, and historically might have had public outreach facilities that functioned similarly to museum exhibits. More recently, FSMLs have been defined as facilities primarily dedicated to research goals at a specific location (McNulty et al., 2017; Struminger et al., 2018; Tydecks et al., 2016). FSMLs are generally grouped as being under four different management levels: government/national parks; non-profits/private; universities/colleges; and research institutions (Tydecks et al., 2016). Over time, FSMLs have shifted their focus to include more primary research (i.e., formal science), and this may be reflective of their close associations with institutions of higher learning. This does not negate the important role in education for which FSMLs continue to contribute (Klug et al., 2002). FSMLs can also often be located in remote areas, far from their home institution, although this is not always the case. Though a widely accepted definition of NCs was not readily accessible in the primary literature, NCs are most often thought of by the authors as hyper-local organizations that are easily accessible and open to the public, conduct K-12 and/or family type programs, and are managed by non-profits or local municipalities such as cities or park districts (Bevan & Semper, 2007). Nature and environmental education (i.e., informal science) play important roles in places like NCs. FSMLs and NCs can vary widely in terms of location (i.e., urban, suburban, rural, remote), property size, staff size, and budgets.

Since they occupy similar places in both the physical and theoretical landscapes, it is important to make at least a broad distinction between the current functionality of FSMLs and NCs. Of course, we expect that there are many instances where the following assumptions may not be true in whole or in part. As such, based on personal knowledge and the available literature, the authors propose that the mission of FSMLs prioritizes research, while NCs are more heavily weighted toward education. Furthermore, FSMLs are more focused on undergraduate and graduate education, whereas NCs are more focused on K-12 education. When we examine two of these primary mission pillars of research and education in terms of known job statistics, we begin to discover demographic differences when it comes to gender (U.S. Bureau of Labor Statistics, 2021).

In the broad category of "Life, physical, and social science occupations," females make up 49.3% of the total U.S. workforce. Within this category, 46% of "biological scientists" are identified as female (U.S. Bureau of Labor Statistics, 2021). This field would appear as fairly equivalent in terms of workforce gender dynamics. In fact, a 2021 National Science Foundation (NSF) report by Hamrick (2021) states that "in biological sciences, women received over 60% of bachelor's and master's degrees, and over half of doctoral degrees" (para. 2). The percentages of women in the "earth sciences" were slightly lower with females obtaining 38.4% of the bachelor degrees, 42.6% of master's degrees, and 44.1% of PhD's (Hamrick, 2021). Compared with something like computer and mathematical occupations where only 25.2% of the more technology-based positions are filled by females (U.S. Bureau of Labor Statistics, 2021), we see a more equal distribution of gender within these "nature-based" occupations. These high-level life and earth science statistics are helpful for thinking about the types of research and education (field and nature-based) that are likely occurring at FSMLs and NCs.

In the broad category of "Education, training, and library occupations," females dominate the field at 73.5% (U.S. Bureau of Labor Statistics, 2021). However, looking at further subcategories in this area shows a slightly different perspective, in that the vast majority of preschool and kindergarten teachers are female (98.8%); the majority elementary and middle school teachers are female (79.6%); most secondary school teachers are female (58.8%); and 51.1% of post-secondary teachers are female (U.S. Bureau of Labor Statistics, 2021). Therefore, we see an equalization of gender in teaching staff in the upper levels of academia. Although raw numbers indicate a more equal distribution of male and female educators in colleges and universities, this actually is a dilution of women's presence in the educational space compared to earlier in the education pipeline (K-12). Additionally, women in the academy are more likely to be employed as lecturers or non-tenure track faculty than as full professors (Harmon et al., 2018).

From these statistics, we can see some potential discrepancies in the composition of males and females in various aspects of STEM (i.e., researchers, educators). It is from this staffing composition breakdown and based on an interview, unrelated to the current study, that the research questions for this study were formulated. During an interview with a female NC executive director, the interviewee mentioned that she had never personally experienced any negative issues because of her gender in her current role but that she was often frustrated by the fact that she could not find many male naturalists/educators to fill job vacancies at her institution. This idea that organizations that identify as NCs were often dominated by female staff was not unknown or even particularly surprising to the authors; however, this concept spurred an interest in the researchers to learn more.

One author identifies as male, uses he/him/his pronouns, and has worked as a science educator for over 20 years in formal and informal science institutions (including natural history museums, an aquarium, science centers, a field station, and NCs). His experience as an educator in all of these organizations has been being one of very few men among the educational staff and many of the leadership positions were held by women. The other author of this chapter identifies as female, uses she/her/hers pronouns and currently works at a university field station. She has graduate degrees in the natural sciences and has worked at a NC as a natural resource specialist and naturalist in the past. Her experience has been that most leadership positions in FSMLs have been held by men, but that women are responsible for the majority of the education and outreach to the general public. Since the authors in some ways represent what may be considered by the general public as "outliers" in their respective fields (a "male educator" and a "female scientist"), the authors wanted to explore the following research questions to investigate whether there any trends related to gender roles within these organizations:

1) What is the staff composition at FSMLs and NCs?
    a) Are traditional research-based and higher educational organizations (Field Stations and Marine Labs) skewed in staff composition toward male staff?
    b) Are traditional youth environmental education organizations (NCs) skewed in staff composition toward female staff?
2) What are the perceptions of gender roles and staffing composition at FSMLs and NCs?

METHODS AND SAMPLING TECHNIQUES

An anonymous survey was developed using Google Forms in order to gain an understanding of the perceived gender discrepancies among staff working at FSMLs and NCs across the United States. The initial survey consisted of 26 questions including demographic information (i.e., respondent's gender identification, which was optional, and position within their organization), information about their organization (such as the founding story, mission, types of activities conducted at the site, and staff makeup), and perceptions of gender bias at their institution (see Appendix A for the full survey). It was anticipated that the survey would take ~20 minutes to complete. Responses were requested from those currently working at FSMLs and NCs via listservs for professional organizations within the United States (Organization of Biological Field Stations [OBFS], Association of Nature Center Administrators [ANCA], and National Association for Interpretation). It is likely that these listservs have hundreds, if not thousands, of subscribers, but there is no way to determine exactly how many people had access to the survey.

There were 84 respondents in total: 20 from FSMLs (14 identified as female, 5 as male, 0 as non-binary), 46 from NCs (44 female, 2 male, 0 non-binary), and 13 institutions were identified as "Both," which could include organizations like museums and arboreta that have clear research and education divisions (13 female, 0 male, 0 non-binary). Five survey submissions were scrubbed from the dataset. Four respondents did not specify any of the above organizations (FSMLs nor as NCs) and one was a duplicate response, bringing the total to 79. It is not the authors' intention to only present a binary viewpoint; however, the lack of non-binary (or other) representation does not allow us to present anything beyond male and female identities. For simplicity and to address the research questions of this study, we also use some terms interchangeably (male, men, boys vs. female, women, girls) while recognizing that gender is a fluid social construct and that this is an oversimplification of a more diverse spectrum in reality.

At the end of the original survey, respondents were invited to participate in a second follow-up survey designed to collect more extensive data on their perceived gendered experiences. Using the email addresses provided by interested participants, the researchers sent a link to a confidential Google Form survey containing 10 additional questions (see appendix B for the complete follow-up survey). Twenty-nine email addresses were provided, and 15 individuals (1 male, 14 females) responded to the follow-up survey, 3 from FSMLs and 12 from NCs.

The open response data were analyzed using a constant comparative approach along with an inductive analysis. Using the initial survey responses and the follow-up survey, we analyzed the data for emerging prevalent and distinct themes across responses. Initially, the responses from all participants were reviewed at the same time in random order. This was done in order to find statements that stood out from the rest. The resulting themes, along with examples of responses for each, will be discussed in the results section below. Each quote was coded with a participant code, i.e., NC 1 = Nature Center participant 1, FSML 2 = Field Station and Marine Lab participant 2, or Both 3 = Both participant 3. "Follow-up" was also included if the quote was from the second follow-up survey. Frequencies of demographics and question responses were also analyzed.

RESULTS

The three overarching themes identified in the survey were: (1) Roles of Staff at FSMLs and NCs, (2) Multiple Viewpoints about Gender Bias, and (3) Directions for Change.

Roles of Staff at Field Stations and Nature Centers

The roles of staff were perceived as vastly different by survey respondents. FSMLs were perceived as research-oriented and the staff were identified as predominantly male, while NCs were perceived to have a focus on education with predominantly female-identifying staff. For example, as one participant wrote, "I feel that a field station is staffed by more scientists whereas a nature center is staffed by educators. If the question is referring to gender, I feel that there may be more male researchers and more female educators" (NC 8). About 61% of the responses indicated a similar viewpoint. See figure 9.1 for the breakdown of degrees by organization type. According to the responses, 65% of FSMLs and 46% of "Both" respondents have PhDs, while only 4% of the NC respondents had PhDs (57% have a bachelor's degree).

Also, as part of the initial survey, participants were asked to estimate the number of full-time, part-time, leadership, and research/field staff at their facilities. Overall, they self-reported 556 staff members at FSMLs, 576 at NCs, 173 at institutions that are "Both." This is 1,305 staff members for all the institutions combined (see figure 9.2).

When coding the reported gender identities of staff, it was noted whether the institution had roughly equal representation (i.e., 50% male, 50% female) or whether one gender was more prevalent than another. If the percentage of one gender was above 60%, it was coded as "more" male or "more" female.

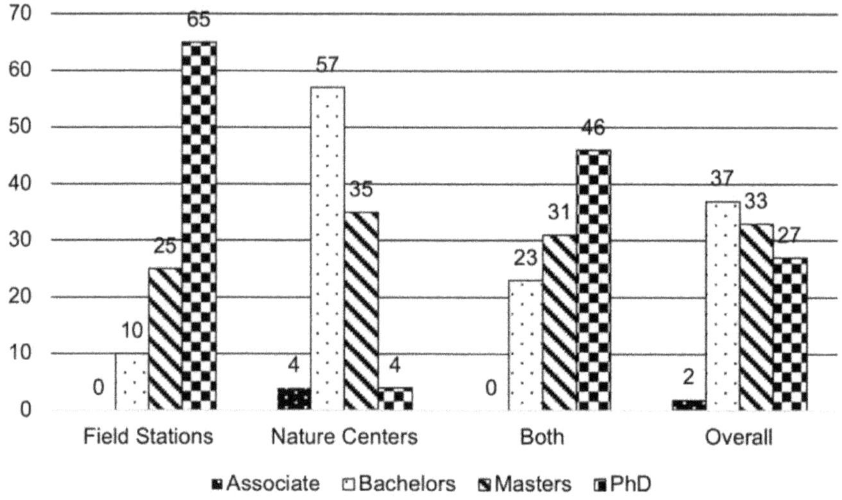

Figure 9.1 Percentage of Degrees by Organization Type (n=79) *Source:* Author data.

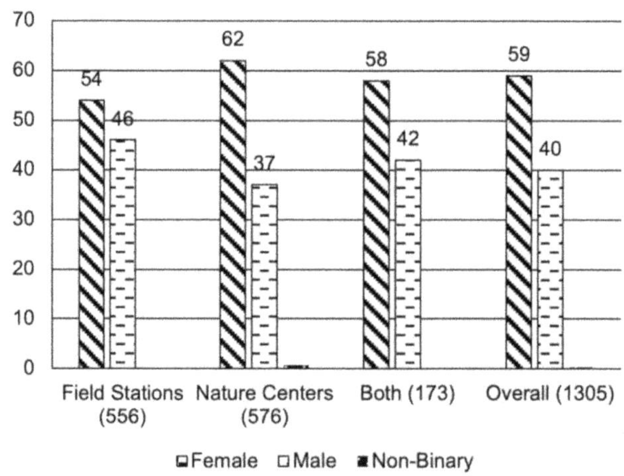

Figure 9.2 Percentage of Reported Staff for Each Organization Type *Source:* Author data.

In some cases, it was as high as 80–100%. Figure 9.3 illustrates the proportion of organizations that had equal representation, more male representation, or more female representation across the three organization types (NCs, FSMLs, or Both). Out of the 46 NCs represented in the initial survey, a higher proportion of respondents reported having a majority of female staff (72%)

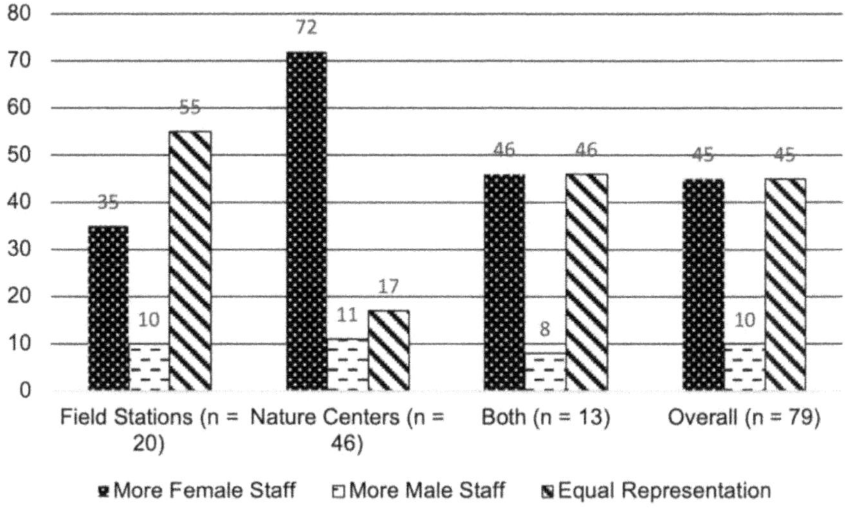

Figure 9.3 Comparison of the Percentage of Staffing and Gender Identities *Source:* Author data.

than the FSMLs (n=20; 35% had a majority female staff) or Both (n=13; 46% had a female majority staff). Note that participants may not necessarily know how their staff members might identify themselves; furthermore, some respondents were unaware of the number of staff within an entire organization if it was large and consequently reported only the staff within their departments. Across all institutions, less than 1% of the staff were reported to identify as non-binary.

The roles at FSMLs and NC could be impacted by their functioning and priorities. When responding to the initial survey, all participants (n=79) indicated that 93% of their sites served the general public, 82% served K-12 schools, 70% had citizen science programs, and 40% had a research focus. Of the research activities, 71% were related to citizen science, and 60% involved researchers.

For education-related activities, 88% offered field trips for K-12 classrooms, 71% provided K-12 classroom visits, and 52% offered professional development opportunities for teachers. Community outreach and engagement were also part of their organizations' activities, with 89% providing lectures and presentations, 79% leading nature hikes, 75% were involved in community events, and offered workshops (70%). Given that the survey was sent out in the midst of a global pandemic, where face-to-face programming was severely limited, it was not surprising to see that 61% of the sites also offered virtual options for their educational and community outreach programming.

Multiple Viewpoints about Gender Bias

When asked on the initial survey "Do you feel that there are gender biases within staffing roles /makeup in NCs and field stations? Please answer Yes, No, or Maybe and briefly explain your answer in the space provided," 38% of respondents said "No." Only 28% said "Yes," followed by 21% saying "Maybe" and another 9% said "Sometimes" (4% of the responses were unclear). Obviously, it is more complicated than these simple responses would indicate, as noted by survey responses clearly expressing perceived bias:

> I do think there are inherent gender biases against the education side from the research side as not being as intelligent and or as educated . . . . There are also pay differences. I know I am not paid as much as males, even though I [*sic*] more qualified than them (NC 1).

> I don't feel direct hiring of Program staff is necessarily impacted, but faculty bias and perception are definitely a challenge. I think cultural practices may have a bigger influence as to qualifications for potential staff versus anything else. Regarding maintenance staff/stewards, those definitely tend to be male dominant. Again, could be a result of cultural practices and exposure to "traditional" skillsets, versus hiring practices. (Both 51)

Some shared challenges on the job as a result of perceived gender bias, as written by a FSML staff member: "I have a Ph.D., but am oftentimes [*sic*] viewed as my department's administrative assistant" (FSML 4 Follow-Up). A NC respondent (a director) shared the following regarding their experiences:

> I have been in many roles that are typically "female"—secretary, communications, environmental education/interpretation. I have felt like I have had to go through a lot of "proving up" to reach my current level—work harder, have more patience, strive for high accolades and advanced degrees, delay family, etc. (NC 15 Follow-up)

Another respondent shared examples of harassment and assault, noting the following:

> I've been sexually harassed and assaulted as a means of bullying me out of the field at the majority of field stations I've worked at. I've been told by hiring managers that I was the most qualified candidate, but they chose a less-qualified male colleague because he had "connections" to male Ph.D. advisers or others that they wanted to gain [access to]. (FSML 5 Follow-Up)

Despite these shared experiences, some participants shared how gender bias was an issue but as a thing of the past, for example, "less so now than 5 years ago when leadership was almost all male" (Both 14). Another respondent suggested gender served as an advantage for their chosen field vs. a perceived barrier, noting how their gender "works" for their chosen field, "My gender really has had no impact on my journey thus far. If anything, my patient demeanor and love of working with children comes from my female instincts" (NC 2). Finally, some participants felt gender bias did not exist in their organization. As stated by another participant, "gender roles or identity have never impacted my work environment or my perceptions of job duties and responsibilities within that environment" (NC 9).

There seems to be some ambiguity about whether gender bias is an issue, especially when gender seems to work in one's favor or since it has been systemic and is pervasive in much of one's life experiences. If the perception was that bias was a thing of the past, there was an attempt to correct these issues. For example, "I think we have had some historic bias, but it has been something we have been working on. As we have added staff, we have been working on diversity" (Both 37).

Furthermore, the applicants for jobs at either type of organization leaned toward a particular gender, as was made evident by this respondent, "there seem to be more females applying for jobs at our non-profit nature center than males" (NC 17) and another respondent noted the following:

> Yes, the research side is definitely more male dominated, and the education side is more female dominated. I also believe that our current research position was going to be filled by a man regardless of the applicants. We also had a lab position where one candidate was female and more qualified, but she did not get the position, a male did. (Both 20)

While this may be the case, it was not seen to be unusual since "people expect women to work with children more" (NC 69) and "educators are typically seen as nurturers (female), directors as male" (NC 28) which suggests confirmation of socially constructed gender norms. One respondent suggested confirmation bias, described as stigmatization, regarding gender norms may influence perceptions of self and others working throughout the organization:

> Most issues in my workplace stem from differences between the all female programs department and the all males operations department. These differences are in temperament, logistical and planning differences, educational differences (degrees in science fields or not), and sometimes even some sexism (in both directions). It feels like our roles are stigmatized, but that also sometimes we are

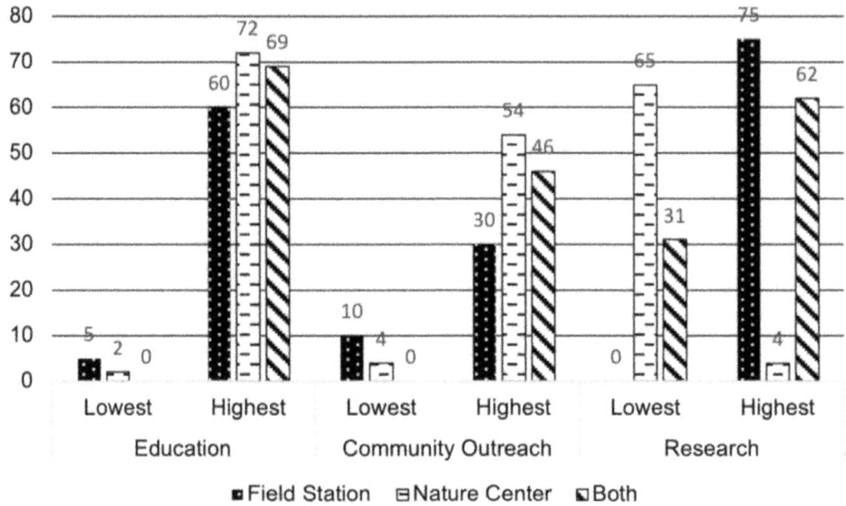

Figure 9.4 Percentage of Low and High Priority Rankings for the Institutional Mission Statement Commitment to Education, Community Outreach, and Research *Source:* Author data.

> the ones doing the stigmatizing because of what we expect of the other departments, or what we ourselves will not do. (NC 3 Follow-up)

Although 60% of FSML respondents indicated that education was a high priority in their mission statements, only 30% ranked education highly in terms of the amount of time spent on such activities. This is compared to 70% of FSMLs ranking research as a time-intensive activity at their institution and 75% ranking this as a priority in their mission statement. The opposite was true for NCs: education was ranked highly in terms of their mission statement priority (72%) and time spent (61%); however, research was often ranked as the lowest priority (65%) for the mission and time spent (67%) (see figures 9.4 and 9.5). In addition, in terms of the mission, community outreach was ranked highly for NCs and "Both" (54% and 46%). However, time spent on such activities was not ranked as highly (28% and 23%). Also of interest, for sites noted as "Both," education and research were ranked highly when considering both the mission statement (69% and 62%, respectively) and time spent on those activities (62% and 54%).

Directions for Change

In the follow-up survey, 60% of the respondents (n=15) indicated that they went into the field due to passion, while 40% had career related or strategic reasons. This passion was demonstrated in the response to the question "What

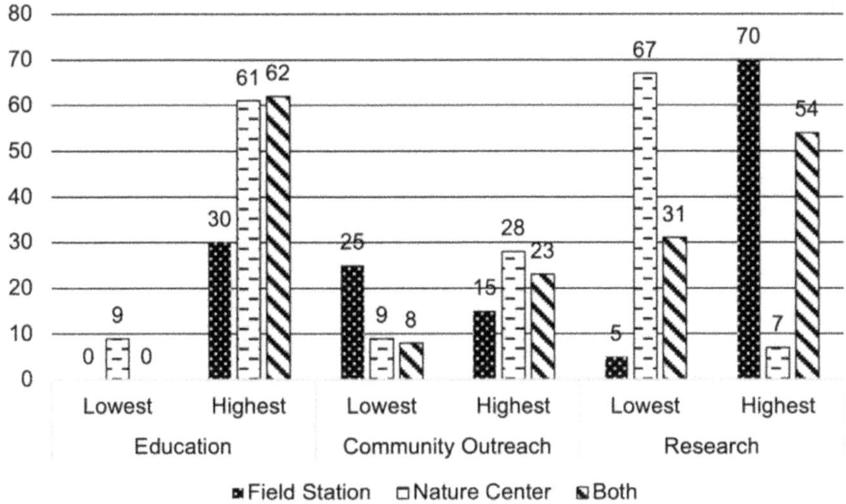

Figure 9.5 Percentage of Low and High Priority Rankings for Estimated Time Spent on an Activity (Education, Community Outreach, and Research) *Source:* Author data.

changes, if any, would you like to see happen in this industry? (These could include culture, policy, funding, relationships, leadership, perceptions, organizational structure, etc.)." One respondent shared the following related to the role of educators:

> I think it is important to have more men in education roles. In the school system there seems to be a lot of progress in this, and there are more and more elementary teachers who are men, but it doesn't feel like this has transferred over well into the natural resources field. It is important for children to learn from a variety of people throughout their lives, both men and women, so staffing locations with both will help to reach and impact the maximum number of children. (NC 3)

Another area of change involved changing the perception of women in other professional areas, outside of education, within FSMLs and NCs:

> The biggest perception change that I would like to see in the industry is that you don't have to be "tough" to work in this field. In the past, I have perceived bias against me from co-workers that I can't handle hikes or long days of field work because of my gender. I was able to show that it wasn't the case and I could actually handle the work that was given to me and the long days outdoors. (NC 4)

This included gear necessary for doing the job, for example, "While it might seem silly I just want field gear that fits! . . . Imagine if diversity of gender and bodies was the assumption instead of the exception" (NC 12). When considering leadership roles within FSMLs and NCs, there was a call for "a more inclusive culture, and that includes fair promotion and compensation for workers at all levels" (FSMLs 5), as well as

> more females in positions of power. . . . Emotional intelligence is hard to come by in any gendered person, and the world needs more of that. Environmentalism and environmental education require compassion, patience and persistence. (NC 7)

DISCUSSION

We found that gender differences in staffing exist in FSMLs and NCs, but that the deep-seated biases related to gender are expressed differently depending upon the type of outdoor research and learning facility (FSML or NC). NCs demonstrated a clear partiality toward women in their staffing composition (72% had more female staff than male) compared to only 35% of FSMLs having more female than male staff, with organizations that identified as "Both" being closer to a middle ground with 46% having more females than males. In all categories independently and overall, only about 10% of FSMLs, NCs, and "Both" indicated that they had an equal distribution of men and women in their workforces. Cumulatively, FSMLs and those identifying as "Both" are much more evenly distributed in terms of gender overall, although it was difficult to determine from the survey data what exact roles within these organizations were held by women and men. These results are consistent with the percentages of men and women in the educational fields (U.S. Bureau of Labor Statistics, 2021), in that women are more likely to be educators for younger children, and that this disparity starts to dissolve at higher education levels. Overall, there still may be an underlying gender bias for females to be in more of the educational roles at FSMLs (depending on how much K-12 education is occurring) while more of the research and leadership positions are held by men. These specific job roles would need to be examined through a different methodology to really tease apart any gender segregation.

The data indicate, however, that job segregation occurs both horizontally (i.e., certain careers are seen as feminine, certain as masculine) and vertically (i.e., even in female-dominated workplaces, bosses may be male) based on gender (Konrad et al., 2000). Furthermore, an even distribution of gender in the workforce does not necessarily mean that gender-based discrimination and harassment does not occur at varying levels of intensity. Although many respondents indicated that there was no current gender bias at their workplace, they qualified their answers in some respects regarding the type of bias, that is, what they seemed to mean in many cases, for example, was that because they were a woman, working with other women, in a career thought to have feminine stereotypes (education), that there was no negative gender bias against them. What these types of conclusions seem to overlook is that a positive (or non-negative) gender bias toward one gender or the other is still a bias (Britton, 2017) and may have repercussions for other genders. This denial of workplace gender bias can continue to perpetuate gender inequality by negating its importance in organizational norms and systemic practices (Gascoigne et al., 2015).

Our research supports the fact that FSMLs are at least perceived as organizations primarily focused on research and therefore run by men, even if this is not entirely true. This widespread perception may be preventing qualified female job candidates from even applying for open positions at FSMLs. Blackburn's (2017) review suggests that the perception of STEM as male-dominated represents one of the biggest hurdles to gender equity in programs because it causes psychological barriers to participation. The job demographics regarding level of degree gathered as part of this study show that the respondents to our surveys were likely highly qualified staffers. When considering the responses concerning educational background, although FSMLs and organizations described as "Both" had more PhDs, the majority of the respondents from the NCs had at least a bachelor's degree and many had master's degrees as well. We did not specifically ask what majors these degrees were from, so this is merely conjecture, but it is conceivable that many NC staffers hold biology or other related degrees like environmental science or geology. It begs the question as to why so many college-educated women might gravitate to jobs in informal science at NCs, rather than potentially higher paying, "more respected" (as implied by survey respondents) jobs in the FSMLs realm. Unfortunately, this tendency to move on from STEM positions into more educational-based positions may have some deep roots in the academic realm.

Much of the literature (Blackburn, 2017; Jacobs, 2003; Kanny et al., 2014) focuses on a culture of a "chilly climate" for women in STEM in academia, and these lingering experiences with less than pleasant interactions may be enough to encourage females to look outside of STEM academic and research portions entirely (Shauman, 2017). Since FSMLs are often associated with universities or colleges, gender gaps at these workplaces could be almost a self-fulfilling prophecy. Cundiff et al. (2013) reminds us that "personal choices [regarding science identity and science career occupations] are made within particular social contexts, and stereotypes are part of that context" (p. 551). Therefore, until better gains for gender equity in STEM are made at the university level, perceptions regarding who is running and working at FSMLs, and who would be welcome at them, may persist into the future (Britton, 2017; DeAro et al., 2019; Shauman, 2017).

Many of the survey respondents supported previous findings in the primary literature that women are drawn to particular careers because they share certain attributes such as the ability to help others (i.e., altruism), flexibility for family obligations (i.e., reasonable working hours, a short commute), and ability to build community with coworkers (i.e., social capital). Gender-based job preferences certainly are evident in both our respondents' survey answers and in the literature (Konrad et al., 2000; Sheppard, 2018). If women feel that NCs support the work-life balance preferences that are more important to them, then they may be more apt to apply for jobs at these types of organizations, even while sacrificing other job attributes like higher pay, leadership opportunities, and autonomy (Konrad et al., 2000; Sheppard, 2018). Another perception about "men's work" is that it is highly physical or extreme in nature and that this means women are not as well suited for the work (Gascoigne et al., 2015; Mitten et al., 2017). Several survey responses indicated that the fieldwork or even lack of appropriately sized gear could contribute to a lack of desire to work at FSMLs. In terms of the sometimes remote location of field stations, the need to live onsite or the perception of safety concerns could also contribute to a gender disparity in certain roles at FSMLs (Gochfeld et al., 2006). A solution here may include developing more inclusive cultural norms. Oversimplified, these could include such things as gender-neutral bathroom facilities, better personnel and field training for staff and management about acceptable conduct, equal pay for equal work, and safety plans for remote/fieldwork environments that specifically include details on sexual harassment. There can be more effort toward building support systems to encourage bonding social capital among staff across genders to create a teamwork approach rather than rewarding individualistic type behaviors (Timberlake, 2005).

CONCLUSION

FSMLs and NCs share many characteristics regarding their missions and everyday activities related to nature/field study and education. They appear to differ mainly in their management (i.e., FSMLs are often associated with universities, and NCs are often associated with municipalities or other nongovernmental organizations), as well as in their constituent base (i.e., FSMLs work with undergraduate/graduate students and NCs work with K-12 and the general public). However, we know from current research and personal experience that FSMLs are greatly expanding their educational missions to also target K-12 and general public audiences (McNulty et al., 2017; Struminger et al., 2018; Tydeks et al., 2016). This trend indicates that FSMLs and NCs may be converging into similar educational and community outreach landscapes. NCs have long been looked to for environmental leaders on issues in their own communities and therefore are important places for increasing science literacy and this is becoming an important area for FSMLs as well (Struminger et al., 2021). These convergences in mission and delivery suggest that both organizations may see benefit from working more purposefully together, especially in the arena of science communication and community literacy (see National Academies of Science, Engineering, and Medicine, 2017). NCs have a long relationship with informal science (i.e., science taught in spaces outside a traditional K-12 classroom) and natural history, which can be traced to roots with "gentlemen naturalists," Victorian age women, and even the seminal text of the *Handbook of Nature Study* by Anna Botsford Comstock from 1911.

Johnson and Dieckmann (2020) found that Americans have more positive and less negative stereotypes around non-profit advocacy groups than with other types of organizations. Therefore, FSMLs may benefit from partnerships with their local non-profit nature center to help disseminate their scientific research findings in a non-threatening and more socially acceptable manner, while NCs may gain credibility by presenting current and cutting-edge scientific research. Beyond that, as FSMLs more fully embrace their role in youth education and public outreach, they could likely benefit from the professional naturalists, educators, and interpreters at their local nature centers in making complex scientific concepts more digestible for general consumption; likewise, NCs could benefit from new partnerships with FSMLs by creating more relevant and compelling curriculum regarding current environmental issues like climate change, invasive species, and habitat degradation that are strongly grounded in science and scientific methods. These positive collaborations and additional interactions between staff, of all genders, at the two types of organizations, could contribute to a breakdown of the perceptions that NCs are for women, by women and FSMLs are for men, by men.

One author had the personal experience of a (male) naturalist at a local NC telling her that she should not be competing with them for their K-12 audience. This statement was quite likely motivated by financial incentives because there are, of course, finite resources (e.g., grants, donations, etc.) around environmental education delivery in certain communities. However, we believe there is no shortage of youth and no maximum number of times for students to have opportunities to learn about nature and science, especially in the field, as these reiterative experiences help shift environmental behaviors over time (Otto & Pensini, 2017).

We should not be thinking of providing experiential learning opportunities in nature as a competition between like-minded institutions. Similar messaging and outreach from multiple organization types on environmental issues and current science to students of all ages and the general public can only help bolster public confidence in such information, especially in an era of misinformation through social media and "fake news" (Lazer et al., 2018). Furthermore, additional opportunities for students to be exposed to genders all along the spectrum, such as male, female, non-binary and other gender scientists and male, female, non-binary and other gender naturalists/educators, may mean a future where perceptions of gender at FSMLs and NCs are less biased.

Indeed, both FSMLs and NCs can move the needle toward gender equity in their workplaces by amplifying their messaging regarding who is a scientist and what is science, as well as who is a naturalist and what is environmental education. The general public needs to see people of all genders doing science and people of all genders teaching about science (Miller et al., 2018). And this is extremely important for more than just the marginalized due to gender, but also other marginalized communities like Black, Indigenous, and People of Color, as well as people with differing physical abilities. The youth of today need diverse role models in both science (i.e., FSMLs) and science communication (i.e., NCs) because as Marian Wright Edelman stated so eloquently, "you can't be what you can't see."

FUTURE WORK

A more comprehensive survey targeted at people who hold specific positions within each of these organizational types may provide a more nuanced view of gender bias within FSMLs and NCs. For example, from the data we collected, it is difficult to determine the breakdown of genders within individual roles within and across organizational types such as executive director, education director, and research director. Determining who holds leadership positions and positions of power may shed light on deeper systemic issues and help guide recommendations for sustainable solutions. The authors believe that more transparent reporting of these types of organizational dynamics (gender, age, race, ability, etc.) could help alleviate incorrect perceptions of place, as well as make organizations accountable to their current and future applicants and employees. Both FSMLs and NCs have robust professional associations in the OBFS and the ANCA, respectively, and it is not outside the scope of their missions to collect and provide demographic data on their members. Not only could this shed light on gender disparities (or not) within these types of organizations but also provide important information regarding racial demographics among employees (Britton, 2017; see Green 2.0 2020 for an example of a transparency report card). Furthermore, although the current research on increased wage transparency's effect on observable reductions in the gender (and race) pay gap is still unclear (Baker et al., 2019), the authors propose that if pay scales were published for jobs by OBFS and ANCA, that applicants could make more informed decisions for which jobs they might be interested in applying. While we are discussing FSMLs and NCs here, if we wish to see equal representation in all professions, this must be a goal for society overall.

APPENDIX A

Initial Survey

1. Name of Organization. Note: If you work at an organization that is a part of a much larger organization (i.e., a nature center in a regional park district that has many NCs), please answer the questions to the best of your knowledge for your specific nature center/field station. If you can only answer questions relevant to your department (i.e., education department), please just indicate that in your answer after the name of your organization in parentheses.
2. What is your discipline/educational background?
3. What is your highest degree level?
   a. PhD
   b. Master's
   c. Bachelor's
   d. Associate
   e. High School
   f. Other
4. What positions have you held in field stations/NCs?
5. What is your current position title? If this role was in the past, please indicate (past). You may also indicate that you prefer not to say.
6. Do you consider your current role to be a leadership position within the organization?
   a. Yes
   b. No
7. Personal Gender Identity (Optional)
   a. Female
   b. Male
   c. Non-binary
   d. Prefer not to say
   e. Other
8. How would you classify your facility? Do you identify as a:
   a. Field Station/Marine Lab
   b. Nature Center

   c. Both
   d. Neither
   e. Other
9. Do you know the founding story/history of your center? If so, please briefly explain. If not, please indicate N/A.
10. What is the organization's mission and/or vision?
11. The next two questions deal with mission rank and percentage. These might correlate in some organizations (highest priority has the highest percentage of time/effort/funding) but it may be uncoupled in other cases. How do you rank the components of your mission in terms of priority (flat number ranking)? (1=highest rank, 5=lowest rank or N/A).
    a. Education
    b. Research
    c. Community Outreach/Engagement
    d. Land Conservation/Preservation
    e. Species Conservation/Preservation
    f. Policy/Advocacy
    g. Other
12. How do you rank the components of your mission in terms of percentage (%) of time/effort/funding? (1=highest rank, 5=lowest rank or N/A).
    a. Education
    b. Research
    c. Community Outreach/Engagement
    d. Land Conservation/Preservation
    e. Species Conservation/Preservation
    f. Policy/Advocacy
    g. Other
13. How many full-time staff? Please indicate gender identity, that is, male/female/non-binary/other in your answer to the best of your knowledge. For example: 2M, 4F, 2NB
14. How many part-time staff? Please indicate gender identity, that is, male/female/non-binary in your answer to the best of your knowledge.
15. How many leadership staff? Please indicate gender identity, that is, male/female/non-binary in your answer to the best of your knowledge.
16. How many research/field staff? Please indicate gender identity, that is, male/female/non-binary in your answer to the best of your knowledge.
17. Do you feel that there are gender biases within staffing roles/makeup in nature center and field stations? Please answer Yes, No, or Maybe and briefly explain your answer in the space provided.
18. How do you define your audience/constituency? Select all that apply.
    a. General Public
    b. K-12

   c. Undergraduates
   d. Graduate Students
   e. Faculty/Researchers
   f. Citizen Science/Specialty-focused (i.e., birding, native plants, etc.)
   g. Other
19. What types of activities do you do for RESEARCH? (include field work?) Select all that apply.
   a. Field
   b. Laboratory
   c. Undergraduate Research
   d. Graduate Student Research
   e. Faculty Research
   f. Citizen Science
   g. None
   h. Other:
20. What types of activities do you do for EDUCATION (specifically with schools/universities)? Select all that apply.
   a. Field trips (K-12)
   b. Classroom Visits (K-12)
   c. Teacher professional development (K-12)
   d. Curriculum Development (K-12)
   e. Curriculum Kits (K-12) for loan to educators
   f. College-level Classes
   g. Overnight/Extended Field Trips/Residential Camps
   h. Virtual
   i. None
   j. Other:
21. What types of activities do you do for COMMUNITY OUTREACH/ENGAGEMENT? Select all that apply.
   a. Lectures/Presentations
   b. Nature Hikes
   c. Workshops
   d. Open Houses
   e. Community Events (Fairs, Art Shows, etc.)
   f. Overnight/Extended Experiences
   g. Virtual
   h. None
   i. Other:
22. What types of activities do you do for OTHER MISSION/VISION COMPONENT? Please list specific mission components and fill in the blank if applicable.

23. If there are other priority activities not mentioned above, or if you would like to comment/elaborate on any other question in the survey, please feel free to do that here.
24. Have you had experience working at a Field Station AND a Nature Center?
    a. Yes
    b. No
    c. Other:
25. Would you be willing to discuss your experiences with us around perceived or real gender biases within these two types of organizations via virtual focus group or through email? We will ask you to provide us with your email address through another survey that will not be linked to the current survey if you answer "yes." If you answer "maybe," you may reach out directly to Dr. Lara Roketenetz at Ldr11@uakron.edu for more information.
    a. Yes
    b. No
    c. Maybe

APPENDIX B

Follow-Up Survey

1. Personal Gender Identity (Optional)
    a. Female
    b. Male
    c. Non-binary
    d. Prefer not to say
    e. Other
2. Current Job Title
3. Length of Time in Industry
    a. 0–5 years
    b. 6–10 years
    c. 11–15 years
    d. 16–20 years
    e. 21+ years
4. Would you BEST describe your organization as a:
    a. Field Station
    b. Nature Center
5. Did you get into this field for:
    a. Career/Strategic Reasons

   b. Passion
   c. Fun
   d. Other
6. How would you describe the overall culture of your organization?
7. What are your perceptions about gender roles within your organization in terms of job duties and responsibilities, if any?
8. How has gender impacted your journey within this field, if at all? Please elaborate.
9. If you work at a Nature Center, what are your perceptions of staffing roles at field stations (or vice versa)?
10. What changes, if any, would you like to see in this industry? (These could include culture, policy, funding, relationships, leadership, perceptions, organizational structure, etc.)

REFERENCES

Arvey, M. D., & Riemer, W. J. (1966). Inland biological field stations of the United States. *BioScience*, *16*(4), 249–254. https://doi.org/10.2307/1293564

Baker, M., Halberstam, Y., Kroft, K., Mas, A., & Messacar, D. (2019). *Pay transparency and the gender gap* (Report No. w25834). National Bureau of Economic Research. http://www.nber.org/papers/w25834

Bevan, B., & Semper, R. J. (2006). *Mapping informal science institutions onto the science education landscape*. Center for Informal Learning and Schools https://www.exploratorium.edu/files/pdf/cils/CILS_BAI_Bevan_&_Semper_Mapping_ISIs.pdf

Blackburn, H. (2017). The status of women in STEM in higher education: A review of the literature 2007–2017. *Science & Technology Libraries*, *36*(3), 235–273. https://doi.org/10.1080/0194262X.2017.1371658

Botella, C., Rueda, S., López-Iñesta, E., & Marzal, P. (2019). Gender diversity in STEM disciplines: A multiple factor problem. *Entropy*, *21*(1), 30. https://doi.org/10.3390/e21010030

Britton, D. M. (2017). Beyond the chilly climate: The salience of gender in women's academic careers. *Gender & Society*, *31*(1), 5–27. https://doi.org/10.1177/0891243216681494

Cundiff, J. L., Vescio, T. K., Loken, E., & Lo, L. (2013). Do gender–science stereotypes predict science identification and science career aspirations among undergraduate science majors? *Social Psychology of Education*, *16*(4), 541–554. https://doi.org/10.1007/s11218-013-9232-8

DeAro, J., Bird, S., & Ryan, S. M. (2019). NSF ADVANCE and gender equity: Past, present and future of systemic institutional transformation strategies. *Equality, Diversity and Inclusion: An International Journal, 38*(2), 131–139. https://doi.org/10.1108/EDI-09-2017-0188

England, P. (2010). The gender revolution: Uneven and stalled. *Gender & Society*, *24*(2), 149–166. https://doi.org/10.1177/0891243210361475

Gascoigne, C., Parry, E., & Buchanan, D. (2015). Extreme work, gendered work? How extreme jobs and the discourse of 'personal choice' perpetuate gender inequality. *Organization, 22*(4), 457–475. https://doi.org/10.1177/1350508415572511

Gochfeld, M., Volz, C. D., Burger, J., Jewett, S., Powers, C. W., & Friedlander, B. (2006). Developing a health and safety plan for hazardous field work in remote areas. *Journal of Occupational and Environmental Hygiene, 3*(12), 671–683. https://doi.org/10.1080/15459620601009201

Green 2.0. *NGO and foundation transparency report card.* (2020). https://diversegreen.org/wp-content/uploads/2021/02/green-2.0-2020-transparency-report-card.pdf

Hamrick, K. (2021). *Women, minorities, and persons with disabilities in science and engineering*. National Science Foundation -National Center for Science and Engineering Statistics. https://ncses.nsf.gov/pubs/nsf21321/report/field-of-degree-women#overview

Harmon, O., Hopkins, B., Kelchen, R., Persky, J., & Roy, J. (2018). The annual report on the economic status of the profession, 2017–18. *Academe*, *104*(2), 4–10.

Hill, C., Corbett, C., & St. Rose, A. (2010). Why so few? Women in science, technology, engineering and mathematics. *American Association of University Women.* https://www.aauw.org/app/uploads/2020/03/why-so-few-research.pdf

Jacobs, J. A. (2003). Detours on the road to equality: Women, work and higher education. *Contexts*, *2*(1), 32–41. https://doi.org/10.1525/ctx.2003.2.1.32

Johnson, B. B., & Dieckmann, N. F. (2020). Americans' views of scientists' motivations for scientific work. *Public Understanding of Science, 29*(1), 2–20. https://doi.org/10.1177/0963662519880319

Kanny, M. A., Sax, L. J., & Riggers-Piehl, T. A. (2014). Investigating forty years of STEM research: How explanations for the gender gap have evolved over time. *Journal of Women and Minorities in Science and Engineering, 20*(2), 127–148. https://doi.org/10.1615/JWomenMinorScienEng.2014007246

Konrad, A. M., Ritchie Jr, J. E., Lieb, P., & Corrigall, E. (2000). Sex differences and similarities in job attribute preferences: A meta-analysis. *Psychological Bulletin, 126*(4), 593.

Kossek, E. E., Su, R., & Wu, L. (2017). "Opting out" or "pushed out"? Integrating perspectives on women's career equality for gender inclusion and interventions. *Journal of Management*, *43*(1), 228–254. https://doi.org/10.1177/0149206316671582

Klug, M. J., Hodder, J., & Swain, H. (2002). The role of biological field stations in education and recruitment into the biological sciences. In Report of the NSF-sponsored workshop, *Education and Recruitment into the Biological Sciences: Potential Role of Field Station and Marine Laboratories.*

Lazer, D. M., Baum, M. A., Benkler, Y., Berinsky, A. J., Greenhill, K. M., Menczer, F., Metzger, M. J., Nyhan, B., Pennycook, G., Rothschild, D. & Schudson, M. (2018). The science of fake news. *Science, 359*(6380), 1094–1096. https://doi.org/10.1126/science.aao2998Martinez, A., & Christnacht, C. (2021). *Women making gains in STEM occupations but still underrepresented.* United States Census Bureau. https://www.census.gov/library/stories/2021/01/women-making-gains-in-stem-occupations-but-still-underrepresented.html.

McNulty, S. A., White, D., Hufty, M., & Foster, P. (2017). The organization of biological field stations at fifty. *Bulletin of the Ecological Society of America, 98*(4), 359–373. https://www.jstor.org/stable/90013298

Miller, D. I., Nolla, K. M., Eagly, A. H., & Uttal, D. H. (2018). The development of children's gender-science stereotypes: A meta-analysis of 5 decades of US draw-a-scientist studies. *Child Development, 89*(6), 1943–1955. https://doi.org/10.1111/cdev.13039

Mitten, D., Gray, T., Allen-Craig, S., Loeffler, T. A., & Carpenter, C. (2018). The invisibility cloak: Women's contributions to outdoor and environmental education. *The Journal of Environmental Education, 49*(4), 318–327. https://doi.org/10.1080/00958964.2017.1366890

National Academies of Sciences, Engineering, and Medicine. (2017). *Communicating Science Effectively: A Research Agenda*. The National Academies Press. https://doi.org/10.17226/23674.

Otto, S., & Pensini, P. (2017). Nature-based environmental education of children: Environmental knowledge and connectedness to nature, together, are related to ecological behaviour. *Global Environmental Change, 47*, 88–94. https://doi.org/10.1016/j.gloenvcha.2017.09.009

Ridgeway, C. L. (2011). *Framed by gender: How gender inequality persists in the modern world.* Oxford University Press.

Shauman, K. A. (2017). Gender differences in the early employment outcomes of STEM doctorates. *Social Sciences, 6*(1), 24. https://doi.org/10.3390/socsci6010024

Sheppard, L. D. (2018). Gender differences in leadership aspirations and job and life attribute preferences among US undergraduate students. *Sex Roles*, *79*(9), 565–577. https://doi.org/10.1007/s11199-017-0890-4

Struminger, R., Zarestky, J., Short, R. A., & Lawing, A. M. (2018). A framework for informal STEM education outreach at field stations. *BioScience, 68*(12), 969–978. https://doi.org/10.1093/biosci/biy108

Struminger, R., Short, R. A., Zarestky, J., Vilen, L., & Lawing, A. M. (2021). Biological field stations promote science literacy through outreach. *BioScience*, biab057. https://doi.org/10.1093/biosci/biab057

Timberlake, S. (2005). Social capital and gender in the workplace. *Journal of Management Development, 24*(1), 34–44. https://doi.org/10.1108/02621710510572335

Toosi, M. (2012). Projections of the labor force to 2050: A visual essay. *Monthly Labor Review*, 3–16. https://stats.bls.gov/opub/mlr/2012/10/art1full.pdf

Tydecks, L., Bremerich, V., Jentschke, I., Likens, G. E., & Tockner, K. (2016). Biological field stations: A global infrastructure for research, education, and public engagement. *BioScience, 66*(2), 164–171. https://doi.org/10.1093/biosci/biv174

U.S. Bureau of Labor Statistics. (2021, January 22). *Employed persons by detailed occupation, sex, race, and Hispanic or Latino ethnicity*. U.S. Bureau of Labor Statistics. https://www.bls.gov/cps/cpsaat11.htm.

Wegemer, C. M., & Eccles, J. S. (2019). Gendered STEM career choices: Altruistic values, beliefs, and identity. *Journal of Vocational Behavior*, *110*, 28–42. https://doi.org/10.1016/j.jvb.2018.10.020

Chapter 10

Women's Perspectives on Building International Community–Field Station Collaborations

Perspectivas de las mujeres sobre la construcción de asociaciones internacionales entre la comunidad y la estación de campo

Rhonda Struminger, Gabriela Maria Vázquez Adame, and Yamila Hussein-Shannan

INTRODUCTION

Field stations and marine laboratories (FSMLs) exist because of the ecological and environmental features of a particular place (Billick et al., 2013). Places that were recognized and named by humans were in existence long before the origin of people throughout geologic time. It is only in the last few thousands of years that there are very few places on earth that have no human history. The notion of a land without people, *terra incognita/terra nullius*, has been used by colonialists for centuries to justify making claims on desirable locations across the planet that undermine established human populations and deny the existence of Indigenous societies (Zukas, 2005). As with any modern institution trying to come to terms with its colonial past and present, FSMLs cannot ignore the human communities in which they reside or the power dynamics that operate between FSMLs and local communities.

The FSML at the center of this chapter is the Centro de Investigaciones Científicas de las Huastecas "Aguazarca" (CICHAZ), established in 2005 in Calnali, Hidalgo Mexico (see figure 10.1). This area is in the bio-geographically

Figure 10.1 Map Showing Mexico and Highlighting the Municipality of Calnali. *Source:* Photo by author based on Google Maps data.

and culturally distinctive Sierra and Huasteca region of central Mexico. The co-founders Rhonda Struminger and Gil Rosenthal founded the field station in Calnali to support Gil's research on the poeciliid fish genus *Xiphophorus*. Rhonda, a social scientist, brings her interest in education policy, informal STEM education, and Indigenous knowledge to the field station. Historically, economically developed and wealthy countries have justified colonialist and exploitative practices by assuming the global scientific directive will benefit both academic and societal values. To help shift this paradigm, from the time of the station's inception and early planning phases, the founders of CICHAZ have partnered with community members, specifically with the Asesoría Social Productiva, A.C. (ASPac), to forge meaningful collaborations that place equal value on the communities' needs, knowledge, and aspirations and the research and policies at CICHAZ.

Gabriela Vázquez Adame (Gaby) and her father, César Vázquez Acosta, founded the Mexican non-profit Asesoría Social Productiva, A.C. (ASPac) in 1994 to promote better business practices among rural producers of coffee, corn, crafts, etc. In 2000, Gaby first came to Calnali to teach an ASPac business course at the invitation of Eduardo Salas (Lalo), president of a local coffee production cooperative. After many return trips to Calnali, Gaby eventually married Lalo and in 2005, they started a small roasted coffee production company at Rancho La Tejería, owned by Lalo and his family. In 2014, the two couples (Rhonda and Gil, Lalo and Gaby) met during the first Day of Science and Sustainability (La Jornada) launched by CICHAZ. The potential for collaborative projects focusing on the environment and conservation in the Sierra and Huasteca region and community outreach was immediately evident. Sharing a deep commitment to research, learning, and community development, the two organizations have since embarked on a number of collaborative projects that seek to improve the quality of the water, promote science education broadly, and advance ranching productivity while protecting the natural resources and biodiversity of the area.

In this chapter, Rhonda and Gaby explore their role in the collaborative work of CICHAZ and ASPac, the international academic/research community, and the local Calnali community. Through dialogue moderated by Yamila Hussein, a scholar, educator, and activist dedicated to social-economic and political justice, Gaby and Rhonda discuss how being women impacts their work and their shared goal of conservation, environmental health, and knowledge-building. Colonialism, social location, identity, and power dynamics are themes that emerged from the dialogue. By analyzing our collaboration and seeking to explore how best to advance our joint commitment, the dialogue allowed us to examine how we position ourselves socially in our families and communities, institutionally within the organizations we operate in, and ultimately, in Calnali, as outsiders—albeit in different ways—to the community where we have planted ourselves.

BACKGROUND: THE AUTHORS AND THE STATION

Gil Rosenthal first came to Calnali in 1997 as a PhD student to study *Xiphophorus malinche and X. birchmanni* (swordtail) fishes. With the help of a National Science Foundation (NSF) Dissertation Improvement Grant, Gil was able to explore the Sierra and Huasteca area extensively and in 1998 stayed at a hotel in Calnali that was run by the Lara family who would become close friends with Gil; they also owned a nearby ranch where they would host Gil, along with his field equipment, over the ensuing years. After identifying hybridization between swordtail species in the region, Gil, who is fluent in Spanish, returned annually to collect fish and in 2003, he met Professor Arnulfo Lara who was a leader and community organizer in Calnali. Arnulfo was very excited about Gil's work in the area and saw economic, cultural, and education-related opportunities for the town.

When Rhonda and Gil married in 2004, the Lara family welcomed Rhonda warmly and continued hosting them at their ranch during the field season. While the ranch was instrumental in building Gil's research and launching his career, Gil dreamt of establishing a field station in Calnali where he could store his equipment, set up laboratory space, host other researchers, and become embedded in the community. A FSML in the region would make it easier to collaborate with Mexican scientists, recruit Mexican students, and work with Mexican postdoctoral scholars to help advance their careers within their own country. Moreover, it was an opportunity to create a space for Mexican researchers to access an understudied region of their own country that may (or may not) be familiar culturally depending on where they originated in Mexico. Creating such an FSML would also serve as a venue through which Rhonda and Gil could address the political nature of their undertaking by intentionally integrating principles, structures, and practices to avoid the pitfalls of colonial relationships and contribute to the community.

When one of the Lara brothers fell ill and needed to move to Mexico City for medical treatment, Arnulfo brokered a deal to sell Gil and Rhonda his home; Arnulfo's brother needed the money, and selling a furnished home in Calnali was not something quickly done. Arnulfo recognized the economic opportunity for his brother, as well as an opportunity to establish a research center in the community that could benefit the town as a long-term partnership between the town and North American scientists. This property soon became CICHAZ and is situated on 2 acres in the Aquazarca neighborhood of Calnali and includes a small portion of the Rio Calnali, where a scientifically important population of swordtails live. In 2006, when Rhonda started her own PhD program in political science and began to study Mexican education policies, especially their impact on community attitudes toward education, Arnulfo introduced Rhonda to the leadership of the local schools and provided demographic data about Calnali. The relationship between Arnulfo, Rhonda, and Gil was critical for helping CICHAZ root itself in the community and advancing its reputation as a valuable resource for the area. To fulfill this vision, the CICHAZ mission became "to bring science and service together," a compass that continues guiding the work internally and through outreach activities.

Gaby spent her first three years in Calnali adapting to the local traditions and culture, as well as observing the society and the nature of the area. By 2008, the vision and mission of ASPac changed from production to social responsibility to "Generate ideas and take action to form sustainable and healthy communities." This shift in mission reflected a change in priorities and recognized the critical work of women, rural, and Indigenous communities, as well as the responsibility groups working with ASPac should have toward the environment. All are interwoven through the reliance on natural resources and their products. At Rancho La Tejería, in addition to producing coffee, Gaby and Lalo harvest fruits, such as oranges and tangerines, raise cattle, catch fish, and collect wood. Taking care of the region and its resources, specifically water and biodiversity, is a priority for Gaby and Lalo. Thus, to maintain their own operations while staying true to their mission and values, they continuously look for creative ways to share their gained knowledge of stewarding the land with the Calnali community, including CICHAZ.

Yamila was invited by Rhonda and Gil to Calnali in the very early stages of the founding of CICHAZ. The intellectual connection she had forged with Rhonda in graduate school had evolved over the years to encompass strong personal and social ties, as well as academic and political collaboration and joint projects. Born in Colombia to Palestinian parents, she grew up in Jerusalem and earned her graduate degrees in the United States, where she lived for over two decades. With Spanish as her first language and a strong command of the English language, she's comfortable navigating multiple spaces and cultures. When she and Gaby met during the CICHAZ–ASPac conference in 2015 (see below), she had been closely following the work of CICHAZ and would eventually join its advisory board. Her research focuses on questions of colonialism, social justice, democratic education, and the interplay between power and knowledge production. Her courses examine institutional practices that sustain or challenge systems of oppression and cultural domination including how power is enacted in dialogue. As such, she was well-positioned to join Rhonda and Gaby in both the dialogue and writing process of this chapter. In addition to facilitating and translating during the Zoom conversations, her contribution to the writing process focused on offering theoretical frameworks and raising probing questions that supported their articulation of, and thinking around, their analysis of their role as women in the field of FSMLs and examination of their collaboration.

Outreach and Projects

"La Jornada, The Day of Science and Sustainability" provided the first opportunity for this collaborative potential to become obvious. Launched by CICHAZ in 2014, La Jornada aimed to present the research program based at CICHAZ and to promote science learning more broadly across the local communities. In addition to an environment awareness poster competition among local high-school students, doctoral and master's students from Gil's lab and collaborating Mexican labs presented their work. Furthermore, Gil addressed topics such as the swordtail hybrid zone, parasites that live on the fish, and Rhonda's presented her educational research into *Oportunidades,* a conditional cash transfer program popular in Mexico at the time. After attending La Jornada events, it was clear to Gaby and Lalo that the goals of CICHAZ complemented those of ASPac's, and gave rise to the idea of working together. Initially, Gaby helped with some fish-collecting bureaucracy, but it was quickly clear that there was alignment in how each organization defined its role in the community and they forged opportunities to advance their impact together.

Now an ongoing collaboration between CICHAZ and ASPac, La Jornada is an annual event for, and with, the Calnali community. While every year is unique, there is always an opportunity for the local public to meet scientists, learn about the research hosted at CICHAZ, and engage with science through outreach activities. The two organizations also sponsor a youth summer camp, set up hiking trails during COVID, and are developing a curriculum for informal learning experiences outside of La Jornada.

A year after the first Jornada, during the summer of 2015, CICHAZ supported a four-day Conference of Science and Sustainability in Calnali, thanks to Broader Impacts funding from NSF. This joint CICHAZ–ASPac Conference hosted 150 participants including researchers from Mexico, the United States, Palestine, and Panama interested in the region's natural and community resources. The visiting scientists, researchers, educators, and environmentalists spent four days learning and teaching with local community members, nonprofits, educators, and government representatives through round table discussions, research presentations, exploratory hikes, and informal settings featuring traditional food, music, and dance with Calnali residents. Discussions centered on existing and potential collaborations and the role of CICHAZ and ASPac in supporting the region's efforts to grow products sustainably and promote environmental responsibility, as well as help grow and promote science education for the general public.

The scientists conducting research in Calnali at CICHAZ have opportunities to interact with the community informally and stimulate the local economy. They visit the Sunday market in town, buy necessities and snacks at the tiendas, eat at the local restaurants, and hang out at coffee shops between field trips. During field trips when the researchers collect their data (fish, soil samples, etc.), they often encounter curious bystanders who engage in knowledge exchanges. The Spanish-fluent researchers can explain their research and learn about the thoughts and experiences of Calanali's residents with the water, land, flora, or fauna. Scientists have gained a lot of insight into the region based on these interactions. However, aside from a familiar wave in passing it is not clear how these moments are generally received by the larger community. Gil, for example, fluent in Spanish, has become a familiar presence in the area after nearly 30 years of collecting fish in the rivers. He is easy to recognize by his large size and distinctive appearance and feels warmly welcomed by community members he has met. From his perspective, he has established a network of contacts with whom he engages and shares insights. This is also true for his students who spend months at a time at CICHAZ, and also for former students who still use CICHAZ as a base for their own lab's research. One student from Mexico is even considering starting his own FSML that would have a different research focus but would share many of CICHAZ's outreach and community-benefiting priorities. These experiences for scientists, especially those who establish long-term personal connections through friendships, can be the most powerful kind of outreach. For scientists who rely on data collected in the field, these interpersonal connections are often as important to their careers as their professional networks. It would be interesting to learn more from the community about how they see these relationships.

In addition to collaborating extensively on all outreach programs, Gaby, now the executive coordinator of CICHAZ, supervises all visitors' comings and goings, often working closely with Lalo on special projects that need attention at CICHAZ. In 2020, CICHAZ and ASPac received funding to study regenerative ranching and water conservation initiatives with Mexican researchers and started applying for funding with European researchers. As the collaboration between the two organizations expands and deepens, across our efforts, we began to take note of our roles as women in biological fields, especially how each of our individual backgrounds affects, and are shaped by our involvement in an FSML in the context of CICHAZ and the larger community of Calnali, as well as how we seek to engage and influence our national and international FSML communities through the professional organizations such as the Organization of Biological Field Stations (OBFS).

DIALOGUE AS METHODOLOGY

In preparation for the reflection and dialogue that informs this chapter, Rhonda and Gaby identified the following questions to help them examine the interplay between their gender and their role in this work, as well as their shared goals around conservation, environmental health, and knowledge-building.

1) How did we find ourselves in Calnali?
2) What does being a woman in the field mean for each of us? How much of our identity is caught up in being a woman?
3) What are the perceptions of Calnali and the community as a place for women?
4) How do our gender and motherhood play into our respective roles at ASPac/the CICHAZ field station? Our collaboration?
5) What goals do we share that drive the collaboration?

While these were articulated questions and themes, the conversation sometimes brought other topics to light. Yamila's perspective and voice were key to this chapter. She facilitated the discussion to both keep the conversation on track and to also open up new topics to unpack assumptions and expand on the central themes of women and biological field stations.

Although Gaby and Rhonda have been working together for seven years and are in constant conversation about the work, they both recognized the need for and value of dedicating time to examine their ongoing collaboration. They wanted to explore how such intentionally guided yet organic dialogue might enrich and expand their work together while helping clarify their positions and roles in the community. The dialogue methodology was chosen given its potential to be socially transformative and to deepen understanding of topics through genuine conversation (Binding & Tapp, 2008). With a focused, intentional, guided discussion, participants in dialogue can build knowledge and unpack assumptions, expectations, and perceptions (Constantino, 2008). Dialogue also creates an opportunity to expose beliefs and/or perceived prejudices, biases, such that agreements of understanding can be established as insights and reflections are put into words (Grondin, 2002). Collaborations that leverage dialogue to keep relationships among participants healthy and honest need to be aware that it is an ongoing, intentional process.

Material realities, including geography and COVID, resulted in two virtual Zoom dialogues with Yamila, who in addition to facilitating the meetings also often helped with translation. More than 150 pages of transcription were typed in both languages and timestamped. All three authors reviewed the transcripts and analyzed them to confirm themes and identify emergent trends. In both two-hour sessions, Rhonda primarily spoke in English and Gaby in Spanish. Rhonda's first language is English and she has limited Spanish fluency, while Gaby's first language is Spanish, and a strong comprehension of English. Yamila would translate between the two and ask clarifying questions when she thought translation might be lost in cultural differences. When participants are communicating in different languages, meaning can get lost and the ideas muddled. Consequently, it is imperative that words and statements are correctly understood, a task that can be complicated when translation is necessary. During the two dialogue sessions, the speakers were more focused on conveying meaning than on carefully selecting words or neatly arranging statements. Yamila's dual role as facilitator and translator helped clarify meaning during the oral dialogue sessions making sure Gaby and Rhonda truly understood the intention of the words used by each. In addition to her multilingual skills and multicultural experiences in South America and the United States, Yamila's familiarity with the field station context and the participants, coupled with her academic background, informed her questions and interventions to pinpoint important nuances in the discussion and highlight ideas that might not have been well conveyed or understood.

Engaging in dialogue demands that participants take the time to fully explain the meaning of their words and clarify their underlying assumptions so together they achieve insight and understanding. It also requires recognition of how, in dialogue, participants construct their identities for others and for themselves (Brubaker & Cooper, 2000; Hopkins, 2008). Fully cognizant that dialogue itself becomes an arena where power is negotiated (Young,

1996), the Zoom conversations also addressed how the intersection of participants' gender, class, age, race, is at play. In other words, their social location, that is, positionality in social structures, became subject for reflection, discussion, and analysis of their collaboration. Equally important, it was agreed that the power dynamic among collaborators (in this case, two women) and the institutions in which they operate in relation to the communities they intend to support should be explored and acknowledged in any healthy, long-term collaboration.

Following the two virtual dialogues moderated by Yamila, Rhonda and Gaby had the chance to deepen the discussion face-to-face during the 2021 field season in Calnali. Reviewing the transcript together and the process of writing created opportunities for them to give examples, clarify meaning or intention and elaborate on and reflect on key aspects of their relationship and activities. Gaby and Rhonda's assumptions and perceptions were unavoidable in the discussion and throughout the writing of this chapter. This was the first time they had discussed many of these topics with each other, or even deeply considered these questions of identity within themselves. In an interview, Audre Lorde once said,

> when we define ourselves, when I define myself, the place in which I am like you and the place in which I am not like you, I'm not excluding you from the joining—I'm broadening the joining . . . what understanding begins to do is to make knowledge available for use, and that's the urgency, that's the push, that's the drive." (as cited by Bereano, 1983, p. 11)

This dialogue enabled Gaby and Rhonda to delve into themselves relative to each other and with respect to the field station. Their commitment to staying candid during this process is grounded both in mutual respect for their relationships and also a firm belief that it is central for their collaboration as it helps expand their vision of how and why they are working together.

Thus, the collaborative writing process created another opportunity for Gaby and Rhonda to pay attention to the specificity of language (e.g., word choice, sentence structure, idioms) and in the process clarify, deepen, and expand analyses, and reflections of ideas. It is through writing that the potential pitfalls of translation were also addressed. The need for translation, in fact, created an opportunity for more scrutiny to make sure ideas were clearly and accurately captured deepening the dialogue in ways that otherwise might not have been felt necessary (i.e., if both spoke the same language, it would be easy to assume that they understood what the other person means, or that they both understood a word or statement similarly). Writing, as a collaborative process, becomes then an extension of dialogue, not simply a written record of what has already been said but also an opportunity to expand, clarify, and question meaning. Writing is a critical part of learning. It is in the process of writing that theoretical frameworks were carefully understood and examined. Yamila's perspective and expertise helped expand and enrich how Rhonda and Gaby made sense of their experiences and dialogue.

In-person interactions have also brought more insight into how each is processing the dialogue and how they want to apply their new understandings. For example, during a focus group that took place while writing this chapter with women involved in the regenerative ranching project, Rhonda and Gaby were asking the women to consider how much knowledge they, the women, had to offer the scientists coming to Calnali to collect data and how much they help with the ranching their husbands do (few are full-time ranchers). The women were quick to minimize their contributions and deferred to their rancher husbands or were deferential to the scientists; one even pointed out that she did not have the education of Gaby and therefore lacked any qualifications to contribute to her husband's ranching practices.

FINDINGS/DISCUSSION

Key themes emerged from the dialogue and we raised more questions than we could reasonably answer. The conversation was dominated by analysis of Gaby and Rhonda's identities and social locations, how each as women, mothers, wives, and professionals were empowered or disempowered in the local, regional, national, and international context, and how their collaboration has developed and continues to change. Ultimately they realized that doing this work broadened their worldview and would enhance their collaboration so that future projects would be more inclusive and successful. Each wanted to dig deeper in their understanding of each other and their shared experiences.

Identities, Social Location, and Action

> *Cuando hablamos con las personas por primera vez, queremos saber "¿quién eres?" - pero solo preguntamos "¿qué haces?" pensando que la respuesta nos dará una idea de quién es esa persona. . .*

Gaby wrote these words when considering identity and what it means when we engage with each other. *When we speak with someone for the first time, we want to know "who are you?" but we only ask "what do you do for a living?" thinking that the answer will give us an idea of who that person is. . .*

Understanding and articulating our identities and social locations is central to unpacking and analyzing our relationships with each other, the organizations, the community, and the work that we do. The social identities we each hold onto emerge from our life experiences, cultural histories, and our interaction with the conditions in which we exist. Kirk and Okazawa-Rey (2006) explain that "Identity formation is the result of a complex interplay among a range of factors: individual decisions and choices, particular life events, community recognition and expectations, societal categorization, classification and socialization, and key national or international events" (p. 9). As such, to construct an understanding of the self, one needs to move beyond an understanding of identity as a list of differences or a set of individual characteristics to interrogate how we are located in formalized and codified systems through social categorization (Brubaker & Cooper, 2000) and understand the political implications of these systems on our lives. Social location, according to Kirk and Okazawa-Rey (2013), is

> a way of expressing the core of a person's existence in the social and political world. It places us in particular relationships to others, to the dominant culture of the United States, and to the rest of the world. It determines the kinds of power and privilege we have access to and can exercise, as well as situations in which we have less power and privilege. (p.15)

Social categorization and classification (race, class, gender, religion, nationality, etc.) are not simply a matter of differences among humans. Instead, it is the *meanings* assigned to these differences that produce unequal proximity to power (Johnson, 2017). In other words, social categorization does not simply rely on difference but assigns hierarchies. Social categories are employed by the modern nation-state as a means to govern (governmentality, in the Foucauldian sense. See Brubaker & Cooper 2000). These codified systems of categorization intersect (Crenshaw, 1991) or interlock (The Combahee River Collective, 1977) locating human beings in particular spheres of group memberships along a spectrum of privilege and oppression. As such, social categories govern social structures and heavily influence unequal power relations between different social groups (men and women; rich and poor; white and Black; colonists and Indigenous). They also create symbolic representations and identity constructions with concrete, tangible albeit differentiated consequences for social groups. Our social location, thus, influences our experiences, practices, access, opportunities, proximity to power hubs, and strongly shapes our views about the world and our place in it (Anthias, 2012; Crenshaw, 1991; Okazawa-Rey, 2013; The Combahee River Collective, 1977; Winker & Degele, 2011).

Social location is not static but rather contextual, fluid, and relational (Anthias, 2012; Brubaker & Cooper, 2000; Okazawa-Rey, 2013). Our positionality in matrices of power (political, economic, social, cultural, etc.) is ultimately a constant negotiation between our material reality and how we make sense of that reality (what we accept, reject, defy, etc.). As contradictions, tensions and conflicts between what we are told we are and who we believe to be inevitably emerge, people can, and often do, resist these imposed meanings, individually and collectively, in the realm of ideas, language, and material reality. It is this contestation that opens spaces for people to engage in social praxis toward social and political change that can benefit the quality of their lives, the health of the environment, and create new opportunities for future generations. Our agency in these imposed social categories can also be understood in the distinction between social position and social positioning that Fiona Anthias (2012) provides. Whereas the former refers to a "concrete position vis-a-vis a range of social resources such as economic, cultural and political" the latter describes the meaning *we* assign to these and, accordingly, "how we articulate, understand and interact with these positions (e.g., contesting, challenging, defining) which relates to the structural and the identificational levels, and their possible Connections" (Anthias, 2012, p.128). Finally, social location cannot be understood without explicit attention to the political and economic landscape and the geographic and historic context.

Social location, as a theoretical and analytical frame, became central to unpacking Gaby's question around active engagement in social needs. So many around us in the scientific community are not actively doing anything to benefit the local community, Gaby wondered aloud, why is this? If we know there is a global problem, like climate change or COVID, why do so many people seem unbothered? Perhaps they are bothered but unable to move beyond their own questions and programs to incorporate these far-reaching issues into their practice. How might social location, that is, our positionality in the webs of power, impact the level and nature of active and intentional effort to attend to communal needs and contribute to collective well-being? This theme kept surfacing in the dialogue between Rhonda and Gaby—*who* is moved to social activism and takes community responsibility and what motivates them? Why are some, like Gaby and Rhonda, Gil and Lalo, and some students and colleagues moved to be active community members when so many are not? Zaytoun (2006) offers some insight into this. Grounded in an understanding of race and gender as social constructs, she opens up new ways to examine how we perceive ourselves and what we believe we are capable of. Zaytoun (2006) contends that

> exploring how sense of self, agency, and connection emerge and change over time is essential to understanding other concepts that are critical to feminist projects, such as social consciousness and movements, and answering questions such as, why are some individuals moved to social activism while others are not, and can social responsibility be fostered? (p. 53)

This suggests that to understand who engages actively in communal responsibility toward collective good, we need to turn our analytical lens both inward, to examine our ways of knowing, conocimiento (Anzaldua & Moraga, 1981), consciousness work and, simultaneously, outward, to understand collective action in the context of a clear read of the reality to be changed (Anzaldua & Moraga 1981). To connect this dual analytical lens to action, an examination of how power operates is helpful. Starhawk's (1987) typology of power can help interrogate how these lenses are related to each other and to action. Examining how power operates in order to act and create positive change, Starhawk (1987) argues that in addition to the widespread understanding of power as a force of domination, coercion, force, and control—an exercise of "power over"—we should examine the flow of "power-from-within" which stands for our inner, personal strength and spiritual integrity, so we can forge "power with" others to engage in collective action for challenging and transforming oppressive realities (pp. 9–10). This notion of "power with" is explained by Starhawk (1987) as "The power of a strong individual in a group of equals, the power not to command but to suggest and be listened to, to begin something and see it happen" (p.10). Since Starhawk's (1987) original article was published, a fourth type of power has emerged focusing on action. "Power To" (Mathie et al., 2017; VeneKlasen & Miller, 2007) describes the power of people to shape their realities, to make a difference, to create new and better conditions. It is the "productive or generative potential of power and the new possibilities or actions" (Mathie et al., p. 57) with intentionality to embody the ideals of equality, equity, and justice we aspire to.

A possible answer to Gaby's question around actively working for positive change, then, would be that once we recognize our power *from within* and nurture it with clarity on our social location, we can share this power with others and activate our power to get involved with others to make a difference. Personal consciousness is therefore connected with social consciousness (Collins, 1998) and collective action. "The work of conocimiento," explained Anzaldua in a 1991 interview, "connects the inner life of the mind and spirit to the outer worlds of action. In the struggle for social change I call this particular aspect of conocimiento spiritual activism" (as cited by Keiting, 2000, p.178). For Gaby, no matter where she finds herself, her aim is to bring hope and support to others that it is possible to make a positive change to the local neighborhoods and environments she's a part of. She has formed a family in Calnali where she lives with her husband and son who was born and is being raised there. Over the years, she has grown and nurtured deep connections to the place, the land, the culture, and the community. After nearly 20 years of actively working and living there, she now considers herself of Calnali and while some see Gaby as part of the community, some may always see her as an outsider. As a non-native to Calnali, Gaby questions the spaces available for her as a mestiza to be involved in defending, protecting, and nurturing her environment fighting for Indigenous land and knowledge. She notes,

> *Es como si los "mestizos" no tuviéramos lugar en las discusiones. Como no somos ni de aquí, ni de allá. No tenemos un lugar para ser fuente de inspiración y sin embargo, lo somos. Porque nos movemos bien en ambientes "privilegiados" y en ambientes no privilegiados.*
>
> *It's like we "mestizos" don't have a place in discussions. Like we are not from here or from there. We don't have a space as sources of inspiration, and yet, we are. Because we move well in "privileged" and unprivileged environments.* (Translated)

Acknowledging how she is positioned through social categories, Gaby reaches into the inner part of her that informs how she positions herself in her world. She is motivated by love, compassion, and concern about a future in which *inaction* will make it even more difficult than she and many others currently anticipate. Motivated to change what is not working, Gaby is carefully navigating the community she has become a part of and focusing on the environment, given her strengths, dedication to the land, and her dedication to supporting the local economy. "I don't seek gratitude from people because of what I do—no one asked me to do it."

Rhonda's relationship with Calnali as a privileged outsider and non-permanent resident influences her sense of moral responsibility and obligation to give back to the community that has made CICHAZ possible. Her complicated relationship to colonialist practices and legacies in which scientific research organizations from the Northern hemisphere are often complicit informs her approach in how CICHAZ relates to its surrounding. Historically, field stations have rarely cared about the places where they operate. Rather, in true colonialist form, they would often place the value of science as the greater good to society than any local values (see chapters 1 by McDermott, Gee, & May, and 3 by McDermott in this edited volume). These pioneering stations would host "parachute science," where scientists would visit a remote field site to conduct their research and take valuable credit for local knowledge and use a local workforce to acquire scientific samples from local natural resources. Foreign scientists would think little of leaving behind a ruined landscape that had been either virtually untouched or managed by native people for generations (de Vos, 2020; Roldan-Hernandez et al., 2020). Within these politics of exploitation and extraction is the practice of erasure of assets which renders local knowledge irrelevant and/or invisible. The knowledge accumulated in communities over centuries and the many local scientists in the community tend to be completely ignored and unseen by the scientists who come from and return to North America and Europe (Raby 2017).

As a research-focused institution that is driven by individual scientific laboratories and supported by U.S. funding, CICHAZ, she believes, should benefit the area in all ways possible and it is well-positioned to do so. CICHAZ is the only field station in the region. As a FSML, CICHAZ is also part of a broader network of stations and researchers who connect this area to other ecological life zones, as well as populations that never otherwise would have known about this part of the Sierra and Huasteca. Throughout the year, CICHAZ promotes and hosts an influx of foreigners to Calnali who often speak little or poor Spanish and take samples of fish, soil, and other natural elements. With the help of ASPac, CICHAZ manages to interact with the community where it makes sense. For some projects, we meet with ranchers and their families, for others we ask to organize outreach events on their land, and often we ask landowners if we can sample on their land. These interactions are carefully done to show respect and inclusion however possible. While most Calnali residents appreciate the international exposure and interest of outsiders, we recognize that for some it can seem intrusive or colonialist in nature depending on how we engage the community and continue to search for ways to mitigate that.

Over the years, CICHAZ has shared scientific knowledge with the community, donated fish tanks to the local school, supported student science projects, and donated to an art initiative to paint murals throughout the Aguazarca neighborhood (see figure 10.2).

Mindful of this legacy, the vision guiding CICHAZ' work prioritizes the advice of those working toward true collaborative science, one that honors local skills and resources and avoids ignorant stereotypes and assumptions.

Figure 10.2 The Front of the Main Building at CICHAZ in the Aguazarca Neighborhood. *Source:* Photo by author.

Among the list of recommendations for change within the scientific community that Roldan-Hernandez et al. (2020) provide, three have become a CICHAZ priority: (1) to invest in local human capacity through training, mentorship, and employment of local members, (2) to ensure that data and results are shared with local partners, and (3) to properly acknowledge the support and contribution of local partners in research manuscripts (pp. 14773–14774). This also aligns with Trask's (1993) argument that non-natives need to understand their place as outsiders: where they are geopolitically, who they are, how they relate to the land, nature, and people native to the land, understand the history of the space and reflect on cultural behaviors that might suggest they equate themselves to natives and/or position themselves as superior (paternalism). This is also true for the scientific community that visits CICHAZ.

Scientists have come to Calnali from throughout the United States and Mexico, as well as countries as far as Uruguay, Canada, Holland, the United Kingdom, Brazil, Spain, Palestine, China, and Japan. This diversity of visitors presents a variety of challenges ranging from how visitors might communicate with one another and with community members, to how they will generally respond to rural Mexico and respect the local community. To orient guests to CICHAZ and the region, we have put together a survival guide that instructs visitors on everything from what to pack to what to expect once they arrive to directions to the station. The guide is available in Spanish and English through the CICHAZ website and all who plan a trip to Calnali are asked to sign a confirmation that they have reviewed the rules. Gaby and a small staff welcome visiting scientists and we continually update the guide to help make expectations clear. As with any field station, there will be research needs that need to be met as well as a period of cultural acclimation. Some scientists come for a week, others a month or longer, and how they fit in and take care of the station and its resources has an impact on everyone who works there, as well as on our collaborations.

Along with Gil, Rhonda is in Calnali at most a few months a year bringing fiscal capital, social capital, and scientific resources (both material and intellectual) that are new to the community. At best, the community sees Rhonda and her family as international members of the Calnali community who bring economic benefits, academic conversations, and entrepreneurial opportunities. At worst, they are seen as wealthy gringos with their own agenda. It's probably somewhere in between. The construction of a new home for the family behind the station complicates matters. From a functional perspective, the family needed a home since the two bedrooms they had been using in the field station were needed for research purposes (one room is now a genetics lab and the other a behavior lab). From a social perspective, building a family home solidifies their commitment to Calnali, the community, and to

CICHAZ while simultaneously signaling their privilege. Although never explicitly stated, this has been embedded in comments from those who work at CICHAZ, including Gaby and Lalo.

Nevertheless, there is an ever-present awareness that the advantages Gil and Rhonda have (e.g., being able to easily cross the Mexico–U.S. border, institutional access to resources, and the strength of their U.S. dollars) places them apart from the community. With this in mind, a top priority in all of CICHAZ's research and programming is to respect, honor, and include the local population. Working with Gaby and Lalo, who have a better grasp of the local customs and attitudes, heightens this awareness and informs decisions in addition to helping validate the station's efforts and Rhonda's social capital, real and perceived.

Social capital is the networks of friendships, acquaintances, and colleagues that are helpful as resources when confronted with life's circumstances such as finding a new job or trying to build a responsible field station (Putnam, 2001; Sammut, 2011). Rhonda and Gil are able to leverage these relationships that stem from their advantaged social locations and life choices. In many ways, this dialogue would not be possible without the friendship Rhonda and Yamila forged at Harvard's Graduate School of Education, their professional choices, and the topics they regularly engage with in their discourse. Rhonda and Gaby each have their own childhood, background, and social location that inform their worldviews, shape their knowledge and their ways of knowing, and give them different types of power in different situations. Each has navigated multiple professional situations before arriving in Calnali. Both are well educated, come from stable families that are financially secure, and are independent thinkers. Both have navigated multiple spaces and operate through multiple roles as professionals, mothers, activists; as women choosing to be in and work for the good of Calnali.

Personal Histories and the Calnali Context

Gaby was born into a large Catholic family (she is the fifth of six children) in Mexico City, where she lived during her youth, and then studied agronomy in Querétaro. Her focus on agronomy was strongly influenced by her Catholic faith and its emphasis on loving God's creation and caring for the poor. She began her professional career in the state of Guerrero, working in a bank in Acapulco, and then in a nongovernmental organization until 1994. That same year, Gaby and her father founded ASPac. Gaby, after her experience working in the bank, recognized that agricultural businesses required not only training and relationship building with people at every level of the operation but also business sense and money. Her father, a businessman, had the needed expertise and was interested in supporting small producers. Together they forged an alliance to support the development of the Mexican countryside and the family moved to the outskirts of Mexico City. Gaby soon began to teach business courses for farmers and lead workshops for groups of farmers in Hidalgo, Puebla, Guerrero, and Tlaxcala. At first, Gaby was not very interested in conserving natural resources; rather the production and generation of economic resources was her priority. As her work progressed, Gaby began to consider her Catholic priorities, and serving others has always been an important component of her motivations. Seeing all the poverty in the outskirts of Mexico City and how it affects people led Gaby to reconsider where she belonged and she knew it was not in the city.

When she met Lalo and Calnali, it was the right time for her to refocus her life's work on promoting a healthy environment through sustainable production and placing importance on the conservation and preservation of natural resources. Calnali, with its coffee and ranching industry, as well as its Indigenous and non-Indigenous communities, provided the right place to live in accordance with its values and to ensure that there is alignment between what she thinks, what she says, and what she does. The death of Gaby's father was the turning point for ASPac; Gaby already lived in Calnali and became executive director. The changes were in her hands and she was able to concentrate on what really interested her—taking care of the land and the poor—in alignment with her Catholic orientation. ASPac's mission then also transformed from one centered on economic development to one centered on forming sustainable and healthy communities within frameworks of equity and nondiscrimination.

Rhonda grew up the youngest of five (and the only daughter) in a conservative Jewish home in Petersburg, Virginia, where she was used to being the only one in her class not going to church on Sundays. Critical of religion and patriarchy from an early age, there was always a curiosity about the world though not so much the environment. Rhonda's first job after college was as a researcher at National Geographic Television in Washington, D.C. and it was there, while working on documentary films, that she began to deeply appreciate natural history and how critical conservation is for the planet. It was in graduate school when Rhonda took a course on social and political change, met Yamila, and began consulting on an all-male software engineering course that Rhonda began to get comfortable in multilingual, multicultural situations. At that time, she also became deeply aware of gender. The course was a virtual environment collaboration between MIT in Cambridge, MA, and CICESE in Ensenada, Mexico. Rhonda was there as an education consultant to study the situation and evaluate the learning of all participants; the experience helped hone her skills as a social scientist. When the course ended, Rhonda took a job at an education startup that sent explorers around the world to report back on the social, environmental, economic, and political situations they encountered in real-time. This work solidified Rhonda's passion for exploring different cultures through informal education experiences to promote multicultural understanding and human rights advocacy. The program was subsequently bought by Houghton Mifflin Publishing where Rhonda moved through the corporate ladder and was exposed to the politics of education publishing. After a few years, Rhonda realized that she wanted to get a doctoral degree in political science to study education policies. It was around this time that Rhonda met Gil, and he was excited to introduce her to Calnali. Given Rhonda's interests in community empowerment and education policies, and Gil's research and dedication to supporting the Calnali community, and their combined goal of promoting a healthy environment, they knew together as a team they could build something special.

At the start of the CICHAZ–ASPac collaboration, Gaby primarily worked with Gil. The first event that really brought Gaby, Rhonda, and Yamila together was the 2015 Conference during which Gaby helped set up a roundtable for Yamila and Rhonda to discuss CICHAZ outreach with local teachers. While many ideas were collected that would inform our outreach programming, it was really after Gaby became the CICHAZ coordinator and started discussing the best way to keep the shared spaces at CICHAZ clean and organized that Rhonda and Gaby became "accomplices." Gil was disinterested and resisted structure in a stereotypically male way, while Rhonda and Gaby, in a stereotypically female and motherly way, wanted to establish norms. We became united then and again over the simultaneous demands of children, husbands, and work obligations. It was through the annual outreach events, however, that we really started collaborating and recognizing each other's voices in the work. It was also around this time that Rhonda got NSF funding to study outreach programming at FSMLs throughout the United States and wanted to apply the knowledge gained to the outreach activities at CICHAZ (Short et al., 2020; Struminger et al., 2018, 2021).

At CICHAZ, Gaby is recognized as the administrator and point person for all logistics or questions while Lalo is seen more as support. Gaby's social and leadership qualities make her very effective at taking care of researchers' needs even though she is not a *traditional academic* researcher. If any researcher seeks to get involved with the community, they quickly recognize that Gaby and Lalo are key to building and strengthening any relationships. This is especially true after a visit to La Tejería where Lalo can explain his work as a rancher and coffee producer, and Gaby can showcase their jams and local products. As the collaboration between Gaby and Rhonda broadens into the regenerative ranching project, some of the visiting researchers are just as focused on the work at La Tejería as they are on the work at CICHAZ. While CICHAZ supports soil, beetle, and cattle scientists who are able to use the laboratory space, Gaby and Lalo are seen as part of the research team.

This has helped to shift the focus a bit for all involved as the work is more diverse and each is given more input into the projects taking place. Whether the focus is on biology or ranching, the role of Lalo and Gil are ever-present at CICHAZ. As the rancher or the biologist, both are key parts of the collaboration and both are very mindful of acknowledging the partnerships they have with Gaby and Rhonda.

In the context of Calnali, Rhonda and Gaby are different types of outsiders and both behave in ways that are outside of what is considered normal culture. For example, nearly all the mothers in Calnali bring their children lunch in the middle of the day, while Gaby would send her son off with a packed lunch so she could use that time to work. Knowing that Gaby comes from Mexico City and is college-educated, a rarity among Calnali women, may have made it easier for some of the other parents to accept Gaby's approach to lunch plans (or to criticize her for not sharing in the tradition).

As an educated woman with economic resources who manages projects and teaches all ages about topics ranging from recycling to regenerative ranching, Gaby is an empowered woman in the Calnali context. She has taken on leadership roles such as being part of the Kindergarten School Council, running church groups, and directing informal learning activities for children together with Rodrigo, her eldest son. In a recent trash crisis wherein garbage was accumulating (the dump closed as it planned to, but Calnali's governing body had not made other arrangements), Calnalenses women who are more involved than men in litter clean-up projects turned to Gaby for help managing the growing piles of trash. On social media, it was clear that Gaby was seen as a knowledgeable, resourceful community member who could help solve the problem. Involved in recycling initiatives over the last decade, Gaby was a known environmental leader and, with this situation, was able to promote composting and other ways of reusing materials instead of adding them to the trash piles. What is becoming clear is that Gaby's abilities and insights are increasingly acknowledged and respected by women though less so among men. It is unfortunate that gender dynamics limit Gaby's ability to lead the broader community when her skills are needed. Gaby feels that she has more recognition for her work and leadership among male or female working professionals and the visiting scholars than with the local Canali community. In general Calnali society, she is recognized by other women but not by men as with the trash crisis discussed above. When working with male ranchers or with men in her local community work, Gaby stresses that Lalo's presence has become necessary to empower her words—without him being in attendance the men do not listen to what she says. Gaby can give her opinion and propose solutions to pressing problems but her voice becomes Lalo's in the eyes of the predominantly male ranching and farming community.

Rhonda is connected to the community in a much different way. With limited Spanish language skills and only a few trips a year to Calnali, Rhonda stays close to CICHAZ and the visiting researchers while in Calnali. Nevertheless, she feels part of the community; some recognize her on sight, others are familiar with her educational research and outreach word, and many welcome her as a neighbor. As co-founder and co-director of CICHAZ, Rhonda has come to rely on Gaby to be the community liaison for CICHAZ and Gil to be the research lead. Finding her footing at the station as co-director and more than an entity who helped found the station has been one of Rhonda's greatest challenges. Still, through her own education research, her children, food, and informal education activities, Rhonda has found ways to connect with her neighbors and build her own network of support. The outreach at CICHAZ has been a pivotal way for Rhonda to connect her own interests in science education with the station's activities. Rhonda does stand out as a Jewish gringa with a doctorate degree. Most in Calnali have never met a Jewish person. To extend her personal culture to the town, Rhonda occasionally makes the traditional Sabbath bread (challah) for the neighbors and enjoys sharing about her religion when the community is interested in her background. Rhonda and Gil's presence is different from the cultural norm in this small town in ways that reach beyond their scientific endeavors and lifestyles. When Gil and Rhonda first bought CICHAZ, it was a furnished, Evangelical home with crosses on every bedroom door. While the Virgin of Guadalupe statue was kept out of respect for the local tradition of having her on an altar in the home, the crosses were given away to the surprise of the neighbors and the previous owner. Upon finding out that Rhonda was Jewish, it became more of a curiosity and a discussion which led to Gil outing himself as Agnostic—another new concept reaching beyond field biology for many of our neighbors. While Judaism and Agnosticism are not missionary in their practice—converting others is not part of the theology—Rhonda and Gil's scientific approach to life and the goals of CICHAZ promote scientific points of view. By centering their lives around doing and teaching science, methodological, and critical thinking are not only intellectual approaches but also the way to raise their children. By working from these margins and focusing on how differences in perspective can enrich our understanding of ourselves, each other, and life more broadly, we can build a creative space in which to do fieldwork, bring communities together, and generate collaborative projects we all can gain knowledge from.

Science and Indigenous Knowledge in Calnali

Currently, at CICHAZ, there are two female technicians who take care of the fish daily living on-site, along with a young male biologist who recently graduated college and grew up helping around the field station. All are local and originally from Calnali. Their observations and input are key to CICHAZ's success from helping with feeding the fish to how observational data is being collected. Rhonda and Gil, both very collaborative in their approach to science, appreciate that everyone with an interest in and curiosity about a topic can contribute to our collective understanding—researchers are not the only people with valuable insights (Gorelick, 2014). Thus, throughout this work, Gil and Rhonda have consciously tried to adopt an attitude "based on the humility of a student rather than the arrogance of a missionary" (Trask, 1993, p. 251). There is a strong recognition that honoring differences between groups and focusing on shared goals is key to working productively with each other.

Though Gaby is not a scientist, she is formally trained and skilled as an agricultural engineer, specializing in agricultural production. She also has a remarkable and natural gift as an ethnobotanist. She collects testimonials to record Indigenous and local knowledge that is invaluable for understanding the medicinal properties of the local flora. Before sharing her own knowledge with locals, Gaby always asks if the person/group she is working with has any hypotheses or knowledge about an issue that she can build on or learn from. This simple question gives a voice and authority to people who study the land in ways that differ from the Western tradition of scholarly investigation. If they do have specific ideas about the medicinal uses of plants and their traditionally accepted applications, she asks who that knowledge came from and under what conditions was that knowledge gained (e.g., was it your aunt who used this plant to calm an upset stomach?). Such first-hand accounts and shared local knowledge are valuable histories and are another way of learning with and from community members in addition to providing useful data points for understanding the medical uses of local plants.

The scientific method gains understanding and paths of discovery when combined with community stories and the associated Indigenous knowledge. These are not conflicting binary methods for understanding ecology, conservation, biology, and the biomedical fields; rather, they are complementary approaches for understanding these and many other fields (Gorelick, 2014; Maracle, 2020; Schmidt & Stricker, 2010), including the social sciences. Surveying and hosting focus groups is how data are often collected to track attitudes and behavioral changes in a studied population. There is an art to asking good questions that will produce useful data. For the research Rhonda and Gaby are collaborating on that is focused on regenerative ranching practices, they need both Rhonda's scientific training and Gaby's cultural and agricultural knowledge to produce reasonable surveys and conduct engaging structured interviews and focus groups of all participants (e.g., scientists and ranchers and their families). This model allows for combining approaches and all participants' perspectives and is useful for helping researchers increase the quality of data collected, the level of rigor, and the scholarship in their research programs, all the while bridging a gap between the two worlds—an element often missing in research.

Given the place-based orientation of the research conducted at field stations, this setting is ideal for bringing these interdisciplinary methods together. In Calnali, there is a local Indigenous Náhuatl community whose knowledge has remained very much untapped in the scientific endeavors that CICHAZ has undertaken. We are mindful of treating the Indigenous community and scientists as equal partners. We do not adopt the Western norm of assessing a research program's worth based on publication and impact factor outcomes, which biases reward in favor of the dominant culture (Davies et al., 2021). At the same time, we acknowledge that including Indigenous knowledge in conventional scientific literature could prove to be challenging, particularly due to linguistic barriers and academic politics. Most influential journals are published in English and are dominated by scientists that derive from Western or other traditional universities and institutions that model the Western system of research priorities (Drori, 2003; Powell & Dusdal, 2017). Finding ways to honor Indigenous knowledge and the scientific method is something CICHAZ is actively trying to address through its outreach programming.

To this end, we are exploring project possibilities with a potential collaborator who is Náhuatl. He speaks the Indigenous language and is trained as an agricultural entomologist. We are also initiating a mobile learning laboratory with the intent to reach different communities within our town and outlying regions and to collaboratively develop a curriculum with these communities to explore and discuss aspects of the environment from both a Náhuatl and scientific perspective; funding for hiring a Náhuatl, Spanish, and English-speaking science educator is being pursued as we work toward new collaborations between CICHAZ and the neighboring communities. Similarly, we are designing science activities that we can bring to communities to begin to establish relationships and interests with the local K-12 community. We recognize that establishing this permanent programming will take years of building trust and establishing our scientific goals and sharing our research activities and discovering collaboratively. With the stability of the CICHAZ–ASPac collaboration, new opportunities emerge frequently at an ever-increasing pace, as does our popularity on social media.

The activism CICHAZ and ASPac engage in to protect the environment has to be guided by the respect both organizations have for the local communities, their cultural traditions, Indigenous knowledge, and welcoming attitude. Promoting change of any sort walks a fine line—often too close to colonialist legacies—between our intentions and commitment to be respectful and our scientific thinking around environmentally sustainable water use, ranching practices, and land conservation. In spite of our constant vigilance, the ASPac–CICHAZ collaboration, though designed to positively impact the community, may be seen by some with suspicion. Are we seen as insincere? Manipulative? Pushy? By some, perhaps yes. Yet others welcome us and hear what we are saying and see that we are also listening and interested in the local perspective. It is central to our mission that Gaby and Lalo are part of the ranching community. With them as stewards in this special place, as well as our observations and communication, our team is learning about the impacts of our activities. Gaby and Lalo bring the power of their local insights and connections to what drives the collaboration between the two organizations. This will hopefully encourage the broader community to investigate their natural surrounding landscape and give them other reasons, such as more productive cattle and more fruit trees, to manage and revere their unique ecological treasures.

Yet through outreach events and participant feedback, it is clear that the intention is mostly well-received by many and conserving Calnali's river waters and biodiversity is increasingly a priority for the town. As the swordtail hybrid zone becomes more recognized internationally, the activities of the community that are having negative impacts on the health of the *poxta* (the Náhuatl name for the swordtails) are increasingly understood. This knowledge is helping create a public push for changing water use habits. As the interests of the community begin to more closely align with those of ASPac and CICHAZ, it may also become easier for us to identify with Calnali and vice versa. We are not from Calnali, but we love Calnali. Knowing a place in depth makes you love it and want to take care of it and preserve it—*How does it become part of your identity? Does that give you consistency to build trust for collaboration?* As representatives of CICHAZ, we come together and present a single voice whether it be at an OBFS meeting or when hosting international researchers and visitors from outside Calnali to feel welcomed. Such opportunities help us further articulate our common goals and our intention to promote the inclusion of often marginalized voices, including our own. Furthermore, it makes it possible for biological field stations to play an effective role in knowledge-building and sharing to support environmental health and conservation in the spaces where they exist.

Environmental Health, Knowledge-building, and Conservation

CICHAZ has become a base for numerous research projects conducted by Gil's own trainees and other scientists from around the world who have come to Calnali to study swordtails. Starting in 2005, on-site research in Calnali has been a key feature of his basic research in behavioral evolution (Schumer et al., 2018; Verzijden et al., 2012; Wong et al., 2005). CICHAZ has also been used as a basis for collaborations in cancer biology (Powell et al., 2020). Both the behavioral triggers of hybridization (Fisher et al., 2006) and its genetic consequences (Culumber et al., 2013) are intertwined with the human footprint on these rivers. The activities of the public are thus playing a key role in the researchers' findings. Consequently, outreach is critical for relaying the impacts of day-to-day life on the local ecosystem, identifying what changes are needed, and sparking a conversation that can serve as a catalyst for behavioral adjustments.

Through science communication and informal learning, scientists can convey to the public what is interesting and relevant to them and can learn about the public's observations, insights, and curiosities. Scientists also advance their own investigations by improving the questions they ask, getting public support for their work, and entering into a dialogue with non-scientists that can remove social barriers that unnecessarily divide them. Finding these common grounds can be challenging but also the most fruitful and with the need for conservation, critical for the health of the flora, fauna, and human populations.

Over the years, we have come to realize that there is great value for the local community to know that the hybrid zone exists and that the biodiversity and ecosystems of the area are important scientifically so there is a better understanding of why we are doing the things we do. The beauty of the area is something the Calnali community is proud of and knowing that the land is so much a part of their everyday life is appreciated beyond those who live there is exciting and invigorating for many whom we have met. A complicating factor in this work is that there is strong evidence that hybridization stems from human pollution. CICHAZ is treading gently in raising the community's awareness of the need for behavioral change, carefully balancing its responsibility to share knowledge that contributes to environmental health and conservation with the need to respect internal dynamics and local processes and norms.

Gaby and Lalo are able to act both institutionally and as individual Calnaleses. Through ASPac and their daily activities as full-time residents of Calnali, Gaby and Lalo are positioned to bring the local community together. Through CICHAZ Rhonda and Gil can provide the human and financial resources, and individually they bring the attitude and care to be collaborative in the way they approach the work of running a field station and doing their research. From Gaby's perspective, each of us contributes and is responsible for our part of the collaboration.

> *Cada uno de nosotros pone algo y tiene poder sobre eso. Me parece que el equilibrio que hemos logrado nace de compartir valores y sueños, donde cada*

uno esta dispuesto a dar lo que tiene, de una manera natural, porque no se cede ante el poder del otro, sino ante el acuerdo de lo que queremos realizar y la forma en que lo vamos a realizar.

It seems to me that the balance we have achieved is born from sharing our values and dreams, where each one of us is willing to give what they have, in a natural way, because they do not give in to the power of the other, but rather to the agreement of what we want to do and the way we are going to do it. (Translated)

Her words offer assurance that CICHAZ so far is doing a judicious job of balancing the work and carefully planning all that we do. In an ongoing journey of learning and methodically collecting feedback from all of the participants in our activities, CICHAZ can better gauge what is going right and where it can do better. Input is regularly collected not only from the participants in our programming but also from all visiting scientists and students. Their insights help CICHAZ accumulate institutional knowledge on how best to implement programs.

COLLABORATION CONSIDERATIONS AND CONCLUSION

Through the dialogue and analysis presented here we have come to realize that for a successful collaboration, every collaborator needs to orient themselves to not just each other but the society in which they are embedded. We also see the necessity for genuine acknowledgment of the differing and often shifting power dynamics within, among, and between participants to reach a shared goal. Women especially can help facilitate conversations to address these topics as the expectations of their role often create opportunities, as well as obstacles. Below we pose the questions we continue to discuss to strengthen and deepen our collaboration. We share these as an invitation to the FSML community to reflect on these questions and consider the impacts of systemic power, barriers, and colonialism on potential local, national, and international collaborations.

1. How is power shared between collaborators and how does this advance the goals of the collaboration?
   a. Identify the shared goals.
   b. Identify who has what power in which collaboration and why does something need to shift? How is this power enacted, employed? How does it serve (or hinder) the shared goals?

2. How is colonialism playing a role in the collaboration and how is this limiting the collaboration?
   a. Address individual and institutional biases toward (or against) science—how might that limit community involvement?
   b. Identify the institutional powers involved and how that is managed?
   c. Consider the social location of the collaborators and how that hinders or helps the collaboration?
3. How does being women in this field hinder or help the collaboration and how do you intend to address the challenges or advantages?
   a. Are there some community members who are more oriented toward working with men? How could that change or how can that be managed?

The dialogue process and the writing of this chapter has helped us better articulate and understand Calnali's social, political, and economic conditions that we navigate in our work. We, and Rhonda especially, are committed to addressing the elements of Western imperialism that surface in the work at CICHAZ. We will hold each other accountable when we see ways that might be replicating and reinforcing white supremacy or a scientific bias in our assumptions. And all of our insights should translate and manifest in our strategic thinking and actions. Constant reflection and evaluation of our roles is "a strategic necessity" according to Trask (1993, p. 259) and we intend to honor that call. We challenge other collaborators to do the same and to share their experiences so all of us can benefit from these activities.

Acknowledgments

Thank you to all the people of Calnali who have allowed us to be a part of their community and welcomed CICHAZ and our many visitors over the years. Another thank you to Lalo and Gil for being reliable, supportive partners, and to our children, for their patience with their mothers! Another thank you goes to all the researchers who have visited CICHAZ over the years and shown their respect to the local population. This work is supported by the USDA National Institute of Food and Agriculture, Hatch projects 1021915 (Struminger).

REFERENCES

Anthias, F. (2012). Hierarchies of social location, class and intersectionality: Towards a translocational frame. *International Sociology, 28*(1), 121–138. https://doi.org/10.1177/0268580912463155

Anzaldua, G., & Moraga, C. (1981). *This bridge called my back*. Kitchen Table Women of Color Press.

Bereano, N. K. (1983). Foreword. In A. Lorde (Eds.). *Sister outsider: Essays and speeches*.

Ten Speed Press. *Sister outsider: Essays and speeches*. Crossing Press.

Billick, I., Babb, I., Kloeppel, B., Leong, J. C., Hodder, J., Sanders, J., & Swain, H. (2013). *Field stations and marine laboratories of the future: A strategic vision*. National Association of Marine Laboratories and Organization of Biological Field Stations.

Binding, L. L., & Tapp, D. M. (2008). Human understanding in dialogue: Gadamer's recovery of the genuine. *Nursing Philosophy, 9*(2), 121–130. https://doi.org/10.1111/j.1466-769X.2007.00338.x

Brubaker, R., & Cooper, F. (2000). Beyond "identity." *Theory and Society, 29*(1), 1–47. https://www.jstor.org/stable/3108478

Collins, P. H. (1998). *Fighting words: Black women and the search for justice*. University of Minnesota Press.

The Combahee River Collective. (1977). A Black feminist statement. *Women's Studies Quarterly, 42*(3/4), 271–280. https://www.jstor.org/stable/24365010

Costantino, T. E. (2008). Dialogue. In L. M. Given (Eds.), *The Sage encyclopedia of qualitative research methods*. Sage.

Crenshaw, K. (1991). Mapping the margins: Intersectionality, identity politics, and violence against women of color. *Stanford Law Review, 43*(6), 1241–1299.

Culumber, Z. W., & Rosenthal, G. G. (2013). Population-level mating patterns and fluctuating asymmetry in swordtail hybrids. *Naturwissenschaften, 100*(8), 801–804. https://doi.org/10.1007/s00114-013-1072-z

Davies, S. W., Putnam, H. M., Ainsworth, T., Baum, J. K., Bove, C. B., Crosby, S. C., Côté, I. M., Duplouy, A., Fulweiler, R. W., Griffin, A. J., Hanley, T. C. Hill, T., Humanes, A., Mangubhai, S., Metaxas, A., Parker, L. M., Rivera, H. E., Silbiger, N. S., Smith, N. S., ... Bates, A. E. (2021). Promoting inclusive metrics of success and impact to dismantle a discriminatory reward system in science. *PLoS Biology, 19*(6), e3001282. https://doi.org/10.1371/journal.pbio.3001282

de Vos, A. (2020). The problem of "colonial science". *Scientific American*. https://www.scientificamerican.com/article/the-problem-of-colonial-science/.

Drori, G. S. (2003). *Science in the modern world polity: Institutionalization and globalization*. Stanford University Press.

Fisher, H. S., Wong, B. B., & Rosenthal, G. G. (2006). Alteration of the chemical environment disrupts communication in a freshwater fish. *Proceedings of the Royal Society B: Biological Sciences, 273*(1591), 1187–1193. https://doi.org/10.1098/rspb.2005.3406

Gorelick, R. (2014). Indigenous sciences are not pseudoscience. *Ideas in Ecology and Evolution, 7*(1), 43–55. https://doi.org/10.4033/iee.2014.7.11.c

Grondin, J. (2002). Gadamer's basic understanding of understanding. In R. J. Dostal (Eds.), *The cambridge companion to Gadamer* (pp. 36–51). Cambridge University Press.

Hopkins, N. (2008). Identity, practice and dialogue. *Journal of Community & Applied Social Psychology, 18*(4), 363–368. https://doi.org/10.1002/casp.954

Johnson, A. (2017). Privilege, power, and difference (3rd ed.). McGraw-Hill Professional.

Keiting, A. (2000). *Gloria E. Anzaldua: Interviews/Entrevistas*. Routledge.

Kirk, G., & Okazawa-Rey, M. (2006). Identities and social locations: Who am I? Who are my people?. In L. P. Rudnick, J. E. Smith, & R. L. Rubin (Eds.), *American identities: An introductory textbook* (pp. 7–16). Blackwell Publishing.

Kirk, G., & Okazawa-Rey, M. (2013). Identities and social locations: Who am I? Who are my people? In M. Adams, W. J. Blumenfeld, R. Castaneda, H. W. Hackman, M. L. Peters, & X. Zuniga (Eds.), *Readings for Diversity and Social Justice*. Psychology Press.

Lorde, A. (1984). *Sister outsider: Essays and speeches*. Ten Speed Press.

Maracle, S. (2020). Effective incorporation of Indigenous Knowledge into biological field stations/place-based research institutes [Bachelor's thesis, Queen's University]. https://qspace.library.queensu.ca/bitstream/handle/1974/27800/Stafford%20Maracle%20Thesis.pdf?sequence=3&isAllowed=y

Mathie, A., Cameron, J., & Gibson, K. (2017). Asset-based and citizen-led development: Using a diffracted power lens to analyze the possibilities and challenges. *Progress in Development Studies, 17*(1), 1–13. https://doi.org/10.1177/1464993416674302

McDermott, V. (2022). "Brush your hair, apply for every grant, and get laid as much as possible": Sensemaking women's experiences conducting fieldwork in the tropics. In V. McDermott, J. Gee, & A. R. May (Eds.), *Women of the wild: Challenging gender disparities in field stations and marine laboratories* (pp. 31–52). Lexington Books.

McDermott, V., Gee, J., & May, A. (2022). Defining the role and value of FMSLs. In V. McDermott, J. Gee, & A. R. May (Eds.), *Women of the wild: Challenging gender disparities in field stations and marine laboratories* (pp. 3–15). Lexington Books.

Powell, D. L., García-Olazábal, M., Keegan, M., Reilly, P., Du, K., Díaz-Loyo, A. P., Banerjee, S., Blakkan, D., Reich, D., Andolfatto, P., & Rosenthal, G. G. (2020). Natural hybridization reveals incompatible alleles that cause melanoma in swordtail fish. *Science, 368*(6492), 731–736. https://doi.org/10.1126/science.aba5216

Powell, J. W., & Dusdal, J. (2017). Science production in Germany, France, Belgium, and Luxembourg: Comparing the contributions of research universities and institutes to science, technology, engineering, mathematics, and health. *Minerva, 55*(4), 413–434. https://doi.org/10.1007/s11024-017-9327-z

Putnam, R. (2001). Social capital: Measurement and consequences. *Canadian Journal of Policy Research, 2*(1), 41–51. https://okat.pw/zup_nized_tahe.pdf

Raby, M. (2017). The Colonial Origins of Tropical Field Stations. *American Scientist, 105*(216). https://www.americanscientist.org/article/the-colonial-origins-of-tropical-field-station

Roldan-Hernandez, L., Boehm, A. B., & Mihelcic, J. R. (2020). Parachute environmental science and engineering. *Environmental Science & Technology, 54*(23), 14773–14774. https://doi.org/10.1021/acs.est.0c07462.

Sammut, G. (2011). Civic solidarity: The negotiation of identity in modern societies. *Papers on Social Representations, 20*(1), 4.1–4.24.

Schmidt, P. M., & Stricker, H. K. (2010). What tradition teaches: Indigenous Knowledge complements western wildlife science. *USDA National Wildlife Research Center - Staff Publications*, 1283. https://digitalcommons.unl.edu/icwdm_usdanwrc/1283

Schumer, M., Xu, C., Powell, D. L., Durvasula, A., Skov, L., Holland, C., Blazier, J. C., Sankararaman, S., Andolfatto, P., Rosenthal, G. G., & Przeworski, M. (2018). Natural selection interacts with the local recombination rate to shape the evolution of hybrid genomes. *Science* 360, 656–660.

Short, R. A., Struminger, R., Zarestky, J., Vilen, L., Wong, M., Pippin, J., & Lawing, A. M. (2020). Spatial inequalities leave micropolitan areas and Indigenous populations underserved by informal STEM learning institutions."*Science Advances, 6*(41), eabb3819. https://doi.org/10.1126/sciadv.abb3819

Starhawk. (1988). *Truth or dare: Encounters with power, authority, and mystery.* HarperSanFrancisco.

Struminger, R., Short, R., Zarestky, J., Vilen, L., & Lawing, A. M. (2021). Biological field stations promote science literacy through outreach. *Bioscience*, biab057. https://doi.org/10.1093/biosci/biab057

Struminger, R., Zarestky, J., Short, R. A., & Lawing, A. M. (2018). A Framework for STEM Educational Outreach at Field Stations. *BioScience, 68*(12), 969–978. https://doi.org/10.1093/biosci/biy108

Trask, H. K. (1993). *From a Native daughter: Colonialism and sovereignty in Hawaii.* University of Hawaii Press in association with the Center for Hawaiian Studies.

VeneKlasen, L., & Miller, V. (2007). *A new weave of power, people & politics: The action guide for advocacy and citizen participation*. Practical Action Publishing.

Verzijden, M. N., Culumber, Z. W., & Rosenthal, G. G. (2012). Opposite effects of learning cause asymmetric mate preferences in hybridizing species. *Behavioral Ecology, 23*(5), 1133–1139. https://doi.org/10.1093/beheco/ars086

Winker, G., & Degele, N. (2011) Intersectionality as multi-level analysis: Dealing with social inequality. *European Journal of Women's Studies,* 18(1), 51–66. https://doi.org/10.1177/1350506810386084

Wong, B. B. M., Fisher, H. S., & Rosenthal, G. G. (2005). Species recognition by male swordtails via chemical cues. *Behavioral Ecology, 16*(4), 818–822. https://doi.org/10.1093/beheco/ari058

Young, I. M. (1996). Communication and the other: Beyond deliberative democracy. In S. Benhabib (Eds.), *Democracy and difference: Contesting the boundaries of the political.* Princeton University Press.

Zaytoun, K. (2006). Theorizing at the borders: Considering social location in rethinking self and psychological development. *NWSA Journal*, *18*(2), 52–72. https://www.jstor.org/stable/4317207

Zukas, A. (2005). Terra incognita/terra nullius: Modern imperialism, maps, and deception. In G. Backhaus, & J. Murungi (Eds.), *Lived Topographies and Their Mediational Forces* (pp. 49–76). Lexington Books.

Chapter 11

A Long (Community) Engagement

From Journalism to Field Stations

Lisa Busch

INTRODUCTION

As a journalist in Alaska in the 1980s, I once interviewed a woman seal scientist who was, by any standard, tough as nails. She worked in subzero temperatures, catching seals from frigid waters, escaping their sharp teeth, radio tagging them and releasing them. When I interviewed her about the challenges women in science face she told me, "I might not be able to do all the heavy physical lifting a man can, but when we work in Alaska Native villages, I can sit down with the women and have a cup of tea and talk." At the young age of 23, I really didn't appreciate the unique role women have in engaging people in science. Now, 30 years later as the director of an Alaskan field station, I know that listening to stories over a cup of tea can make a monumental difference in building an appreciation for science and laying the foundation for research that reflects community interests. This chapter frames the special role that field station and marine laboratory (FSML) leaders can play when they engage in the communicative behaviors pioneered by many women and minority science communicators. It will provide reflections from a woman-led field station wherein communication, specifically science communication, is highly valued. Open and effective communication can result in genuine community engagement, highlighting the human experience behind the science. The communicative skills regularly used by women can be utilized by all field station leaders to create more equitable and inclusive relationships between FSMLs and local communities.

THE PUBLIC AND SCIENCE

For decades scholars have argued, "the STEM fields—disengaged from the real needs of people—have neglected their social and environmental commitments" (Boucher et al., 2020, p. 2). However, engaging the public in science is vital for developing stronger connections and trust between the scientific community and the greater public (Martin, 2017; Struminger et al., 2018). Currently, many models of communication surrounding science limit the publics' engagement with the scientific community. For example, Bush (1960) outlined the distinctions between "basic" and "applied" research that resulted in a linear communication model intended to isolate science from the value-laden world (Byerly & Pielke, 1995; Pielke, 1997; Stokes; 1997). As a result, the audiences for scientific information have traditionally been treated as consumers who get the information at the end of the process—referred to as the "deficit model" or "loading dock" approach to science communication (Brossard & Lewenstein, 2010; Bubela et al., 2009; Cash et al., 2006; Nisbet & Scheufele, 2009). In the deficit model of science communication, the audience is perceived to be lacking a specific type of knowledge, and the purpose of science communication is to convey information to fill this deficit (Brossard & Lewenstein, 2010; Nisbet & Scheufele, 2009).

The simplistic "deficit model" of science communication assumes that undesirable public actions regarding science are caused by a lack of knowledge, and the role of science communication is therefore to translate complex science into simplified and digestible facts to fill this gap (Ballantyne, 2016; Dahlstrom, 2014; National Academies of Sciences, Engineering, & Medicine, 2017). This model treats audiences as passive recipients of information and overlooks the influence of cultural values and worldviews. For example, research by Kahan et al. (2012) found that in highly contentious scientific contexts, such as climate change, the audiences with more accurate knowledge are also often the most polarized. Even when individuals agree on the scientific facts, their preexisting and contrasting values can lead them to interpret the application of those facts in opposing directions.

Improving science communication therefore requires a more audience-centered model. This alternative, the interactive paradigm, emphasizes that audiences are active consumers of information and will interact with and interpret science in ways guided by their needs and worldviews (Ballantyne, 2016; Dahlstrom, 2014; National Academies of Sciences, Engineering, & Medicine, 2017). Under this model, communicating science represents an interaction where all parties involved have a role in shaping the meaning of the content to be understood, that is, "co-production of knowledge."

FSMLs offer an ideal opportunity to facilitate the interactive paradigm of science communication and broaden participation in science, technology, engineering, and mathematics (STEM) through informal science learning (Baker, 2015; National Research Council NRC, 2014). With over 984 FSMLs across the United States, FSMLs provide access to the environment, logistical support for a wide range of scientific research and student training, and foster a community of learning (Billick et al., 2013). Primarily established by universities and governments to serve researchers and students conducting fieldwork, FSMLs recognize the importance of providing informal STEM learning programs to the general public (Billick et al., 2013).

Engaging the public in science is vital for inspiring public interest in STEM and building trust in the scientific community (Martin, 2017). Due to their often-remote nature, FSMLs have the opportunity to be a reciprocal hub, providing the space for citizens to connect with scientists and where researchers can learn local knowledge from people who live in rural areas. With the advent of COVID-19 pandemic, a team of FSML directors has launched a National Science Foundation (NSF)-sponsored project to explore novel virtual teaching methods to bring the field station experience to audiences who might not otherwise visit or have access to FSMLs, field station personnel, and researchers (see The Virtual Field for more information).

Although FSMLs provide an opportunity to connect the scientific community and local communities, there can be barriers to creating effective partnerships. One of the biggest problems is that conventional scientific training does not prepare scientists to communicate their research effectively to the public nor does it prepare scientists to listen to local people. During their college careers, undergraduates are rarely required to take science communication, intercultural communication, or social science classes (Eise, 2019), resulting in a lack of understanding related to the "psychological, social, geographic, health, cultural, infrastructural and technology vulnerabilities" that impact the communities where FSMLs are located (Potnis & Gala, 2020, p. 2). This means that researchers working in rural areas, specifically, may not be adequately prepared to work alongside local and Indigenous populations (Graham et al., 2019). Overall, without trusted relationships between scientists and community members, it can be difficult to have impactful and long-lasting engagement (see chapter 1 by McDermott, Gee, & May in this edited volume for more information).

Science communication is an interdisciplinary endeavor requiring knowledge of scientific thinking and concepts, psychology, anthropology, sociology, communication, understanding of audiences, and strong writing and verbal skills. Women and other groups underrepresented as leaders at field stations may have a rare opportunity to break new ground in science communication in these nontraditional academic career paths. Although not all marginalized groups may want to assume the communicator role or recognize the complexities associated with communication as a discipline, this may be a niche in which groups that have been excluded from academia can lead the charge to further interdisciplinary collaborations. Research has argued that women and minorities have been early adopters of interdisciplinary studies (Rhoten & Pfirman, 2007), finding niches in relatively unexplored cross-sectional areas of research that have not yet been discovered by traditional power structures.

SITUATING MYSELF

I became a field station director through an unusual route of journalism and community organizing. Though I received a BS in geology and environmental science, my dismal college grades did not portend a successful career as a researcher. My college adviser, who recognized that my grades did not reflect my enthusiasm for science, helped me find internships and get established in the budding field of science journalism. Eventually journalism opened the door to the idea of a career in which I could work *around* scientists but not *do* science.

My first paid job was as a general public radio reporter at KCAW in Sitka, Alaska. Here I learned the technical basics of how to cut tape (yes, it was actual tape back then) and operate a recording machine. But more importantly, I got to know my community. I attended hundreds of community meetings and events and became familiar with the individuals and the processes that operate in a rural place. A reporter in a small town has a rare perspective on community issues: I met decision makers, community agitators, and organizers and learned how government, nonprofits, and academia can work together to bring about change. Attending a breadth of community events from city council to hospital board and animal control commission meetings meant hearing from neighbors and city officials, observing how a community evolves, and learning strategies for engaging the public. In spite of my aptitude for field trips, not writing, I learned the formula for magazine writing at *U.S. News and World Report*, *Science* and *Bioscience* magazines covering Alaska science issues.

Early on in my science journalism career, I saw myself as a translator with a mission to decode scientific language into words that those outside the scientific community could understand. I was told by countless editors and scientists that researchers could not possibly speak to the general public, so it was up to journalists to translate for them.

"I majored in geology," I would say as a way to reassure an apprehensive scientist that they were in trusted hands. But I was quick to tell them that I got a D in physics after taking it for the second time, so they would not expect me to understand the technical language of their discipline, because I didn't. Enamored with science, my early stories were very "Gee Whiz" about "cool" and "amazing" scientific discoveries that were published in *Popular Mechanics* and trade journals.

In 1999, I received the Ted Scripps Fellowship for Environmental Journalism at the University of Colorado Boulder. I plunged into the study of the history and philosophy of science. And that's when my love affair with science ended. The history of scientific ideas reveals how white men have excluded women, minorities, and Indigenous ways of knowing from the sciences for centuries. I learned that in spite of its claim of objectivity, scientific thinking can be swayed by the economic, social, and political issues of the day (Avraamido & Schwartz, 2021; Tseng et al., 2020). In studying history and culture, I was also exposed to a variety of worldviews. Indigenous worldview, for example, had a holistic view of the natural world that siloed scientists often lacked. Indigenous worldview looked at the habitats and animals in the environment on equal footing as humans and respected the natural world in a way that sometimes seemed lacking in non-native cultures.

At the same time, the fellowship brought into focus the true essence of what made science reporting so interesting and so much fun to be—the scientists themselves. Seeing scientists as people with hobbies, foibles, egos, families, and ideas brought me close to the data and content side of science. I appreciate the way scientists think about problem-solving and use critical thinking, validation, and experimentation to create new ideas. Along with the reading or listening audience, I am often drawn to scientific ideas by a scientist's background, culture, and what motivates them. Failures and stories of humility are also engaging. I admire the courage it takes to postulate a new scientific idea, experiment, and be open to the idea that it might be wrong. I am drawn to people who are enthusiastic about understanding the natural world.

When I returned from my fellowship, I began producing a local public radio program that was hosted by a volunteer named Richard Nelson, a famed cultural anthropologist who lived with Alaskan Indigenous communities for more than 40 years. The show which was eventually distributed to 187 stations across the nation, called *Encounters: Radio Experiences in the North,* had the host provide first-person accounts of wild locations around the circumpolar north while weaving together a rare narrative of natural history and Indigenous knowledge on the northern subject (polar bears, muskox, wilderness, wind, whales, salmon, etc.)

Alongside my professional trajectory in journalism, I am also a community member. As a resident of a small town, each person's contribution to the common good seems amplified. I co-founded a trails group, Sitka Trail Works, that trained displaced timber workers to be a trail construction crew. Ultimately, with an enthusiastic constituency, this nonprofit built $20 million of trails in our area. I also helped to start a local Tree and Landscape Commission that planted and maintained trees and greenery in our downtown area. I participated in sports teams and after-school activities that my kids were involved with by writing small grants and organizing fundraising events, coordinating volunteers, and advocating at the city, state, and federal level for a variety of causes. I built trusted relationships just by being an engaged citizen.

CASE STUDY: DIRECTING THE SITKA SOUND SCIENCE CENTER

These experiences, together with my background in journalism and science helped lay the ideal groundwork for a position as a field station director. In this position, I oversee a nonprofit organization, develop programs that help us meet our science research and education mission, collaborate with community partners, develop funding streams, and create a team of science education and researchers that serves the community. All of the aspects of my job require an understanding of communication. As the leader of a field station, I have a unique position in developing ways and methods for connecting our community and researchers. I have come to understand that good science communication at a field station can strengthen the relationship between scientists and community members. It can connect and ground research questions in a community. Furthermore, when Indigenous knowledge is integrated into scientific discovery, it can deepen and enrich our understanding.

Since its inception in 2007, Sitka Sound Science Center (SSSC) has had women—from the board and from the staff—directing its development. I was the first full-time employee hired in 2010. Since then, our team has developed some signature informal science education programs that have been critical in engaging the community in scientific research and scientific thinking. Below I will outline two themes with specific examples that have been invaluable in building the reputation and integration of the SSSC in the local community. These themes are the role a community-based field station can have on incorporating Indigenous knowledge, the second is that FSMLs provide the space for scientists to practice and engage in communication skills.

One advantage that a community-based field station has is its proximity and ability to understand local and Indigenous culture enough to be able to integrate scientific thinking, findings, and questions

Example Scientists in the Schools (SIS)

Through our SIS program, we strategically and carefully integrate working scientists into the existing science curriculum and the Indigenous culture. SIS is a program that brings scientists from a variety of disciplines into every K-12 classroom each year in the Sitka School District and into Mt. Edgecumbe High School, a state-operated boarding school that is 90% Alaska Native. The program is carefully and strategically coordinated between SSSC educational staff, scientists, and teachers at the school districts to bring scientists into the classrooms to help teachers meet certain state education standards, expose our rural and Alaska Native students to new scientific disciplines, and build enthusiasm for STEM careers. The scientists receive training in how to work with the developmental age of the students and where the students are in their curriculum. SSSC conducts pre-lessons in advance of the classroom visit and helps scientists design fun, hands-on, age-appropriate, engaging activities. The award-winning program (OBFS, 2020) has brought 118 scientists to our community since 2012, teaching 403 classes and more than 90 different topics.

This program has been credited with helping to raise science standardized test scores among economically disadvantaged students and Alaska Native students (SSSC, n.d.). Alaska Native and rural children build relationships with scholars, allowing them to experience science through contact with a real human being. Scientists learn about local culture and through the interaction with children learn about the local culture, classroom parameters, and how to communicate to a nonscientific audience.

A Field Station Provides an Ideal Platform for Scientists to Practice Communication Skills and to Learn from Community Members

Example Required Science Communication Training

At the SSSC, we facilitate hundreds of community engagement activities each year with professional scientists. From these experiences, we have learned that even good science communicators need training before interacting with the public. Scientists rarely receive science communication training in their academic careers. SSSC requires science communication training from our staff members to anyone using our field station. The training is intended to prepare scientists to work in our rural Alaskan community. The short, required course is an overview of knowing the audience, storytelling, the use of technical language, and listening. The training is usually 90 minutes, so scientists are not meant to be experts by the time it's over. Rather the purpose is to expose scientists to the perceptions of science, the pitfalls in communicating their research, and share our experiences in what makes for effective engagement. Our field station also facilitates cultural training with local Indigenous culture bearers and basics on how to navigate a rural community. Our hope is that scientists would feel

Figure 11.1 Field Stations Can Promote Scientists as "Super Stars" as a way to Engage the Community in Science. *Source*: Photo by author.

comfortable drinking a cup of tea with locals when they have completed the training.

Example Scientists in Residency Fellowship (SIRF)

We encourage scientists to show their human side, what they dream about, what their failures and successes are. In showing their humanity, they connect more fully with community members. The SIRF program brings scientists from around the United States to our field station for a one-month mini-sabbatical (see Figure 11.1). Three or four selected applicants per year come to Sitka for a month to work on anything they need time to do (e.g., analyze data, study a new aspect of their work, prepare a manuscript, develop a new collaboration) and get a full immersion experience in engaging with our rural geographically isolated community. SSSC staff facilitates a schedule in advance for the SIRF to participate in existing programs, such as our SIS program, community lecture series, after-school programs, summer camps, interviews on public radio, profiles in the newspaper, tribal council meetings, or work with a specific population. Sometimes the researchers want to meet with fishermen or hear from Alaska elders in the state-operated nursing home. As scientists are known by the community, they get invitations to go on hikes and boat rides, fishing and berry picking dates and are provided a myriad of opportunities to get to know the issues that concern our citizens. Our field station makes science fun and integrates it into local arts, food, and recreational activities.

Example WhaleFest

Sitka WhaleFest is one of Alaska's premier informal science education events. WhaleFest is an annual community celebration of the marine environment. It brings nine speakers from around the nation to talk about their current research to a general audience including commercial fishermen, visitors, and students. The science symposium is surrounded by a host of other eating, art, music, and whale-watching community events. Rural high school, community college, and university undergraduates attend the festival and participate in a variety of workshops, as well as discussion groups led by the scientists who are presenting with the intention of giving students closer access to real working scientists. Overall, infusing fun into STEM education is a way to encourage STEM majors, while exposing students to a breadth of marine science issues and potential careers. Sitka WhaleFest committee is committed to equity, diversity, and inclusion and emphasizes traditional knowledge by inviting Alaska Native culture bearers to speak alongside scientists. Sitka WhaleFest speakers are required to attend a half-day science communication workshop where we describe the audience and prepare scientists for speaking to a general audience.

DISCUSSION/REFLECTIONS

Overall, these informal science education experiences and training have resulted in students and community members becoming more engaged in scientific thinking and ideas. We know this in part by the improvements we have seen to state science standardized testing among low income and Alaska Native students and by the increases in attendance at community science-based events. Our summer camps have waiting lists and our science center memberships are ever increasing. We believe the emphasis on communication, namely training both researchers in the classrooms and scientists in the community, has been helpful in connecting our community with scientific thinking and ideas.

We know FSMLs can play an important role in connecting the community to research (Billick, 2013; Struminger et al., 2018). However, the connection requires strategic and thoughtful planning, understanding of how the community operates, and training to better communicate science (Scuber, 2002). While the above examples are for the most part positive programs, not every attempt at community engagement is a success. As a director of an organization that has grown quickly in the last decade, I sometimes forget that not everyone is enthusiastic about science and there are still those who are surprised to see women leading in science disciplines. I have made missteps culturally with Indigenous organizations by being too direct or acting on ideas too quickly. However, I still maintain that experimenting with a variety of approaches is worthwhile. Progress happens at the speed of trust. And trust takes time to establish.

RECOMMENDATIONS

From my reflections, I provide four important recommendations for FSML leadership to consider:

Build up women's strengths in community-based facilitating and communicating

Communication is often relegated as an add-on to an existing job and very often women take on this responsibility. Instead, FSMLs might consider building up positions around community engagement and provide training that build on communication strengths that some women possess.

Science communication does not need to be limited to just women

Although women are often communicators in a variety of fields, science communication does not have to be limited to women. By setting a culture of engagement, FSMLs can encourage people from all backgrounds to communicate well.

Require scientists working at a FSML to get training in communication, local culture, and the history of the region

By requiring science communication, culture, and history training, and then providing real-life opportunities to practice, FSMLs are in a unique position to educate researchers. This emphasis on communication, culture, and history training may create better long-term relationships between the local and scientific communities.

Build trusted relationships in the community

Trust takes time to build. It requires getting to know individual people in a variety of organizations. Getting to know people means going for coffee or a beer, providing services like free passes or lectures, sending a note when you notice something positive, or calling just to talk or introduce yourself. Then when you do need another organization or want to work together, there is a foundation of trust.

REFERENCES

Avraamidou, L., & Schwartz, R. (2021). Who aspires to be a scientist/who is allowed in science? Science identity as a lens to exploring the political dimension of the nature of science. *Cultural Studies of Science Education, 16*, 337–344. https://doi.org/10.1007/s11422-021-10059-3

Baker, B. (2015). The way forward for biological field stations. *BioScience 65*(2), 123–129. https://doi.org/10.1093/biosci/biu210

Ballantyne, A. G. (2016), Climate change communication: what can we learn from communication theory? *WIREs Climate Change, 7*, 329–344. https://doi.org/10.1002/wcc.392

Billick, I. Babb, I., Kloeppel, B., Leong, J., Hodder, J., Sanders, J., & Swain, H. (2013). *Field stations and marine laboratories of the future: A strategic vision.* National Association of Marine Laboratories and Organization of Biological Field Stations.

Boucher, J. L., Levenda, A. M., Morales-Guerrero, J., Macias, M. M., & Karwat, D. M. A. (2020). Establishing a field of collaboration for engineers, scientists, and community groups: incentives, barriers, and potential. *Earth's Future, 8*(10). https://doi.org/10.1029/2020EF001624

Brossard, D., & Lewenstein, B. V. (2010). A critical appraisal of models of public understanding of science. In L. A. Kahlor & P. Stout (Eds) *Understanding and communicating science: New agendas in communication* (pp. 11–39). Routledge

Bubela, T., Nisbet, M. C., Borchelt, R., Brunger, F., Critchley, C., Einsiedel, E., Geller, Gupta, A., Hampel, J., Hyde-Lay, R., Jandciu, E. W., Jones, A. S., Kolopack, P., Lane, S., Lougheed, T., Nerlich, B., Ogbogu, U., O'Riordan, K. O., Oullette, C., Spear, M, Stauss, S., Thavaratnam, T., Willemse, L., & Caulfield, T. (2009). Science communication reconsidered. *Nature Biotechnology, 27*(6), 514–518.

Bush, C. R. (1960). A system of categories for general news content. *Journalism Quarterly, 37*(2), 206–210. https://doi.org/10.1177/107769906003700205

Byerly, R., & R. A. Pielke, (1995). The changing ecology of United States science. *Science*, 269(5230), 1531–1532. https://doi.org/10.1126/science.269.5230.1531

Cash, D. W., Borck, J. C., & Patt, A. G. (2006) Countering the loading-dock approach to linking science and decision making—Comparative analysis of El Niño/Southern Oscillation (ENSO) forecasting systems. *Science, Technology, & Human Values, 31*(4), 465–494. https://doi.org/10.1177/0162243906287547

Dahlstrom, M. F. (2014). Storytelling in science. *Proceedings of the National Academy of Sciences, 111*(4), 13614–13620. https://doi/org/10.1073/pnas.1320645111

Eise, J. (2019, December 3). What institutions can do to improve science communication. *Nature*. https://www.nature.com/articles/d41586-019-03869-7

Graham, I. D., McCutcheon, C., & Kothari, A. (2019). Exploring the frontiers of research co-production: The Integrated Knowledge Translation Research Network concept papers. *Health Research Policy & Systems, 17*(88), 1–4. https://doi.org/10.1186/s12961-019-0501-7

Kahan, D., Peters, E., Wittlin, M., Slovic, P., Ouellette, L. L., Braman, D., & Mandel, G. (2012). The polarizing impact of science literacy and numeracy on perceived climate change risks. *Nature Climate Change, 2*, 732–735.

Martin, V. Y. (2017). Citizen science as a means for increasing public engagement in science: Presumption or possibility? *Science Communication, 39*(2), 142–168. https://doi.org/10.1177/1075547017696165

McDermott, V., Gee, J., & May, A. (2022). Defining the role and value of FMSLs. In V. McDermott, J. Gee, & A. R. May (Eds.), *Women of the wild: Challenging gender disparities in field stations and marine laboratories* (pp. 3–15). Lexington Books.

National Academies of Sciences, Engineering, & Medicine. (2017). *Communicating science effectively: A research agenda.* Washington, DC: The National Academies Press.

National Research Council [NRC]. (2014). *Enhancing the value and sustainability of field stations and marine laboratories in the 21st century.* https://www.nap.edu/catalog/18806/enhancing-the-value-and-sustainability-of-field-stations-and-marine-laboratories-in-the-21st-century

Nisbet, M. C., & Scheufele, D. A. (2009). What's next for science communication? Promising directions and lingering distractions. *American Journal of Botany, 96*(10), 1767–1778.

OBFS. (2020). OBFS human diversity committee. https://www.obfs.org/human-diversity-committee

Pielke, R. (1997). Asking the right questions: Atmospheric sciences research and societal needs. *Bulletin of The American Meteorological Society, 78*, 255–255.

Potnis, D., & Gala, B. (2020). Best practices for conducting fieldwork with marginalized communities. *Information Processing & Management, 57*(3), 1–4. https://doi.org/102144.10.1016/j.ipm.2019.102144.

Rhoten, D., & Pfirman, S. (2007). Women in interdisciplinary science: Exploring preferences and consequences. *Research Policy, 36*, 56–75. https://doi.org/10.1016/j.respol.2006.08.001

Scuber, A. C. (2002) *Working with differences in communities: A handbook for those who care about creating inclusive communities.* Oregon State University.

Sitka Sound Science Center. (n.d.). SIS impacts. https://sitkascience.org/education/education programs/scientists-in-the-schools/sis-impacts/

Stokes, D. E. (1997). *Pasteur's quadrant: Basic science and technological innovation.* Brookings Institution Press.

Struminger, R., Zarestky, J., Short, R. A., Lawing, A. M. (2018). Framework for informal STEM education outreach at field stations. *BioScience*, 68(12), 969–978. https://doi.org/10.1093/biosci/biy108

The Virtual Field. (n.d.). About. https://thevirtualfield.org/

Tseng, M., El-Sabaawi, R. W., Kantar, M. B., Pantel, J. H., Srivastava, D. S., & Ware, J. L.(2020). Strategies and support for Black, Indigenous, and people of colour in ecology and evolutionary biology. *Nature Ecology & Evolution, 4*, 1288–1290. https://doi.org/10.1038/s41559-020-1252-0

Part III

RECOMMENDATIONS FOR FSMLS

Chapter 12

Recommendations for Developing More Diverse, Equitable, Accessible, and Inclusive FSMLs

Amy R. May, Victoria M. McDermott, and Jennifer M. Gee

INTRODUCTION

Field stations and marine labs (FSMLs) are microcosms of society at large, providing a unique lens to explore the barriers we face as educators, scholars, and practitioners as we push toward equity and inclusion. Through the lived experience of our contributors navigating these spaces, we have started to unpack the unique challenges women face working, living, and supporting the larger scientific community. From the narrative form used to tell women's stories of sexual harassment to the importance of building community-field station partnerships, our diverse range of authors sought to not only explicate their experiences but provide readers with practical recommendations for building equitable spaces. Gender disparities remain a significant issue in science, technology, engineering, and math (STEM) (Hill et al., 2010), underscoring the urgency for the greater scientific community to pursue "research outside of their comfort zone" (Interdisciplinarity, 2015, para. 3). Utilizing an interdisciplinary approach, each chapter supports the larger call for STEM and social science collaborations "to solve the grand challenges facing society—energy, water, climate, food, health" (Interdisciplinarity, 2015, para. 1).

RECOMMENDATIONS

Critically evaluating the lived experiences of educators, scholars, and practitioners living and working at FSMLs through this edited volume has identified opportunities to redress gaps in support structures and build programs to support not only women choosing to pursue careers in STEM but all members of the scientific community who work at over 1,260 FSMLs across the globe and the surrounding communities in which they are situated (Billick et al., 2013; Tydecks et al., 2016). As demonstrated through the interdisciplinary scholarship in this edited volume, challenging cultural norms at FSMLs and the larger institutions in which they serve has the potential to promote scientific discovery, support different ways of knowing, and build relationships that support citizen science, and engage future generations of scientists. Moreover, evaluating organizational climates and associated risk factors has been cited as critical to understanding the scope and nature of concerns that perpetuate a "culture of silence" (U.S. Equal Employment Opportunity Commission EEOC, 2017, p. 6) and prevent further marginalization and disenfranchisement of members of our community. As such, we provide readers with final recommendations for supporting women scientists and staff working at FSMLs with full acknowledgment of their limitations and potential for bias as women navigating these patriarchal and often misogynistic institutions. Furthermore, we recognize each FSML represents a unique culture defined by its history, leadership, supporting institutions, stakeholders, location, and peoples that inhabit these spaces. As such, these recommendations are offered as a starting point for continuing the conversation while recognizing what works at some FSMLs may not work at others. Our goal is to challenge and inspire FSMLs to work within their systems and cultures to support inclusive practices that promote scientific discovery and community engagement. To facilitate this process, we have broken down these recommendations into strategies for institutions, policymakers, funding agencies, and the FSML community at large.

Recommendations for Administrators/ Policymakers/Funding Agencies

Shift Values of Funding Agencies to Change Cultural Values

Funding to Support Women Scientist Parents. Early-career advancement for many women often overlaps with prime reproductive years where they are forced to make critical decisions regarding marriage and family (Cardel et al., 2020). For many women, these decisions may represent a "forced choice" due to a lack of perceived institutional and social support (Cardel et al., 2020). STEM has been especially hard hit by the loss of women as a result of the decision to parent. Cech and Blair-Loy (2019) investigated the career choices for women faculty members in STEM to better understand how parenthood impacts their career decision-making process. Their findings indicate over 43% of early-career women holding an academic appointment make the decision to leave after the birth of their first child compared to 23% for their male counterparts (Cech & Blair-Loy, 2019). These findings quantify the gender gap, its impact on institutions, and underscore the urgency for administrators, policymakers, and funding agencies to identify and redress equity gaps. As noted in chapter 4 by Debinski of this edited volume, some FSML leaders have been able to balance the competing needs of parenthood and a scientific career with partner and community support. However, partner and community support are not available to all those considering parenthood. Therefore, more large-scale support systems need to be in place to fully support women seeking to have a family and a successful field-based research career.

Federal grant funding agencies, such as the National Science Foundation (NSF), have recognized the urgency to support women researchers who historically have been underfunded compared to their male peers (Else, 2019). NSF's Career-Life Balance Initiative (n.d.b.), for example, provides funding for researchers to provide dependent care. This support most commonly comes in the form of granting a leave of absence and funding temporary replacement personnel. There is limited support, however, for women scientists who wish to parent while simultaneously continuing their scholarship. Moreover, access to these funds is tied to "established awardee institutional policy as approved by the cognizant agency and consistently applied to both Federal and non-Federal sponsors" (NSF, n.d.a, FAQ#3). Burdened by legalese, these policies vary from institution to institution, creating potential barriers to access which may result in unequal dispersion of dependent-care funding for women scientists across the larger scientific community.

In addition, funding support is not provided for dependent care while traveling to conferences or attending workshops (NSF, n.d.a., FAQ #4, 5), creating additional disparities for women. Presenting research at conferences provides access to a global stage to showcase one's scholarship, establish one's reputation in the discipline, and often provides a platform for fostering future collaborations and network development. Funding agencies and grant administrators are encouraged to consider additional avenues for funding dependent care and associated costs for women scientists to ensure equal access to the larger scientific community.

Defund Stations and People Who Violate Sexual Harassment and Bullying Policies. Discussions of ethical research practice have long been part of the scientific community. Required training related to responsible data management is a critical part of the funding process; however, only high-profile cases of researcher misconduct make headlines that often result in termination of funding. In recent years, major funding agencies, such as the National

Institutes of Health (NIH), have "[bolstered] policies, guidelines, requirements, and communications to make . . . expectations clear . . . and to take appropriate actions within [their] authority" (NIH, n.d., para. 1). However, prior to 2018, no principal investigator (PI) had ever been removed as a result of allegations related to sexual harassment (Kaiser, 2021).

To their credit, their commitment to ending sexual harassment and other forms of harassment has resulted in 75 PIs being removed from grants, promoting accountability (Kaiser, 2021). However, the editors underscore the concerns raised by critics who challenge these efforts as not enough to create safe workspaces free of harassment (Subbaraman, 2020) as the behavior must be deemed "severe or pervasive" (Kaiser, 2021, para. 5). Additionally, NIH does not require funded institutions to disclose sexual harassment investigations; disclosure is encouraged but not mandated as part of the funding process (Subbaraman, 2020). This is problematic because even if a PI is removed from a grant, the funds remain at the institution; with no real consequence for lack of reporting, there is no significant motivator to promote transparency or ethical practices (Subbaraman, 2020; Witze, 2016). Moreover, policies regarding sexual harassment along with reporting, investigative practices, and protection from retaliation vary from agency to agency as "the United States (U.S.) government does not classify sexual infractions as research misconduct" (Witze, 2016, para. 2). The end result is a lack of consistency and accountability across agencies and institutions, which ultimately has the potential to trickle down to individual FSMLs.

The challenge becomes how to promote and regulate the beast, that is, the funding structure of the U.S. government along with private institutions that are not bound by the same rules of engagement, that is, taxpayer-supported enterprises. Maybe part of the solution requires women to mobilize locally to force change globally. Women have incredible power to mobilize and bring about change. #MeToo, #TimesUp, and other calls to share stories of sexual harassment and sexual assault in STEM have resulted in a community of activism and directly influenced NIH's anti-harassment policy stance (Subbaraman, 2020). Moreover, the current administration has committed to ending violence against women (Biden|Harris, 2021). Part of this plan is an increased commitment to researching issues impacting women, partnering with colleges and universities to promote training and create safe spaces, and holding offenders accountable (Biden|Harris, 2021). Since many FSMLs are affiliated with colleges and universities, there may be an opportunity for lobbying and working within the system to bring about an increased awareness for reform at the federal level. The larger field station community is also challenged to work within their institutional support structures to increase awareness of gender-related funding disparities, gender harassment, and the need for reform.

Curricular Level

A growing body of literature recognizes the importance of interdisciplinary scholarship to promote not only scientific discovery but develop other once deemed "soft" skills relegated exclusively to the social sciences and humanities. Interdisciplinarity is a term used to describe the integration of multiple approaches or disciplines into the curriculum, research process, or institutional practice (Okamura, 2019). As we seek to understand the larger social processes impacting FSMLs, such as gender harassment, the need to support cultural change, and complexities associated with communication as a discipline, promoting interdisciplinarity may provide current and future researchers additional resources for navigating these spaces and bridging the cultural divide that separates the sciences (Snow, 1959).

In practice, interdisciplinarity can be integrated across the curriculum, and STEM educators are encouraged to challenge their students to explore the social sciences. As communication scholars, specifically, we recognize the value of communication studies for FSML communities. Students of communication learn the importance of inclusive language and audience analysis, conflict management, relationship development, how information flows within an organization, group norms, and the importance of intercultural competence to support diversity and inclusion initiatives. Likewise, psychology, anthropology, sociology, and other social science disciplines provide an opportunity for students and practitioners to learn more about the historical, political, and sociocultural influences impacting scientific discovery and field research.

In addition to integrating the social sciences into the curriculum, interdisciplinary research teams that bring together specific expertise are encouraged to design, execute, and interpret research data to explicate the larger implications of the findings within a global context. At the Cold Climate Research Center in Fairbanks, Alaska, for example, one deficiency noted in their current research practice was communicating results to the local community and "closing that loop" (M. O'Neall, personal communication, July 27, 2021). Future research projects will include a social scientist as part of the research team from inception to planned communication strategies and more fully partner with local community members. Additionally, this edited volume consists of interdisciplinary research teams and collaborators, including an interdisciplinary editorial team, which represents both the social sciences and biological sciences. While not without its challenges, the different perspectives and ways of knowing significantly enhanced our scholarship and collaboration.

Finally, advocating for interdisciplinarity offers different ways of knowing. Introducing native science, for example, into the curriculum provides an opportunity for students to explore the scientific method through a different lens. Dividing knowledge into different departments or disciplines is a

Western model for scientific discovery. Native science offers a more holistic approach to understanding the natural world, challenges the notion of what constitutes "good data," and instills the importance of respecting local communities and knowledge systems when doing field research at FSMLs (Black Elk, 2016, para. 10).

Stations/FSML Community

Gender Harassment and Reporting Structures

Women and non-gender conforming peoples remain underrepresented at FSMLs (see chapter 9 by Roketenetz & Holliday in this edited volume). Moreover, FSMLs have a history of excluding women to ensure they remain "a place where real research men can find quiet, keen intellectual stimulation, freedom from any outside distractions" (as cited in Henson, 2002, p. 586) (see Torti's chapter 2 and McDermott's chapter 3 in this edited volume). As women increasingly occupy these spaces dominated by hegemonic masculinity, providing opportunities to report gender harassment and other forms of harassment is critical to changing the culture and creating more inclusive spaces. Gender harassment is cited in the literature as the most common form of harassment and includes a variety of communication constructs that demean, devalue, and degrade based on one's gender (National Academies of Sciences, Engineering, and Medicine, 2018). Left unchallenged, gender harassment has the potential to negatively impact the emotional, mental, and physical health of targets and may play a critical role in the decision process for women and non-gender conforming peoples who consider leaving STEM (National Academies of Sciences, Engineering, and Medicine, 2018). Redressing gender harassment in a meaningful and inclusive way provides a starting point for creating more inclusive spaces and changing cultural norms.

Similarly, when considering how we invite people who are/have experienced gender harassment to disclose, it is also important to consider the language used to describe the formal process and how these messages are integrated into the physical space. "Victim" or "target" or other legalese-based terms may be perceived as negative framing and further inhibit disclosure. The U.S. Equal Employment Opportunity Commission (EEOC) (2017) encourages using descriptors such as "a person seeking resources" (p. 11) to help remove perceived stigma and normalize disclosure. Finally, displaying posters in bathrooms, common areas, and throughout the facility may help inform and empower FSML community members to use the resources at their disposal by fully integrating them into the space.

In addition to considering language and framing, providing easy access to reporting channels allows site directors and support staff to ensure problematic behaviors are identified and addressed, challenging the idea "this is just how science is." Multiple reporting channels that allow for privacy and anonymity are critical (EEOC, 2017); moreover, reporting channels should be representative of the available technology at the FSMLs. Once FSML personnel, be it staff, researchers, visiting scholars, and/or community visitors, voice their concerns, investigations need to be prompt, thorough, and resolute to ensure trust is built into the reporting system to promote disclosure and utilization as issues occur (EEOC, 2017). Similarly, investigations need to be as transparent as possible (respecting legal boundaries) with the FSML community to highlight that the specific station holds perpetrators responsible for their actions. Since some FSMLs are situated within larger institutional frameworks, for example, colleges and universities, identifying how to facilitate communication to reduce the cumbersome nature of the bureaucracies that may impede many of these institutions is worthy of additional consideration and research.

Codes of Conduct

FSMLs welcome scientists, practitioners, and support staff from across the globe, bringing together people from different cultures, generations, and educational backgrounds. As argued in chapter 7 by Becker, Griffin, and Miller, the climate fostered at FSMLs can have considerable impact on the students and staff who frequent them. The workplace culture, communication, and inequities that cultivate positive or negative experiences can greatly impact long-term career trajectories. To ensure a shared understanding of acceptable and unacceptable behaviors, site directors are encouraged to consider drafting a code of conduct that must be acknowledged prior to granting access to their respective facilities. A code of conduct defines appropriate and inappropriate behaviors along with consequences for violations, emphasizes the treatment of people, and explains the reporting process (ADVANCEGeo Partnership, 2021). The EEOC (2017) recommends using clear descriptions and detailed examples of prohibited conduct; in other words, communicate using words and images. Moreover, this code of conduct should be translated into multiple languages and cultural contexts to ensure shared understanding (EEOC, 2017). This would guarantee shared accountability and prevent "I didn't know" being used as a justification for an offensive behavior that devalues or degrades a community member.

In chapter 2, Torti shared a fictional account of a lone woman researcher working at a remote field station with three other men who experienced repeated sexual harassment. Although fiction, this piece was based on historical and representative experiences of women. While it is easy to assume adults understand consent, for example, do not invade another community member's personal space without invitation, following the old adage of ass-u-me seems particularly relevant as sexual harassment, sexual aggression, and sexual violence remain a major concern for women navigating spaces that continue to be dominated by men.

Sharing Narratives through Interdisciplinary Research

In chapter 3, McDermott argues that women and other "muted groups," that is, marginalized groups, need channels for sharing their stories in their "language," representing their ways of knowing. How a story is told should be as open as possible to include not only the dominant language of science but also other means of narration. In chapter 2, Torti uses a fictional narrative to represent historical accounts of women navigating sexual harassment at a field station. In chapter 4, Debinski tells her story using pictures, recollections from family, and old publications to reimagine more inclusive spaces for women scientists who choose to parent. Struminger, Adame, and Shannan (chapter 10) engage in a translated dialogue to make sense of their experiences as women, mothers, and field station leaders seeking to engage their local community in scientific inquiry. As a former science writer, Busch (chapter 11) uses a journalistic style to share her path from journalist and community member to executive director of the Sitka Sound Science Center. Thus, some of the most powerful stories and contributions regarding women's experiences in FSMLs may come from more "non-traditional" scientific writing formats. Expanding what is considered credible and scholarly work will give voice to those currently muted by colonialist, male-dominated institutional language.

Professional Development: The Importance of Training and Mentoring

Decades of research have explicated the gender gap in STEM, identifying systemic disparities that continue to plague the scientific community (Martinez & Christnacht, 2021; McCollough, 2011). As we continue to seek strategies for promoting the inclusion of more women and gender non-conforming researchers and practitioners into FSMLs, one area requiring additional scholarships is how we promote women into positions of leadership as the data indicate an even wider gender gap (McCollough, 2011). As such, leadership development programs for women with aspirations to occupy field director positions and other roles within the executive suite are critical to promoting equity and creating more inclusive cultures.

In chapter 5, Oktay shared her experiences as a woman leader at FSMLs, highlighting the opportunities and challenges for women seeking to occupy these roles. From the lack of affirming mass media representations of women in leadership positions (Simon & Hoyt, 2013) to socialization processes that challenge gender norms (Dennehy & Dasgupta, 2017), there are significant barriers to inviting women and gender non-conforming peoples into leadership positions. Adding a layer of complexity, McDermott and May (see chapter 6 in this edited volume) identified a significant disparity in requirements for leadership positions at FSMLs and the available opportunities to gain the training and/or leadership experience to compete and occupy these positions. On one side, we advocate for more women and gender non-conforming peoples in leadership positions, but we fail to provide the resources to help them prepare for these roles.

Formal leadership training programs provide participants tangible and immediate strategies for developing leadership skills. National Academies of Sciences (2014) highlights the importance of leadership training for current directors to help them accomplish their strategic goals for their respective centers but also "for developing the next generation of effective science administrators" (p. 58). A variety of organizations in the scientific community, such as the NSF, offer training; however, researchers, support staff, and other community members are often limited in terms of time and resources to complete needed training. Access, funding, and time away from assigned responsibilities are required to help create a cultural norm surrounding professional development.

Although formal training provides access to critical knowledge required to develop as leaders, so much of what it means to be an "effective" or "strategic" leader develops over time through experience and everyday interactions with the people in our communities. Oktay and Kloeppel (see chapter 8 in this edited volume) facilitate a rich discussion on the importance of mentorship as integral to the development of leadership, highlighting how the needs of mentees develop over time as their career progresses. For women and gender non-conforming peoples, mentoring plays a critical role in recruitment and retention (Hill et al., 2010) and representative mentors are needed to fully support the unique lived experiences of these scholars, researchers, and practitioners (Scheinert, 2015). Moreover, mentoring networks have been cited as a tool for shifting power dynamics, especially within the context of higher education and STEM for minoritized populations (Yang & Katz, 2020). Oktay and Kloeppel's (see chapter 8 in this edited volume) scholarship highlight the multitude of ways mentorship programs can be implemented, and readers are encouraged to consider how mentorship offered through professional organizations, such as the NSF and 500 Women Scientists, may support their leadership development efforts.

Understanding the Legacy of Colonization

Raby (2017) argues "to confront persistent geographic and demographic biases in environmental science, researchers must understand the history of their field sites" (para. 1). For many field stations, this history is one of colonization whereby early members of the scientific community seized Native and Indigenous lands without consideration of the people and the cultures subjugated as a result (Zukas, 2005). During this process, a power structure was established whereby "true" scientific discovery was facilitated by the scientists claiming the right to lands seized to build FSMLs while the "other ways of knowing" cultivated over centuries by Native and Indigenous peoples through "participation in the natural world" (Black Elk, 2016, para. 9; Trisos et al. 2021) were discredited and deemed inferior. The end result can be distrust, disengagement, or lack of community partnerships. Partnerships with local communities are critical as we promote inclusive practices, but it's also just good science:

> In discussions with locals who have inhabited a particular area for hundreds or even thousands of years, we will find a deep understanding of our surroundings that can enhance our research in a variety of ways. It is obvious that, if we are open to it, Native science can give us "new" ways of looking at the landscape and all that it has to offer in terms of chemical, physical and ecological processes and communities. (Black Elk, 2016, para. 11)

Our contributors offer additional examples of how to foster local community relationships. In chapter 10 of this edited volume, Struminger, Adame, and Shannan share the story of *C*entro de *I*nvestigaciones *C*ientíficas de las Huastecas "Aguazarca" (CICHAZ) in Calnali, Hidalgo, Mexico, and its commitment to rebuilding trust and learning from the community in which it is situated through partnerships and policies that focus on the following: (1) Needs of the local community and its peoples; (2) Knowledge systems and different ways of knowing cultivated by the local peoples, and (3) The aspirations of the community. In chapter 11, Busch shares her experiences as a director at Sitka Sound Science Center. Situated among the Native peoples of Alaska, their center offers integrated programming in the local schools, sponsors community-wide educational events, and educates incoming scientists and visiting scholars on the local community and inclusive science communication.

As we consider the larger power structures impacting the experiences of women at FSMLs, we would be remiss not to mention the important role Native and Indigenous women play in our understanding of the natural world. Using generational knowledge with a focus on interconnectedness, "native women use keen observational skills to improve crop yields, restore bee populations, or manage scarce water supplies in response to a changing climate" (Walton, 2016, para. 7). In chapter 11, Busch opens with the powerful story of a woman seal scientist using gender as a tool to navigate the space between Western science and Native science so beautifully, summing up her experience with the following: "I might not be able to do all the heavy physical lifting a man can, but when we work in Alaska Native villages, I can sit down with the women and have a cup of tea and talk" (p. 225). Through connections with Native women that affirm shared lived experiences, women scientists may be uniquely positioned to occupy spaces not readily available to men to further scientific discovery, learn from different ways of knowing, and build relationships with the communities they serve.

More Inclusive Job Descriptions/Recruitment Practices

Recruiting more diverse applicants and helping them navigate the hiring process is critical for addressing the gender gap at FSMLs (see chapter 6 in this edited volume). Directors are challenged to consider how power is framed in the job description and how hiring committees are selected to ensure women and other marginalized groups are invited to apply and share their lived experiences during the interview and selection process. In the job descriptions analyzed by McDermott and May (chapter 6), several issues were identified which may limit the applicant pool. Since job descriptions are often an applicant's first impression of a potential employer, we have to challenge biases and create more inclusive job descriptions. Specifically, male-themed words and phrases, such as expert, driven, strong, may dissuade female applicants with concerns regarding "fit" (Gaucher et al., 2011). These male-themed words and phrases in job descriptions are more likely to appear in industries dominated by the masculine, that is, STEM and FSMLs (Gaucher et al., 2011). Additionally, FSML job descriptions often present a list of required or preferred experiences and skill sets, which may discourage women from applying (Mohr, 2014). For women who choose to parent, lack of access to dependent care may limit the available time for them to conduct field research, for example.

For women who do move through the hiring process, the job description and actual role responsibilities do not match. Employers are encouraged to be transparent about the job role responsibilities and time breakdowns, as well as position reporting structures so that actual and perceived expectations are aligned. Long-term role ambiguity, as well as inadequate time to complete required tasks, can lead to directorship burnout and turnover (Hill et al., 2015; Schmidt et al., 2014; Tang & Chang, 2010).

Developing Stronger Partnerships among FSML Professional Communities

Professional societies are "organizations comprising individuals and groups (e.g., corporations, guilds, etc.) who share common interests, work domain

. . . [and] serve to facilitate engagement between their members in ways that promote the community's goals, efforts, work products, and services" (Andreatta et al., 2018, p. 91). Research shows that relationships built through professional societies play a significant role in the retention and satisfaction of members (Feingold & Estes, 2016; Greer et al., 2020; Nettleton et al. 2008). Anecdotally, as members of the Organization of Biological Field Stations (OBFS), we have often heard that OBFS provides an invaluable community of support for FSML leaders, staff, and researchers who must often do a very unique job (i.e., everything from making beds to building trails to writing million-dollar budget proposals). Therefore, it is imperative that stronger partnerships and networking opportunities be fostered in current FSML-oriented professional societies and across research reserves, national parks, wildlife refuges, public agencies, and nongovernmental organizations. Resource-sharing and networking among professional societies will help emerging scholars find these organizations, as well as build valuable mentorship networks as mentioned in chapter 8 by Oktay and Kloeppel. Professional societies have been known to play an integral role in the development of graduate students, not just for technical skills, but for developing "work-ready skills," that is, communication, problem-solving, decision-making, and application of knowledge (Nettleton et al., 2008, p .1). Moreover, building the presence and value of FSML professional societies can result in more advocates for FSMLs at the local, national, and international levels. Research has found that professional societies have greater relevance and impact on societal and global issues showing a collective force for change (Feingold & Estes, 2016). Furthermore, professional societies can act as community builders, highlighting that education continues throughout careers and emphasizing the value of knowledge-sharing and mentorship with future generations of scholars, practitioners, researchers, and students (Greer et al., 2020).

Inclusive and Family-Friendly Spaces

FSMLs exist within the natural environment. These sites may be situated in remote and isolated conditions; moreover, the facilities provided vary widely from modern research centers to tents providing basic shelters for researchers collecting data (National Academies of Sciences, 2014). As such, FSMLs represent a defined community often separate and distinct from their home institutions. Although this serves to facilitate research and advance knowledge of the natural world, there are challenges especially for women and gender non-conforming peoples occupying these spaces, as facilities are often shared open spaces. For example, lack of privacy is a reality at many field stations as facilities are often shared due to limited availability (Golden et al., 2018; McDermott, 2019). This may also contribute to a perceived lack of safety and inability to distinguish between public and private spaces (McDermott, 2019). While funding and sustainability are significant concerns for many FSMLs, creating a culture that prioritizes safety, defines public and private spaces, and ensures boundary management may be more tangible and realistic goals as people seek to find the money and space to build gender-inclusive facilities.

Another challenge for FSMLs is the lack of family-friend spaces to help community members balance work-life responsibilities. For community members choosing to parent, working at FSMLs often requires leaving their children and intimate partners behind. While this decision is deeply personal, the literature (Mason & Goulden 2004; Williams 2000) emphasizes how difficult it is for mothers to leave their children, especially infants and toddlers who may be nursing. The decision to parent and lack of perceived support for mothers significantly contributes to the leaky pipeline (Cech & Blair-Loy, 2019). When forced to choose due to lack of access to facilities, such as nursing stations or family housing, women may choose to leave field station work and/or higher education. Creating inclusive spaces for families, such as the facilities and support highlighted by Debinski in chapter 4, allows for more work-life balance and ensures the scientific community doesn't miss out on the unique perspectives offered by women scientists who choose to parent.

FUTURE RESEARCH AND CONCLUSION

As noted at the beginning of this edited volume, there are some "blind" spots and some voices left out. For instance, we use the term women to include all people who identify and experience FSMLs as women and womxn. We acknowledge all people who work at FSMLs from the margins. At the same time, we hope that our readers from non-academic and non-traditionally represented groups have found support and a collection of ideas to explore and reflect on their own perspectives and experiences. We encourage future research and scholars to study the intersection of gender with race, ethnicity, sexuality, socioeconomic status, and other socially constructed aspects that define power, privilege, ability, and status within STEM and related fields. In addition, exploring the impact of mass media messages on women and their experiences in relationship to STEM are worthy of additional investigation.

Although FSMLs represent unique and defined cultures, they exist within the context of larger societal institutions and may experience the same challenges that prevent progress toward equity. For women living and working in FSML communities, gender harassment continues to plague and challenge their ability to thrive within these communities of inquiry. As we look to the future and the increasing importance of FSMLs in understanding the impact of climate change the intersection of communication and STEM provides a rich landscape for pushing the larger research community forward, as well as for making all of academia and scientific inquiry more inclusive, diverse, accessible, and equitable for everyone.

REFERENCES

ADVANCEGeo Partnership. (2021, March 12). *Code of conduct.* https://serc.carleton.edu/advancegeo/resources/codes_conduct.html

Andreatta, P. B., Freeman, K. J., & MacKinnon, R. J. (2018). The value of professional societies to the healthcare simulation community of practice. In D. Nestel, M. Kelly, B., Jolly, & M. Watson (Eds.), *Healthcare simulation education: Evidence, theory, and practice* (pp. 90–104). John Wiley & Sons.

Becker, D. M., Griffin, J. E., & Miller, C. M. L. (2022). Identifying factors that contribute to positive and negative student experiences at field-based institutions. In V. McDermott, J. Gee, & A. R. May (Eds.), *Women of the wild: Challenging gender disparities in field stations and marine laboratories* (p. 143–168). Lexington Books.

Biden|Harris. (2021). *The Biden plan to end violence against women.* https://joebiden.com/vawa/

Billick, I., Babb, I., Kloeppel, B., Leong, J. C., Hodder, J., Sanders, J., & Swain, H. (2013). *Field Stations and Marine Laboratories of the Future: A strategic vision.* National Association of Marine Laboratories and Organization of Biological Field Stations. http://www.obfs.org/fsml-future.

Black Elk, L. (2016). Native science: Understanding and respecting other ways of thinking. *Rangelands, 38*(1), 3–4. https://doi.org/10.1016/j.rala.2015.11.003.

Busch, L. (2022). A long (community) engagement: From journalism to field stations. In V. McDermott, J. Gee, & A. R. May (Eds.), *Women of the wild: Challenging gender disparities in field stations and marine laboratories* (p. 255–266). Lexington Books.

Cardel, M. I., Dean, N., & Montoya-Williams, D. (2020). Preventing a secondary epidemic of lost early career scientists. Effects of COVID-19 pandemic on women with children. *Annals of the American Thoracic Society, 17*(11), 1366–1370. https://doi.org/10.1513/AnnalsATS.202006-589IP

Cech, E. A., & Blair-Loy, M. (2019). The changing career trajectories of new parents in STEM. *PNAS, 116*, 4182–4187. https://doi.org/10.1073/pnas.1810862116

Debinski, D. (2022). Make the approach and get the data: Challenges, teamwork, and culture of support for women who are scientists and parents at field stations and marine labs. In V. McDermott, J. Gee, & A. R. May (Eds.), *Women of the wild: Challenging gender disparities in field stations and marine laboratories* (p. 53–88). Lexington Books.

Dennehy, T. C., & Dasgupta, N. (2017). Female peer mentors early in college increase women's positive academic experiences and retention in engineering. *Proceedings of the National Academy of Sciences of the United States of America, 114*(23), 5964–5969. https://doi.org/10.1073/pnas.1613117114

Else, H. (2019, March 20). Female scientists get less money and staff for their first labs. *Nature*. https://www.nature.com/articles/d41586-019-00933-0
Feingold, R. S., & Estes, S. G. (2016). The politics, roles, and future of professional societies. *Quest, 68*(3), 284–291. https://doi.org/10.1080/00336297.2016.1175952
Gaucher, D., Friesen, J., & Kay, A. C. (2011). Evidence that gendered wording in job advertisements exists and sustains gender inequality. *Journal of Personality and Social Psychology, 101*(1), 109–128. https://doi.org/10.1037/a0022530
Golden, S. J., Chang, C., & Kozlowski, S. (2018). Isolated, confined, and extreme (ICE) environments: Review and integration. *Journal of Organizational Behavior, 39*, 701–715. https://doi.org/10.1002/job.2288
Greer, M. L., Akman, O., Comar, T. D., Hrozencik, D., & Rubin, J. E. (2020). Paying our dues: The role of professional societies in the evolution of mathematical biology education. *Bulletin of Mathematical Biology, 82*, 1–17. https://doi.org/10.1007/s11538-020-00728-9
Henson, P. (2002). Invading Arcadia: Women scientists in the field in Latin America, 1900 1950. *The Americas, 58*(4), 577–600. https://doi.org/10.1353/tam.2002.0045
Hill, C., Corbett, C., & Rose, A. S. (2010). *Why so few?* https://www.aauw.org/app/uploads/2020/03/why-so-few-research.pdf
Hill, K., Chênevert, D., & Poitras, J. (2015). Changes in relationship conflict as a mediator of the longitudinal relationship between changes in role ambiguity and turnover intentions. *International Journal of Conflict Management, 26*(1), 44–67. https://doi.org/10.1108/IJCMA-11-2013-0091
Interdisciplinarity. (2015, September 17). *Nature*, *525*, 305. https://www.nature.com/articles/525305a.pdf
Kaiser, J. (2021, June 11). More than 70 lab heads removed from NIH grants after harassment findings. *Science Magazine*. https://www.sciencemag.org/news/2021/06/nih-removed-more-70-lab-heads-grants-after-harassment-complaints
Martinez, A., & Christnacht, C. (2021). Women are nearly half of U.S. workforce but only 27% of STEM workers. https://www.census.gov/library/stories/2021/01/women-making-gains-in-stem-occupations-but-still-underrepresented.html
Mason, M. A., & Goulden, M. (2004). Marriage and baby blues: Redefining gender equity in the academy. *The ANNALS of the American Academy of Political and Social Science, 596*, 86–103.
McCollough, L. (2011). Women's leadership in science, technology, engineering & mathematics: Barriers to participation. *Forum on Public Policy, 2*, 1–11. https://eric.ed.gov/?id=EJ944199
McDermott, V. (2019). *'It's a magnifying glass': The communication of power in a remote Field station* [Unpublished master's thesis]. University of Alaska Fairbanks.
McDermott, V. (2022). "Brush your hair, apply for every grant, and get laid as much as possible": Sensemaking women's experiences conducting fieldwork in the tropics. In V. McDermott, J. Gee, & A. R. May (Eds.), *Women of the wild: Challenging gender disparities in field stations and marine laboratories* (p. 31–52). Lexington Books.
McDermott, V., & May, A. (2022). From the standpoint of women FSML directors: Communication, leadership, and the impact of gender norms. In V. McDermott, J.

Gee, & A. R. May (Eds.), *Women of the wild: Challenging gender disparities in field stations and marine laboratories* (p. 115–142). Lexington Books.

Mohr, T. S. (2014, August 25). Why women don't apply for jobs unless they're 100% qualified. *Harvard Business Review.* https://hbr.org/2014/08/why-women-dont-apply-for-jobs-unless-theyre-100-qualified

National Academies of Sciences. (2014). *Enhancing the value and sustainability of field stations and marine laboratories in the 21st century.* National Academies Press. https://ib.berkeley.edu/labs/power/publications/Schubel_2014_NatAcadSciences.pdf

National Academies of Sciences, Engineering, and Medicine. (2018). *Sexual harassment of women: Climate, culture, and consequences in academic sciences, engineering, and medicine.* The National Academies Press. https://doi.org/10.17226/24994.

National Institutes of Health [NIH]. (n.d.). Anti-sexual harassment. https://www.nih.gov/anti-sexual-harassment

National Science Foundation. (n.d.a). Frequently Asked Questions (FAQs) on career-life balance. https://www.nsf.gov/career-life-balance/clbfaqs.jsp

National Science Foundation. (n.d.b.). Balancing the scale: NSF's career-life balance initiative. https://www.nsf.gov/career-life-balance/index.jsp

Nettleton, S., Litchfield, A., & Taylor, T. (2008). Engaging professional societies in developing work-ready graduates. In *Higher Education Research and Development Society of Australasia Annual Conference.*

Okamura, K. (2019). Interdisciplinarity revisited: Evidence for research impact and dynamism. *Palgrave Communications, 5,* 141. https://doi.org/10.1057/s41599-019-0352-4

Oktay, S. D. (2022). Experiences of a female leader in FSMLs. In V. McDermott, J. Gee, & A. R. May (Eds.), *Women of the wild: Challenging gender disparities in field stations and marine laboratories* (p. 89–114). Lexington Books.

Oktay, S. D., & Kloeppel, B. D. (2022). The gift relationship: How mentoring leads to success for women in field station leadership. In V. McDermott, J. Gee, & A. R. May (Eds.), *Women of the wild: Challenging gender disparities in field stations and marine laboratories* (p. 169–198). Lexington Books.

Raby, M. (2017). The colonial origins of tropical field stations. *American Scientist, 105*(4), 216–223.

Roketenetz, L. D., & Holliday, G. M. (2022). Are field stations and nature centers gendered work spaces?. In V. McDermott, J. Gee, & A. R. May (Eds.), *Women of the wild: Challenging gender disparities in field stations and marine laboratories* (p. 199–224). Lexington Books.

Scheinert, R. (2015). The science of mentoring women in science. *The NIH Catalyst, 23*(2), 6–7. https://irp.nih.gov/sites/default/files/catalyst/catalyst_v23i2.pdf

Schmidt, S., Roesler, U., Kusserow, T., & Rau, R. (2014). Uncertainty in the workplace: examining role ambiguity and role conflict, and their link to depression—A meta-analysis. *European Journal of Work and Organizational Psychology, 23*(1), 91–106. http://doi.org/10.1080/1359432X.2012.711523

Simon, S., & Hoyt, C. (2013). Exploring the effect of media images on women's leadership self-perceptions and aspirations. *Group Processes & Intergroup Relations, 16,* 232–245. https://doi.org/10.1177/1368430212451176.

Snow, C. P. (1959). *The two cultures.* Cambridge University Press.

Struminger, R., Adame, G. M. V., & Shannan, Y. H. (2022). Women's perspective on building international community-field station partnerships. In V. McDermott, J. Gee, & A. R. May (Eds.), *Women of the wild: Challenging gender disparities in field stations and marine laboratories* (p. 225–254). Lexington Books.

Subbaraman, N. (2020, June 25). NIH's new sexual harassment rules are still too weak, say critics. *Nature.* https://www.nature.com/articles/d41586-020-01921-5

Tang, Y. T., & Chang, C. H. (2010). Impact of role ambiguity and role conflict on employee creativity. *African Journal of Business Management, 4*(6), 869–881.

Torti, S. (2022). The Isthmus. In V. McDermott, J. Gee, & A. R. May (Eds.), *Women of the wild: Challenging gender disparities in field stations and marine laboratories* (p. 17–28). Lexington Books.

Trisos, C. H., Auerbach, J., & Katti, M. (2021) Decoloniality and anti-oppressive practices for a more ethical ecology. *Nature Ecology & Evolution.* https://doi.org/10.1038/s41559-021-01460-w

Tydecks, L., Bremerich, V., Jentschke, I., Likens, G. E., & Tockner, K. (2016). Biological field stations: A global infrastructure for research, education, and public engagement. *BioScience, 66,* 164–171. https://doi.org/10.1093/biosci/biv174

U.S. Equal Employment Opportunity Commission [EEOC]. (2017). Promising practices for preventing harassment. https://www.eeoc.gov/laws/guidance/promising-practices-preventing-harassment

Walton, M. (2018). Recognizing the crucial scientific contributions of Indigenous People. *American Association for the Advancement of Science.* https://www.aaas.org/membership/member-spotlight/recognizing-crucial-scientific-contributions-indigenous-people

Williams, J. (2000). *Unbending gender. Why family and work conflict and what to do about it.* Oxford University Press.

Witze, A. (2016, February 9). Science funders struggle to deal with sexual harassers. *Nature.* https://www.nature.com/articles/d41586-020-01921-5

Yang, J. R., & Katz, B. (2020). *Promising practices for addressing harassment in the STEM workplace: How to lead in today's environment.* Urban Institute. https://www.urban.org/sites/default/files/publication/102045/promising-practices-for-addressing-harassment-in-the-stem-workplace.pdf

Zukas, A. (2005). Terra incognita/terra nullius: Modern imperialism, maps, and deception. In G. Backhaus, & J. Murungi (Eds.), *Lived topographies and their mediational forces* (pp. 49–76). Lexington Books.

Index

Note: Page locators in italics refer to figures and tables.

About the Contributors

Victoria M. McDermott (MA University of Alaska Fairbanks) is instructor at the University of Maryland and adjunct faculty at the University of Alaska Fairbanks. Her research explores the communication of power in traditionally masculine environments specifically within the military and science fields (i.e., field stations and marine laboratories, FSMLs). She has worked with members of the FSML community to unpack and explore their lived experiences through trainings, workshops, and research. As the social science consultant on a National Science Foundation grant, she seeks to continue improving the inclusion, equity, diversity, and access to FSMLs for all. Her research has been published in the *Ecology Society of America Bulletin* and the *Journal of Communication Pedagogy*. Other work has included paper presentations, panels, and short courses at the National Communication Association Conference in 2018, 2019, 2020, 2021, and the Organization of Biological Field Stations Annual Conference. Previously, Victoria has been the first editor of an edited volume exploring how to better support military-affiliated learners in higher education, *Supporting the Military-Affiliated Learner: Communication Approaches to Military Pedagogy and Education* (Lexington, 2020).

Jennifer M. Gee (PhD, Princeton University) is director of the James San Jacinto Mountains and Oasis de los Osos Reserves, field research stations that are a part of the University of California Natural Reserve System and the University of California, Riverside. She is an evolutionary biologist who conducts research on speciation in New World quail, which she has blogged about as a scientist at work for *The New York Times*. Her professional writing documents the natural world under shifting natural and artificial ecological conditions. It includes scientific articles that are published in such journals as *Evolution, the American Naturalist, the Journal of Animal Ecology* and *Cornell Lab of Ornithology's Birds of North America and Birds of the World.*

Amy R. May (PhD, University of Wisconsin–Milwaukee) is assistant professor in the Department of Communication and Journalism at the University of Alaska Fairbanks. She designs and delivers training programs to promote effective communication at FSMLs, providing both an in-depth understanding of how communication (dis)functions in these environments along with the practical recommendations to create more inclusive and equitable spaces. She has also supervised graduate student research in FSMLs. Her current scholarship focuses on understanding gender and power disparities in the #MeToo movement along with how power may be used in digital media to silence marginalized and disenfranchised populations, excluding them from conversations regarding climate change and environmental science. Amy's research has been published in *Journal of Communication Pedagogy, Teaching in Higher Education*, and *Qualitative Research Reports in Communication.* She also presents at regional, national, and international conferences, including the National Communication Association (NCA) and International Communication Association (ICA). She also served as editor for *Supporting the Military-Affiliated Learner: Communication Approaches to Military Pedagogy and Education* (2020).

Gabriela María Vázquez Adame is agricultural engineer, educated at the Monterrey Institute of Technology and Higher Education (ITESM) in Querétaro, Mexico. Gabriela specializes in agricultural production and producers' professional development. She, along with her family, run La Tejería ranch where in addition to ranching, produce coffee and tropical fruits. She is also the executive director of Productive Social Consulting, A.C. (ASPAC) and works on gender and sustainability issues in Calnali and throughout Mexico. For CICHAZ, Gabriela plays a key role, overseeing day-to-day operations, coordinating summer outreach program activities, and working closely with the local community. In addition, Gabriela sits on the international committee of the Organization of Biological Field Stations.

Danielle M. Becker is current PhD student in Dr. Hollie M. Putnam's Eco-Physiology and Environmental Epigenetics of Marine Invertebrates Lab at the University of Rhode Island. She is broadly interested in the ecophysiology within coral reef ecosystems and how global climate change and genomic processes influence coral population dynamics for generations to come. Her fascination and curiosity with the underwater world, especially coral reef ecosystems, developed into an innate passion for research-based science. Her passion for coral reefs is entwined with her interest in conservation and environmental justice initiatives that understand the importance of supporting STEM education and furthering policy agendas for the future of oceanic ecosystems.

Lisa Busch is executive director of the Sitka Sound Science Center (SSSC) where she oversees a team of researchers and science educators for the non-profit she has led since 2010. Before SSSC, she produced the award-winning *Encounters: Radio Experiences in the North* hosted by Richard Nelson and Elizabeth Arnold that aired on 180 stations around the nation and on XM Satellite radio. She holds a BS in geology from Tufts University and a MA in northern studies from University of Alaska Fairbanks. She worked as a general reporter at KCAW in Sitka, and then as a science journalist covering Alaska environmental and science issues for *Science, Popular Mechanics, Bioscience, Discovery* and *U.S. News and World Repor*t magazines. She is an active community member in Sitka, Alaska, where she spends her free time ocean sculling and hiking.

Diane Debinski is ecologist, and field stations have always played an important role in her life. As an undergraduate at University of Maryland Baltimore County, Diane took a field course through Frostburg State University and stayed at a field station for a week, with some memorable sampling of swamps where one student purposefully became immersed up to their armpits. As an undergraduate, Diane conducted spider research at the Patuxent Wildlife Research Station in Maryland for four summers. As an MS student, she spent a summer studying piping plover shorebirds at the University of Michigan's Biological Station. So perhaps it is not surprising that shortly after completing her PhD, Diane began conducting research at the University of Wyoming-National Park Service (UW-NPS) research station in Grand Teton National Park in 1992. Diane started that research funded by a $500 grant from the University of Kansas in 1992 followed by a $5K grant from UW-NPS Research Station in 1993 entitled "A Remote Sensing and GIS-based Model of Habitat as a Predictor of Biodiversity." Collaborating with geographer Mark Jakubauskas and botanist Kelly Kindscher, their preliminary data set them up for a larger grant ($709K) from the EPA entitled "Modeling Spatial and Temporal Dynamics of Montane Meadows and Biodiversity in the Greater Yellowstone Ecosystem." Diane's research at the UW-NPS research station has continued annually since that time, except during COVID years. In 2014, she served as a panel member and coauthor of a National Academy of Sciences report entitled "Enhancing the Value and Sustainability of Biological Field Stations and Marine Laboratories in the 21st Century" and in 2016, Diane served on the external review team to review the University of Minnesota's Itasca Biological Station and Laboratories. Field stations have, and continue to be, a major focus in her life.

Marilyn L. Fogel has conducted fieldwork that has taken her to the deserts of Australia, the Sargasso Sea in the infamous Bermuda Triangle, the cold Mars-like island of Svalbard north of Norway, and other desolate regions of the world. She received her BS from Penn State and a PhD in botany and marine science from the University of Texas's Marine Science Institute. Fogel joined the Carnegie Institution's Geophysical Laboratory in 1977. In 2013, she joined the faculty at UC Merced, then came to UC Riverside in 2016 as director of the EDGE Institute. Marilyn is now a distinguished professor emerita. Marilyn is a fellow of the Geochemical Society, the American Association for the Advancement of Science, and the American Geophysical Union. In 2014, she received the Alfred Treibs Medal in Organic Geochemistry for lifetime achievement and is the first woman to be awarded this honor. She was elected to the National Academy of Sciences in 2019.

Jessica E. Griffin is PhD candidate in marine ecology at University of California, Davis, and San Diego State University. She was born and raised in Connecticut and received her BS in ecology and evolutionary biology from the University of Connecticut. Her current research focuses on how species interactions in California eelgrass beds are affected by climate change and eutrophication. She is a National Science Foundation Graduate Research Fellow, and her research has also been funded by University of California, Davis, San Diego State University, and the California State University Council on Ocean Affairs, Science, & Technology.

Gary M. Holliday is associate professor of science education in the LeBron James Family Foundation School of Education at The University of Akron in Ohio. He earned both his M.Ed. and his PhD in science education. His dissertation addressed the impact of professional development in informal science contexts on teachers' content knowledge and discourse. To date, his research has focused on informal settings (museums, science centers, etc.) specifically addressing the learning of science, nature of scientific knowledge, inquiry, and bridging the informal and K-12 learning environments. He has published in the *International Journal of Science Education,* the *Ohio Journal of Teacher Education*, and the *Journal of Science Teacher Education.* He has also coauthored a number of book chapters and has presented his work at professional meetings in the United States and in Finland, France, Greece, South Africa, Taiwan, Sweden, and Turkey.

Brian D. Kloeppel is forest ecologist, field station leader, and university administrator. He completed his PhD at the University of Wisconsin–Madison comparing water and nutrient dynamics in evergreen and deciduous conifer trees in Montana and Wisconsin. He served as site director for the Long-Term

Ecological Research program at Coweeta Hydrologic Laboratory for 13 years and was a member of the steering committee for an extensive strategic planning effort for field research science and conservation that was published as "Field Station and Marine Laboratories of the Future: A Strategic Vision." He has had the good fortune of serving as the lead reviewer or committee member of 24 strategic plans or program reviews at field stations or graduate schools. He is currently a faculty member in Geosciences and Natural Resources and serves as the dean of the Graduate School and Research at Western Carolina University.

Cassandra M. L. Miller is PhD student at the University of New Mexico. She was born and raised in Las Vegas, New Mexico. She attended Grinnell College, IA, where she studied biology and discovered her passion for microbial ecology. A positive undergraduate research experience at Sevilleta LTER enabled her to see herself as an ecologist and opened a window to desert ecology, an enduring interest that has subsequently driven her academic career. Cassandra is grateful to be a home-grown scientist who is researching ways to alleviate the impacts of extreme drought at Sevilleta LTER. Her research aims to characterize multiple dimensions of microbe-plant interactions in order to better understand ecosystem functioning across NM ecosystems and drylands worldwide. Cassandra enjoys giving back to her community by serving in local government where she assists in the development of climate change policies. She also leverages her position as a Latina scientist to mentor to uplift young students from underrepresented backgrounds to ensure that they feel welcome in academia.

Sarah D. Oktay has held leadership and executive team positions at field stations and marine labs for almost 20 years. She is the director of strategic engagement for the University of California Davis' Natural Reserve System. She received her BS in marine science and a PhD in Chemical Oceanography from Texas A&M University–Galveston. She is the past president of the Society of Women Geographers and has been on the boards of many civic and nonprofit groups. She served as president of the Organization of Biological Field Stations (OBFS) from 2014 to 2016 and has been on the board for twelve years. She is also a nonfiction writer with 175 science essays published in Nantucket's *Yesterday's Island* and a poet. Her chapbook *Sifting Light from the Darkness* was released in 2020. She was the senior science advisor for actor/activist Mark Ruffalo's nonprofit organization, providing advice on climate change, fracking, and water quality.

Lara D. Roketenetz is field station manager at The University of Akron in Ohio. She has a MS in biology from John Carroll University and a PhD in integrated bioscience from The University of Akron. She has also received a graduate certificate in nonprofit management from Cleveland State University. She is on the boards of several local, regional, and national nonprofits, including the Organization of Biological Field Stations. Lara was the recipient of the "Cleveland Museum of Natural History Conservation Educator of the Year in 2017" and the "Diversity Award" from the University of Akron in 2020. She is a national geographic certified educator and a certified interpretive guide through the National Association of Interpretation. She is responsible for oversight and curriculum development of the K-12 programming at her field station. She has conducted research on aquatic ecosystems, as well as more recently on environmental education in informal settings.

Yamila Hussein-Shannan, EdD is scholar, educator, activist, and public speaker dedicated to socioeconomic and political justice. Her work examines how matrices of oppression and liberation operate in the context of settler colonialism and anti-Black racism. Yamila teaches at the graduate level on the intricate relationship between language, power, and (in)justice, critical race theory, the institutionalization of oppression, and liberation. She has designed, directed, and taught academic programs for teachers in Boston (Harvard University, Boston College, Goddard College, Lesley University, BTR/UMass Boston), and internationally (Morocco, Jordan, Spain, Palestine, Mexico, and the Balkans). Prior to her doctorate, Yamila founded and ran Yammita Activity Center for Children, co-founded the Teacher Creativity Center, and worked for Defense for Children International in Palestine. A Palestinian born in Colombia and raised in Jerusalem she is fluent in Spanish, Arabic, and English. After spending 23 years in the United States, she is currently back home in Palestine.

Rhonda Struminger, EdM, PhD, is co-founder and co-director of the CICHAZ field station in Calnali, Mexico. She is also an assistant research professor and assistant professor of the practice at Texas A&M University. Her investigations, in which Participatory Action Research has become central, focuses on informal STEM education at field stations, the role of science and education in democratic societies, and science communication. Rhonda's interdisciplinary background in education, applied history, industrial management, and political science gives her a unique perspective on the teaching and learning experiences she studies. In all of her research projects and teaching, Rhonda explores ways to bring theory and practice together. With this intention, Rhonda is now a board member of the Organization of Biological Field Stations and sits on the international committee.

Sylvia Torti is ecologist and writer. She completed her PhD at the University of Utah focusing on the unique and little understood phenomenon of tropical monodominance in the Democratic Republic of Congo. She is also a creative writer. Her first novel, *The Scorpion's Tail* (2005) won the "Miguel Mármol Award" for best debut fiction by an American Latino. Her second novel, *Cages* (2017) won the "Nicholas Schaffner Award for Music in Literature." Her short stories and essays have been published in numerous magazines and edited volumes. She currently serves as the dean of the Honors College at the University of Utah.

www.ingramcontent.com/pod-product-compliance
Ingram Content Group UK Ltd.
Pitfield, Milton Keynes, MK11 3LW, UK
UKHW021904150926
475560UK00004B/339

9 781793 629401